Transforming Remote Work and Tourism in the Digital Nomad Era

Ricardo Correia
Polytechnic University of Bragança, Portugal

Márcio Martins
Polytechnic University of Bragança, Portugal

Ruta Fontes
University of Aveiro, Portugal

IGI Global
Scientific Publishing
Publishing Tomorrow's Research Today

Vice President of Editorial Melissa Wagner
Managing Editor of Acquisitions Mikaela Felty
Managing Editor of Book Development Jocelynn Hessler
Production Manager Mike Brehm
Cover Design Phillip Shickler

Published in the United States of America by
IGI Global Scientific Publishing
701 East Chocolate Avenue
Hershey, PA, 17033, USA
Tel: 717-533-8845
Fax: 717-533-8661
Website: https://www.igi-global.com E-mail: cust@igi-global.com

Library of Congress Cataloging-in-Publication Data

Names: Correia, Ricardo Fontes, 1978- editor. | Martins, Márcio Ribeiro, 1979- editor. | Fontes, Ruta, 1985- editor.
Title: Transforming remote work and tourism in the digital nomad era / [edited by] Ricardo Correia, Márcio Martins, Ruta Fontes.
Description: Hershey, PA : IGI Global Scientific Publishing, [2025] | Includes bibliographical references and index. | Summary: "This book examines how the digital nomad movement impacts tourism, particularly how destinations are evolving to cater to this group's needs. It explores essential infrastructure like coworking spaces and reliable internet, alongside nomad-specific services and experiences that promote productivity, leisure, and cultural exchange"-- Provided by publisher.
Identifiers: LCCN 2024061711 (print) | LCCN 2024061712 (ebook) | ISBN 9798337300764 (hardcover) | ISBN 9798337300771 (paperback) | ISBN 9798337300788 (ebook)
Subjects: LCSH: Telecommuting. | Virtual work teams. | Tourism. | Work environment.
Classification: LCC HD2336.3 .T74 2025 (print) | LCC HD2336.3 (ebook) | DDC 658.3/123--dc23/eng/20250228
LC record available at https://lccn.loc.gov/2024061711
LC ebook record available at https://lccn.loc.gov/2024061712

British Cataloguing in Publication Data
A Cataloguing in Publication record for this book is available from the British Library.

Table of Contents

Detailed Table of Contents

One of the many after effects of the COVID 19 epidemic is the birth of a new work culture known as remote working/wfh or agile working. This pandemic has a lot of after affects in every part of the planet. The need for digital wellness has increased all around the world as a result of this work practice, which was seen to have varying effects depending on factors such as gender, area, and industry. People in recent years have begun to embrace this work culture for a variety of reasons, one of the most important outcome, being the fact that it introduces an opportunity to work from anywhere and flexibility in their work environments. The purpose of this chapter is to look deeply into the many facets of Remote Working/Work From Anywhere culture and its positive effects on employee welfare as a result of the growing number of flexible working possibilities and the emerging work cation practices among job doers.

Increasingly, people are traveling while working online, driven by new technologies and remote work styles. This chapter examines the financial, social, and environmental impacts of digital nomads on tourist destinations, emphasizing their unique characteristics and role in reshaping tourism. Digital nomads stimulate economic growth by generating income, fostering services, and sparking innovation. However, challenges like gentrification, cultural disconnection, and environmental sustainability demand well-designed public policies. Through in-depth interviews with digital nomads, the chapter explores their experiences and needs while analyzing policies implemented by countries to attract these workers. Sustainable measures are proposed to balance economic benefits with cultural and environmental preservation. This analysis aims to inform future research and innovative practices at the intersection of remote work and global tourism.

This study explores the factors that attract digital nomads to Istanbul, a dynamic city. Digital nomads use technology to work remotely, allowing them to travel freely and embrace a flexible lifestyle. They value independence, exploration, and balancing work with leisure, seeking to escape traditional office environments. While facing challenges such as visa procedures, reliable infrastructure, and time zone differences, digital nomads contribute to local economies and immerse themselves in new cultures, forming diverse identities. Push factors, like the desire for relaxation or adventure, and pull factors, such as a destination's attractions, climate, and culture, influence their travel decisions. Istanbul offers numerous attractions, including natural beauty, outdoor activities, and vibrant urban life, making it ideal for both work and leisure. This study examines how Istanbul can attract digital nomads and provides insights into destination marketing strategies tailored to their needs.

This study investigates the interrelationships among Digital-Nomads, marketing of destination, and economies of tourism based destinations to comprehend the influence of digital nomadism on tourism based economies. Utilizing structural equation modeling with 302 sample size, output manifested that Digital-Nomads meaningfully enhance both the marketing influence of destinations and their economic performance. The outcomes manifest a strong direct influence of Digital-Nomads on economies of tourism based destinations, as well as a substantial indirect influence mediated by marketing of destination. This proposes that influence marketing strategies are essential for maximizing the economic contributions of Digital-Nomads. Our research manifest the necessity for tourism stakeholders to adopt targeted marketing approaches that resonate with the unique preferences of Digital-Nomads, thereby fostering enhanced economic growth in tourism destinations. The implications extend to practical recommendations for emphasizing the need for infrastructure and services tailored to this demographic.

Digital nomadism, characterised by location-independent work and enabled by digital technologies, represents a promising path for destinations seeking to revitalise their economies and attract new residents, associated to their quality of life, welcoming communities and interesting leisure and tourism proposals. This study examines the interplay between digital nomads and local communities by examining host-guest interactions, their influence on perceived quality of life, and the evolving attitudes of residents towards tourism development. In-depth interviews with residents from a low-population density rural area and representatives from the local Destination Management Organization (DMO) were conducted. The findings from this case study provide valuable insights into how rural communities can manage and benefit from the growing trend of 'remote working tourism', while also addressing potential challenges related to cultural integration, economic disparities, and community cohesion.

This chapter critically examines digital nomadism and its transformative impact on the ethical dimensions and sustainability of tourism in India. With remote work transcending geographic constraints, digital nomads are reshaping tourism in regions like Goa, Bangalore, and Rishikesh, where cultural richness, ecological diversity, and conducive work environments converge. Using secondary data from academic literature, industry reports, and case studies, the chapter explores digital nomads' nuanced impacts on local socio-economic structures, environmental sustainability, and cultural integrity. While benefiting local economies and fostering community-driven initiatives, they risk overtourism, cultural commodification, and ecological strain. The chapter proposes actionable strategies, including region-specific policies, digital nomad visas, and eco-conscious travel behaviors, to sustainably integrate

Preface

The emergence of digital nomadism and remote work has redefined the global landscape of employment and travel. Once considered a niche lifestyle, remote work has become a mainstream phenomenon, driven by technological advancements and shifting workplace cultures. The COVID-19 pandemic accelerated this transition, compelling businesses and individuals alike to embrace flexible work arrangements. As a result, the intersection of remote work and tourism has sparked significant transformations in local economies, urban planning, and cultural dynamics. This volume delves into the multifaceted implications of digital nomadism, exploring its impact on workforce mobility, tourism economies, and sustainable development.

The chapters in this book collectively highlight the evolving role of digital infrastructure, policy adaptation, and economic strategies that cater to digital nomads. From urban centers to rural retreats, destinations worldwide are reimagining their offerings to accommodate this new breed of travelers who seek work-life integration beyond traditional office spaces. As digital nomads contribute to local businesses and cultural exchanges, their presence poses both opportunities and challenges. Questions surrounding gentrification, infrastructure demands, and environmental sustainability underscore the need for balanced, well-informed strategies to ensure mutually beneficial outcomes for both host communities and digital workers.

By compiling research from distinguished scholars across diverse geographical contexts, this book offers an in-depth examination of how remote work and digital nomadism are reshaping industries, policies, and societal structures. The insights presented herein aim to provide policymakers, tourism stakeholders, and scholars with valuable perspectives on the evolving future of work and travel. Through empirical studies, conceptual frameworks, and comparative analyses, this volume serves as a critical resource for understanding the broader implications of digital nomadism and its role in shaping tomorrow's world.

CHAPTER OVERVIEW

Chapter 1: Navigating the New Frontier: Remote Work and the Rise of the Digital Nomads explores the transformative impact of remote work on employment cultures worldwide, highlighting the advantages of work-from-anywhere models and their effects on digital wellness and employee well-being.

Chapter 2: New Frontiers of Tourism: The Transformation of Tourism in the Era of Remote Work and Digital Nomads examines the economic and social influences of digital nomads on global tourism, analyzing their contributions and the policy measures required to balance their presence with sustainability concerns.

Chapter 3: Tourism in the Age of Remote Work: How Digital Nomads Are Changing the Game investigates the role of digital nomads in local economies and cultural exchanges, emphasizing the challenges and benefits associated with this emerging form of tourism.

Chapter 4: Transition from Traditional Tourism Destinations to Digital Nomad-Friendly Destinations: A Conceptual Perspective presents a conceptual analysis of how tourism destinations can adapt to accommodate digital nomads while ensuring long-term viability and sustainable growth.

Chapter 5: Push and Pull Factors Making Istanbul an Attractive Destination for Digital Nomads explores the motivations behind digital nomads' choice of Istanbul, considering factors such as infrastructure, cultural experiences, and economic opportunities.

Chapter 6: Digital Nomads on Tourism Destinations Economies by Mediation of Marketing of Destinations in Horn of Africa examines the relationship between digital nomads, destination marketing, and economic performance, offering insights into the potential of influence marketing strategies.

Chapter 7: Promoting Digital Nomads in Rural Japan investigates how rural Japanese destinations can leverage digital nomadism to stimulate economic and cultural development through strategic infrastructure enhancements and policy adaptations.

Chapter 8: The Role of Digital Infrastructure in Shaping Digital Nomad Tourism: A Comparative Analysis of Urban and Rural Nomad Hubs compares the influence of digital infrastructure in urban and rural settings, analyzing its role in sustainable tourism and economic resilience.

Chapter 9: The Role of Host-Guest Interactions in Remote Work-Driven Tourism Development discusses how interactions between digital nomads and local communities shape tourism experiences, with a focus on rural development and socio-economic impact.

Chapter 10: Digital Nomads as Catalysts for Change: Enhancing Ethical Travel and Sustainability in Indian Tourism delves into the ethical dimensions of digital nomad tourism in India, proposing strategies for sustainable integration into local economies.

Chapter 11: Transforming Remote Work and Tourism in the Digital Nomad Era: Rural and Low-Density Destinations: The New Frontier for Digital Nomads explores the potential of rural and low-density areas to serve as digital nomad hubs, emphasizing technological advancements and work-life balance considerations.

The discussions in this book illustrate the significant changes taking place in the worlds of work and travel. As digital nomadism continues to gain momentum, its effects on economic structures, cultural exchanges, and environmental sustainability must be examined critically. The insights presented throughout these chapters provide a nuanced understanding of how digital nomads are reshaping the tourism industry and local economies.

As we move forward, collaboration between policymakers, business leaders, and local communities will be essential in maximizing the benefits of digital nomadism while mitigating potential drawbacks. Destinations must strike a balance between economic development, environmental stewardship, and cultural preservation to ensure that digital nomadism remains a sustainable and mutually beneficial phenomenon.

We hope this book serves as a valuable resource for scholars, industry professionals, and policymakers seeking to navigate the rapidly evolving landscape of digital nomadism. By fostering informed discussions and evidence-based policy recommendations, we aspire to contribute to a future where remote work and tourism coexist harmoniously, enriching both travelers and the communities they engage with.

Chapter 1
Navigating the New Frontier:
Remote Work and the Rise of the Digital Nomads

Roma Singh
https://orcid.org/0000-0003-0683-1051
Tezpur University, India

Runumi Das
Tezpur University, India

ABSTRACT

One of the many after effects of the COVID 19 epidemic is the birth of a new work culture known as remote working/wfh or agile working. This pandemic has a lot of after affects in every part of the planet. The need for digital wellness has increased all around the world as a result of this work practice, which was seen to have varying effects depending on factors such as gender, area, and industry. People in recent years have begun to embrace this work culture for a variety of reasons, one of the most important outcome, being the fact that it introduces an opportunity to work from anywhere and flexibility in their work environments. The purpose of this chapter is to look deeply into the many facets of Remote Working/Work From Anywhere culture and its positive effects on employee welfare as a result of the growing number of flexible working possibilities and the emerging work cation practices among job doers.

DOI: 10.4018/979-8-3373-0076-4.ch001

INTRODUCTION

The prevalent transition from traditional, face-to-face employment to remote work can be attributed to the enactment of work-from-home (WFH) legislation in the 1970s. This move was prompted by the significant increase in petrol costs resulting from the 1973 OPEC oil embargo, which made travelling more costly (Choudhury, 2023). Later, the 1984 research by Pratt explored the concept of pioneers engaging in home telework or working from home (WFH). It began by presenting a futuristic perspective of white-collar workers operating from their home offices. In the past, the motive for WFH was mostly driven by either energy constraints and the need to reduce daily commuting (Halford, 2005) or a perceived gender-based segregation (Šmite et al., 2023). Nevertheless, the unexpected outbreak of the pandemic and the swift advancement of information and communication technology (ICT) resulted into many changes in the way people work. This shift in perspective has led to the emergence of a novel concept of enduring and adaptable work practices, known as remote working (RW) or working from home (Nagel, 2020). This arrangement particularly benefits individuals engaged in knowledge-based tasks, as they can now conveniently access their work using laptops, tablets, and smartphones, regardless of their location or time (Maitland & Thomson, 2014). Such work practises adapted by organisations worldwide have given new concepts and meanings to the then called telework or Work From Home (WFH). Still having no standard definition of telework, studies in the previous two years found alternative labels for new working patterns. The same phrase is usually used for many sorts of jobs causing overlap. WFH (Ortiz & Bluyssen, 2022), RW (Prodanova & Kocarev, 2021; Satpathy et al., 2021), telecommunicating (Magnavita et al., 2021) and e-working (Taser et al., 2022) are various terminology for professionals working remotely. These are the most common terms for work practices outside of work place. Similarly, Work From Anywhere (WFA) refers to a form of evolving remote work practice which allows employees with geographic flexibility to choose where to live and carry on their work tasks (Choudhury et al., 2020).

The COVID 19 pandemic also gave a mushroom hike into terms like digital nomads and slomads. Digital nomads were pioneering individuals who combined remote work agreements along with vacation travel, sometimes including leisurely and continuous trips without any fixed place of residence (Chevtaeva & Denizci-Guillet, 2021). Lately the nomads are accompanied by a new group of travellers called 'workationers', who opt for short-term adventures rather than long-term commitments. These folks opt to enjoy the advantages of being deployed at a foreign place for a specific period of time before going back to their native country. The duration of their journeys often varies from a few days to many months. Usually, they operate remotely under the supervision of their employer while being fully employed. A new addition to the work-from-anywhere (WFA) trend is the increasing number of individuals known as 'flexcationers'. This word refers to people who prolong their vacation in other countries by working remotely for a period of one to two weeks.

According to a study conducted by IWG in 2023, about 60% of the participants extended their holidays in this manner during the year 2022. To illustrate, Ter Hoeven & van Zoonen, in 2015 argued that increased flexibility in work location leads to improved WLB, job autonomy, effective communication, and overall well-being. Regardless of the prevailing empirical data demonstrating the correlation amidst flexible working practices, such as ‘e-working, and employee well-being’, studies so far lack compelling inference (De Menezes & Kelliher, 2011). Warr (1987) and Warr (1999) proposed that well-being at workplace must be evaluated based on three primary dimensions: “pleasure-displeasure”, “anxiety-comfort”, and “depression-enthusiasm”. Studies on wellbeing have indicated that individuals who engage in distant e-working practices often face feelings of guilt (Moe & Shandy, 2010) and may labor excessively to requite the granted flexibility. However, there is insufficient empirical data to support the notion that distant e-working is unequivocally advantageous for the well-being of employees, leaving organizations, employers, and managers unable to depend on such evidence in general (Charalampous et al., 2018). Moreover a rising interest in studying the arrangements of remote work and the tourist industry's efforts to lure remote workers have been witnessed (Ferreira et al., 2021; Sorensen et al., 2021a), but with a dearth of a speculative evaluation on remote work travels and their possible impact on wellbeing (Chevtaeva et al., 2022).

Given the absence of consensus about the ramifications of remote working on employee well-being, the objective of this study is to offer insight into a relatively new and significant type of remote work called work-from-anywhere (WFA), the recent advances in this area which has received limited research attention so far. Workers are no longer obligated to reside in the same geographical area as the company, with increased freedom to select their place of residence. This in turn have given rise to workation practices and terms like digital nomadism, blurring work-leisure boundaries. Therefore, this chapter also aims to study the implications of such emerging modern work practices on employee wellbeing, business houses and environment at large. The central focus of this argument revolves around the fundamental aspect of the virtual office, particularly its inherent ability to be accessed from anywhere.

ADVANCES IN WFA/REMOTE WORKING TECHNOLOGIES

The enticing potential of ICTs has created new opportunities in communities. Undoubtedly, digital technology has become an essential component of contemporary life, leading to an increasing digitalization of communities. According to Jacobs and

Cooper, the digital revolution and the employment of digital technologies have a substantial impact on several aspects of people's life (Jacobs & Cooper, 2018). The term "co-workplace" came into being in the early 2000s to refer to an innovative local facility that made use of information and communication technologies (ICTs) to support distant working (Di Marino et al., 2023). Very recently, facilities like cloud computing has fundamentally altered the way people work since the pandemic. As a result, digital nomads, "workationers", and "flexcationers" are all results that may be assigned to cloud computing (IWG, 2023a).

Video Conferencing and Virtual Communication Platforms

The terms 'hybrid work' and 'hybrid workplace' have been more prominent throughout the pandemic due to the move towards remote interactions in various working practices (Florida et al., 2021; Petani & Mengis, 2021a; Gratton, 2021). In recent times, the public media and press have spread the notion that place-independent, nomadic employment allows all individual online workers with the flexibility to work from anywhere (WFA) (Adams, 2017; Chayka, 2018).

Nomadic workers may have the freedom to move about, but their ability to work is limited to locations where their technology can function effectively. Their capacity to acquire and disseminate information is greatly dependent on their access to ICTs. The technology and platforms that facilitate networking, obtaining projects, sharing work, and receiving money are essential to the work practices of individuals (Jarrahi et al., 2018). Essential amenities like reliable charging outlets and Wi-Fi connections are not universally available in all spaces, requiring nomads to actively search for sites that offer these facilities (Hemsley et al., 2020). Those facilities comprise of both physical tools and software apps. Following the pandemic, the alterations in the location and manner of employment present a chance to reconsider the culture, structure, and purpose of the workplace (Tredinnick & Laybats, 2021, p.109). In recent times, managers, IT professionals, and space designers have created several hybrid environments that are specifically designed to be used when crises disrupt or halt current working processes. Given the circumstances, it is advisable for them to modify and reuse their workspaces (Petani & Mengis, 2021b). Information technology enables individuals to engage in flexible work arrangements, allowing them to effectively allocate their time across many locations, such as their homes, corporate offices, and co-working spaces.

Cyber security in the remote working environment

Security has not been a prominent concern in the context of RW, despite the fact that RW is not a recent idea. Several firms and their employees were preparing for the unforeseen breakout of RW, along with the increased cyber dangers that coincided with it (Furnell & Shah, 2020). However, the WFH employees have exhibited a tendency to forget about security measures, leading to the abandonment of routine office security practices. These Practices encompass abstaining from transmitting dubious Emails, SPAM, Vlogs, Texts, Invitations, links, and attachments to the Information Technology Department. The CyberArk Report identified several prominent cyber security threats, including insider threats (51%), ransomware/malware (48%), targeted phishing attacks (56%), unsecured privileged accounts (42%), and unprotected data stored in the cloud. For those working remotely, there are several recommendations for their personal well-being (Ahmad, 2020; Borkovich & Skovira, 2020).

- Try to utilize a VPN solution with an encrypted network connection.
- Enable multi-factor authentication wherever possible.
- Organizations must update their cyber security policy along with encompass home and RW.
- For official matters, the employees must interact with colleagues by utilizing IT equipment.
- Organizations require encompassing RW access management, the usage of private devices, along with updated data privacy deliberations for employees access to documents along with varied information.

Artificial Intelligence Facilitating WFA

Digitisation significantly contributes to labour and operational flexibilities, including numerical, temporal, and locational flexibilities. It facilitates smarter working and assists in managing work-life balance (Strauss, 2018). The process of transforming various organizational processes and activities into data has enabled algorithms to gather and evaluate information. This, in turn, aids in the management and decision-making processes (Newell & Marabelli, 2015).

Data is kept in cloud and network systems which may be accessed using a little device. Ultimately, this alters our impression of telework. One may perform tasks such as checking emails, reviewing previous transactions, reading messages, and accessing news with immediate speed and convenience using a handheld device. This allows for remote work to be completed with ease, without being physically present at the employer's location (Sayah, 2013). Virtual reality has the potential to replace video conferencing technologies by providing a more authentic environment for impromptu collaboration and sharing of information. As an avatar, a knowledge worker has the ability to navigate the virtual workplace and interact with colleagues (other avatars) to exchange ideas (Kirchner & Nordin Forsberg, 2021). Augmented reality has the potential to aid knowledge workers in training and distant collaboration. It enables the superimposition of virtual reality onto the actual world. Employees facilitate the transfer of knowledge by engaging in a shared augmented environment. An office-based knowledge worker can acquire the skills to operate a 3D printer using augmented reality technology, with guidance from a remote experienced colleague (Chantziaras et al., 2021).Within the realm of digital labor platforms, algorithmic management has evolved as a mechanism for organizing and managing extraordinarily large groups of workers and clients in an automated manner. Consequently, the digital platform functions as an organizational model that generates flexibility by means of a process that involves scale and automation (Sutherland & Jarrahi, 2018; Newlands et al., 2018). Also, cloud technology has emerged as a viable means of conducting WFA, contingent upon the availability of a dependable internet connection of superior quality. It is therefore unsurprising that an increasing number of people are favouring the concept of combining work and travel, whether it be a long-run commitment of being a digital nomad, spending a few months or weeks at a new location, or simply adding a few days before the conclusion of a vacation, as said by Mark Dixon, Founder & CEO, (IWG, 2023b).

EMPLOYEE WELLBEING IN REMOTE WORK ENVIRONMENTS

Balancing Work and Personal Life

Remote work can promote work-life balance by eliminating commutes, giving workers more time for family, increasing job productivity, and giving them more control over their day (Shockley & Allen, 2007; Ferreira et al., 2021). By virtue of its location independence, no other form of employment may more effectively integrate work life with individual interests and travel, therefore enhancing employee's autonomy and capacity to establish their own equilibrium betwixt work and personal life (Orel et al., 2021). Integrating personal and work life can be facilitated by adhering to professional deadlines while still fulfilling family obligations and pursuing personal hobbies. Adapting flexibly to objectives and needs, might once again untangle the trade-offs in the work-life interaction (Allen et al., 2013a). Due to the fact that employees are afforded greater freedom and independence when they are able to work from home, there are a number of assumptions that are associated with remote employment. In the first place, it is presumed that working from home may lessen the stress and burnout experienced by employees, as well as minimize work tiredness and conflicts between work and home. This, in turn, raises the level of work engagement and job satisfaction among workers, which in turn leads to an improvement in job performance (Allen et al., 2015). However, knowledge workers may lack social connection, feel bound to their computers, lose significance at work, or lack vital tools (Ipsen et al., 2021). The academy and industry should do greater research and promotion on strategies to mitigate stress and enhance general well-being in the remote working context (Sorensen et al., 2021b).

Mental Health Considerations

Anxiety and its associated problems are prevalent within the realm of mental disorders. The reported lifetime prevalence of anxiety disorders is as high as 31%, surpassing the lifetime incidence of mood disorders and substance use disorders (SUDs) (Martin-Merino et al., 2010). Regrettably, anxiety disorders suffer from a lack of proper diagnosis and treatment (Kroenke et al., 2007). Global data from the World Health Organisation (WHO, 2017) indicate the widespread occurrence of depression and anxiety disorders. The negative consequences of this phenomenon are widely recognised, since they significantly diminish the overall quality of human existence and impose substantial social and economic burdens (Rapaport, 2005). Research undertaken during the predominance of COVID-19 has found that remote work has had a substantial and adverse effect on job-related stress. Remote employees have heightened levels of work-related stress and employees who regularly works remote may feel disconnected from in-person social ties (Donnelly & Johns, 2021; Shakti et al., 2021). The imposition of pandemic limitations exacerbated the sense of social isolation and the strain associated with remote employment. The shift to a remote work paradigm, particularly amidst the heightened stress of a pandemic, has demonstrated its potential to diminish the overall well-being or even cause the deterioration of workers' health (Toscano & Zappalà, 2020). Given the rising prevalence of e-working, which is likely to persist after the conclusion of the COVID-19 pandemic, it is crucial to establish preventative strategies to address the health hazards associated with this work arrangement (Buomprisco et al., 2021). In its 2020 ad hoc brief, the International Labour Office offered a set of valuable suggestions to mitigate the health hazards associated with e- work during the COVID-19 pandemic, such as; Notifying employers on the potential hazards to health and safety and dangers associated with the home office setting, including apparatus, occupational ergonomics, stress, and additional mental health concerns, offer occupational safety and health (OSH) guidelines and ergonomic measures particularly tailored for those working remotely and offer psychological assistance to employees, allowing them to anonymously express their fears and concerns through helplines, counselling, or support groups.

Strategies for Combatting Remote Work Burnout

Burnout and mental stress are terms that are frequently associated with difficulties in balancing the demands of working remotely or effectively fulfilling professional duties. A sense of alienation and ineffectiveness in their professional duties is experienced by employees who are isolated and do not get assistance from their employers. This results in the employee being disengaged from their work, experiencing higher demands on the workplace, experiencing burnout, and experiencing emotional exhaustion (Rapp et al., 2021; Singh et al., 2022). According to the findings of the studies that have been conducted so far, there are certain measures that can be taken to reduce the occurrence of burnout in remote workers. These measures include shifting the focus of one-on-one sessions with the boss from professional advancement to individual well-being, increasing the duration of stand-up meetings to thirty minutes in order to include personal status updates and having conversations about well-being. In situations when the use of a computer is not required, walking meetings should be substituted for virtual meetings. Create a timetable that allows you to take relaxation and rest breaks at regular intervals. The establishment of a fixed end time for work, wherein the computer is turned off at a specified hour, is recommended by researchers (Šmite et al., 2023b).

WORKATION PRACTICES: BLURRED THE LINES BETWEEN WORK AND LEISURE

A workation is an emerging trend when people engage in remote work while also traveling. The excursions, along with other concepts such as "hush trips," have surged in popularity as employees strive to capitalise on flexible-working rules (Nolan, 2023a). It was particularly in the United States of America when the idea started to gain traction. For the purpose of providing employees with the opportunity to refresh and recover (Retreat), participate in activities such as cruising (Activity), while spending time with their spouses and children (Family Trip), in addition to carrying out work tasks such as networking, coding, and instruction, the primary objective of a work cation is to provide employees with the opportunity to take a vacation. In most cases, employees will mix these components in a work vacation environment (Allen et al., 2013c). At first sight, the work cation might provide the impression of being a way to work and relax away from the hustle and bustle of city and the computer screen. On the other hand, in practice, it is a technique of being employed and relaxing which can only be constructed on the basis of an online environment with the keywords "mobile" and "sharing" as its driving forces (Hart, 2015). Both geographical independence and mobility are two views that may be taken into consideration while thinking about work cations as a work style. The term "location independent" denotes to the growing trend of remote work and telecommuting, that encompasses telecommuting, co-working spaces and satellite offices rather than traditional office settings. Numerous studies on nomads, including those on immigration and migration, have focused on mobility as a topic of investigation. Since the middle of 2010s, there has been a growing body of study that focuses on digital nomads in terms of their patterns of employment (Cook, 2020b).

Considering the subsequent study, involving "WTTC, Trip.com Group, and now Deloitte Global", some enduring and reinforced individual travel patterns that have persisted beyond 2022. One notable trend was the enduring appeal of "blended" travels, when individuals include both professional and leisure travel. This involves individuals taking advantage of work visits to also engage in exploration or extending their stay after a conference to enjoy a vacation. Technology is also significantly influencing the work, especially in terms of employee's decision-making (Trip.Com Group & Deloitte Global, 2023).

Those individuals who desire to live a lifestyle that blends work and pleasure are referred to as digital nomads. Through the utilisation of digital technology and working remotely, they are able to perform their jobs from any location in the world. Because of advancements in technology that have made it easier for young people to move about, there has been a considerable increase in the number of young people traveling in recent decades. This trend has been increasingly noticeable. As a result of their use of digital technologies to work while traveling, digital nomads are able to create their own work schedules and live freely from specific locations. According to Cook, this way of living not only creates a unique work-life balance, but it also incorporates a new kind of lifestyle that combines work and leisure (Cook, 2020a). Additionally, the growth of ICT has led to the development of broader social connections, further encouraging mobility (Richards, 2015). As perspectives shift, work is now being viewed more as a component of one's lifestyle, where individuals prioritise their work environment on the basis of personal preferences of leisure rather than professional factors (Allen et al., 2013b). As a result of the proliferation of digital work, the line between leisure and labor has become increasingly blurry, facilitating both the elements of life to live simultaneously and calling into question the definitions of both of them (Sintas, De Francisco, & Álvarez 2015). According to Colbert, Yee & George (2016), this presents a challenge to the conventional ideas regarding the timing, location, and manner in which leisure activities and work is carried out. These future pursuits of work and leisure inclinations, which hint in the direction of a confiscation of space and time limitations, shall have a variety of repercussions on the recreational and tourism sector, several of which are subsequently apparent (Rainoldi et al., 2022). These ramifications include the fact that time and place limitations will probably be confiscated.

Popular Workation Destinations

Research conducted by Qiu et al., (2021) has demonstrated that engaging in nature-based travel has a greater capacity to enhance the overall wellbeing of employees. Work-cations are leisure trips that provide the opportunity to unwind and appreciate the attractions of a selected location while engaging in remote work. Given the ability to work remotely, many are seeking to break out from their homes and opting for staycations. This trend is particularly popular among urban residents who need greater living space, autonomy, and access to fresh air following an extended period of lockdown restrictions (Faulmann, 2022). As defined by IWG, employees who work form destinations abroad with extended vacations have become popular since the epidemic and resulted into the rise of "Work cations". Destinations like Barcelona, Toronto, and Beijing were named among the top cities for those who are adopting the "work from anywhere" lifestyle. Milan, New York, Rio de Janeiro, Amsterdam, Paris, Jakarta and Lisbon were some of the other hotspots in the list (Nolan, 2023b). The cities were evaluated based on many criteria, such as visa policies, quality of remote-working facilities, level of safety, ease of travel, overall satisfaction, cost of living, and income tax rate. The **table 1** presented below showcases the results obtained from evaluating the workation qualifications of each city. The study examined the factors that lead to a pleasant workation and ranked each city based on their level of enjoyment, from the most joyful to the least enjoyable. Additionally, it determined whether each city has enacted legislation to entice remote workers through the implementation of specific visa choices, such as a digital nomad visa. In addition, they assessed the calibre of the infrastructure necessary for remote workers, including factors such as the availability of co-working spaces and the speed of internet connection. The scores vary between 50 and 100, where 100 denoting the maximum achievable score.

Table 1. Results on the International Ranking of Best Cities for Remote Work

		Workation		
City	**Country**	**Remote Work Visa (Score)**	**Remote Work Infrastructure (Score)**	**Visitor Experience (Score)**
Zagreb	Croatia	Digital Nomad Visa	72.2	70.9
Wichita	USA	None	92.6	75.4
Wellington	New Zealand	Restricted Work & Travel Visa	96.7	63.6
Warsaw	Poland	None	60.2	71.3
Vienna	Austria	None	92.6	74.3

continued on following page

Table 1. Continued

		Workation		
City	**Country**	**Remote Work Visa (Score)**	**Remote Work Infrastructure (Score)**	**Visitor Experience (Score)**
Vancouver	Canada	None	97.1	66.1
Toulouse	France	None	93.2	60.6
Toronto	Canada	None	97.1	80.6
Tokyo	Japan	None	88.9	100.0
Tampa	USA	None	92.6	72.7
Tallinn	Estonia	Digital Nomad Visa	93.8	63.5
São Paulo	Brazil	None	51.5	79.5
Sydney	Australia	Restricted Work & Travel Visa	99.0	79.5
Stockholm	Sweden	None	96.4	56.5
Singapore	Singapore	None	95.8	76.6
Shanghai	China	None	93.8	73.4
Seattle	USA	None	92.6	80.4
San José	Costa Rica	Digital Nomad Visa	67.7	64.4
San Francisco	USA	None	92.6	95.1
Rome	Italy	Freelancer visa only	64.1	83.3
Rio de Janeiro	Brazil	None	51.5	79.8
Reykjavík	Iceland	Digital Nomad Visa	90.4	74.0
Prague	Czechia	Digital Nomad Visa	84.3	87.1
Portland	USA	None	92.6	80.3
Pittsburgh	USA	None	92.6	65.1
Phoenix	USA	None	92.6	65.9
Paris	France	None	93.2	94.2
Oslo	Norway	Digital Nomad Visa	99.4	63.3
New York	USA	None	92.6	93.8
New Orleans	USA	None	92.6	81.9
Nashville	USA	None	92.6	73.3
Nantes	France	None	93.2	57.8
Munich	Germany	Freelancer visa only	88.1	65.6
Montréal	Canada	None	97.1	77.6
Miami	USA	None	92.6	80.7
Mexico City	Mexico	Digital Nomad Visa	53.4	77.4

continued on following page

Table 1. Continued

		Workation		
City	**Country**	**Remote Work Visa (Score)**	**Remote Work Infrastructure (Score)**	**Visitor Experience (Score)**
Melbourne	Australia	Restricted Work & Travel Visa	99.0	89.1
Medellín	Colombia	Digital Nomad Visa	50.0	75.2
Marrakech	Morocco	None	69.7	75.8
Madrid	Spain	Digital Nomad Visa	84.4	92.1
Louisville	USA	None	92.6	75.4
Los Angeles	USA	None	92.6	87.3
London	UK	None	85.6	95.2
Lisbon	Portugal	Digital Nomad Visa	82.2	91.8
Istanbul	Turkey	None	68.6	73.1
Indianapolis	USA	None	92.6	64.2
Houston	USA	None	92.6	71.2
Honolulu	USA	None	92.6	81.4
Hong Kong	Hong Kong	None	94.2	70.4
Helsinki	Finland	Freelancer visa only	98.4	63.3
Hamburg	Germany	Freelancer visa only	88.1	60.7
Gran Canaria	Spain	Digital Nomad Visa	84.4	76.5
Gothenburg	Sweden	None	96.4	50.0
Glasgow	UK	None	85.6	72.4
Gdańsk	Poland	None	60.2	62.7
Frankfurt	Germany	Freelancer visa only	88.1	61.1
Edinburgh	UK	None	85.6	75.4
Dublin	Ireland	None	94.9	74.4
Dubai	UAE	Digital Nomad Visa	90.7	87.8
Denver	USA	None	92.6	73.4
Denpasar	Indonesia	Announced Legislation	72.6	76.8
Dallas	USA	None	92.6	64.7
Copenhagen	Denmark	None	100.0	71.7
Colorado Springs	USA	None	92.6	75.4
Cologne	Germany	Freelancer visa only	88.1	61.8
Chicago	USA	None	92.6	88.2

continued on following page

Table 1. Continued

		Workation		
City	**Country**	**Remote Work Visa (Score)**	**Remote Work Infrastructure (Score)**	**Visitor Experience (Score)**
Chiang Mai	Thailand	Restricted Work & Travel Visa	74.1	84.7
Charlotte	USA	None	92.6	75.4
Cape Town	South Africa	Announced Legislation	81.0	89.3
Buenos Aires	Argentina	Digital Nomad Visa	56.9	89.7
Budapest	Hungary	Digital Nomad Visa	68.7	81.1
Brussels	Belgium	None	92.3	65.6
Boston	USA	None	92.6	75.0
Bologna	Italy	Freelancer visa only	64.1	71.6
Bern	Switzerland	None	98.6	51.8
Berlin	Germany	Freelancer visa only	88.1	89.4
Bari	Italy	Freelancer visa only	64.1	62.2
Barcelona	Spain	Digital Nomad Visa	84.4	95.5
Bangkok	Thailand	Restricted Work & Travel Visa	74.1	81.6
Bangalore	India	None	63.9	61.2
Austin	USA	None	92.6	77.4
Auckland	New Zealand	Restricted Work & Travel Visa	96.7	75.5
Atlanta	USA	None	92.6	70.7
Athens	Greece	Digital Nomad Visa	78.1	84.9
Amsterdam	Netherlands	Digital Nomad Visa	98.7	80.6

Source: Workmotion.com

The COVID-19 epidemic has had a substantial influence on our lifestyles, occupations, and travel patterns during the past year. The global travel industry has experienced significant changes as a result of widespread lockdowns and restrictions, leading to it to be one of the sectors most profoundly impacted by the epidemic, according to the World Tourism Organisation. During the initial six months of 2020, there was a significant decline of more than 65% in international visitor arrivals. Nevertheless, among the prevailing uncertainty in the tourism sector, one notable trend that has experienced a substantial surge this year is the concept of 'workation', which combines work with vacation (AMEX, 2021). Accommodation operators have responded to market developments by offering long-term rates and discounts for visitors staying weeks or months. Airbnb found that remote workers are booking two plus weeks of stay in smaller cities with natural environs, with a growing interest in cabins, cottages, and yurts. Hyatt, Limelight Hotels, and citizenM have also created long-stay packages and discounts in the US with remote worker-friendly amenities (Faulmann, 2022a). Ultimately, sustainability has consistently upheld its significance as a fundamental component of the travel itinerary. Travellers are progressively seeking methods to diminish the 'carbon footprint' and endorse 'sustainable tourism practices'. Approximately sixty percent (60%) of participants in the Trip.com study have chosen to engage in sustainable travel practices in recent times. Additionally, approximately 60% of respondents are either currently making financial contributions to compensate for their carbon emissions or express their willingness to do so at an acceptable cost (Trip.Com Group & Deloitte Global, 2023). This practice seems to be increasing among corporate travellers as well (2022).

CHALLENGES AND SOLUTIONS IN IMPLEMENTING WORK FROM ANYWHERE

Technological Challenges

It is possible that increased levels of tension and weariness will come from work that is carried out from a remote place and can only be accomplished via the use of digital connectivity. This has the potential to result in a range of consequences, including improved coordination, a rise in the frequency of virtual meetings, and the possibility of experiencing zoom fatigue and technostress (Richter, 2020). In addition, the lack of access to information that is both relevant and up to date can result in emotions of aggravation and anxiety, as well as the recurrence of errors and the loss of time owing to the necessity of obtaining the same information many times (Ipsen and Jensen, 2012). There are still certain places where poor or sluggish internet access continues to be a serious concern, according to an article that was published by Forbes. This is despite the fact that remote business destinations such as Mexico and Antigua may seem appealing owing to their sunny weather. Tech monitor found that out of the 85 countries taken into consideration for the Digital Nomad Index, 56 of them had an average internet speed that was lower than 100 megabits per second (mbps), which is the minimum required for effective remote work (Faulmann, 2022b).

Managing Remote Teams Effectively

Managers may have a distinct effect from remote working compared to workers, since overseeing operations remotely presents an extra difficulty. Managers must establish communication with their personnel and ensure intercommunication among them. Engaging in conversations on an employee's welfare is more challenging during online meetings. Additionally, the process of integrating new workers or terminating employees is more strenuous compared to in-person interactions (Kirchner et al., 2021).

Depending on their value extraction viewpoint line, HR managers may want to monitor remote workers' activities. The degree of monitoring may be impacted by the interplay between the organization's and individuals' involvement in hard (seeing human resources as replaceable commodities) and soft (treating them as valuable assets) HRM methods, as well as remote working. This was discussed by Boxall & Purcell in 2016. In addition to the alterations in monitoring style, the epidemic also prompted modifications in utilisation of the software. This widespread adoption of Google Meet and other video conferencing softwares like, Zoom and Microsoft Teams etc are widely recognised and widely publicised, yet the impact extends far beyond only video communication solutions. Managers also sought project productivity software and corporate management tools (Ozimek, 2020). Mistrust and the urge to manage work practices might have led to intensive digital surveillance for remote workers as part of a rising emphasis on measuring performance indicators and utilizing human resources analytics (Abraham et al., 2019).

FUTURE TRENDS AND IMPLICATIONS

Anticipated Developments in Work From Anywhere (WFA)

Alvin Toffler, in his influential book The Third Wave, missed to anticipate the significant impact of the Internet on the utilisation of ICTs. Toffler observed that in the information society, work locations shifted from the employer's facilities to the homes of employees. In the early 1990s, this appeared to be a viable hypothesis. In spite of this, as the 21st century drew closer, it became abundantly clear that the author's point of view required certain adjustments. The authors Makimoto and Manners made a forecast in their book "Digital Nomad" that the nature of employment in the future will not be set in one area, but rather will be marked by everlasting mobility (Messenger & Gschwind, 2016; Thompson, 2018).

It is possible that the COVID 19 has contributed to an increase in the average amount of time that persons spend traveling, which might be attributable to the rising trend of blended travel. In 2019, the typical amount of time required to make a reservation on Trip.com for a round-trip flight was nine days. The length has increased to around 14 days by the year 2022. From twenty percent of all reservations in 2019 to twenty-six percent in 2022, the percentage of prolonged stays, which are defined as visits (lasting two weeks or more), experienced a considerable increase. The pandemic which expedited the adoption of flexible working/WFA, being one of the factors driving the increase in 'blended' trips (AMEX, 2022). It should, however, be noted that this pattern varied throughout different regions of the world, with the regions of North America and Asia-Pacific exhibiting significantly greater rates of increase in comparison to regions such as the Middle East and the Caribbean (Paula, 2023). There are a number of countries throughout the world that are introducing specific visas in order to profit on the growing popularity of blended holidays. These licenses, which are sometimes referred to as "digital nomad" visas, make it possible for foreign visitors to participate in remote work in a foreign jurisdiction for an extended period of time, and they are generally completely free from paying taxes. According to Forbes (2022), the Spanish government has introduced its very own "Digital Nomad" visa as of the year 2023 within the European Union.

Opportunities and Challenges for Businesses

In a highly competitive industry, the need to create intricate products and services within a rapidly shrinking timeframe is imperative. Furthermore, having a workforce that is adaptable enables organizations to switch between personnel in a seamless manner and swiftly respond to the unique requirements that arise inside the processes that have been established for work (Kalleberg, Reynolds, & Marsden, 2003). According to Lipsey et al., the growing acceptance of fully remote work brings about major changes to the dynamics of the workplace, which go beyond the simple geographical presence of personnel (Lipsey et al., 2005). Efficiently collaborating and communicating on work, monitoring progress, and assigning action items have become significantly crucial for firms in many sectors. Upon closer examination, it becomes evident that these managerial changes have a wide-ranging impact, influencing virtually every facet of a business's operations (Ozimek, 2020a). Buomprisco et al., (2021) in their study suggest certain advantages and disadvantages relating to business houses which includes enhanced efficiency, decreased expenses, and streamlined organisation scale enhanced employee motivation, decrease in the quantity and responsibilities of middle management reduce expenses associated with property rentals and enhanced capacity for adaptability within an organisation (Toscano & Zappalà, 2020). However, the management of remote employees, the reorganisation of corporate processes to align with cultural values and practices, the use of multiple employment agreements to regulate disagreements among middle-level managers, the increased costs of telecommunication equipment and training, and the analysis of the corporate structure are some of the challenges that are associated with this situation.

DISCUSSING KEY FINDINGS

Emphasising the Interplay Between Advances, Wellbeing, and Workation Practices

As per the Upwork survey Remote work forecasts indicate robust growth. Within the next five years, a total of 40.7 million professionals in the United States will transition to working exclusively from distant locations. Out of the total respondents in the report, almost 35% of them felt working remotely was better now compared to the pandemic restrictions (Ozimek, 2020b).

The popularity of co-working settings is steadily increasing each year. According to Statista (2023) "There will be around 41,975 co-working spaces worldwide by the end of 2024". With co-working spaces now available in every continent, excluding Antarctica, and a rising number of users who operate in a mobile and nomadic manner, it is important to comprehend the advantageous function of these settings and the motivations behind their usage. In addition to the necessary hardware and software for digital work, it also decreases the use of paper and other resources, which might be regarded as a favourable environmental factor (Green et al., 2018). Furthermore, virtual work has the capacity to reduce traffic congestion by reducing the number of commutes. Implementing digital working options would yield multiple benefits, including reducing environmental impact by decreasing $CO2$ emissions, as well as enhancing efficiency, productivity, and overall well-being of individuals (Messenger et al., 2017). Nevertheless, there is a scarcity of literature specifically addressing the subject of combining holidays with a focus on tourism. The available scholarly works mostly examine this question from the perspective of work-life balance, and the notion of workation has not received significant attention in academic discussions. The scarcity of pertinent research is partially attributed to the absence of a theoretical framework, and this findings of the current chapter collides with the notion of Brigitta Pecsek (2018) and her study, even till date there is a nascent growth witnessed in the studies related to work cation concepts and its implications, especially in different sectors and for different genders or on demographic status of employees round the globe.

The pertinent research in geography, as determined by comprehensive literature searches, may be categorised into three distinct domains: (1) The field of study that deals with the transmission of information by electronic means, such as the Internet and virtual reality environments known as 'cyberspace'. (2) Altering geographical aspects of labour and employment experiences and (3) the positioning of organisations and individuals within value chains. Current study have demonstrated its explanatory nature by highlighting the increasing prevalence of digital nomadism and the co-working space utilisation to enhance employee's standard of life, increase efficiency, and address the work-leisure balance difficulties. The chapter findings clearly indicates that the co-working business is seeing significant growth as a result of the increased demand from the rapidly expanding group of mobile workers who seek to combine work and pleasure by travelling around the world (Orel, 2019). However, digital workers experience a constant sense of duty to be accessible at all times, which negatively impacts their personal lives. They often experience feelings of guilt if they are unable to meet this expectation. To safeguard against such emotions and the disparity between work and personal life, individuals should establish distinct boundaries between these two positions or adhere to structured schedules to avoid excessive labour (Cook, 2020c). Figure 1 below explains the multi-facet impact of remote work practices on different spheres of individual, organisational and environmental outcomes.

Figure 1. The Multifaceted Impact of Work From Anywhere (WFA) & Remote Work Practices

CONCLUSION

Implication and Future scope

The current study is an effort to bring researchers and managerial attention to the growing potential for digital nomadism and work-from-anywhere opportunities. It is a review of available scholarly articles and think tank reports citing the need and implications of this work culture. This kind of research might prove to be helpful for firstly the organisations, to know the choices and preferences of today's employees and how their well-being can be taken care of by the management. Ground-level strategies can be drafted by organisations for employee flexibility and well-being policies, whereas government policymakers will need to frame policies to safeguard the environmental surroundings and deal with sustainability issues if and when caused by such exposures to tourist destinations.

This area of research can be further analysed empirically and real-time data can be collected from white-collar employees, who had an experience of WFA or are still working from outside the traditional office spaces along with their leisure trips. The impact of such overflow of educated tourists to nearby places or untouched hill stations can also be studied in countries which are not future-ready or highly populated but low-income economies, as to how the tourist spots or naturally rich places have been suddenly over-exposed to a big lot of crowd as a result of rising digital nomadism work culture and cowering spaces round the globe.

Closing Thoughts on the Future Face of Work

'Employees' willingness to change jobs in the current economic environment for flexible opportunities and autonomy to choose their place of work is a game-changer. The COVID-19 pandemic has shown that flexibility can work for both employees and employers, and flexible working is the new currency for attracting and retaining top talent," Liz Fealy, EY Global People Advisory Services Deputy Leader and EY Global Workforce Advisory and Solutions Leader, stated in a press release (2021). The trend of working from anywhere is gaining momentum and is spreading at a rapid rate. The benefits for workers are readily apparent, particularly in terms of establishing a good balance between their professional and personal lives and experiencing general well-being. Additionally, businesses who implement Work From Anywhere (WFA) policies stand to benefit from a number of advantages, including increased productivity, greater talent recruiting and retention, and improved employee retention (IWG, 2023c). According to the data that has been collected up to this point, the majority of people who are reaping the benefits of working remotely are persons who are not married and belong to the millennial and Gen-Z groups. These folks are choosing to integrate their job activities with their holidays, and they are staying in their destination cities for an average of six months. In addition, according to the statistics, a sizeable number of foreign workers are increasingly opting to go back to their home countries in order to participate in remote work options (WorkMotion).

REFERENCES

Abraham, M., Niessen, C., Schnabel, C., Lorek, K., Grimm, V., Möslein, K., & Wrede, M. (2019). Electronic monitoring at work: The role of attitudes, functions, and perceived control for the acceptance of tracking technologies. *Human Resource Management Journal*, *29*(4), 657–675. DOI: 10.1111/1748-8583.12250

Adams, R. L. (2017). *How to become a digital nomad and travel the world.* Forbes Magazine., Retrieved from https://www.forbes. com/sites/robertadams/2017/01/20/how-to-become-a-digital- nomad-and-travel-the-world/

Ahmad, T. (2020). Corona Virus (COVID-19) Pandemic and Work from Home: Challenges of Cybercrimes and Cybersecurity. SSRN Electronic Journal. https://doi.org/DOI: 10.2139/ssrn.3568830

Allen, T. D., Golden, T. D., & Shockley, K. M. (2015). How Effective Is Telecommuting? Assessing the Status of Our Scientific Findings. *Psychological Science in the Public Interest*, *16*(2), 40–68. DOI: 10.1177/1529100615593273 PMID: 26403188

Allen, T. D., Johnson, R. C., Kiburz, K. M., & Shockley, K. M. (2013). Work–Family Conflict and Flexible Work Arrangements: Deconstructing Flexibility. *Personnel Psychology*, *66*(2), 345–376. DOI: 10.1111/peps.12012

Borkovich, D. J., & Skovira, R. J. (2020). Working from home: Cybersecurity in the age of COVID-19. *Issues in Information Systems*. Advance online publication. DOI: 10.48009/4_iis_2020_234-246

Brigitta Pecsek, B. (2018, December 31). Working on holiday: The theory and practice of workcation. *Balkans Journal of Emerging Trends in Social Sciences*, *1*(1), 1–13. DOI: 10.31410/Balkans.JETSS.2018.1.1.1-13

Buomprisco, G., Ricci, S., Perri, R., & De Sio, S. (2021, February 13). Health and Telework: New Challenges after COVID-19 Pandemic. *European Journal of Environment and Public Health*, *5*(2), em0073. Advance online publication. DOI: 10.21601/ejeph/9705

. Chantziaras, G., Triantafyllidis, A., Papaprodromou, A., Chatzikonstantinou, I., Giakoumis, D., Tsakiris, A., Votis, K., & Tzovaras, D. (2021). An Augmented Reality-Based Remote Collaboration Platform for Worker Assistance. Pattern Recognition. ICPR International Workshops and Challenges, 404–416. https://doi.org/DOI: 10.1007/978-3-030-68787-8_30

Charalampous, M., Grant, C. A., Tramontano, C., & Michailidis, E. (2018, November). Systematically reviewing remote e-workers' well-being at work: A multidimensional approach. *European Journal of Work and Organizational Psychology*, *28*(1), 51–73. DOI: 10.1080/1359432X.2018.1541886

Chayka, K. (2018). When you're a "digital nomad," the world is your office, New York: The New York Times. Retrieved from https://www. nytimes.com/2018/02/08/magazine/when-youre-a-digital-nomad- the-world-is-your-office.html

Chevtaeva, E., & Denizci-Guillet, B. (2021). Digital nomads' lifestyles and coworkation. *Journal of Destination Marketing & Management*, *21*, 100633. DOI: 10.1016/j.jdmm.2021.100633

Chevtaeva, E., Neuhofer, B., & Rainoldi, M. (2022). THE "NEXT NORMAL" OF WORK: HOW TOURISM SHAPES THE WELLBEING OF REMOTE WORKERS. ResearchGate. https://www.researchgate.net/publication/360216936

Choudhury, P. (2023, November 27). Our Work-from-Anywhere Future. Harvard Business Review. https://hbr.org/2020/11/our-work-from-anywhere-future

Choudhury, P. R., Foroughi, C., & Larson, B. (2020, November 22). Work-from-anywhere: The productivity effects of geographic flexibility. *Strategic Management Journal*, *42*(4), 655–683. DOI: 10.1002/smj.3251

Colbert, A., Yee, N., & George, G. (2016). The Digital Workforce and the Workplace of the Future. *Academy of Management Journal*, *59*(3), 731–739. DOI: 10.5465/amj.2016.4003

Cook, D. (2020). The freedom trap: Digital nomads and the use of disciplining practices to manage work/leisure boundaries. *Information Technology & Tourism*, *22*(3), 355–390. DOI: 10.1007/s40558-020-00172-4

De Menezes, L. M., & Kelliher, C. (2011, April 7). Flexible Working and Performance: A Systematic Review of the Evidence for a Business Case. *International Journal of Management Reviews*, *13*(4), 452–474. DOI: 10.1111/j.1468-2370.2011.00301.x

Di Marino, M., Tabrizi, H. A., Chavoshi, S. H., & Sinitsyna, A. (2023, April). Hybrid cities and new working spaces – The case of Oslo. *Progress in Planning*, *170*, 100712. DOI: 10.1016/j.progress.2022.100712

Donnelly, R., & Johns, J. (2021). Recontextualising remote working and its HRM in the digital economy: An integrated framework for theory and practice. *International Journal of Human Resource Management*, *32*(1), 84–105. DOI: 10.1080/09585192.2020.1737834

Faulmann, A. (2022). The Rise of the Workation. Nezasa Blog. https://nezasa.com/blog/the-rise-of-the-workation/

Ferreira, R., Pereira, R., Bianchi, I. S., & da Silva, M. M. (2021, March). Decision Factors for Remote Work Adoption: Advantages, Disadvantages, Driving Forces and Challenges. *Journal of Open Innovation*, *7*(1), 70. DOI: 10.3390/joitmc7010070

Florida, R., Rodríguez-Pose, A., & Storper, M. (2021, June 27). Critical Commentary: Cities in a post-COVID world. *Urban Studies (Edinburgh, Scotland)*, *60*(8), 1509–1531. DOI: 10.1177/00420980211018072 PMID: 38602910

Forbes, 2022, 'Digital Nomads Alert: Spain Set to Launch New Visa in 2023'. https://www.forbes.com/sites/ceciliarodriguez/2022/12/20/ digital-nomads-alert-spain-set-to-launch-new-visa-in-2023/

Furnell, S., & Shah, J. N. (2020, January). Home working and cyber security – an outbreak of unpreparedness? *Computer Fraud & Security*, *2020*(8), 6–12. DOI: 10.1016/S1361-3723(20)30084-1

Gratton, L. (2021). Four principles to ensure hybrid work is productive work. *MIT Sloan Management Review*, *62*(2), 11A–16A.

Green, D. D., McCann, J., Vu, T., Lopez, N., & Ouattara, S. (2018). Gig Economy and the Future of Work: A Fiverr.com Case Study. *Management and Economics Research Journal*, *4*(2), 281. DOI: 10.18639/MERJ.2018.04.734348

Hart. (2015). Living and working in paradise: the rise of the "digital nomad." Telegraph.Co.Uk. https://www.telegraph.co.uk/news/features/11597145/Living-and-working-in-paradise-the-rise-of-the-digital-nomad.html

Hemsley, J., Erickson, I., Jarrahi, M. H., & Karami, A. (2020, February 15). Digital nomads, coworking, and other expressions of mobile work on Twitter. *First Monday*. Advance online publication. DOI: 10.5210/fm.v25i3.10246

Ipsen, C., & Jensen, P. L. (2012). Organizational options for preventing work-related stress in knowledge work. *International Journal of Industrial Ergonomics*, *42*(4), 325–334. DOI: 10.1016/j.ergon.2012.02.006

Ipsen, C., van Veldhoven, M., Kirchner, K., & Hansen, J. P. (2021). Six Key Advantages and Disadvantages of Working from Home in Europe during COVID-19. *International Journal of Environmental Research and Public Health*, *18*(4), 1826. DOI: 10.3390/ijerph18041826 PMID: 33668505

Jacobs, N., & Cooper, R. (2018). *Living in Digital Worlds*. Routledge., http://books.google.ie/books?id=uClKDwAAQBAJ&pg=PT569&dq=Jacobs,+N.,+%26+Cooper,+R.+(2018).+Living+in+Digital+Worlds:+Designing+the+Digital+Public+Space.+New+York:+Routledge.&hl=&cd=2&source=gbs_api DOI: 10.4324/9781315592787

Jarrahi, M. H., Philips, G., Sutherland, W., Sawyer, S., & Erickson, I. (2019). Personalization of knowledge, personal knowledge ecology, and digital nomadism. *Journal of the Association for Information Science and Technology*, *70*(4), 313–324. DOI: 10.1002/asi.24134

Kalleberg, A. L., Reynolds, J., & Marsden, P. V. (2003). Externalizing employment: Flexible staffing arrangements in US organizations. *Social Science Research*, *32*(4), 525–552. DOI: 10.1016/S0049-089X(03)00013-9

Kirchner, K., Ipsen, C., & Hansen, J. P. (2021). COVID-19 leadership challenges in knowledge work. *Knowledge Management Research and Practice*, *19*(4), 493–500. DOI: 10.1080/14778238.2021.1877579

Kirchner, K., & Nordin Forsberg, B. (2021). A Conference Goes Virtual: Lessons from Creating a Social Event in the Virtual Reality. Innovations for Community Services, 123–134. https://doi.org/DOI: 10.1007/978-3-030-75004-6_9

Kroenke, K., Spitzer, R. L., Williams, J. B., Monahan, P. O., & Löwe, B. (2007). Anxiety Disorders in Primary Care: Prevalence, Impairment, Comorbidity, and Detection. *Annals of Internal Medicine*, *146*(5), 317–325. DOI: 10.7326/0003-4819-146-5-200703060-00004 PMID: 17339617

Lipsey, R. G., Carlaw, K. I., & Bekar, C. T. (2005). Economic Transformations. OUP Oxford. http://books.google.ie/books?id=tSrGTMtBv50C&printsec=frontcover&dq=Lipsey,+Richard+G.,+Kenneth+I.+Carlaw,+and+Clifford+T.+Bekar.+Economic+transformations:+general+purpose+technologies+and+long-term+economic+growth.+OUP+Oxford,+2005.&hl=&cd=1&source=gbs_api

Magnavita, N., Tripepi, G., & Chiorri, C. (2021, March 24). Telecommuting, Off-Time Work, and Intrusive Leadership in Workers' Well-Being. *International Journal of Environmental Research and Public Health*, *18*(7), 3330. DOI: 10.3390/ijerph18073330 PMID: 33804828

Maitland, A., & Thomson, P. (2014, March 20). Future Work (Expanded and Updated). Springer. http://books.google.ie/books?id=7kcfAwAAQBAJ&pg=PT5&dq=Maitland,+A.,+%26+Thomson,+P.+(2014).+Future+work+(expanded+and+updated):+Changing+organizational+culture+for+the+new+world+of+work.+London,+UK:+Springer.&hl=&cd=2&source=gbs_api

Martin-Merino, E., Ruigomez, A., Wallander, M. A., Johansson, S., & Garcia-Rodriguez, L. A. (2010). Prevalence, incidence, morbidity and treatment patterns in a cohort of patients diagnosed with anxiety in UK primary care. *Family Practice*, *27*(1), 9–16. DOI: 10.1093/fampra/cmp071 PMID: 19884124

Messenger, J., Vargas, O. L., Gschwind, L., Boehmer, S., Vermeylen, G., & Wilkens, M. (2017). *Working anytime, anywhere: The effects on the world of work*. Publications Office of the European Union.

Messenger, J. C., & Gschwind, L. (2016, November). Three generations of Telework: New ICTs and the (R)evolution from Home Office to Virtual Office. *New Technology, Work and Employment*, *31*(3), 195–208. DOI: 10.1111/ntwe.12073

Moe, K., & Shandy, D. (2010). *Glass ceilings & 100-hour couples: What the opt-out phenomenon can teach us about work and family*. The University of Georgia Press. DOI: 10.1353/book11402

Newell, S., & Marabelli, M. (2015, March). Strategic opportunities (and challenges) of algorithmic decision-making: A call for action on the long-term societal effects of 'datification.'. *The Journal of Strategic Information Systems*, *24*(1), 3–14. DOI: 10.1016/j.jsis.2015.02.001

Newlands, G., Lutz, C., & Fieseler, C. (2018, September 6). Collective action and provider classification in the sharing economy. *New Technology, Work and Employment*, *33*(3), 250–267. DOI: 10.1111/ntwe.12119

Nolan, B. (2023). Zero income tax and tight security makes Dubai one of the best destinations for a "workation," study finds. Business Insider. https://www.businessinsider.in/thelife/news/zero-income-tax-and-tight-security-makes-dubai-one-of-the-best-destinations-for-a-workation-study-finds/articleshow/104776184.cms

Nolan, B. (2023). Barcelona, Toronto, and Beijing are some of the best cities to work remotely while traveling, study finds. Business Insider. https://www.businessinsider.com/remote-work-best-cities-work-while-traveling-study-2023-8?r=US&IR=T

Number of coworking spaces worldwide | Statistica. (2023). Statista. Retrieved December 15, 2023, from https://www.statista.com/statistics/554273/number-of-coworking-spaces-worldwide/

Orel, M. (2019). Coworking environments and digital nomadism: Balancing work and leisure whilst on the move. *World Leisure Journal*, *61*(3), 215–227. DOI: 10.1080/16078055.2019.1639275

Orel, M., Dvouletý, O., & Ratten, V. (Eds.). (2021). *The Flexible Workplace*. Human Resource Management., DOI: 10.1007/978-3-030-62167-4

Ortiz, M. A., & Bluyssen, P. M. (2022, March). Profiling office workers based on their self-reported preferences of indoor environmental quality and psychosocial comfort at their workplace during COVID-19. *Building and Environment*, *211*, 108742. DOI: 10.1016/j.buildenv.2021.108742 PMID: 35002047

Ozimek, A. (2020). Future Workforce Report. SSRN Electronic Journal. https://doi.org/DOI: 10.2139/ssrn.3787530

Paula. (2023). Global Travel Trends 2023. ForwardKeys. https://forwardkeys.com/global-travel-trends-2023/

Petani, F. J., & Mengis, J. (2021, November 17). Technology and the hybrid workplace: The affective living of IT-enabled space. *International Journal of Human Resource Management*, *34*(8), 1530–1553. DOI: 10.1080/09585192.2021.1998186

Prodanova, J., & Kocarev, L. (2021, August). Is job performance conditioned by work-from-home demands and resources? *Technology in Society*, *66*, 101672. DOI: 10.1016/j.techsoc.2021.101672 PMID: 34840365

Purcell, J., & Boxall, P. (2017). Strategy and Human Resource Management. Bloomsbury Publishing. http://books.google.ie/books?id=oCVHEAAAQBAJ&printsec=frontcover&dq=Boxall,+P.,+%26+Purcell,+J.+(2016).+Strategy+and+human+resource+management.+Palgrave&hl=&cd=1&source=gbs_api

Qiu, M., Sha, J., & Scott, N. (2021, February 26). Restoration of Visitors through Nature-Based Tourism: A Systematic Review, Conceptual Framework, and Future Research Directions. *International Journal of Environmental Research and Public Health*, *18*(5), 2299. DOI: 10.3390/ijerph18052299 PMID: 33652652

Rainoldi, M., Ladkin, A., & Buhalis, D. (2022, May 10). Blending work and leisure: A future digital worker hybrid lifestyle perspective. *Annals of Leisure Research*, •••, 1–21. DOI: 10.1080/11745398.2022.2070513

Rapaport, M. H., Clary, C., Fayyad, R., & Endicott, J. (2005). Quality-of-life impairment in depressive and anxiety disorders. *The American Journal of Psychiatry*, *162*(6), 1171–1178. DOI: 10.1176/appi.ajp.162.6.1171 PMID: 15930066

Rapp, D. J., Hughey, J. M., & Kreiner, G. E. (2021, August). Boundary work as a buffer against burnout: Evidence from healthcare workers during the COVID-19 pandemic. *The Journal of Applied Psychology*, *106*(8), 1169–1187. DOI: 10.1037/apl0000951 PMID: 34424001

Richter, A. (2020). Locked-down digital work. *International Journal of Information Management*, *55*, 102157. DOI: 10.1016/j.ijinfomgt.2020.102157 PMID: 32836629

Satpathy, S., Patel, G., & Kumar, K. (2021, November 12). Identifying and ranking techno-stressors among IT employees due to work from home arrangement during Covid-19 pandemic. *Decision (Washington, D.C.)*, *48*(4), 391–402. DOI: 10.1007/s40622-021-00295-5

Sayah, S. (2013, November). Managing work–life boundaries with information and communication technologies: The case of independent contractors. *New Technology, Work and Employment*, *28*(3), 179–196. DOI: 10.1111/ntwe.12016

Shakti, D., Ray, D., & Gupta, D. (2021). Factors affecting Work from Office and Work from Anywhere for Employees: A Study. [IJSRP]. *International Journal of Scientific and Research Publications*, *11*(10), 251–256. DOI: 10.29322/IJSRP.11.10.2021.p11827

Shockley, K. M., & Allen, T. D. (2007). When flexibility helps: Another look at the availability of flexible work arrangements and work–family conflict. *Journal of Vocational Behavior*, *71*(3), 479–493. DOI: 10.1016/j.jvb.2007.08.006

Singh, P., Bala, H., Dey, B. L., & Filieri, R. (2022, November). Enforced remote working: The impact of digital platform-induced stress and remote working experience on technology exhaustion and subjective wellbeing. *Journal of Business Research*, *151*, 269–286. DOI: 10.1016/j.jbusres.2022.07.002 PMID: 35847196

Sintas, J. L., de Francisco, L. R., & Álvarez, E. G. (2015). The Nature of Leisure Revisited. *Journal of Leisure Research*, *47*(1), 79–101. DOI: 10.1080/00222216.2015.11950352

Šmite, D., Moe, N. B., Klotins, E., & Gonzalez-Huerta, J. (2023). From forced Working-From-Home to voluntary working-from-anywhere: Two revolutions in telework. *Journal of Systems and Software*, *195*, 111509. DOI: 10.1016/j.jss.2022.111509 PMID: 36105918

Sorensen, G., Dennerlein, J. T., Peters, S. E., Sabbath, E. L., Kelly, E. L., & Wagner, G. R. (2021, January). The future of research on work, safety, health and wellbeing: A guiding conceptual framework. *Social Science & Medicine*, *269*, 113593. DOI: 10.1016/j.socscimed.2020.113593 PMID: 33341740

Strauss, K. (2018). Labour geography 1. *Progress in Human Geography*, *42*(4), 622–630. DOI: 10.1177/0309132517717786

Sutherland, W., & Jarrahi, M. H. (2018, December). The sharing economy and digital platforms: A review and research agenda. *International Journal of Information Management*, *43*, 328–341. DOI: 10.1016/j.ijinfomgt.2018.07.004

Taser, D., Aydin, E., Torgaloz, A. O., & Rofcanin, Y. (2022, February). An examination of remote e-working and flow experience: The role of technostress and loneliness. *Computers in Human Behavior, 127*, 107020. DOI: 10.1016/j.chb.2021.107020

Ter Hoeven, C. L., & van Zoonen, W. (2015, November). Flexible work designs and employee well-being: Examining the effects of resources and demands. *New Technology, Work and Employment, 30*(3), 237–255. DOI: 10.1111/ntwe.12052

The Cities Best Facilitating Remote Work. Workation Edition. Workmotion.com. Retrieved December 2023, from https://workmotion.com/best-remote-work-cities-workation-edition/

The world's best 'work from anywhere' cities and the rise of the digital nomad. (2023). In assets.iwgplc.com. IWG PLC. Retrieved December 18, 2023, from https://assets.iwgplc.com/image/upload/v1694070764/IWG/MediaCentre/IWG_White_Paper_Work_From_Anywhere_Cities_Rise_of_the_Digital_Nomad_Sept_2023.pdf

Thompson, B. Y. (2018, December 19). The Digital Nomad Lifestyle: (Remote) Work/Leisure Balance, Privilege, and Constructed Community. *International Journal of the Sociology of Leisure*, *2*(1–2), 27–42. DOI: 10.1007/s41978-018-00030-y

Toscano, F., & Zappalà, S. (2020, November 24). Social Isolation and Stress as Predictors of Productivity Perception and Remote Work Satisfaction during the COVID-19 Pandemic: The Role of Concern about the Virus in a Moderated Double Mediation. *Sustainability (Basel), 12*(23), 9804. DOI: 10.3390/su12239804

Tredinnick, L., & Laybats, C. (2021, September). Blended workplaces. *Business Information Review, 38*(3), 108–110. DOI: 10.1177/02663821211042474

Trip.Com Group & Deloitte Global. (2023). A World In Motion: Shifting consumer travel trends in 2022 and beyond. In WTTC. Retrieved December 16, 2023, from https://www2.deloitte.com/content/dam/Deloitte/fr/Documents/consumer-business/Publications/wttc-consumer-trends-report-2023.pdf

Warr, P. (1999). Well-being and the workplace. In Kahneman, D., Diener, E., & Schwarz, N. (Eds.), *Well-being: The foundations of hedonic psychology* (pp. 392–412). Russel Sage.

Warr, P. B. (1987). *Work, unemployment, and mental health*. Oxford University Press.

World Health Organization. (2017). *Depression and other common mental disorders: global health estimates (No. WHO/MSD/MER/2017.2)*. World Health Organization.

Chapter 2
New Frontiers of Tourism:
The Transformation of Tourism in the Era of Remote Work and Digital Nomads

Noelia Araújo Vila
https://orcid.org/0000-0002-3395-8536
University of Vigo, Spain

Almudena Otegui Carles
https://orcid.org/0000-0003-4112-8580
University of Vigo, Spain

ABSTRACT

Increasingly, people are traveling while working online, driven by new technologies and remote work styles. This chapter examines the financial, social, and environmental impacts of digital nomads on tourist destinations, emphasizing their unique characteristics and role in reshaping tourism. Digital nomads stimulate economic growth by generating income, fostering services, and sparking innovation. However, challenges like gentrification, cultural disconnection, and environmental sustainability demand well-designed public policies. Through in-depth interviews with digital nomads, the chapter explores their experiences and needs while analyzing policies implemented by countries to attract these workers. Sustainable measures are proposed to balance economic benefits with cultural and environmental preservation. This analysis aims to inform future research and innovative practices at the intersection of remote work and global tourism.

DOI: 10.4018/979-8-3373-0076-4.ch002

INTRODUCTION

The intersection between tourism and remote work has given rise to a phenomenon of global proportions: digital nomads. These individuals, driven by technological advances and a cultural shift in the way we work, are redefining the dynamics of traditional tourism and creating new opportunities and challenges for tourist destinations worldwide. This chapter aims to analyze the impact of digital nomads on tourism, their distinctive characteristics, and the ways they are "changing the game" in an ever-evolving industry (Hannonen, 2020).

Remote work, previously limited to specific sectors, has gained new prominence due to advances in communication technologies, global Internet access, and more recently, the COVID-19 pandemic, which accelerated the adoption of flexible and ubiquitous work models. The growing popularity of this model has allowed workers to overcome the geographical and cultural barriers that once limited them to living and working in a single location, facilitating their transition to an itinerant lifestyle (Nash et al., 2018).

Digital nomads represent a unique category of workers who not only choose to work remotely but make mobility and tourism an integral part of their working life. This group has highly differentiated characteristics: they are highly skilled, possess a global mindset, value flexibility, and seek diverse cultural and life experiences while advancing their careers. Moreover, this labor mobility represents a growing trend among young workers and entrepreneurs who view remote work to explore the world without compromising their professional growth (Mouratidis, 2018).

Unlike conventional tourists who travel for recreational purposes and on a limited basis, digital nomads seek destinations where they can establish a temporary base while they work. This implies that tourist destinations must adapt to their specific needs, such as reliable Internet access, collaborative workspaces, and supportive communities. Furthermore, many digital nomads tend to stay in a location for extended periods, resulting in a more sustained economic impact on the local economy than traditional short-term tourism (Woldoff & Litchfield, 2021).

In this sense, digital nomads resemble "temporary residents" more than tourists, which requires tourist destinations to change their offerings and marketing strategies. Destinations like Bali, Lisbon, and Medellin have started actively promoting themselves as "digital nomad hubs" and have invested in infrastructure to attract these mobile workers. These destinations leverage their climate, culture, and relatively low cost of living to attract a global community of remote workers, creating a new economic model based on digital tourism and remote work (Hannonen, 2020).

Digital nomad tourism can revitalize local economies, especially in underserved areas that were not previously considered popular tourist destinations. However, its impact is not only economic; it also presents challenges and tensions in local communities. One of the most notable effects is digital gentrification, where the influx of digital nomads raises living costs and displaces low-income local residents, affecting social cohesion and generating tensions (Ji et al., 2024).

Still, there are significant positive effects: digital nomads promote infrastructure development, such as coworking spaces and digital services, which benefit both locals and visitors (Ji et al., 2024). They also help diversify the local economy by encouraging the creation of businesses related to technology, wellness, and services, stimulating entrepreneurship and innovation in host communities. On the other hand, the environmental impact of digital nomads is a relevant aspect, as the increased influx of travellers to natural or historically less-frequented areas may affect their long-term sustainability. Destination managers must consider these variables and adapt their policies to create tourism models that are not only economically viable but also environmentally responsible and culturally respectful.

The growth of digital nomads also raises questions about the role of public policy in this new context. Countries like Estonia and Croatia have already implemented special visas to attract these workers and stimulate economic growth through the temporary residence of digital nomads. These public policies seek to harness the benefits of this new type of tourism by facilitating the entry of digital nomads through flexible visa requirements, tax incentives, and support for creating coworking spaces, as well as developing regulations that protect both residents and visitors (Lazarević-Moravčević, & Domazet, 2025). As other countries and regions consider implementing similar policies, it is essential that strategies for attracting and retaining digital nomads consider the long-term social and environmental impacts. To achieve this, governments and the tourism industry must collaborate to create a sustainable tourism model that balances economic benefits with environmental preservation and the protection of local cultural identity.

The expansion of remote work and the growth of digital nomads also open new opportunities for innovation in tourism. The digital economy enables the development of specialized platforms offering services tailored to this segment, such as searching for temporary accommodation, coworking spaces, and access to professional networks in specific destinations. Additionally, destinations can benefit from the global visibility that digital nomads provide, as they act as ambassadors for the places they visit through social networks and digital platforms (Lazarević-Moravčević & Domazet, 2025).

However, the challenge for tourism in the digital nomad era lies in balancing the attraction of these visitors with the social and environmental sustainability of destinations. This requires an integrative approach that not only facilitates these workers' stays but also preserves resources and the quality of life of host communities. The future of tourism will largely depend on the adaptability and collaboration between the tourism industry, governments, and the digital nomads themselves, who must assume shared responsibility to minimize their environmental and social footprint.

Objective and Structure of the Chapter

The objective of this chapter is to analyze the transformation of tourism in the era of remote work, highlighting how digital nomads are redefining traditional paradigms in the tourism industry. This analysis will provide insights into the economic, social, and environmental impact of digital nomads on tourist destinations and discuss the opportunities and challenges that arise in this context.

The chapter structure will be developed as follows:

1. Introduction to the Digital Nomad Phenomenon and Remote Work: A historical and conceptual review of how remote work and technological advances have led to the rise of digital nomads.
2. Characterization of Digital Nomads as Tourists: An analysis of the distinctive characteristics of digital nomads, differentiating them from traditional tourists and describing their travel needs and behaviors.
3. Economic, Social, and Environmental Impact on Tourist Destinations: A study of the positive and negative repercussions of the presence of digital nomads in various local economies and destination sustainability.
4. Public Policies and Destination Adaptation: An analysis of how destinations and governments are implementing policies to attract and manage the influx of digital nomads, including examples of best practices and proposals for improving digital tourism sustainability.
5. New Opportunities for Tourism and Digital Innovation: Identification of emerging opportunities for the tourism industry related to digital nomads and analysis of how digital platforms can support this new tourism model.
6. Analysis of the Reality of Digital Nomadism: A qualitative analysis through in-depth interviews with digital nomads.
7. Conclusions and Recommendations: A synthesis of the main findings and recommendations for the sustainable development of digital nomad tourism, suggesting measures that maximize economic benefits and minimize negative effects on local communities and the environment.

This chapter will contribute to a comprehensive, multidimensional analysis of tourism in the era of digital nomads, providing a foundation for future research and innovative practices at the intersection of remote work and global tourism.

INTRODUCTION TO THE DIGITAL NOMAD PHENOMENON AND REMOTE WORK

Being part of the digital age has transformed numerous aspects of our society, including the world of work, giving rise to new organizational structures and modalities such as telecommuting and the phenomenon of digital nomadism. Today, factors such as information technology, mobility, and access to high-speed internet converge, enabling a segment of the workforce to perform their duties from anywhere in the world. This has given rise to what is now known as digital nomads. This phenomenon represents a profound shift in how people live and work, presenting new challenges and opportunities for both employees and companies.

Recent studies suggest that this is not a passing trend but a growing movement (Buffer, 2023). "97% of remote workers do not want to return to a traditional office full-time," emphasizing that flexibility and the freedom to choose where and when to work are the main drivers for adopting this mode (Buffer, 2023). This shift toward decentralized work is facilitated by a suite of digital tools, including project management platforms and video conferencing applications, allowing employees to fulfill their responsibilities from virtually any location.

While this may seem like a very recent phenomenon, its origins date back several decades, even though technological advancements have significantly accelerated its adoption. Moreover, the COVID-19 pandemic prompted a massive adoption of this modality. During lockdowns, millions of workers had to rapidly transition to remote work, demonstrating the feasibility of this option across various sectors and roles. The pandemic accelerated a trend already underway, forcing companies and workers to adapt to a new work paradigm at unprecedented speed (McPhail et al., 2024).

Digital nomadism is not the same as telecommuting or remote work. While remote work involves individuals working from a fixed location, such as their home or an alternative office space outside their company's headquarters, digital nomads take it a step further by combining work with constant geographic mobility. A digital nomad is someone who "uses technology to work from anywhere in the world, often moving between countries and cities without a fixed residence" (Makimoto & Manners, 1997). This lifestyle has become particularly appealing to workers in sectors such as technology, consulting, digital marketing, and content creation—roles that can often be performed anywhere with a reliable internet connection.

However, being a digital nomad is not always easy. Constant mobility requires strong self-management skills and a high level of adaptability to navigate different time zones, cultural barriers, and, at times, loneliness. The lack of stability and ephemeral connections that often characterize the life of digital nomads can sometimes have negative effects on mental health (Jaiswal et al., 2024). Therefore, while this modality is ideal for individuals with a high degree of independence and resilience, it may prove unsustainable for those who value stability and strong community ties.

Digital nomads are driven to adopt this lifestyle by both intrinsic and extrinsic factors. From an intrinsic perspective, the freedom of movement, autonomy, and the opportunity to explore new destinations are key attractions. Many digital nomads regard the ability to work from anywhere as the primary motivation for choosing this way of life. This underscores the idea that the appeal of this phenomenon lies not only in the ability to work remotely but also in the chance to travel and experience diverse cultures. Extrinsic factors include the rising cost of living in major cities and the desire to avoid high urban housing prices. Location flexibility allows remote workers to live in areas with a lower cost of living, optimizing their income and reducing significant expenses. This is particularly relevant for digital nomads, who can strategically choose locations with lower living costs that enable them to maintain a comfortable lifestyle without compromising the quality of their work (Orel, 2019).

As previously mentioned, technology is a key enabler of this phenomenon. On one hand, digital platforms like Microsoft Teams allow entire teams to communicate and coordinate tasks regardless of each member's location. On the other hand, internet connectivity has improved exponentially in recent decades, and high-speed networks are now accessible in many parts of the world. This is essential for remote work activities that require real-time data transmission (Ahlberg, 2021).

CHARACTERIZATION OF DIGITAL NOMADS AS TOURISTS

Digital nomadism attracts individuals because it allows them to work anytime, anywhere, and in ways that align with their interests (Hall et al., 2019). This newfound freedom extends beyond the professional realm, blending tourism, leisure, and professional activities to create a unique lifestyle based on remote work, global travel, and multi-location living (Mancinelli, 2020).

Despite its frequent use in tourism marketing, the term "digital nomad" is often used interchangeably with "remote worker" and lacks precision. Reichenberger (2018, p.364) defines them as "young professionals who work exclusively in an online environment and lead a location-independent, often travel-dependent lifestyle, where the boundaries between work, leisure, and travel appear blurred." Richter and Richter (2020, p.78) state that this emerging group is redefining professional life by seeking employment that enables international travel, flexible working hours, and a departure from traditional office environments. More recently, Nash et al. (2021, p.273) define them as "independent digital workers with extreme forms of spatial mobility and nonexistent or loose organizational affiliations."

In contrast to traditional tourists, digital nomads carry out work tasks while exploring different places. Thus, it is vital for them to strike a balance between their travels and work performance to meet the demands of this lifestyle. Productivity is a critical concern for digital nomads, given their constant work rhythm. The seamless combination of endless travel and work poses significant challenges for them. Their strong preference for tropical and subtropical climates may adversely impact their motivation and productivity due to the dynamic lifestyles that prevail in these regions (Arslan, 2024).

Reichenberger (2018) identified the importance of conceptualizing the digital nomad phenomenon and classified them based on their geographic mobility. He suggested three degrees of digital nomads: 1) versatile employees whose work does not demand travel and who have limited travel schedules; 2) those who maintain a permanent residence but take numerous trips; and 3) those who are fully committed to a life of mobility. On the other hand, Richards (2015) established three fundamental categories of digital nomads: the backpacker nomad, the flashpacker nomad, and the global nomad. He argued that, in contrast to the conventional backpacker, nomadism represents a personalized way of life. Global and digital nomads practice downshifting, which includes long-term travel and a minimalist lifestyle.

What various authors highlight is that the main motivation for this group is the pursuit of a better quality of life. Additionally, digital nomads are motivated by the desire to explore the world while maintaining their professional careers (Prabawa et al., 2020). This phenomenon is made possible by technology, which allows work to be performed from anywhere in the world with an internet connection. Instead of confining themselves to conventional offices, digital nomads seek destinations where they can enjoy unique cultural experiences, pleasant climates, and lower living costs compared to their home countries (Hall et al., 2019).

The mobility that characterizes these travellers also reflects a need for flexibility and autonomy, values increasingly appreciated by current generations. This suggests that digital nomads not only seek a change of environment to work but also value the freedom to experience diverse lifestyles in different geographic locations, avoiding routine and urban stress. Many choose destinations for their tourist and natural appeal, strengthening their connection to the category of tourist (Hermann & Paris, 2020).

As a hybrid profile of tourist and employee, digital nomads require infrastructure that combines connectivity and comfort. This includes appropriate workspaces, such as coworking spaces or cafés with strong internet connections, as well as versatile and comfortable accommodations. Moreover, the quality of internet connectivity in the destination is one of the most determining factors in selecting a temporary living site. Locations with robust and developed digital infrastructure become preferred choices for this type of traveler (Mouratidis, 2018).

In contrast to traditional tourists, digital nomads demand longer stays. According to various studies on digital tourism, the stays of digital nomads typically last several weeks to several months, as opposed to the short stays of a few days or weeks that define conventional tourists. This extended presence leads digital nomads to have a different impact on destinations, as they not only use tourist services but also integrate into the local economy by renting apartments or using transportation services over longer periods (Vagena, 2021).

ECONOMIC, SOCIAL, AND ENVIRONMENTAL IMPACT ON TOURIST DESTINATIONS

Digital nomads, a new generation of travelers and workers, exert considerable influence on tourist destinations where they settle temporarily. Their impact is broad and multifaceted, affecting not only the local economy but also the social fabric and environment of the places they choose to inhabit. This section examines how digital nomads transform tourist destinations, addressing economic impacts, social repercussions, and environmental effects.

First, it is important to note that the economic impact of digital nomads on tourist destinations is both direct and indirect. Their continuous consumption promotes the development of various local industries, particularly those providing services tailored to their needs, such as coworking spaces, technological infrastructure, and medium- and long-term accommodations. The digital economy and remote work have enabled tourist destinations to become temporary hubs for digital workers who, by staying longer, contribute more sustainably to local economies (Floričić & Pavia, 2021).

Moreover, the preference of digital nomads for cities with a lower cost of living creates opportunities for many local economies to diversify their income sources. Digital nomads generally earn higher incomes than local residents, enabling them to invest in products and services not typically associated with short-term tourism. Digital nomads often represent adaptable spending, supporting both luxury tourism and the development of small and medium enterprises in emerging destinations (Mourato et al., 2023). However, this spending has also led to increased living costs in some cities, such as Lisbon and Bali, driven by higher demand for tourist accommodations.

The social impact of digital nomads on tourist destinations is a topic of significant discussion. On one hand, their presence promotes cultural exchange and introduces new global perspectives into local communities. This cultural exchange process can benefit communities by fostering broader openness and tolerance. Digital nomads bring a global outlook and help enrich the cultural life of the cities they visit by engaging in local events and sharing knowledge (Chevtaeva & Denizci-Guillet, 2021).

However, the adoption of digital nomads is not always beneficial. The economic disparity between these remote employees and local residents can lead to social conflicts, particularly when rising prices limit residents' access to essential resources like housing. In cities like Mexico City and Lisbon, the impact of these new temporary residents on the real estate sector has caused a phenomenon of "digital gentrification," pushing local inhabitants to peripheral areas due to increasing rental costs (Bahri & Widhyharto, 2021). This situation has raised concerns about the social and economic viability of welcoming digital nomads without clear regulations that consider community interests.

Additionally, the rapid emergence of digital nomads can generate a sense of "temporary colonization" in certain places. Unlike other types of visitors, digital nomads tend to establish routines and forge connections within local communities. While this can be beneficial in many cases, it may cause tensions if residents feel their culture and spaces are being invaded or altered without consent. This is one reason some tourism specialists advocate for the importance of "careful and regulated management" of the rise of digital nomads (Cook, 2020).

Another important factor is the environmental impact of the growing presence of digital nomads in tourist destinations. Like traditional visitors, digital nomads contribute to resource consumption and waste generation. However, because they often stay for extended periods, their consumption patterns also remain stable over time, which can lead to both positive and negative environmental impacts.

On one hand, digital nomads tend to be aware of the ecological impact of their choices and seek destinations that promote sustainability practices. Research by Reichenberger (2018) indicates that digital nomads show a tendency to support sustainability initiatives, such as using eco-friendly accommodations and opting for low-carbon transportation options. This suggests they can become partners in fostering responsible tourism in certain locations, particularly those aiming to build more environmentally friendly infrastructure. On the other hand, their presence also increases pressure on local ecosystems, especially in popular tourist areas and protected natural zones. The concentration of smartphones in certain locations can overload local services and contribute to the deterioration of natural resources, such as water and electricity. Furthermore, the intensive use of digital infrastructure requires significant energy investment, impacting the environment, particularly in areas where sustainable energy sources are scarce (Zhou et al., 2024).

PUBLIC POLICIES AND DESTINATION ADAPTATION

Digital nomads are growing as a phenomenon that is changing tourism norms and creating different requirements for the places they visit. Governments and local communities are implementing policies and strategies to attract and sustainably manage the economic, social, and environmental impact of these travelers.

Many areas are adjusting their structures and regulations to meet the specific needs of digital nomads. For example, Thailand and Croatia have created special visas that allow these professionals to legally reside while working remotely. These policies not only help regularize the migratory status of nomads but also increase revenue through specific fees and promote longer stays, thereby benefiting local economies with a more stable and predictable income flow (Tourism Authority of Thailand, 2022).

In contrast, programs like Spain's Tourism Sustainability Strategy 2030 aim to incorporate sustainability into tourism growth through participatory and collaborative approaches. This strategy emphasizes financial, social, and environmental sustainability, ensuring that tourism development does not harm local resources or community well-being (Spanish Ministry of Industry and Tourism, 2022).

Another part of these policies involves creating infrastructure that meets the needs of digital nomads. Investments in coworking spaces, fast internet, and flexible accommodations are common practices. In regions like Bali or Lisbon, such services have become essential offerings for attracting this group and promoting competition in the international market. There is also an increasing emphasis on using modern technologies, such as digital platforms for managing smart tourism destinations. Standards like UNE 178504, developed in Spain, guide hotels and other tourism stakeholders in efficiently managing information, improving service planning, and personalizing the tourist experience. These technologies also facilitate impact monitoring and the development of sustainable measures (UNE, 2019).

In online tourism management, the concept of sustainability aligns with the overarching definition governing the industry. In countries like Costa Rica and Colombia, programs have been implemented involving local populations to promote authentic tourism activities. These models not only generate financial returns but also foster cultural exchanges and heritage preservation (UNWTO, 2018).

Madeira in Portugal, for instance, offers excellent examples of innovative solutions sought in the context of digital nomadism. The archipelago launched the "Digital Nomads Madeira" program, providing coworking spaces located in beautiful ecological areas. This model has shown how to attract this type of visitor while minimizing adverse impacts on local populations and the environment (Digital Nomads Madeira Islands, 2024).

However, while the migration of digital nomads is viewed positively by most, it also brings challenges. One significant issue is gentrification, which increases living costs and displaces local populations from their areas. Governments must promote social welfare by balancing the needs of tourists with those of the local population to avoid adverse effects on host communities. This can be achieved through measures like regulating short-term rental prices and implementing programs that engage with local culture. Additionally, the environmental impact of nomadism—particularly the carbon footprint from frequent travel—requires well-thought-out responses. Destinations can encourage renewable energy use, facilitate sustainable transportation systems, and conduct awareness campaigns.

Finally, the social and cultural disconnection that characterizes the transient lifestyle of these professionals can be addressed by promoting meaningful interactions between visitors and local communities. Volunteering programs and community events are examples of how to strengthen cultural ties and foster a sense of belonging (UNWTO, 2018).

NEW OPPORTUNITIES FOR TOURISM AND DIGITAL INNOVATION

Digital nomads represent a market segment characterized by constant mobility, a focus on cultural experiences, and a reliance on high-quality technological infrastructure. According to a Statista report (2023), there are an estimated 35 million digital nomads worldwide, and this number is continually growing. This demographic, primarily composed of young and middle-aged professionals with stable incomes and advanced technological skills, offers significant opportunities for tourism destinations that know how to attract them.

The adoption of digital platforms in the tourism sector presents both challenges and significant opportunities. According to Heredia et al. (2024), technological and economic barriers are key obstacles to integrating these tools. However, they also highlight that diversifying the tourism offering and increasing visibility in broader markets are emerging opportunities. Additionally, their research suggests that training in digital competencies is essential for tourism service providers to adapt to the demands of digital nomads. In this context, digital platforms not only facilitate marketing but also enable the creation of personalized experiences that appeal to this new segment of travelers. Thus, the integration of digital technologies becomes a crucial factor for the competitiveness and sustainability of tourism in the region.

One of the main opportunities this group offers is the deseasonalization of tourism. Unlike conventional tourists, digital nomads are not tied to scheduled vacations; they can settle in a destination for weeks or months, contributing to a constant and diversified demand throughout the year. Cities like Bali, Lisbon, and Mexico City have emerged as hubs for digital nomads, benefiting from a continuous flow of visitors who consistently consume local services.

Moreover, this traveler profile tends to favor authentic and sustainable experiences. This encourages tourism businesses to develop more personalized products, such as coworking spaces in rural settings, wellness retreats with high-speed internet access, or travel packages that integrate cultural activities. According to an HBR study (2022), digital nomads are willing to pay up to 20% more for experiences that combine work and leisure, provided they offer stable connectivity and stimulating environments.

The rise of platforms like Airbnb, Nomad List, and Selina has transformed how digital nomads choose their destinations. These platforms not only provide accommodations but also access to communities and essential resources for remote work, such as integrated coworking spaces and connectivity guides. For instance, Selina combines lodging with collaborative workspaces and leisure activities, specifically designed for this group. This hybrid model has enabled less conventional destinations, such as coastal towns or rural areas, to position themselves as viable options.

Artificial intelligence (AI) is being used to create more personalized travel experiences. Advanced algorithms can analyze the preferences and travel patterns of digital nomads to recommend destinations, activities, and accommodations tailored to their needs. Platforms like Booking.com and Expedia have begun implementing these technologies to enhance user experiences and facilitate planning for flexible travel.

Virtual reality (VR) is also emerging as a key tool to attract digital nomads. Immersive simulations allow travelers to explore destinations before committing, helping them visualize their living and working experience in a particular location. This is especially useful for emerging destinations seeking to compete with established hubs.

Beyond the advantages for the tourism sector, the digital nomad model has significant implications for local communities. Economically, these travelers often spend more than conventional tourists due to their extended stays and need for additional services. According to a Forbes report (2023), the average monthly expenditure of a digital nomad ranges between $1,500 and $3,000, depending on the destination.

However, challenges also arise regarding housing access and cultural integration. In some cities, increased demand for accommodations by digital nomads has contributed to rising prices, displacing local residents. To mitigate these effects, some destinations, such as Barcelona and Amsterdam, have implemented regulations to balance economic benefits with social sustainability.

What measures can destinations and tourism businesses take to capitalize on the opportunities digital nomads offer? Key actions include:

1. Investing in technological infrastructure: Ensuring reliable connectivity is essential. Countries like Estonia have led this trend with their e-Residency program, which allows digital nomads to establish businesses and work from anywhere in the world.
2. Promoting collaborative hubs: Creating vibrant communities that offer coworking spaces, networking events, and cultural activities encourages digital nomads to stay longer in destinations.
3. Encouraging public-private collaboration: Partnerships between local governments and tech companies can drive the development of innovative solutions, such as specialized visas for digital nomads, already implemented in countries like Portugal and Croatia.
4. Focusing on a sustainable approach: Incorporating sustainable practices in tourism services not only meets the demands of digital nomads but also helps mitigate their environmental impact.

Analysis of the Reality of Digital Nomadism

After conducting a theoretical review of digital nomadism, including its conceptualization, its characterization as a form of tourism, its impact and adaptation to destinations, and the new opportunities this group generates, a practical analysis was carried out based on the collection of primary data.

To deeply explore the experiences of digital nomads, a qualitative analysis was conducted using in-depth interviews. A qualitative approach for researching underexplored topics offers an in-depth understanding of key problems (Brown et al., 2020). Qualitative analysis produces descriptive data in the form of written or spoken words and observable behavior (Za et al., 2020). This approach allowed for an understanding of the motivations, challenges, and perspectives of those who adopt this lifestyle, as well as the identification of relevant patterns for the tourism and technology industries. The analysis was based on the responses of four digital nomads currently practicing this way of life.

To ensure the collection of relevant and meaningful data, the interviews were structured around a script of 14 questions (Table 1), which included open-ended questions to thoroughly explore key aspects of digital nomadism, such as: Motivations for becoming a digital nomad; Major challenges in living as a digital nomad; Selection of destinations; Necessary services to sustain a digital nomad lifestyle; and Relationship with the local community.

The questions were chosen based on the objectives of the research, and the literature review provided the initial foundation of knowledge. The structure of the interview was designed to encourage reflection and elicit extensive, detailed responses, allowing for the identification of recurring themes and individual nuances in the narrated experiences.

Table 1. Interview Script

1	**From where are you attending this interview?**
2	Since becoming a digital nomad, in which places have you lived?
3	Where is the company you work for located?
4	What type of work do you do remotely, and what technological tools do you consider essential for your daily work?
5	How did you become a digital nomad?
6	How do you choose the destination(s) you travel to? What factors influence your decision (culture, cost of living, infrastructure, connectivity)?
7	Unlike conventional tourists, you stay in destinations for longer periods. How does this impact your relationship with the places you visit and their communities?
8	Have you ever experienced a situation where your presence as a digital nomad caused conflict or tension with local residents? How did you handle it?
9	In your opinion, how do you think your presence as a digital nomad affects the local economy of the destinations you visit? Do you think your presence has a positive or negative impact?
10	From your experience, do you believe digital nomad tourism can contribute to the sustainable development of a destination, or do you think it can cause negative effects (gentrification, resource strain)?
11	How do you evaluate the infrastructure available in the destinations you visit (coworking spaces, internet services, accommodation options)? Is there anything you always look for when choosing a place to work remotely?
12	Have you had any positive or negative experiences with local or national policies related to digital nomads (special visas, tax incentives, labor regulations)? What improvements would you like to see in policies to attract and manage this type of tourism?
13	How do you see the future of tourism for digital nomads? What trends do you think will shape the evolution of remote work and its integration with tourism?
14	Is there anything else you'd like to share about your experience as a digital nomad and how you think this phenomenon is changing the way we understand tourism?

Source: Own elaboration

A phenomenological approach was employed, ideal for capturing the subjective experiences and perceptions of participants. The interviews were conducted remotely using videoconferencing platforms, which facilitated interaction with interviewees located in different countries. Each session lasted an average of 45 minutes and was recorded with the participants' consent for later transcription and analysis.

Although for in-depth interviews, the recommended number of interviewees is the smallest number that provides sufficient information to meet the research objectives (Izcara Palacios & Andrade Rubio, 2003), additional interviews were initially planned to explore the possibility of uncovering new insights. However, no new relevant information emerged after the third interview. Consequently, it was decided not to proceed with further interviews from the pool of volunteers.

Once the interviews were completed, manual transcriptions were reviewed, and the data were classified, organized, and translated from Spanish into English to present the results and draw conclusions. The analysis was conducted using thematic coding, which allowed the identification of key patterns in the responses.

To ensure the validity of the study, data triangulation was employed. This involved comparing individual narratives with prior research and trends observed in the literature, reinforcing the reliability of the findings.

ANALYSIS OF THE REALITY OF DIGITAL NOMADISM

Table 2 presents the profile of the four interviewees, detailing their current work location at the time of the interview, the location of their company headquarters, the places they have visited as digital nomads, how and when they became digital nomads, and their reasons for doing so, as well as their different job positions.

Table 2. Interviewees' profile

	Current location	Company headquarters	Places visited as digital nomad	How he/she became a digital nomad	Job Position
Interviewee 1	Valencia	London	Lisbon Berlin Prague Krakow	During pandemic as a result of remote work	Digital design
Interviewee 2	Berlin	Stockholm	Amsterdam Dublin Stockholm	Five years ago, when discovered he/she could work from anywhere and live in different countries and experience new cultures.	Web design
Interviewee 3	Lisbon	Madrid	Málaga Other many places	He/she reached an agreement with the company to work remotely to have the freedom to travel.	Technology programmer
Interviewee 4	Las Palmas de Gran Canaria	Berlin	Norway Canary Islands	During pandemic as a result of remote work	Web programmer

Source: Own elaboration

From the places where they have lived as digital nomads, the four interviewees highlighted aspects such as having "good Wi-Fi," "views," a "peaceful and welcoming atmosphere," "good weather," "excellent food," "opportunities to connect with other professionals," "quality of life," an "abundance of coworking spaces," "good digital infrastructure," and "different cultures." The characteristics they seek in the destinations they travel to include "Internet connectivity," "low cost of living," "climate," "cultural diversity and offerings," "good quality of life," "opportunities for outdoor activities," "communities of other digital nomads," and "safety." They all agree on prioritizing an affordable cost of living and good Internet quality. These preferences align with those presented in previous literature, except for the climate, which does not emerge as a relevant topic in prior studies.

All the interviewees work in technology-related fields, such as web development, design, or programming. These are remote jobs that only require a computer, hardware such as headphones, and specialized software, conditions shared by all the interviewees and deemed essential for being a digital nomad. Software like Figma, GitHub, or Notion is necessary for their work. Another common condition is that their companies adopted remote work. One interviewee emphasized that this shift happened due to COVID-19, while the others did not specify if it was pandemic-related. While previous literature highlights the role of COVID-19 in the rise of digital nomads, the interviews suggest that the primary condition is the companies' provision of remote work opportunities. Should companies cease to offer this type of work, it would have severe negative consequences for this form of tourism.

All the interviewees agreed that they differ from conventional tourists in that, by spending more time in a destination, they integrate more deeply, getting to know the locals and better understanding the places they visit. This allows them to "create deeper connections" and authentic relationships with locals, experiencing "more meaningful" interactions. This is something not emphasized in previous literature, which tends to overlook the experiences generated by this type of tourism and lifestyle and the feelings experienced by these workers. They did not report any negative experiences with local residents, something that is repeatedly mentioned in previous literature. However, they are aware that tensions are growing in some destinations due to gentrification and rising living costs. To address this issue, they emphasize the importance of being mindful of the problem, staying in less touristy areas, and supporting local businesses. They claim to have a positive impact on the destinations they visit, contributing through the income spent on accommodation, restaurants, and other local services. They consciously aim to consume from small, local businesses and promote the growth of coworking spaces.

They believe that digital nomad tourism can be sustainable if managed with that goal in mind, creating policies that balance the interests of locals and visitors, with collaboration among locals, governments, and nomads. Supporting local businesses and respecting communities is vital, according to the interviewees. They do not think the scale of digital nomad tourism is currently large enough to cause an unsustainable burden. When asked about positive or negative experiences, they highlighted only positive ones, such as in the Canary Islands, the "Digital Nomad Visa" initiative, and the lower taxes under the REF (Régimen Económico y Fiscal de Canarias - The Economic and Tax Regime of the Canary Islands), as well as special digital nomad visas in Estonia.

When specifically asked about available and necessary infrastructure, all the interviewees highlighted the same requirements: well-designed and equipped coworking spaces, fiber-optic broadband with good Wi-Fi, and comfortable accommodations for long stays. Much of the previous literature emphasizes that digital nomad tourism can revitalize local economies, especially in underserved areas not previously considered popular tourist destinations. However, this is incompatible with the basic characteristics required by these digital workers, especially those related to good Internet connectivity and well-designed, equipped spaces. There will be areas that are less touristy where providing these features is not feasible, posing a significant challenge to adapting such destinations to the requirements of digital nomads.

As mentioned in previous literature, they believe that digital nomad tourism will continue to grow for several reasons: the increase in remote work, destinations competing to attract more digital nomads, and improvements in coworking infrastructure. However, they consider it necessary to adopt a more sustainable approach with greater integration into local communities and cultures. This approach is important because it characterizes this type of tourist and tourism as responsible and conscious of the problems that may arise due to their professional activities and lifestyle.

When asked for any additional thoughts or comments, they responded:

Interviewee 1: "Being a digital nomad is not just about traveling; it's about learning to adapt and being aware of the impact you leave."

Interviewee 2: "Being a digital nomad has taught me that remote work is not just a way of working but an opportunity to build bridges between cultures and rethink tourism in a more responsible way."

Interviewee 3: "Overall, I'm very happy with the experience of being able to work and travel."

Interviewee 4: "Being a digital nomad not only redefines how we work but also how we live. This lifestyle has taught me to be more flexible, adaptable, and mindful of the impact I leave on the places I visit."

CONCLUSIONS

The phenomenon of digital nomadism has emerged as an intersection between remote work and tourism, driving significant transformations in both areas. This lifestyle reflects a cultural and technological shift that redefines traditional patterns of employment and travel, while simultaneously creating opportunities and posing challenges for tourist destinations worldwide.

Digital nomads are not just an emerging segment of workers but also a new type of tourist with specific characteristics and needs. By seeking destinations with advanced technological infrastructure, affordable living costs, and diverse cultural experiences, these individuals are pushing tourist destinations to innovate and adapt their offerings. Destinations like Bali and Lisbon have become key hubs for attracting this community, showcasing the long-term economic impact this type of tourism can generate. However, digital nomadism also presents significant challenges, such as digital gentrification, pressure on local resources, and the environmental impact of prolonged tourism. Host communities must balance economic benefits with preserving their cultural identity and quality of life.

The future of tourism in the remote work era will depend on the ability of governments, the tourism industry, and digital nomads to collaborate in creating sustainable models that maximize economic benefits while minimizing social and environmental negative impacts. Striking this balance will be essential to ensure digital nomadism evolves as a positive force in transforming global tourism.

Digital nomads are a transformative force in tourist destinations, with diverse economic, social, and environmental impacts. Their presence stimulates local economies through sustained consumption and income diversification, though it may drive up living costs and exacerbate inequalities. Environmentally, their inclination toward sustainability is a positive trend, but their prolonged presence increases pressure on natural resources and energy infrastructure. Implementing management strategies is crucial to balancing benefits and mitigating negative impacts.

The adaptation of tourist destinations to the phenomenon of digital nomadism is essential to maximize benefits and address associated challenges. Public policies, such as specialized visas and sustainability programs, have proven effective in attracting and managing these remote workers. Investments in technological infrastructure, collaborative spaces, and rent price regulation are necessary to balance local interests with the demands of digital tourism. Additionally, fostering cultural interactions and adopting innovative technologies such as artificial intelligence and virtual reality can enhance the competitiveness and sustainability of emerging destinations.

REFERENCES

Ahlberg, E. (2021). The Development of the Digital Nomad During the Course of the Pandemic: The digital nomad workforce, a study looking into the power of digital tools allowing people to work remotely.

Arslan, E. (2024). From tourists to nomads: Unveiling the transformative potential of digital nomads in travel and tourism. *Worldwide Hospitality and Tourism Themes*, *16*(3), 269–281. DOI: 10.1108/WHATT-03-2024-0046

Bahri, M. T., & Widhyharto, D. S. (2021). Social network analysis (SNA) on# Kristengray Hashtag: Understanding gentrification side effects behind the digital nomad phenomenon. *Jurnal Studi Pemuda*, *10*(1), 75. DOI: 10.22146/studipemudaugm.65255

Brown, L., Buhalis, D., & Beer, S. (2020). Dining alone: Improving the experience of solo restaurant goers. *International Journal of Contemporary Hospitality Management*, *32*(3), 1347–1365. DOI: 10.1108/IJCHM-06-2019-0584

Buffer. (2023). *The Global Rise of Remote Work*. Recuperado de: https://buffer.com/state-of-remote-work

Chevtaeva, E., & Denizci-Guillet, B. (2021). Digital nomads' lifestyles and coworkation. *Journal of Destination Marketing & Management*, *21*, 100633. DOI: 10.1016/j.jdmm.2021.100633

Cook, D. (2020). The freedom trap: Digital nomads and the use of disciplining practices to manage work/leisure boundaries. *Information Technology & Tourism*, *22*(3), 355–390. DOI: 10.1007/s40558-020-00172-4

Digital Nomads Madeira Islands. (2024). https://digitalnomads.startupmadeira.eu/

Floričić, T., & Pavia, N. (2021). Linkage of leisure with remote work and digital nomadism in tourist accommodation facilities. *ToSEE*, *6*, 247–268. DOI: 10.20867/tosee.06.17

Forbes. (2023). *How digital nomads are transforming global tourism*. Recuperado de https://www.forbes.com

Hall, G., Sigala, M., Rentschler, R., & Boyle, S. (2019). Motivations, mobility and work practices; the conceptual realities of digital nomads. In *Information and Communication Technologies in Tourism 2019:Proceedings of the International Conference in Nicosia, Cyprus, January 30–February 1, 2019* (pp. 437-449). Springer International Publishing.

Hannonen, O. (2020). In search of a digital nomad: Defining the phenomenon. *Information Technology & Tourism, 22*(3), 335–353. DOI: 10.1007/s40558-020-00177-z

Harvard Business Review. (2022). *The rise of digital nomads: How remote work is reshaping the workforce*. Recuperado de https://hbr.org

Heredia, C. G. M., Layedra, C. A. S., Prado, R. R. G., & León, P. M. (2024). Barreras y oportunidades en la adopción de plataformas digitales por parte de los prestadores de servicios turísticos en el cantón Alausí: Barriers and opportunities in the adoption of digital platforms by tourism service providers in Alausi´ s town. *LATAM Revista Latinoamericana de Ciencias Sociales y Humanidades, 5*(5), 648–660.

Izcara Palacios, S., & Andrade Rubio, K. (2003). *La entrevista en profundidad teoría y práctica*. Universidad Autónoma de Tamaulipas.

Jaiswal, R., Gupta, S., & Gupta, S. K. (2024). The impending disruption of digital nomadism: Opportunities, challenges, and research agenda. *World Leisure Journal*, •••, 1–31. DOI: 10.1080/16078055.2024.2346091

Ji, Y., Kim, S. M., & Kim, Y. (2024). A way to attract digital nomads to tourist destinations in the new normal era. *Sustainability (Basel), 16*(6), 2336. DOI: 10.3390/su16062336

Kasman Arifin, Z. A., & Syapsan, D. P. S. (2020). Optimization of Tourism Industry by Supply Chain Strategy of Rokan Regional District to Increase Original Revenue. Int. J Sup. Chain. *Mgt, 9*(1), 1036.

Lazarević-Moravčević, M., & Domazet, I. S. (2025). Attraction of Digital Nomads as Significant Tourism Potential: Evidence From Serbia. In *Tracking Tourism Patterns and Improving Travel Experiences With Innovative Technologies* (pp. 191–214). IGI Global.

Makimoto, T., & Manners, D. (1997). *Digital nomad*. John Wiley & Sons.

Mancinelli, F. (2020). Digital nomads: Freedom, responsibility and the neoliberal order. *Information Technology & Tourism, 22*(3), 417–437. DOI: 10.1007/s40558-020-00174-2

McPhail, R., Chan, X. W., May, R., & Wilkinson, A. (2024). Post-COVID remote working and its impact on people, productivity, and the planet: An exploratory scoping review. *International Journal of Human Resource Management, 35*(1), 154–182. DOI: 10.1080/09585192.2023.2221385

Ministerio de Industria y Turismo de España. (2022). Estrategia de Turismo de España 2030. Recuperado de https://turismo.gob.es/es-es/estrategia-turismo-sostenible/paginas/index.aspx

Mouratidis, G. (2018). Digital nomads: travel, remote work and alternative lifestyles.

Mourato, I., Dias, Á., & Pereira, L. (2023). Estimating the impact of digital nomads' sustainable responsibility on entrepreneurial self-efficacy. *Social Sciences (Basel, Switzerland)*, *12*(2), 97. DOI: 10.3390/socsci12020097

Nash, C., Jarrahi, M. H., Sutherland, W., & Phillips, G. (2018, March). Digital nomads beyond the buzzword: Defining digital nomadic work and use of digital technologies. In *International conference on information* (pp. 207-217). Cham: Springer International Publishing. DOI: 10.1007/978-3-319-78105-1_25

Orel, M. (2019). Coworking environments and digital nomadism: Balancing work and leisure whilst on the move. *World Leisure Journal*, *61*(3), 215–227. DOI: 10.1080/16078055.2019.1639275

Prabawa, I. W. S. W., & Pertiwi, P. R. (2020). The digital nomad tourist motivation in Bali: Exploratory research based on push and pull theory. *Athens Journal of Tourism*, *7*(3), 161–174. DOI: 10.30958/ajt.7-3-3

Reichenberger, I. (2018). Digital nomads–a quest for holistic freedom in work and leisure. *Annals of Leisure Research*, *21*(3), 364–380. DOI: 10.1080/11745398.2017.1358098

Richter, S., & Richter, A. (2020). Digital nomads. *Business & Information Systems Engineering*, *62*(1), 77–81. DOI: 10.1007/s12599-019-00615-1

Secretaría de Turismo de Tailandia. (2022). *Digital Nomad Visa Policies in Thailand*. Recuperado de https://www.tourismthailand.org

Statista. (2023). *Number of digital nomads worldwide from 2020 to 2023*. Recuperado de https://www.statista.com

UNE. (2019). UNE 178504:2019. Recuperado de https://www.une.org/encuentra-tu-norma/busca-tu-norma/norma?c=N0062377

UNWTO. (2018). *Tourism and the Sustainable Development Goals: Good Practices in the Americas.* Madrid, España. Recuperado de https://www.unwto.org

Vagena, A. (2021). Digital nomads and tourism industry. *Academia Letters*, *765*, 1–6.

Woldoff, R. A., & Litchfield, R. C. (2021). *Digital nomads: In search of freedom, community, and meaningful work in the new economy*. Oxford University Press.

Zhou, L., Buhalis, D., Fan, D. X., Ladkin, A., & Lian, X. (2024). Attracting digital nomads: Smart destination strategies, innovation and competitiveness. *Journal of Destination Marketing & Management, 31*, 100850. DOI: 10.1016/j.jdmm.2023.100850

KEY TERMS AND DEFINITIONS

Digital Nomad Visa: A type of visa that allows individuals to work remotely in a foreign country while legally residing there, typically for an extended period. It is designed for remote workers, freelancers, or entrepreneurs who can perform their work online.

Digital Nomadism: A lifestyle where individuals use technology to work remotely while traveling or living in different locations, often without being tied to a single workplace or office.

Figma: A web-based collaborative design tool used for interface design, prototyping, and team collaboration. It allows multiple users to work on the same project in real time.

GitHub: A platform for version control and collaboration, primarily used for software development. It allows developers to host and manage code repositories, track changes, and collaborate on projects using Git, a version control system.

Notion: An all-in-one productivity and organizational tool that allows users to manage tasks, create databases, write notes, and collaborate on projects. It is highly customizable and used for both personal and team productivity.

The Economic and Tax Regime of the Canary Islands (REF): A special fiscal framework that provides tax incentives and reduced rates to promote economic activity and investment in the Canary Islands. Key features include lower indirect taxes (IGIC instead of VAT) and benefits like the Canary Islands Special Zone (ZEC).

Chapter 3
Tourism in the Age of Remote Work:
How Digital Nomads Are Changing the Game

Gaye Deniz
https://orcid.org/0000-0002-9980-8506
Nevşehir Hacı Bektaş Veli University, Turkey

Şule Ardıç Yetiş
https://orcid.org/0000-0002-8792-9079
Nevsehir Haci Bektas Veli University, Turkey

ABSTRACT

Digital nomads are individuals who leverage the flexibility afforded by technology to perform their work remotely from diverse global locations over extended periods. This chapter explores the economic contributions of digital nomads to local communities, their role in fostering cultural exchange, and their potential impact on sustainable tourism practices. It also examines the opportunities that digital nomads offer to the hospitality and service sector, as well as the challenges such as increasing costs of living, demand for infrastructure, and loss of authenticity. In particular, the focus is on how destination managers and local governments can balance economic development and environmental sustainability when attracting digital nomads. In this context, the strategies and policies necessary to achieve sustainable tourism goals are discussed. In the near future, digital nomad tourism is expected to transform the tourism industry significantly, introducing lasting changes driven by this innovative working style.

DOI: 10.4018/979-8-3373-0076-4.ch003

INTRODUCTION

In today's world, working models are transforming massively due to the rapid growth of technology and the impact of digitalization. Enforcement of social distancing policies compelled the en masse adoption of remote working, and it altered the very nature of the concept of 'work, workplace, and workforce.' These modifications are also inextricably linked with several other concepts (Yılmaz Güzey & Çelik, 2022). The expansion of remote working practices, especially in recent years, has brought about deep transformations in the tourism industry, as it has for many other industries (Lanza et al., 2022; Chevtaeva et al., 2022). However, it is noted when going through the supporting literature that very little research has attempted to seriously challenge what effect the digital nomadism phenomenon imposes on host regions. In this, there is a requirement for extensive analysis to be in a position to achieve the balance between the economic, social, and cultural contributions of digital nomad tourism to destinations and the challenges emanating from this model.

Digital nomads have emerged as one of the striking outcomes of this new working order. In recent years, digital nomadism has become widespread as a lifestyle and has emerged as an alternative that challenges traditional working models (Nash et al., 2018). The term 'digital nomads,' employed by Makimoto and Manners (1997), best describes the way people entirely redefine their lifestyle as technology advances. The term 'digital nomads' best describes people who are on-the-move professionals who work anywhere and at any time globally with digital technologies. Alternatively, 'digital nomadism' best describes the lifestyle of highly mobile professionals who appreciate geographical independence with the assistance of technology (Hannonen, 2020). Digital nomads are defined in this context as people who can work from anywhere in the world indefinitely and yet be free of the tether of a physical office through technology. However, it is seen that the studies in the literature on the effects of digital nomads on the tourism sector have largely focused on individual experiences and work dynamics, and the economic, social, and cultural reflections of this new form of mobility on a destination basis have not been adequately addressed. This study aims to fill a gap at this point and holistically address the effects of digital nomadism on tourism destinations.

The emergence of digital nomads has also created a radical change in the tourism sector. Unlike typical tourists, who visit destinations for a brief duration, digital nomads work while renting long-term residences but delve deeper into the cultural and social framework of the destinations they travel to. This long-term accommodation and work model has changed the structure of tourism and has led many destinations to develop service models for digital nomads. However, the long-term stay of digital nomads in destinations should be evaluated in terms of their effects on local economies, social dynamics, and sustainable tourism. Considering that the current literature contains limited studies that systematically address this issue, this section aims to contribute to the literature by deeply analyzing the interaction between digital nomadism and tourism. Digital nomadism has many economic, social, and environmental impacts on tourism destinations. This study presents a conceptual framework to explain these impacts and the role of destination policies (See Figure 2).

This section examines the effects of digital nomads on the tourism sector, focusing on their economic, social, and cultural contributions to destinations, as well as the opportunities and challenges they generate. In particular, the contributions of digital nomad tourism to the local economy, the requirements it creates in terms of destination management, and its effects in the context of sustainability will be detailed. In this context, the opportunities offered by digital nomad tourism and the problems it faces will be detailed, and a comprehensive analysis will be presented on this new tourism model.

MAIN FOCUS OF THE CHAPTER

The main focus of this section is to examine the transformations created by digital nomads in the tourism sector and the impacts of this new travel model on destinations. In contrast to tourism with the classical definition, digital nomads combine travel and work and bring in new income sources with their long-term residences. This section addresses how digital nomads mingle with local cultures, how they contribute towards sustainable tourism, and what opportunities they present to destination managers. It addresses features like increased cost of living and infrastructure stress due to digital nomad tourism.

The Concept of Digital Nomadism

Since the 1980s, international mobility has become an important trend worldwide due to the change in individuals' lifestyles, freedom of choice, and desire for self-realization. Such various forms include but are not limited to second-home tourism, seasonal migration, and digital nomadism. Globalization, built around individualism, technological advancements in communication and transport, flexible working conditions, and changing digital real estate, reveals the most significant socio-political factors that fuel the aforementioned trend. Digitalization and mobile lifestyles have played an important role in the emergence of some new social and way-of-life forms, standing halfway between tourism and migration in their effects (Hannonen, 2020).

This lifestyle of digital nomadism is emerging when opportunities are made available under globalization and developments in technology. The concept was first introduced in the work "Digital Nomad" by Makimoto and Manners in 1997 (Birtchnell, 2019). Digital nomads are thus professionals who do work digitally and travel around constantly without the need for any physical office. They do not have fixed working hours as they opt to use the flexible work models provided by technology, thus combining work with traveling (Hensellek & Puchala, 2021; Nash et al., 2018). More and more people are embracing this way of life with the development of technologies and the increase in remote working models. Bozdoğan and Dağdelen (2022) preferred the conceptualization of lifestyle mobility in their study, as they emphasize the fluidity between travel, leisure, and migration. Digital nomadism is a concept that expresses a significant transformation in working and lifestyles, especially after the COVID-19 pandemic. The post-pandemic America has recorded a 50% rise in the number of digital nomads, an increase reaching up to 10.2 million. This increase will likely continue. 71% of digital nomads work full-time, 29% work part-time, and 85% are satisfied with their current job status. In terms of categories, digital nomads show the following proportion age share: 44 percent are millennials, 23 percent are Gen X, 21 percent are Gen Z, and 12 percent are baby boomers. In terms of gender, males (59%) are more common than females (41%). Quite a significant population of digital nomads, around 70%, belong to the racial group known as White, while around 14% identify as African American, 7% claim to be of Hispanic ethnicity, and 7% belong to Asian ethnicities. In terms of education level, 72% have at least a bachelor's degree, while 33% have a master's degree (FlexJobs, 2022).

Current approaches to digital nomadism can be evaluated under two main perspectives: work-life and lifestyle dimensions (Stumpf et al., 2022). The work-life perspective defines digital nomads as mobile professionals who can work remotely (Mouratidis, 2018). While Liegl (2014) describes digital nomads as mobile knowledge workers equipped with digital technologies and able to work anywhere, anytime, Müller (2016) describes this group as location-independent freelancers, online workers, and young entrepreneurs. However, Nash et al. (2021) challenge the rhetoric of spatial independence of digital nomads, emphasizing the critical role of space in business processes. Digital nomadism provides an important basis for understanding the dynamic relationship between technology and space. On the other hand, the lifestyle perspective evaluates digital nomadism not only as a way of working but also as a way of life. In this context, digital nomads are individuals continuing their work from anywhere in the world while traveling constantly (Wang et al., 2018). Digital nomadism is emerging as a lifestyle that allows individuals to travel the world independently of a fixed office (Thompson, 2019). Wanderlust along with a facility for it is one of the fundamental ingredients of digital nomadism (Makimoto & Manners, 1997). Both approaches emphasize that digital nomadism is an important element in the context of employment relations and labor productivity, while semi-permanent or permanent international travel is one of the distinguishing features of this lifestyle.

Digital nomads differ from traditional tourists in many ways. These two categories of travelers are introduced. Traditional tourists are expected to take vacation trips, whereas short-term travelers can just be defined as vacations (Gao & Song, 2024; Gess, 1975). Digital nomads, on the other hand, prefer long-term stays and seek a place where they can still do their work (Hall et al., 2019; Hannonen et al., 2023). Unlike traditional tourists, digital nomads stay longer in the destinations they visit because they continue to work, allowing them to integrate more deeply into the local culture (Reichenberger, 2018). Such long-term stays contribute more sustainably to local economies and social configurations and create new dynamics in the tourism sector (Gupta et al., 2024). Digital nomads have different needs than tourists who come for vacation, and they prioritize elements such as good internet infrastructure, affordable accommodation, and access to social networks (Sutherland & Jarrahi, 2017).

The emergence of the concept of digital nomadism has been made possible largely by technological developments and flexible working models (Wang et al., 2020). Advice rapid development of the infrastructure of the internet, cloud computing, electronic communications tools, and spreading remote-working systems made the Work become independent of physical offices. The pandemic period in particular has accelerated the permanence of remote working, which has strengthened the digital nomad movement (Holleran, 2022). The remote working arrangements or flexible working hours offered by companies to workers have facilitated many professionals to continue working from different parts of the globe, which has increased the number of people turning into digital nomads (Demaj et al., 2021).

Figure 1. Digital Nomadism as a Combination of Personal Choice, Corporate Growth, and Technological Innovation

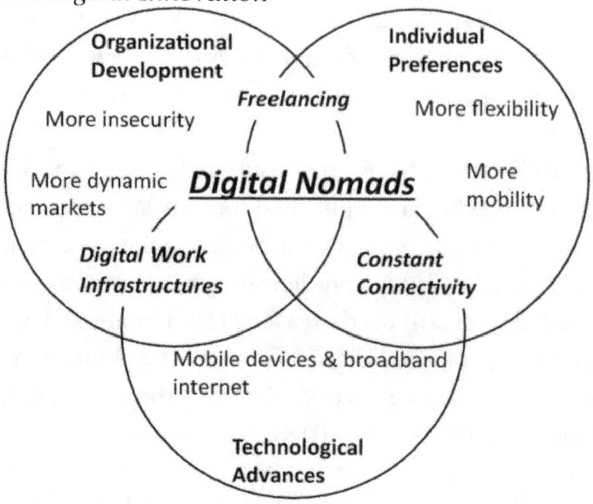

Source: Richter & Richter, 2020.

Figure 1 explores digital nomadism at the intersection of organizational expansion, technological transformation, and individual choices. As far as individual choices are concerned, autonomy-favorable traits such as flexibility and mobility take precedence. The process of a market economy and issues related to security are the main forces behind digital nomadism when it comes to organizational expansion. Innovations in technology make possible the infrastructure supporting this lifestyle, from mobile and broadband internet access. Furthermore, digital nomadism is influenced not just by these three aspects but also by their mutual interaction, producing a self-sustaining circle. For instance, as advances in technology expand remote employment opportunities, so they also influence corporate practice and individual vocational decision-making, fueling the further evolution of digital nomadism. Similarly, the demand for flexible work arrangements encourages the use of digital infrastructures by organizations, resulting in the acceleration of technology advancements in remote working solutions. There are forces such as freelancing, digital business infrastructures, and constant connectedness that help to propel an individual like the digital nomad around the globe despite all the challenges created by these three forces. By integrating these dynamics, Figure 1 diagrammatically illustrates the multifaceted nature of digital nomadism and its consequences for the tourism sector, illustrating how digital nomads place themselves in this evolving environment.

The best destinations for digital nomads tend to be destinations with low living expenses, solid internet infrastructure, and high cultural diversity (Zhou et al., 2024). Such places contribute to the local economy in terms of sustainable long-term thinking and completely change the models of tourism by offering services for the digital nomads. In this context, cities such as Bali (Indonesia), Chiang Mai (Thailand), and Lisbon (Portugal) are among the popular destinations for digital nomads (Bozdoğan & Dağdelen, 2022). On the contrary, it became a hotspot for digital nomads in which the tropics and huge coworking spaces have set the stage for Bali (Rakhmadi, 2021), while Chiang Mai is still the city that piques the interest of such a group, given its lower cost of living and rich cultural heritage (Pongruengkiat et al., 2023). In Europe, Lisbon has become an attractive center for digital nomads thanks to its modern infrastructure and dynamic technology sector (Braathen, 2022). For digital nomads, the preferred types of accommodation are hotels (51%), staying with friends or host families (41%), and by using Airbnb (36%). On average, digital nomads visit 3-4 countries, and 88% say this lifestyle has positive effects on their lives. According to projections made in the future, 24 million people in the U.S. as well plan to become digital nomads currently or within the next 2 to 3 years (FlexJobs, 2022).

Figure 2. Conceptual Framework: Digital Nomadism & Tourism Impact

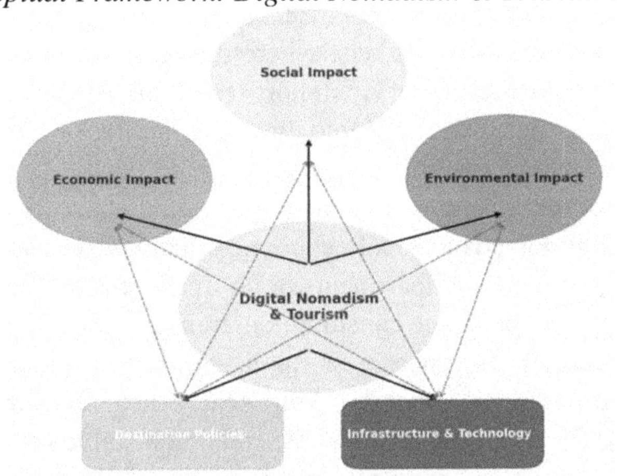

Source: Created by author

Figure 2 presents the economic, social, and environmental impacts of digital nomadism on tourism destinations within a conceptual framework. This framework shows how digital nomadism shapes destinations beyond being just an individual lifestyle. In addition, destination policies and infrastructure factors are considered as the main elements that determine the success of this process.

Economic Impact on Local Destinations

Digital nomads are creating a major transformation in the tourism sector and have significant economic impacts on local destinations. Compared to typical tourists, digital nomads reside in destinations for extended durations, thus contributing more sustainably and consistently to the local economies (Zhou et al., 2024). This long-term stay model allows local businesses to generate income not only from short-term tourist expenditures but also from services that nomads use regularly. The contribution of digital nomads to the local economies increases and brings a significant source of income, particularly for small and medium enterprises (Håkansson & Bejaković, 2023).

New service models are emerging to meet the needs of digital nomads. Coworking spaces are very much becoming a norm to fulfill the working requisites of a digital nomad (Chevtaeva & Denizci-Guillet, 2021). Such establishments not only serve the professional needs of digital nomads but also equip them with the ability to expand their business and social connections. In addition, the option of long-stay accommodation has been modified to suit the purpose of digital nomads who seek to stay for longer durations (Floričić & Pavia, 2021). These types of accommodation support local accommodation markets, where digital nomads make longer-term contributions compared to temporary and short-term tourists. The economic impacts of digital nomads can be categorized into direct and indirect effects.

- ***Direct economic effects:*** These include the immediate financial contributions of digital nomads to local economies. Examples include expenditures on housing (e.g., renting apartments or co-living spaces), co-working memberships, food and beverage consumption, transportation, entertainment, and professional services such as visa applications and insurance. Businesses like cafes, restaurants, and coworking spaces benefit from the consistent consumption habits of digital nomads, creating a stable revenue stream that makes local economies more resilient to seasonal fluctuations (Mouratidis, 2018; Zhou et al., 2024).
- ***Indirect economic effects:*** These effects stem from the secondary economic activities generated by digital nomads' presence (Jiwasiddi et al., 2024). For example, their prolonged stays create employment opportunities in hospitality, technical support, and small business entrepreneurship. Additionally, increased demand for housing often results in higher rental prices, which can have a mixed impact—benefiting property owners but potentially displacing residents. Moreover, the influx of digital nomads often attracts foreign investment in co-working spaces, digital services, and infrastructure develop-

ment, further stimulating economic activity in host destinations (Policarpio & Pacete, 2024).

Digital nomad tourism offers significant opportunities for destinations to diversify their tourism strategies (Bednorz, 2024). Unlike traditional tourism, which often leads to seasonal revenue spikes, digital nomads contribute to stable, year-round income streams. This allows local businesses to maintain financial stability and encourages long-term urban and rural development. Furthermore, the long-term and sustainable lifestyle of digital nomads creates opportunities for economic development through more balanced contributions to local economies (Jiwasiddi et al., 2024). As shown in Figure 2, digital nomads contribute to destination economies through long-term accommodation, interaction with local businesses, and remote working systems. However, while digital nomads contribute positively to local economies, their presence can also create economic challenges. As digital nomads seek comfortable accommodations for extended stays, rental prices in popular destinations often rise, sometimes making housing unaffordable for local residents (Radha et al., 2024). The growing presence of digital nomads can put pressure on essential services such as healthcare, public transportation, and internet infrastructure, requiring additional investments by local government (Ji et al., 2024). Many digital nomads work remotely for foreign companies and do not contribute to local tax systems. This creates a gap in government revenues while still increasing demand for public resources (Coursesidekick, 2024).

Cappadocia, one of the important tourism regions of Turkey, stands out as an important case study where we can observe such effects of digital nomads on the local economy (Akgün, 2024). While Cappadocia is traditionally known for its historical and cultural tourism appeal, it is now developing new infrastructure, including co-living spaces and eco-friendly accommodations, to attract long-term digital nomads (Coban Yildiz & Yildiz, 2024). Small and medium-sized businesses in the region benefit from the continuous consumption habits of digital nomads and achieve a more sustainable structure economically (Erdoğan & Özdemir, 2021; Hovardaoglu & Calisir-Hovardaoglu, 2024). Digital nomad tourism is a model, just like Cappadocia's example, which allows local economies to be tied to longer segments of the tourism market and encourages sustainable development of destinations.

Radha et al. (2024) examined the social and economic impacts of digital nomads in Canggu village, Bali. Generally, it leads to an increase in housing prices, and the living expenditures to allow space for growth in services in addition, social relationships have shifted from face-to-face communication to digital platforms, influencing traditional social values and harmony. This study suggests the adoption of a more inclusive management strategy for digital nomad tourism while emphasizing the development of infrastructure and environmental sustainability.

There was a study conducted by UNSW Business School that centered on the impact of digital nomads on the local community in Chiang Mai. The study identified the good and bad aspects to the existence of digital nomads in the local economy and culture in general (Businessthink, 2020). Positive impacts are the economic contribution to local businesses and the service sector in the region by digital nomads, encouraging local entrepreneurship, and raising international connections, which turns Chiang Mai into an international hub. Negative impacts are increased rental prices, changing the cultural identity of local communities, and little interaction with locals on the part of some digital nomads, leading to social fragmentation. By revealing the multidimensional impacts of digital nomadism on the host context, this study makes important conclusions about how such forms of mobility should be managed within the sphere of sustainable tourism.

It is estimated by the World Economic Forum that there are as many as 63 million digital nomads in the world today, who together contribute around $787 billion worth of economic value annually. Capitalizing on this trend, states have launched temporary residence visas for digital nomads to spur their economies (World Economic Forum, 2024a). Visa programs provide a structured framework whereby governments can regulate taxation, business contribution, and social responsibilities of digital nomads while maximizing the maximum economic benefit.

Digital nomads offer a sustainable alternative to traditional tourism models as individuals who can work from anywhere in the world with the flexibility provided by technology. Especially for developing countries, digital nomadism provides year-round economic stability and local development opportunities by reducing dependence on seasonal tourism (World Economic Forum, 2024b). However, managing digital nomad tourism effectively requires policies that balance economic growth with sustainable urban planning, ensuring that locals benefit from the influx of remote workers while avoiding economic displacement and social inequities.

Social and Cultural Dynamics

Digital nomads not only provide economic contributions to tourism destinations but also offer significant impacts on social and cultural transformations. The social impacts of digital nomadism on tourism can be considered in terms of the dynamics of community integration, cultural changes, and social isolation, as summarized in Figure 2. Such tourists are not only purely tourists but can also be viewed as prototype workers. Long periods are spent by them such that they not only visit the places but also integrate more into the local social fabric. This interaction often occurs through co-working spaces, local cafés, networking events, and social gatherings, where digital nomads connect with both other nomads and residents. Additionally, participation in cultural activities such as language exchanges, community projects, and workshops enables them to integrate more deeply into the cultural landscape of their chosen destinations. Cultural integration entails an unforeseen carving out of a niche beyond the bounds of established tourism and multidimensional inputs concerning cultural mix and social harmony (Gupta et al., 2024; Hall et al., 2019).

Digital nomads convey a wonderful impression of places as they assimilate perfectly into the social framework and encourage cultural integration (Reichenberger, 2018). They make themselves part of communities through the local events, social activities, and collaboration projects they take part in, and ultimately may even deepen connections with the local cultures. However, their immersion in digital work can sometimes act as a barrier to deeper cultural engagement. The constant need to remain connected through digital tools and remote work platforms can limit their ability to fully participate in local traditions, leading to a form of cultural engagement that is more surface-level rather than deeply integrated. Lifestyle in terms of mobility, adventure, and fulfillment presents another strong challenge against consumer-oriented ideologies and traditional definitions of success. It has us all downsized towards minimalism (Chevtaeva & Denizci-Guillet, 2021). Digital nomads seek more than just the price tag of a place where they choose to be; they experience everything from food to local arts and become part of cultural diversity (Bertola et al., 2022). Nevertheless, that can often bring about problems like the commercialization of culture and loss of originality because of high demand.

Digital nomadism, as a lifestyle shaped by the combination of mobility, flexibility, and technology, responds to the search for remote work, the sharing economy, and work-life balance. This lifestyle allows individuals to constantly travel, adapt to different cultural contexts, and rebuild their identities (Coursesidekick, 2024). Kuzheleva-Sagan and Nosova (2016) evaluated digital nomadism as a product of the modern information-communication society and examined this phenomenon with an interdisciplinary approach. Ontologically, digital nomadism transforms individuals' lifestyles and identities; anthropologically, it has been analyzed in the context of identity construction and sustainability of social relations. From a semiotic perspective, the culture of digital nomads has been addressed through symbolic systems and technological tools. While digital nomads are highly mobile, their ability to form long-term relationships with local communities varies. In destinations with well-established digital nomad communities, interactions are more structured and frequent, whereas, in emerging digital nomad hotspots, engagement with locals may be limited to commercial interactions rather than meaningful social exchanges.

Digital nomadism is part of a global movement that encourages individuals to interact with different cultures and create new communities. Günay et al. (2024) have presented a phenomenological case study examining the experiences of digital nomad families, revealing why a digital nomad family chooses this lifestyle, how they experience this process, and the challenges they face. Better quality of life, flexibility, and spending more time with family are the main motivations. Nature access, the quality of life, and proximity to other nomad families are key considerations for determining the destination. While there is liberation in digital nomadism, limitations such as internet access, continuity of work, and children's education are drawbacks. While the pandemic has spread the lifestyle, sustainability and how artificial intelligence will affect entrepreneurship are some of the uncertainties in the future. Additionally, digital nomadism is challenging in the establishment of a sense of belongingness due to its transient nature. Digital nomads commonly struggle to balance their mobile lifestyles with their desire for stability, and as a result, social isolation can be experienced amid frequent social interactions. Kunda et al. (2024) identify the basic requirements for sustainable development of digital nomad tourism, such as fair distribution of economic benefits, environmental sustainability, and promoting social harmony.

Kunda et al. (2024) identify the basic requirements for sustainable development of digital nomad tourism, such as fair distribution of economic benefits, environmental sustainability, and promoting social harmony. Environmental sustainability in this regard implies the responsible utilization of natural and cultural resources in the destinations that receive digital nomads. These include reducing carbon footprints, promoting sustainable accommodations, and ensuring increased tourism does not deplete local resources (Mourato et al., 2023). However, this lifestyle can also hurt substantially, such as high rents, gentrification problems, and tax regulations (Bozzi, 2024).

Bahri and Widhyharto (2021) cover digital nomadism and its impacts on local communities, in this case, specifically regarding gentrification, cultural interaction, and migration policies in Bali. Using Kristen Gray's controversial experience as an example or case study, this study illustrates how digital nomads from Western countries shape and characterize the social and economic organization in their host countries. Based on the analysis of online forums through social network analysis, the study recognizes the need for adequate policies to foster fair relationships between digital nomads and local communities and prevent the negative consequences of gentrification. To address these challenges, "smart destination" initiatives have been introduced in certain destinations, embracing digital infrastructure and data-driven policies to manage tourism flows effectively (Sorokina et al., 2022). Smart destinations leverage technology to enhance visitor experience, optimize local resources, and promote sustainable tourism practices so that digital nomads can contribute positively to their host destinations. Specific digital nomad visa schemes with taxation provisions, coupled with the removal of socio-economic inequalities, are some of the requisite suggestions.

Information about the lifestyles of digital nomads holds significant keys regarding the economic and demographic aspects of this group. Research from 2023 shows that the vast majority of digital nomads are from the United States, their average age is 32, and their annual income is around $117,959. These individuals generally represent a young population with high-income levels and allocate more resources to social and cultural experiences in the destinations they visit. The most preferred destinations include Thailand, Portugal, Mexico, Indonesia, Spain, and the United States; it is emphasized that these preferences are attractive in terms of cultural diversity, social dynamics, and adaptability to the lifestyles of digital nomads (Dream Big, Travel Far, 2023; Localyze, 2023).

Digital nomads are considered an innovative model that pushes the boundaries of modern life on both an individual and social level. While they provide sustainable contributions to destinations with their long-term stays, they establish strong social and cultural ties with local people and encourage intercultural dialog (Jiwasiddi et al., 2024). Digital nomads make interaction among people with cultures different. This is making a highly alternative reality that goes beyond conventional tourism. Indeed, digital nomadism is synonymous with a lifestyle that, by definition, completely revolutionizes the present form of society.

Environmental and Sustainability Considerations

Digital nomads, as a demographic that prioritizes environmental sustainability, present both opportunities and challenges in this area with their travel preferences and lifestyles. In the framework shown in Figure 2, the environmental impacts of digital nomadism include carbon footprint, natural resource use, and sustainability practices. The literature is rife with assertions about the ability of this way of living to reduce carbon emissions. For example, Jaiswal et al. (2024) state that digital nomads contribute to environmental sustainability by reducing the need for fixed office use and the frequency of daily commuting. Above all else, long-term accommodation trends will assist in the reduction of the carbon footprint from transport (Betre, 2022).

However, despite these advantages, digital nomadism also poses some risks in terms of environmental sustainability. Development is hampered by frequent traveling and its most carbon-intensive means, such as air travel (Widmoser, 2024). In addition, increasing demand in environmentally sensitive regions can put pressure on local ecosystems and threaten the sustainability of tourist activities (Christiansen, 2023). Such areas as e-waste management are also among the environmental problems caused by high technology in the life of the digital nomad. In this context, adopting sustainable consumption practices and promoting collaboration with local communities play a critical role in managing these risks.

Digital nomads stand out with their contributions to sustainable tourism. Such include profound importance in attaining sustainable development goals, including the preference to have accommodations that favor environmental consideration plus the preference to engage continuously with the local communities (Basu, 2024). Unlike short-term tourists, digital nomads stay in a destination for longer periods, providing more opportunities for the rest and renewal processes of local communities and the natural environment (Wang et al., 2024). However, these benefits usually come at the expense of increased pressure on destination infrastructure and natural resources for such types of travel. For example, increasing demand for accommodation and digital services in popular destinations can increase the cost of living for locals and lead to social injustice (Kocaman, 2021).

In particular, environmentally friendly tourism practices and sustainable destinations are becoming attractive to digital nomads (Yayla et al., 2024). Thus, a destination should prepare an appropriate plan to manage digital nomad tourism for a sustainable development goal. Local governments should increase their efforts to protect natural resources and local ecosystems while developing the necessary infrastructure for digital nomads (Ji et al., 2024). These infrastructure projects are part of a whole process through which the transition to renewable energy sources is possible, with environment-friendly means of transport, new initiatives to benefit local communities, and many more (Chakraborty, 2024). For example, Bali and Chiang Mai are striving to create this equilibrium with green lodgings and earth-friendly businesses aimed at targeting low carbon emissions of the digital nomads (Jiwasiddi et al., 2024; Lhakard, 2022; Xiao & Lutz, 2024). These places include amenities for long-term habitation of digital nomads, but they also emphasize the health of the local ecosystems.

Digital nomadism must be integrated into sustainable tourism practices, in the opinion of Boluda Chova and von Ehrlich-Treuenstätt (2023). The long-term benefits to the individuals and communities would be accrued by the destinations that formulate policies on environmental sensibilities and enhance efforts in natural resource protection development. Achieving a balance between sustainable consumption and mobility is key to minimizing the environmental impact of this lifestyle. In such a way it is important to align sustainable tourism policies with that of the digital nomad tourism activity and strategy that also incorporate the interests of the local populace.

Challenges Posed by Digital Nomadism

While the digital nomad lifestyle offers flexibility and freedom to individuals, it also brings with it various challenges, and addressing it solely within this framework ignores the position of these individuals within the global workforce and their relationship with the neoliberal transformation (Ersöz, 2024). It is emphasized that digital nomadism offers flexibility and freedom, but it also has negative aspects such as insecurity and social isolation (Bozdoğan & Dağdelen, 2022). To provide a clearer and more structured discussion, the challenges associated with digital nomadism can be categorized into four main areas: economic, social, cultural, and environmental challenges.

- ***Economic Challenges:*** One of the most significant challenges of digital nomadism is financial instability. Digital nomads lack the equivalent financial security that regular employees enjoy, including healthcare insurance, retirement plans, and fixed income (Verma, 2023). Furthermore, taxation and the law are also ambiguous for digital nomads, where several countries have conflicting regulations regarding work permits, social security, and taxation, creating bureaucratic hassles for the workers as well as the employers (Broek et al., 2023). Another economic issue is the rising cost of living in digital nomad locations. Excessive demand for short-term rentals and common work areas increases rental fees, which is not good for the residents (Radha et al., 2024). In Lisbon, for example, gentrification by digital nomads and foreign investors has driven many locals to the suburbs due to rising rents and the cost of living (Braathen, 2022). While digital nomads contribute to the local economy, their economic impact on the local population can cause economic disparity and displacement (Jaiswal et al., 2024).
- ***Social Challenges:*** Their very mobile way of life makes it difficult to establish long-term relationships with communities at the residence, leading to isolation and feelings of not belonging (Broek et al., 2023). Although they participate in social events and networking activities, because of their temporary presence, it is difficult to establish strong social bonds. Increased reliance on Internet communication also contributes to this problem, as people's one-on-one contacts are substituted for online networking (Elad, 2024). Another socio-issue is that local social order is disrupted. As digital nomads create high-end service demands, economic differences between foreign workers and local service workers grow stronger, leading to social tensions and local people feeling excluded (Jaiswal et al., 2024). Additionally, the rest are living in the remotest expat communities thus minimizing contact with native populations (Boluda Chova & von Ehrlich-Treuenstätt, 2023). Psychologically, the nomadic way of life can also be to blame for mental health problems such as loneliness, anxiety, and burnout due to the absence of stability, frequent travel, and absence of support system (Silva Hunt, 2024). Work-life balance is particularly difficult because time zones, changing work environments, and travel plans are accompanied by another host of stressors (Elad, 2024).

- ***Cultural Challenges:*** Another key challenge is cultural integration. Even though digital nomads become integrated into local societies to some extent, their cultural integration is superficial due to their temporary nature (Reichenberger, 2018). Compared to traditional expats, digital nomads are not necessarily invested in spending time learning the host country's language, customs, or traditions, which can limit their ability to form deeper cultural connections (Bertola et al., 2022). Furthermore, the increasing number of digital nomads accelerates the commercialization of local cultures. As destinations cater to the preferences of global remote workers, traditional cultural practices and local identities may become commodified to attract more digital nomads, potentially leading to the loss of authenticity (Glaeser, 2022). Moreover, demographic changes brought by digital nomads can lead to tensions between long-term residents and temporary inhabitants, particularly in small and medium-sized tourism destinations (Jaiswal et al., 2024). The transformation of residential areas into digital nomad hubs often shifts the local economy toward serving foreign professionals rather than local communities.
- ***Environmental Challenges:*** The environmental impact of digital nomadism is an emerging concern. Frequent international travel contributes to a significant carbon footprint due to excessive air travel and increased energy consumption in co-working and co-living spaces (Boluda Chova & von Ehrlich-Treuenstätt, 2023). While some destinations promote eco-friendly accommodations and sustainable travel initiatives, digital nomads' highly mobile nature makes it difficult to enforce environmentally responsible behavior (Silva Hunt, 2024). Moreover, over-tourism and increased digital nomad activity in certain areas put a strain on natural resources and local infrastructure (Glaeser, 2022). In destinations like Bali and Chiang Mai, abrupt surges in digital nomad populations have led to waste management issues, overuse of public utilities, and environmental degradation due to amplified urban development demands (Businessthink, 2020).

In order to create a more balanced and sustainable environment for local communities and digital nomads, policy interventions and strategic planning are essential (Elad, 2024).

- ***Economic Solutions:*** Digital nomads should be made to contribute their share to local economies through taxation policies and visa regulations while being allowed to maintain financial independence (Sánchez-Vergara et al., 2023).

- ***Social Strategies:*** Encouraging community-based initiatives can help facilitate deeper integration between digital nomads and locals, reducing social isolation and fostering cultural exchange (Betre, 2022).
- ***Cultural Preservation:*** Tour destinations should embrace sustainable models of tourism that conserve local heritage and avoid commercialization of cultures (Jaiswal et al., 2024).
- ***Environmental Responsibility:*** Sustainable environmental regulations, adoption of green infrastructure, and digital nomad sustainability measures can ensure minimized environmental harm (Basu, 2024).

One such instance is the urban regeneration of the Perpetuo Socorro neighborhood of Medellín which demonstrates how local governments and private sectors can collaborate to provide balanced urban development, shared workspace, and social innovation projects to digital nomads as well as local communities (Boluda Chova & von Ehrlich-Treuenstätt, 2023). Despite all these challenges, digital nomadism has become a fundamental aspect of the world economy. With the right policies and strategies, it can be made a more inclusive and sustainable model that balances economic growth, social cohesion, cultural integrity, and environmental responsibility.

Strategies for Destination Managers and Policymakers

Digital nomads represent the new target market for tourist destinations because they are individuals who can sustain work while traveling. The new tourism niche that emerges provides great opportunities but also presents challenges to destination managers and policymakers. Smart destinations must be prepared and apply measures that render them more competitive to capture this growing market (Zhou et al., 2024). Digital nomads are individuals who continue their lives regardless of where they are through the utilization of digital infrastructures and sociotechnical systems in their daily lives (Lee et al., 2019). Infrastructures are required for their work, especially the presence of a stable internet connection, cheap accommodation, and coworking spaces. These infrastructures are bare essentials for destinations that want to host digital nomad tourism (Chevtaeva, 2021). There is a necessity to develop a more robust internet infrastructure, expand coworking facilities, and develop housing solutions that are sustainable for the long term to meet the demands of this new population.

Digital nomad destinations must be positioned with long-term and sustainable planning to attract them. Digital nomads care not only about a good work environment, but also value aspects like environmental sustainability, cultural exchange, and affordability. In this context, supporting sustainable social harmony between digital nomads and local people, addressing housing problems, and promoting accessible, environmentally friendly accommodation options within the framework of sustainable tourism requires strategic approaches (Gupta et al., 2024). The era of the new normal, coming after the COVID-19 pandemic, has hastened changes in digitization innovation and has allowed workspaces to cross times and spaces. In this process, the increasing presence of digital nomads on a global scale, combined with the decrease in the economically active population, has made it necessary to develop sustainable tourism strategies in local cities. After the pandemic, there should be new tourism attractions that combine social objectives, economic value-adding, and regional factors to achieve non-traditional approaches as contrasted with existing development strategies in any region (Ji et al., 2024). In this context, destination managers must develop a sustainable tourism approach for digital nomads and create strategies that encourage it. Such policy recommendations would include enhancing tax policies for the effective safeguarding of the tax base, collaboration-oriented economic models, as well as environmental regulations. In addition, integrating community planning infrastructure and implementing demographic strategies to manage population changes are of vital importance. Suitable policies of education, training, health, and welfare lay the groundwork for both sustainable tourism and social vitality (Gupta et al., 2024).

The performance of a destination is usually evaluated in line with management and marketing strategies. Globalization, digitalization, and increasing complexity processes cause destinations to constantly evolve in an unpredictable tourism environment (Morrison, 2023). Marketing campaigns to be developed to attract digital nomads should be shaped in line with their values and preferences. Özgen Çiğdemli et al. (2024) emphasize that Destination Management Organizations (DMOs) should develop targeted marketing strategies by taking into account the emotional preferences of digital nomads, increasing destination attractiveness, and integrating these strategies into strategic planning processes. Digital nomads want to not only work in the places they travel to but also explore cultural richness and integrate with local life. Betre (2022) stated in her study that none of the organizations considered digital nomads as an element of their future marketing strategies in targeting digital nomads and long-term stays. However, the marketing strategies of destination managers should highlight destinations that offer sustainable tourism and affordable living opportunities to digital nomads.

Tourism agencies and destinations adopt various strategies to promote destinations on a global scale. In the context of targeting digital nomads, branded content production stands out as an effective promotion method (Lacárcel et al., 2024). Branded content will most likely appeal to potential visitors with the philosophy and stories of destinations in the form of brief video content (Jacobson et al., 2022). These contents, along with user-generated content (UGC), become more discoverable on social media and provide a reliable, authentic source of information (Borges-

Tiago et al., 2019). Playing this part of social media for public sharing (Gretzel, 2017), UGC enables the practical identification of places to become possible and implementable for digital nomads (Khan and Mujitaba, 2023; Zhang et al., 2021). In addition to UGC, online paid campaigns are also one of the most important sources of information for digital nomads. They include sponsored content, programmatic advertising, and social media marketing used to increase destination visibility, attract digital nomads, and market UGC (Chamboko-Mpotaringa & Tichaawa, 2021; Kaur, 2017). They contribute immensely to increasing destination appeal on the basis of influencing digital nomads' choices.

To make places digital nomad-friendly, it is of the utmost importance that governments develop policies. These policies should have in place controls such as special visas for digital nomads to stay and work for a certain duration with tax breaks. In the UNWTO (2024) report on digital nomad visa schemes, digital nomadism is defined as an emerging phenomenon that has enabled the majority of countries to design digital nomad visas (DNV) as a consequence of the process of digitalization which gained pace during the COVID-19 pandemic. The different nations have developed different policies such as special tax legislation for digital nomads so that visa-free residence, residence benefits, and special visa schemes are provided to digital nomads intending to relocate to another nation (Hannonen et al., 2023; Ersöz, 2024). Digital nomad visas targeting this segment of tourists are among the most important policy changes states are undertaking and are being promoted extensively (Bednorz, 2024; Sánchez-Vergara et al., 2023). Designing channels through which digital nomads can plug into the local economy should be beneficial for both communities and nomads. Remote work visas, for example, can allow digital nomads to work in a country for a certain period while also benefiting the local economy. Likewise, it could help if local governments would consider providing incentives for the development of things like coworking spaces and digital infrastructure to help support digital nomad tourism.

Digital nomads can stay in various parts of the world thanks to remote work opportunities. This has led many countries to offer digital nomad visas. First introduced by the Caribbean islands in 2020, these visas aimed to compensate for the losses experienced by tourism-based economies due to the pandemic. In Europe, Estonia became the first country to issue a digital nomad visa in August 2020, followed by countries such as Croatia, Cyprus, Greece, and Malta (IOM, 2023). Digital nomad visas stand out with their tax advantages, low cost of living, and flexible application processes. Indeed, Bednorz (2024) demonstrates how digital nomad visas can support the broader strategic priorities of governments, which are often focused on tourism development, their potential to stimulate competition between countries, and how they contribute to broader discussions in the context of corporate tourism by redefining the concept of 'digital nomad' from the perspective of host countries. These visas allow digital nomads to reside legally for a certain period, and in the process, countries benefit from the economic contributions of digital nomads. Ahmed et al. (2024) evaluate the impact of digitalization on international tax policies through the concepts of "digital nomads" from developed countries and "digital freelancers" from developing countries. While digital nomads benefit from flexible working arrangements by moving freely, digital freelancers often work in their own countries due to restrictive visa and travel policies. This situation challenges the tax allocation rules of Article 15 of the United Nations Model Tax Convention and demonstrates the need for fair regulations in the international tax system. Likewise, the Portuguese government has developed a special visa program to attract digital nomads. However, the four times minimum salary income requirement of this visa widens the economic gap between locals and foreigners (Braathen, 2022). Countries offering digital nomad visas aim to attract individuals working remotely and provide non-tourism income streams to their economies. Table 1 lists some of the key features of leading European countries offering visas for digital nomads.

Table 1. Digital Nomad Visas

Country	Ease of Obtaining Visa	Online Application	Visa Duration	Income Requirement	Visa Fee	Processing Time	Permanent Residence	Average Cost of Living (Monthly)
Albania	Easy	Yes	1-7 years	€9,800/year	Unspecified	12 weeks	Yes	€1,108
Armenia	Easy	Yes	1-5 years	Unspecified	€250-330	2 months	Yes	€1,506
Croatia	Easy	Yes	6-12 months	€2,245/month or €26,930/ year	€56-186	4 weeks	No	€1,269
Cyprus	Difficult	No	1-3 years	€3,500/month	€70	5-7 weeks	No	€1,659
Czechia	Difficult	No	1-3 years	€6,706 accumulation	€282	90 days	No	€1,808
Estonia	Difficult	No	3-12 months	€3,504/month	€80-100	30 days	No	€1,403
Georgia	Easy	-	1 year Visa-free	-	-	-	Yes	€600
Germany	Middle	No	1 year	Unspecified	€75	1-5 months	Yes*	€2,368
Greece	Difficult	No	1-2 years	€3,500/month	€225	10 days	No	€1,312
Hungary	Difficult	No	1-2 years	€2,000/month	€110	30 days	No	€1,312
Iceland	Difficult	No	180 days	€6,680/month	€82	Uncertain	No	€3,439
Latvia	Difficult	No	1 year	€3,193/month	€60	15 days	No	€1,274
Malta	Easy	Yes	1-3 years	€2,700/month or €32,400/ year	€300	15 days	No	€1,970
Norway	Easy	Yes	2 years	€38,700/year	€650	4 months	No	€2,479

continued on following page

Table 1. Continued

Country	Ease of Obtaining Visa	Online Application	Visa Duration	Income Requirement	Visa Fee	Processing Time	Permanent Residence	Average Cost of Living (Monthly)
Portugal	Difficult	No	1-5 years	€10,644/ year (D7) or €35,485/year (D8)	€500	3-4 months	No	€1,583
Romania	Easy	Yes	1-3 years	€3,300/month	€173	10-14 days	No	€995
Spain	Difficult	No	1-5 years	€2,334/month or €28,000/ year	€80	15-45 days	Yes	€1,568

Source: Where to Flow, 2023.
* Germany offers permanent residence under certain conditions.

Lisbon stands out as a successful example of digital nomad tourism. Lisbon has become one of the leading digital nomad centers in Europe with the infrastructure investments it has made to attract digital nomads and the living opportunities it offers (Glaeser, 2022). The city is quite a lovely place for digital nomads with high-speed internet, cheap accommodation, and large coworking spaces. It also represents a lot in terms of social and cultural diversity (Beaumont, 2019). Lisbon's digital nomad-friendly policies are also supported by policies such as tax incentives and remote work visas offered for digital nomads by local authorities. These strategies have placed Lisbon as a center for work, but have also endowed it with rich cultural and sustainable qualities as a living space. The presence of foreigners contributes to Lisbon's economic growth and cultural diversity. Many new restaurants are being opened, and several events and social spaces are shaping up (Braathen, 2022). This successful example also offers important lessons for other destinations on how digital nomad tourism can be integrated. The destinations will have to harmonize their infrastructure investment, marketing strategies, and government policies even as they recognize the potential for digital nomad tourism to develop. Destination managers and policymakers can develop a sustainable and attractive tourism model by understanding the values and needs of digital nomads.

The Future of Digital Nomadism in Tourism

Digital nomadism stands out as one of the most important trends of the future in tourism. The segment of the population embracing this lifestyle is transforming traditional tourism models through long-term travel, sustainability-oriented lifestyles, and deeper engagement with local communities (Woldoff & Litchfield, 2021). To thrive in embracing this trend, destinations need to invest in digital infrastructure, implement sustainable tourism policies, and put in place active strategies for integrating digital nomads into the host economy and society. Digital nomads prioritize the most excellent climatic conditions, landscape features, and societal atmosphere when choosing destinations (Zhang et al., 2024). Future studies might, thus, focus on how several environmental and social conditions influence destination selection and long-stay patterns among digital nomads.

Digital nomadism is intrinsically connected with travel and tourism. In contrast to conventional tourists, digital nomads are differentiated by their extended stay accommodation options, use of co-working areas, and input into local economies. This new category of traveler has prompted academics to refer to them as "noma-tourists" (Arslan, 2024). Yet, future research must explore the effects of this new type of tourism on established models of tourism, examining how destinations can find a balance between the demands of short-term and extended-stay visitors.

Also, the economic dimensions of digital nomadism become evident. Digital nomads engage in geographic arbitrage, taking advantage of price differentials between their home and destination countries in order to maximize the quality of life at a low cost (Akın, 2021). While this brings economic gains, it also sustains inflationary pressures on local markets. Research in the future could examine the long-term impacts of digital nomads on local labor markets, housing markets, and service sector dynamics.

One of the emerging trends among digital nomads is "slomading"—staying longer in fewer places to build deeper connections with local culture and splitting work and life more evenly. However, the long-term implications of the trend are not particularly well examined. Future studies could ascertain whether slomading minimizes some of the negative impacts associated with high digital nomad churn in certain destinations (MBO Partners, 2023).

As remote work continues to evolve, the digital nomad movement is expected to expand further. Flexible work policies are being increasingly adopted by companies, allowing them to attract and retain top talent while benefiting from advances in digital communication technologies (Eversole et al., 2012). Moreover, as more destinations realize the economic benefits of attracting digital nomads, the number of digital nomad visas is expected to rise. Future research could compare the effectiveness of different visa models and evaluate how they influence digital nomad mobility patterns and economic contributions.

To advance the knowledge in this field, future studies should focus on the following key areas:

- ***Long-term socio-economic impacts on host communities:*** How do digital nomads contribute to or challenge local economic stability, housing markets, and labor dynamics over extended periods? What are the long-term effects of digital nomadism on local entrepreneurship, innovation, and cultural heritage preservation?

- ***Comparative studies of digital nomad destinations:*** How do destinations with different levels of digital nomad presence (e.g., established hubs vs. emerging hotspots) experience economic, social, and cultural transformations? What factors make certain destinations more resilient to the potential negative effects of digital nomadism, such as gentrification and rising costs?
- ***Psychosocial well-being and work-life balance of digital nomads:*** How does long-term digital nomadism affect mental health, productivity, and social connectedness? What role do co-living and co-working spaces play in fostering digital nomads' sense of belonging and well-being?
- ***Digital infrastructure and policy development:*** What are the best practices for governments seeking to develop infrastructure that supports digital nomads while ensuring sustainable local development? How do different taxation policies and visa regulations affect the mobility and economic integration of digital nomads?
- ***Environmental sustainability and digital nomad mobility:*** What are the carbon footprints of digital nomads, and how can sustainable travel practices be encouraged? How can digital nomad tourism be aligned with sustainable tourism policies to minimize negative environmental impacts?

As digital nomadism continues to grow, a more comprehensive understanding of its implications is necessary to ensure it remains a sustainable and beneficial model for both travelers and host communities. The integration of multidisciplinary research approaches, including qualitative ethnographic studies, economic impact assessments, and policy analyses, can provide deeper insights into the evolving landscape of digital nomad tourism. By addressing these research gaps, scholars can contribute to shaping the policies and frameworks that will define the future of digital nomadism in a way that benefits both digital workers and the communities they engage with.

SOLUTIONS AND RECOMMENDATIONS

To benefit from the opportunities offered by digital nomad tourism sustainably and to solve the challenges created by this tourism model, comprehensive strategies need to be developed. First, infrastructure development efforts should be brought to a level that will meet the needs of digital nomads. In this context, fast and reliable internet infrastructure, affordable long-term accommodation opportunities, and the creation of workspaces should be priority investment areas. It is particularly going to be a long inhale about energy-efficient housing and green building practices as it is a long-term focused solution for such needs. It is important that policies are designed to support digital nomad tourism and at the same time protect the interests of local communities. There should be special visas for digital nomads and those specifically targeted at providing opportunities to spend time in a local economy while permitting legitimate work. At the same time, economic incentives such as tax advantages can be seen to ensure social justice. They may be multicultural events, language courses, or shared activities of local projects aimed at stimulating direct face-to-face interaction of digital nomads with locals. These practices can ensure long-term benefits by fostering not only economic but also social integration. Environmental sustainability remains a matter of prime importance in the context of digital nomad tourism in the future. Models of building endeavors working towards realizing aims of minimizing the carbon impact of digital nomads, upscaling the exploitation of renewable energies, and helping accountable travel offerings for making such benefits easier. Moreover, drives on important issues such as dealing with e-waste should also be initiated. Protection schemes would have to be launched to minimize the severity of the heavy tourist pressure on ecosystems. Environmental laws can be framed for digital nomad operations in sensitive ecosystems and a balanced management can be provided in such ecosystems. Restructuring the marketing strategy of destinations for digital nomads to include higher value propositions would be a good idea to make this tourist segment re-invent itself in some kind of interesting tourism. Social media marketing, user-generated content, and sponsored campaigns can be used as effective tools in the international promotion of destinations. Also, the updating of visas, accommodation, and local amenities provided by digital platforms can greatly influence the destinations chosen by digital nomads. Branding destinations with their unique cultural and environmental assets is an important part of this strategy. Lastly, new forms particularly meant for digital nomads will maximize both the economic and social benefits of this tourism model.

FUTURE RESEARCH DIRECTIONS

Future research on the development of digital nomad tourism should be approached with a multifaceted approach. In-depth studies are especially needed in the dimensions of economic impacts, social dynamics, and sustainability. Determining the contribution of digital nomads to local economies can reveal the economic potential of this tourism model. It is possible to enhance different perspective through the impacts that non-tourism areas like real estate, technology, and education suffer from. In terms of social dynamics, understanding the long-term interactions of digital nomads with local cultures is of critical importance. For their part, risks regarding cultural commodification and social stratification should be explored in net terms. At the same time, the integration of digital nomads into local communities and the effects of community-based tourism practices should also be the focus of research. This area of environment should attend to evaluation techniques for the carbon mitigation strategy related to digital nomadism, and also extend beyond other measures to incorporate renewable energy. The digital divide and technological equality issues are other important areas that need to be addressed in order for digital nomad tourism to become more inclusive. The study on effects of technologies like blockchain and artificial intelligence on digital connectives will also add innovative applications. Finally, studies examining the mental health and well-being of digital nomad communities can guide the development of social policies to support this new lifestyle.

CONCLUSION

Digital nomadism has become an innovative model that has radically transformed modern working and living models and is redefining global tourism dynamics. Flexibility in technology has made all such knit lifestyles a blend of many destinations and the chances they offer for digital home nomads. Supporting economic development, cultural integration, and environmental sustainability goals, this model also brings with it social, economic, and environmental challenges. The effect of tourist services among digital migrants will be determined by the degree to which planning and management strategies of the services are aligned with the perspectives of sustainable development. Achievement of success in cooperation between governments, local communities, and the private sector will realize the maximum advantages of this type of tourism while minimizing the potential negative effects. Thus, investment in infrastructure, green protection programs, social adjustment programs, and the use of new technology will be some of the basic elements for facilitating the long-term sustainability of digital nomad tourism. It is of utmost importance that local governments invest in infrastructure that will cater to the unique needs of digital nomads and adopt eco-friendly policies. At the same time, social adaptation schemes must be drawn up to merge the digital nomads into local culture. These projects can increase the economic contribution of digital nomads and reduce negative impacts on local communities. To conclude, tourism underlies the concept of modern tourism in the sense that it shapes an approach to which digital nomadism can be called as a formal alternative for contemporary society. The conceptual framework (Figure 2) discussed in this study provides a systematic structure to understand the effects of digital nomadism on tourism. In addition to economic, social, and environmental impacts, how this process is shaped by destination policies and infrastructure is also evaluated. The successful implementation of this model can positively transform not only the tourism sector but also social structures and environmental systems. It will be future research, which may guide one understanding much more deeply into all sides of the electric effects of digital nomadism and reveal the contributions of that tourism model to sustainable development.

REFERENCES

Ahmed, M. A., Nazir, H., & Haider, M. (2024). UN MTC Article 15: Reconciling the global north's 'digital nomad' with the global south's 'digital freelancer': Will the rising tide lift all boats? [pre-publication]. *Intertax, 52*(6/7), 455–475. DOI: 10.54648/TAXI2024050

Akgün, A. C. (2024). Kültürel diplomasi bağlamında dijital göçebelerin Türkiye izlenimleri üzerine bir inceleme. *Erciyes İletişim Dergisi, 11*(2), 673–682. DOI: 10.17680/erciyesiletisim.1437918

Akın, M. Ş. (2021). Dijital göçebelik: Deneyim ve özgürlük. *Sosyal Ekonomik Araştırmalar Dergisi, 21*(1), 41–52. DOI: 10.30976/susead.799881

Arslan, E. (2024). From tourists to nomads: Unveiling the transformative potential of digital nomads in travel and tourism. *Worldwide Hospitality and Tourism Themes, 16*(3), 269–281. DOI: 10.1108/WHATT-03-2024-0046

Bahri, M. T., & Widhyharto, D. S. (2021). Social network analysis (SNA) on #Kristengray hashtag: Understanding gentrification side effects behind the digital nomad phenomenon. *Jurnal Studi Pemuda, 10*(1), 75–90. DOI: 10.22146/studipemudaugm.65255

Basu, M. (2024). Tech-driven horizons: Pioneering sustainable tourism for environmental resilience and SDGs triumph. In *The need for sustainable tourism in an era of global climate change: Pathway to a greener future* (pp. 215–247). Emerald Publishing Limited. DOI: 10.1108/978-1-83608-668-020241032

Beaumont, J. (2019). *Digital nomads and sense of place: A case study of Lisbon.* Wageningen University.

Bednorz, J. (2024). Working from anywhere? Work from here! Approaches to attract digital nomads. *Annals of Tourism Research, 105*, 103715. DOI: 10.1016/j.annals.2023.103715

Bertola, P., Iannilli, V., Spagnoli, A., & Vandi, A. (2022). Cultural and creative industries as activators and attractors for contemporary culture-driven nomadism. In *Cultural leadership in transition tourism: Developing innovative and sustainable models* (pp. 51–74). Springer International Publishing. DOI: 10.1007/978-3-031-14121-8_4

Betre, H. K. (2022). Reconceptualising the potential of digital nomads to transform community-based and sustainable tourism [Master's thesis]. Retrieved from ProQuest Dissertations and Theses.

Big, D., & Far, T. (2023). 65+ fascinating digital nomad statistics [Fresh for 2023!]. Retrieved from https://www.dreambigtravelfarblog.com/blog/digital-nomad-statistics

Birtchnell, T. (2019). Digital nomads and (im)mobile identities. In *Routledge handbook of identity studies* (pp. 274–282). Routledge. DOI: 10.4324/9781315626024-16

Boluda Chova, J., & von Ehrlich-Treuenstätt, K. T. (2023). Nomadism without borders: Exploring connections in digital nomad destinations: An ethnographic multiple-case study in Malaysia and Colombia [Dissertation]. Retrieved from https://urn.kb.se/resolve?urn=urn:nbn:se:hj:diva-60385

Borges-Tiago, M. T., Tiago, F., & Cosme, C. (2019). Exploring users' motivations to participate in viral communication on social media. *Journal of Business Research, 101*, 574–582. DOI: 10.1016/j.jbusres.2018.11.011

Bozdoğan, M., & Dağdelen, E. Ö. (2022). Seyahat, çalışma ve boş zamanın kesişiminde yeni bir grup: Dijital göçebeler. *İnsan Hareketliliği Uluslararası Dergisi, 2*(2), 270–297.

Bozzi, A. (2024). Digital nomadism from the perspective of places and mobilities: A literature review. *European Transport Research Review, 16*(1), 50. DOI: 10.1186/s12544-024-00663-z

Braathen, N. S. (2022). Virtually anywhere, physically in Lisbon: A study of gentrification and the new work-lifestyle among digital nomads in Lisbon [Master's thesis]. Retrieved from Lund University Repository.

Broek, T. V. D., Haubrich, G. F., Razmerita, L., Murero, M., Marx, J., Lind, Y., & Boer, P. D. (2023). *Digital nomads: Opportunities and challenges for the future of work in the post-COVID society*. Aurora Universities Network.

Businessthink. (2020). Digital nomads: Five key insights into the future of knowledge work. Retrieved from https://www.businessthink.unsw.edu.au/articles/digital-nomads-five-key-insights-future-of-knowledge-work

Chakraborty, P. P. (2024). Tourism in transition in a sustainable world: Embracing technology and sustainability in the post-pandemic era. In *Special interest trends for sustainable tourism* (pp. 348–374). IGI Global. DOI: 10.4018/979-8-3693-5903-7.ch017

Chamboko-Mpotaringa, M., & Tichaawa, T. M. (2021). Tourism digital marketing tools and views on future trends: A systematic review of literature. *African Journal of Hospitality, Tourism and Leisure, 10*(2), 712–726. DOI: 10.46222/ajhtl.19770720-128

Chevtaeva, E. (2021). Coworking and coliving: The attraction for digital nomad tourists. In *Information and communication technologies in tourism 2021:Proceedings of the ENTER 2021 eTourism Conference,January 19–22, 2021* (pp. 202–209). Springer International Publishing.

Chevtaeva, E., & Denizci-Guillet, B. (2021). Digital nomads' lifestyles and coworkation. *Journal of Destination Marketing & Management, 21*, 100633. DOI: 10.1016/j.jdmm.2021.100633

Chevtaeva, E., Neuhofer, B., & Rainoldi, M. (2022, January). The "next normal" of work: How tourism shapes the wellbeing of remote workers. In *CAUTHE 2022 Conference Online: Shaping the Next Normal in Tourism, Hospitality and Events: Handbook of Abstracts of the 32nd Annual Conference* (p. 33). Council for Australasian University Tourism and Hospitality Education (CAUTHE).

Christiansen, R. A. (2023). Development of digital nomads as a new market segment and their role in the local digital ecosystem [Doctoral dissertation].

Coban Yildiz, G., & Yildiz, O. S. (2024). A debate on Turkey tourism's adaptation to climate change. In *Tourism and climate change in the 21st century: Challenges and solutions* (pp. 197–223). Springer Nature Switzerland. DOI: 10.1007/978-3-031-59431-1_9

Coursesidekick. (2024). The social dynamics of digital nomadism: Exploring work, lifestyle, and community in a borderless world. Retrieved from https://www.coursesidekick.com/sociology/3350886

De Almeida, M. A., Correia, A., Barbosa, C. E., de Souza, J. M., & Schneider, D. (2024). AI and digital nomads: Glimpsing the future human-computer interaction [Preprint]. Retrieved from https://www.researchgate.net/publication/385611257

Demaj, E., Hasimja, A., & Rahimi, A. (2021). Digital nomadism as a new flexible working approach: Making Tirana the next European hotspot for digital nomads. In *The flexible workplace: Coworking and other modern workplace transformations* (pp. 231–257).

Elad, B. (2024, May 20). Digital nomad statistics 2024: Demographics, gender, background, salaries, education levels, nationalities, and preferred activities. *Enterprise Apps Today*. Retrieved from https://www.enterpriseappstoday.com/stats/digital-nomad-statistics.html

Erdoğan, Y., & Özdemir, E. G. (2021). Sales effect of digital marketing in small and medium-sized accommodation enterprises in core Cappadocia. *Karadeniz Uluslararası Bilimsel Dergi, 1*(51), 1–23. DOI: 10.17498/kdeniz.944276

Ersöz, B. (2024). Removing the boundaries of flexibility: A critical evaluation on digital nomadism. *Sosyal Bilimler Araştırmaları Dergisi, 19*(2), 241–252. DOI: 10.48145/gopsbad.1540618

Eversole, B. A., Venneberg, D. L., & Crowder, C. L. (2012). Creating a flexible organizational culture to attract and retain talented workers across generations. *Advances in Developing Human Resources, 14*(4), 607–625. DOI: 10.1177/1523422312455612

FlexJobs. (2022). Digital nomad survey: Insights into the remote lifestyle. Retrieved December 6, 2024, from https://www.flexjobs.com/blog/post/digital-nomad-survey-insights-remote-lifestyle/

Floričić, T., & Pavia, N. (2021). Linkage of leisure with remote work and digital nomadism in tourist accommodation facilities. *ToSEE, 6*, 247–268. DOI: 10.20867/tosee.06.17

Gao, J., & Song, L. (2024). A cross-cultural comparison of island vacation experience: Empirical evidence from the Maldives. *Asia Pacific Journal of Tourism Research, 29*(7), 1–14. DOI: 10.1080/10941665.2024.2351124

Gess, K. (1975). A study of Mexican travel habits and patterns: Results of an exploratory study assimilating secondary data and personal interviews with individuals representing organizations of the Mexican travel trade (Vol. 1). The Office.

Glaeser, J. (2022). The effects of digital nomads on housing affordability for local populations in Ericeira (Master's thesis). ISCTE-Instituto Universitario de Lisboa.

Gretzel, U. (2017). Influencer marketing in travel and tourism. In *Advances in social media for travel, tourism and hospitality* (pp. 147–156). Routledge. DOI: 10.4324/9781315565736-13

Günay, F., Toksöz, D., & Aslan, Z. (2024). The causes, process and result of becoming a digital nomad family: A phenomenological case study. *Worldwide Hospitality and Tourism Themes, 16*(3), 294–302. DOI: 10.1108/WHATT-03-2024-0042

Gupta, S., Jaiswal, R., & Gupta, S. K. (2024). Digital nomads: A systematic literature review and future research agenda. *Tourism Review*. Advance online publication. DOI: 10.1108/TR-12-2023-0869

Hackl, A. (2018). Mobility equity in a globalized world: Reducing inequalities in the sustainable development agenda. *World Development, 112*, 150–162. DOI: 10.1016/j.worlddev.2018.08.005

Håkansson, P. G., & Bejaković, P. (2023). Can digital nomads solve the problem of tourist economy? The case of Croatian islands. *Eastern Journal of European Studies, 14*(Special Issue), 116–134. DOI: 10.47743/ejes-2023-SI07

Hall, G., Sigala, M., Rentschler, R., & Boyle, S. (2019). Motivations, mobility and work practices; the conceptual realities of digital nomads. In *Information and Communication Technologies in Tourism 2019:Proceedings of the International Conference in Nicosia, Cyprus, January 30–February 1, 2019* (pp. 437–449). Springer International Publishing.

Hannonen, O. (2020). In search of a digital nomad: Defining the phenomenon. *Information Technology & Tourism, 22*(3), 335–353. DOI: 10.1007/s40558-020-00177-z

Hannonen, O., Quintana, T. A., & Lehto, X. Y. (2023). A supplier-side view of digital nomadism: The case of destination Gran Canaria. *Tourism Management, 97*, 104744. DOI: 10.1016/j.tourman.2023.104744

Hensellek, S., & Puchala, N. (2021). The emergence of the digital nomad: A review and analysis of the opportunities and risks of digital nomadism. In *The flexible workplace: Coworking and other modern workplace transformations* (pp. 195–214). DOI: 10.1007/978-3-030-62167-4_11

Holleran, M. (2022). Pandemics and geoarbitrage: Digital nomadism before and after COVID-19. *City (London, England), 26*(5–6), 831–847. DOI: 10.1080/13604813.2022.2124713

Horton International. (2023). The rise of digital nomadism in remote working. Horton International. Retrieved from https://hortoninternational.com/the-rise-of-digital-nomadism-in-remote-working/

Hovardaoglu, O., & Calisir-Hovardaoglu, S. (2024). Estrategias de supervivencia de las PYMEs en la pandemia Covid-19 en los sitios de turismo patrimonial en Turquía. *Pasos (El Sauzal), 22*(1), 125–145. DOI: 10.25145/j.pasos.2024.22.008

Hunt, S. (2024). 6 most common challenges of a digital nomad lifestyle and how to overcome them. Retrieved December 6, 2024, from https://www.silvahunt.ee/business-in-estonia/6-most-common-challenges-of-a-digital-nomad-lifestyle-and-how-to-overcome-them/

International Organization for Migration (IOM). (2023). Overview: Digital nomad policies in the European context. IOM. Retrieved December 13, 2024, from https://denmark.iom.int/sites/g/files/tmzbdl1306/files/documents/TalentHub/overview.-digital-nomad-policies-in-the-european-context_clean.pdf

Jacobson, J., Hodson, J., & Mittelman, R. (2022). Pup-ularity contest: The advertising practices of popular animal influencers on Instagram. *Technological Forecasting and Social Change*, *174*, 121226. DOI: 10.1016/j.techfore.2021.121226

Jaiswal, R., Gupta, S., & Gupta, S. K. (2024). The impending disruption of digital nomadism: Opportunities, challenges, and research agenda. *World Leisure Journal*, •••, 1–31. DOI: 10.1080/16078055.2024.2346091

Ji, Y., Kim, S. M., & Kim, Y. (2024). A way to attract digital nomads to tourist destinations in the new normal era. *Sustainability (Basel)*, *16*(6), 2336. DOI: 10.3390/su16062336

Jiwasiddi, A., Schlagwein, D., Cahalane, M., Cecez-Kecmanovic, D., Leong, C., & Ractham, P. (2024). Digital nomadism as a new part of the visitor economy: The case of the "digital nomad capital" Chiang Mai, Thailand. *Information Systems Journal*, *34*(5), 1493–1535. DOI: 10.1111/isj.12496

Kaur, G. (2017). The importance of digital marketing in the tourism industry. *International Journal of Research-Granthaalayah*, *5*(6), 72–77. DOI: 10.29121/granthaalayah.v5.i6.2017.1998

Khan, K., & Mujitaba, A. (2023). Development and validation of brand strategies evaluation scale for mobile network users. *ESIC Market*, *54*(1), e291–e291. DOI: 10.7200/esicm.53.291

Kocaman, S. (2021). Nomadlist'de dijital göçebeler tarafından 2020'de en fazla tercih edilen destinasyonların destinasyon seçim kriterlerine göre küme lendirilmesi. *Türk Turizm Araştırmaları Dergisi*, *5*(2), 799–815. DOI: 10.26677/TR1010.2021.739

Kunda, N. L. R., Sunarta, I. N., & Bhaskara, G. I. (2024). The impact of social and economic changes of digital nomadic on tourists and the local community in Canggu. [IJETER]. *International Journal of Technology and Education Research*, *2*(4), 50–55. https://e-journal.citakonsultindo.or.id/index.php/IJETER

Kuzheleva-Sagan, I., & Nosova, S. (2016). Culture of digital nomads: Ontological, anthropological, and semiotic aspects. In *Proceedings of the World Congress of the IASS/AIS 12th WCS Sofia 2014 - New Semiotics. Between tradition and innovation* (pp. 131–141). Sofia: IASS Publications & NBU Publishing House.

Lacárcel, F. J. S., Huete, R., & Zerva, K. (2024). Decoding digital nomad destination decisions through user-generated content. *Technological Forecasting and Social Change*, *200*, 123098. DOI: 10.1016/j.techfore.2023.123098

Lanza, G., Pucci, P., Carboni, L., & Vendemmia, B. (2022). Impacts of the Covid-19 pandemic in inner areas. Remote work and near-home tourism through mobile phone data in Piacenza Apennine. *TEMA*, *2*, 73–89.

Lee, A., Toombs, A. L., Erickson, I., Nemer, D., Ho, Y. S., Jo, E., & Guo, Z. (2019). The social infrastructure of co-spaces: Home, work, and sociable places for digital nomads. *Proceedings of the ACM on Human-Computer Interaction, 3*(CSCW), 1–23. DOI: 10.1145/3359244

Lhakard, P. (2022). Destination city for digital nomads in Thailand: A case study of digital nomad community in Chiang Mai. *Journal of Humanities and Social Sciences Studies (JHSSS), 4*(1). Available at *SSRN*: https://ssrn.com/abstract=4053619

Liegl, M. (2014). Nomadicity and the care of place—On the aesthetic and affective organization of space in freelance creative work. [CSCW]. *Computer Supported Cooperative Work, 23*(2), 163–183. DOI: 10.1007/s10606-014-9198-x

Localyze. (2023). Digital nomad statistics & trends: 2023 & 2024. Retrieved from https://www.localyze.com/blog/digital-nomad-statistics-trends-2023-2024

Makimoto, T., & Manners, D. (1997). *Digital nomad*. John Wiley & Sons.

Mariati, S., Gilitasha, A., Rahmanita, M., Djati, S. P., & Adawiyah, R. (2023). Analysis of sustainable tourism destination development for digital nomads (Comparative study: Lisbon-Portugal and Canggu, Bali-Indonesia). *Technium Social Sciences Journal, 43*, 403–415. DOI: 10.47577/tssj.v43i1.8773

Morrison, A. M. (2023). *Marketing and managing tourism destinations*. Routledge. DOI: 10.4324/9781003343356

Mouratidis, G. (2018). Digital nomadism: Travel, remote work and alternative lifestyles [Master's thesis, Department of Arts and Cultural Sciences]. Lund University.

Mourato, I., Dias, Á., & Pereira, L. (2023). Estimating the impact of digital nomads' sustainable responsibility on entrepreneurial self-efficacy. *Social Sciences (Basel, Switzerland), 12*(2), 97. DOI: 10.3390/socsci12020097

Müller, A. (2016). The digital nomad: Buzzword or research category? *Transnational Social Review, 6*(3), 344–348. DOI: 10.1080/21931674.2016.1229930

Nash, C., Jarrahi, M. H., & Sutherland, W. (2021). Nomadic work and location independence: The role of space in shaping the work of digital nomads. *Human Behavior and Emerging Technologies, 3*(2), 271–282. DOI: 10.1002/hbe2.234

Nash, C., Jarrahi, M. H., Sutherland, W., & Phillips, G. (2018, March). Digital nomads beyond the buzzword: Defining digital nomadic work and use of digital technologies. In *International Conference on Information* (pp. 207–217). Cham: Springer International Publishing. DOI: 10.1007/978-3-319-78105-1_25

Özgen Çiğdemli, A. Ö., Yayla, Ş., & Çiğdemli, B. S. (2024). The world from the perspective of digital nomads: Exploring sentiments in destination reviews. *Worldwide Hospitality and Tourism Themes*, *16*(3), 303–315. DOI: 10.1108/WHATT-03-2024-0044

Partners, M. B. O. (2023). New survey reveals rise of tethered nomading: Digital nomads answer the office's beckoning. Retrieved from https://www.mbopartners.com/blog/press/new-survey-reveals-rise-of-tethered-nomading-digital-nomads-answer-the-offices-beckoning/

Policarpio, J. E. A., & Pacete, J. L. B. (2024). Co-Working Spaces and Digital Nomadism in the Philippines: Understanding Bleisure Tourism's Role in Diffusion of Culture. In *Bleisure Tourism and the Impact of Technology* (pp. 190-211). IGI Global.

Pongruengkiat, W., Tippayawong, K. Y., Aggarangsi, P., Pichayapan, P., Katongtung, T., & Tippayawong, N. (2023). Assessing sustainability of Chiang Mai urban development. *Discover Sustainability*, *4*(1), 54. DOI: 10.1007/s43621-023-00174-2

Pumble. (2024). Digital nomad visa statistics. Retrieved December 6, 2024, from https://pumble.com/learn/digital-nomad-visa/statistics/

Radha, N. L. R. K., Sunarta, I. N. S., & Indra, G. I. B. (2024). The impact of social and economic changes of digital nomadic on tourists and the local community in Canggu. *International Journal of Technology and Education Research*, *2*(4), 50–55. https://e-journal.citakonsultindo.or.id/index.php/IJETER/article/view/1196

Rakhmadi, R. (2021, December). Role of digital nomad in supporting tourism in Indonesia: Case study Bali. In *Proceedings of the 2nd International Indonesia Conference on Interdisciplinary Studies (IICIS 2021)* 606(2), 143–148 DOI: 10.2991/assehr.k.211206.020

Reichenberger, I. (2018). Digital nomads–A quest for holistic freedom in work and leisure. *Annals of Leisure Research*, *21*(3), 364–380. DOI: 10.1080/11745398.2017.1358098

Richter, S., & Richter, A. (2020). Digital nomads. *Business & Information Systems Engineering*, *62*(1), 77–81. DOI: 10.1007/s12599-019-00615-1

Sánchez-Vergara, J. I., Orel, M., & Capdevila, I. (2023). "Home office is the here and now." Digital nomad visa systems and remote work-focused leisure policies. *World Leisure Journal*, *65*(2), 236–255. DOI: 10.1080/16078055.2023.2165142

Singh, B., & Kaunert, C. (2025). Innovative business models in digital and virtual reality for the gig economy: Space-age sustainable development projecting smart business practices. In *Business transformation in the era of digital disruption* (pp. 127–156). IGI Global.

Sorokina, E., Wang, Y., Fyall, A., Lugosi, P., Torres, E., & Jung, T. (2022). Constructing a smart destination framework: A destination marketing organization perspective. *Journal of Destination Marketing & Management*, *23*, 100688. DOI: 10.1016/j.jdmm.2021.100688

Stumpf, T. S., Califf, C. B., & Lancaster, J. (2022). Digital nomad entrepreneurship and lifestyle design: A process theory. *Proceedings of the 55th Hawaii International Conference on System Sciences*, 5201–5210. Retrieved from https://hdl.handle.net/10125/79972

Sutherland, W., & Jarrahi, M. H. (2017). The gig economy and information infrastructure: The case of the digital nomad community. *Proceedings of the ACM on Human-Computer Interaction, 1*(CSCW), 1–24. DOI: 10.1145/3134732

Thompson, B. Y. (2019). The digital nomad lifestyle: (Remote) work/leisure balance, privilege, and constructed community. *International Journal of the Sociology of Leisure*, *2*(1), 27–42. DOI: 10.1007/s41978-018-00030-y

UNSW Business School. (2024). How digital nomads impact local communities: A Chiang Mai case study. Retrieved from https://www.businessthink.unsw.edu.au/articles/digital-nomads-local-communities-chiang-mai

UNWTO. (2024). *UNWTO brief: Digital nomad visas*. World Tourism Organization., DOI: 10.18111/9789284424481

Verma, M. (2023). The future of work for digital nomads: The benefits and risks of automation. *IJSART, 9*(4), 339–343. Retrieved from https://www.researchgate.net/publication/370099953

Wang, B., Schlagwein, D., & Cecez-Kecmanovic, D. (2024). Critical-theoretic review and research agenda on digital nomadism. *ICIS 2024 Proceedings, 14*. Retrieved from https://aisel.aisnet.org/icis2024/lit_review/lit_review/14

Wang, B., Schlagwein, D., Cecez-Kecmanovic, D., & Cahalane, M. C. (2018). Digital work and high-tech wanderers: Three theoretical framings and a research agenda for digital nomadism. In *ACIS 2018 Proceedings. Australasian Conference on Information Systems*. Retrieved from https://aisel.aisnet.org/acis2018/55

Wang, B., Schlagwein, D., Cecez-Kecmanovic, D., & Cahalane, M. C. (2020). Beyond the factory paradigm: Digital nomadism and the digital future (s) of knowledge work post-COVID-19. *Journal of the Association for Information Systems, 21*(6), 10. DOI: 10.17705/1jais.00641

Where to Flow. (2023). *Digital nomad visas in Europe*. Retrieved December 23, 2024, from https://wheretoflow.com/digital-nomad-visas-europe/

Widmoser, L. (2024). Digital nomads: Balancing mobility and sustainability in the liquid modern world (Master's thesis, University of Innsbruck). University of Innsbruck Repository. Retrieved from https://repository.university-innsbruck.edu

Woldoff, R. A., & Litchfield, R. C. (2021). *Digital nomads: In search of freedom, community, and meaningful work in the new economy*. Oxford University Press. DOI: 10.1093/oso/9780190931780.001.0001

World Economic Forum. (2024a). How digital nomads can transform tourism and the economy of Small Island Developing States. Retrieved from https://www.weforum.org/stories/2024/10/how-digital-nomads-can-transform-tourism-and-the-economy-of-small-island-developing-states/#:~:text=Digital%20nomadism%20emerged%20as%20a,a%20more%20sustainable%20economic%20model

World Economic Forum. (2024b). *The rise of global digital jobs.* Retrieved from https://www3.weforum.org/docs/WEF_The_Rise_of_Global_Digital_Jobs_2024.pdf

Xiao, Y., & Lutz, C. (2024). Wayfarers in cyberspace: A temporal investigation of digital nomads based on liquid modernity theory. *Journal of Travel Research, 00472875231224242*. Advance online publication. DOI: 10.1177/00472875231224242

Yayla, Ö., Özgür Göde, M., & Ekincek, S. (2024). Global palates: Unraveling digital nomads' culinary journeys and gastro-tourist profiles. *Worldwide Hospitality and Tourism Themes, 16*(3), 329–344. DOI: 10.1108/WHATT-03-2024-0045

Yılmaz Güzey, Y., & Çelik, D. (2022). COVID-19 ve çalışma hayatının dönüşümü. In *COVID-19'un ekonomi politiği* (pp. 116–136). Beykent Üniversitesi.

Zhang, M., Yu, Y., Liu, M., & Liu, J. (2024). Opportunities for China's agricultural heritage systems under the "Digital Nomadism" trend—A stakeholder-weighted approach. *Sustainability (Basel), 16*(7), 2918. DOI: 10.3390/su16072918

Zhang, Y., Gao, J., Cole, S., & Ricci, P. (2021). How the spread of user generated contents (UGC) shapes international tourism distribution: Using agent-based modeling to inform strategic UGC marketing. *Journal of Travel Research*, *60*(7), 1469–1491. DOI: 10.1177/0047287520951639

Zhou, L., Buhalis, D., Fan, D. X., Ladkin, A., & Lian, X. (2024). Attracting digital nomads: Smart destination strategies, innovation and competitiveness. *Journal of Destination Marketing & Management*, *31*, 100850. DOI: 10.1016/j.jdmm.2023.100850

ADDITIONAL READING

Arisoy, B. (2024). Digital nomadism and the tourism industry labor markets. *Worldwide Hospitality and Tourism Themes*, *16*(3), 383–395. DOI: 10.1108/WHATT-03-2024-0062

Arslan, E. (2024). From tourists to nomads: Unveiling the transformative potential of digital nomads in travel and tourism. *Worldwide Hospitality and Tourism Themes*, *16*(3), 269–281. DOI: 10.1108/WHATT-03-2024-0046

Chevtaeva, E., & Denizci-Guillet, B. (2021). Digital nomads' lifestyles and coworkation. *Journal of Destination Marketing & Management*, *21*, 100633. DOI: 10.1016/j.jdmm.2021.100633

Cook, D. (2023). What is a digital nomad? Definition and taxonomy in the era of mainstream remote work. *World Leisure Journal*, *65*(2), 256–275. DOI: 10.1080/16078055.2023.2190608

Floričić, T., & Pavia, N. (2021). Linkage of leisure with remote work and digital nomadism in tourist accommodation facilities. *ToSEE*, *6*, 247–268. DOI: 10.20867/tosee.06.17

Hensellek, S., & Puchala, N. (2021). The emergence of the digital nomad: A review and analysis of the opportunities and risks of digital nomadism. *The flexible workplace: Coworking and other modern workplace transformations*, 195-214.

Hermann, I., & Paris, C. M. (2020). Digital Nomadism: The nexus of remote working and travel mobility. *Information Technology & Tourism*, *22*(3), 329–334. DOI: 10.1007/s40558-020-00188-w

Ji, Y., Kim, S. M., & Kim, Y. (2024). A way to attract digital nomads to tourist destinations in the new normal era. *Sustainability (Basel)*, *16*(6), 2336. DOI: 10.3390/su16062336

Lee, P. (2022). Digital Nomadism: A New Era of Remote Work and Travel. *International Journal of Business Management and Visuals, ISSN: 3006-2705, 5*(1), 22-27.

Thompson, B. Y. (2019). The digital nomad lifestyle: (remote) work/leisure balance, privilege, and constructed community. *International journal of the sociology of leisure, 2*(1), 27-42.

Zerva, K., Huete, R., & Segovia-Pérez, M. (2022, May). Digital nomad tourism: The experience of living at the destination. In *International Conference on Modern Trends in Business Hospitality and Tourism* (pp. 15-26). Cham: Springer International Publishing.

KEY TERMS AND DEFINITIONS

Digital Nomad: Individuals who work location-independently through digital technologies, carrying out their tasks from anywhere without being tied to a physical office.

Remote Work: A flexible working model where tasks are carried out online without the need to commute to an office.

Destination Attractiveness: Factors such as infrastructure, cost of living, safety, and community that influence the preferences of digital nomads.

Association with Local Culture: The relationships digital nomads establish with local communities and cultures during their long-term stays.

Travel Dynamics: Digital nomads shaping new trends in the tourism sector with their behaviors differing from traditional tourists.

Sustainable Tourism: Managing the environmental and social impacts of long-term accommodation and lifestyle on destinations.

Work-Life Balance: The desire of digital nomads to work while traveling and enjoying the pleasures of vacation.

Chapter 4
Transition from Traditional Tourism Destinations to Digital Nomad-Friendly Destinations:
A Conceptual Perspective

Ali Yuce
https://orcid.org/0000-0003-4700-2006
Cappadocia University, Turkey

ABSTRACT

The main aim of this study is to clarify how destinations should be developed to offer a more natural and unobstructed environment where digital nomads can attain comfort, security, and tranquility. Several studies show how smart cities or tourism attractions affect traveler behavior. Nonetheless, there is a dearth of study examining the impact of digital nomadism on tourism destinations as a whole, especially with the benefits and challenges it entails. Consequently, the study does a conceptual analysis, rigorously evaluating relevant resources and interacting with the area of tourism. This study utilized a hermeneutic methodology to examine the available literature, providing varied views that enrich the present understanding of the topic. Lastly, it is discovered that visitors' objectives to enjoy their work while on the go are not substantially impacted by the use and adjustment of these technologies.

DOI: 10.4018/979-8-3373-0076-4.ch004

INTRODUCTION

The world has been evolving at a never-before-seen rate, changing everything in its immediate environment. This dynamic Earth also influences technological advancement, which pervades every facet of human existence, from entertainment to healthcare (Yuce, 2021). A correlation exists between technology advancement and the manner in which humans execute their daily activities. From an individualistic standpoint, technology profoundly impacts individuals' lifestyles, needs, expectations, cultural connections, and social relationships (Pencarelli, 2020). From the supply perspective, technology offers various advantages, including enhanced product quality, reduced labor and other production-related expenses, increased efficiency, lowered maintenance costs, and heightened satisfaction among customers and employees (Buhalis & Law, 2008). Digital nomadism has arisen due to the continuous and rapid growth of technology, allowing individuals to work remotely (Ji, Kim, & Kim, 2024; Mandić & Garbin Praničević, 2019; Vagena, 2021). Nonetheless, in addition to technological progress, digital nomadism arose from the necessity to escape the traditional work environment, often characterized as toxic, where employees encounter clichés, monotonous routines, and even concerns related to well-being (Rainoldi, 2024). Recent research studies have significantly focused on the connection between technology and digital nomadism (Jacobs & Gussekloo, 2016; Nash, Jarrahi, Sutherland, & Phillips, 2018; Reichenberger, 2018). However, there are two major factors that trigger digital nomadism: one is rejection, and the other one is longing (Wang, Schlagwein, Cecez-Kecmanovic, & Cahalane, 2024; Woldoff, Woldoff, & Litchfield, 2021). Studies, such as Cook (2023) and Wang et al. (2024), indicate that rejection is related to the current office or work norms and lifestyles such as feeling obligated to wear white shirts and ties and a hectic, but not productive work environment with the small-sized cubical 'cave' offices. In other words, they reject the classical work environment, which is generally described as a 'toxic' work environment (Woldoff et al., 2021).

The widespread impact of technological innovation on businesses, organizations, and individuals leads to the adoption of progressive techniques that change how we engage in doing our job duties (Pencarelli, 2020; Yuce, 2021). As digital nomadism expands, the investigation into the fundamental motivations for individuals choosing remote employment is increasingly relevant. What compels individuals to leave their hometowns and separate from their friends and sometimes their families? This section will examine nomadism, starting from the archaic period. This chapter aims to clarify the key factors influencing the relationship between smart destinations and digital nomadism, providing a thorough understanding of the fundamental reality rather than merely examining superficial elements. This study will employ a qualitative methodology, focusing on secondary sources including current literature and supplementary digital databases. This current study also seeks to create new frameworks about the influence of smart destinations on digital nomadism, particularly in promoting healthier and safer work and living conditions that extend beyond conventional smart tourism destinations.

Who are digital nomads? Digital nomads are now as location-free individuals as "extraterritorial elites" (Dobrinskaya, 2016). Another study (Wang, Schlagwein, Cecez-Kecmanovic, & Cahalane, 2020) cited from Davenport (2005) "Knowledge workers, in general, are people whose jobs entail "thinking for a living ... [and] the creation, distribution or application of knowledge" (Davenport, 2005, p. 9). Digital nomads are unwilling to invest their knowledge, skills, and effort in an environment where they see a repetitive daily routine. The author describes digital nomads as those who reject the 'circulus vitiosus,' also known as the 'vicious circle.' According to Bachmann (2019), a circulus vitiosus is characterized by a negative emotional condition that prompts an increased reliance on coping mechanisms providing rapid yet transient emotional comfort, subsequently intensifying the negative emotional state. Consequently, they favor locations that allow them to engage with diverse societal values and natural settings. For digital nomads, being trapped in a detrimental cycle is intolerable, as it frequently appears to be an unending loop. Rather than enduring this perpetual cycle, characterized by a traditional or antiquated work environment, they aspire to maximize their potential in an atmosphere where they feel liberated, autonomous, and at ease.

Numerous locations globally are altering their approaches to attract digital nomads (Gupta, Jaiswal, & Gupta, 2024; Jaiswal, Gupta, & Gupta, 2024; Zhou, Buhalis, Fan, Ladkin, & Lian, 2024). Furthermore, research within tourism academia investigates this burgeoning sector of tourism and underscores the significance and potential of digital nomadism. Nonetheless, both destinations and academics are neglecting the significant underlying factors that drive digital nomads to remain mobile. Destinations try to attract digital nomads with their technological developments, while literature highlights how digital nomadism generates economic chances, which are the primary incentives of avaricious capitalist philosophy. Despite the substantial research available in the existing literature, to the author's best knowledge, no study has investigated the motivations behind digital nomads leaving their traditional employment environments and their home regions. Identifying the primary underlying elements is crucial for localities to foster further contributions beyond providing a favorable environment for digital nomads. A relationship exists between digital nomadism and the primitive nomadism of the Paleolithic period. Hence, this study tries to define digital nomadism as a "regression in progression." It might be metaphorically perceived as humanity climbing the modernizing ladder, experiencing estrangement from their roots, and finally repudiating this cycle. The present research also examines digital nomadism through Maslow's Hierarchy of Needs presented below.

Most studies concerning digital nomads indicate that Makimoto and Manners (1997) were the inaugural academics to introduce the phrase "digital nomad" in academic literature. Arslan (2024), cited from Roberts (1984), asserts that Steve K. Roberts is the inaugural individual characterized in literature as a high-tech nomad. Roberts (1984) articulated in the paper, "I observe it daily—the yearning, the jealousy, the distant gaze." He repeatedly stated that he was living someone else's fantasy while riding his mobile office on the bicycle. Conversely, Makimoto and Manners (1997) were pioneers in forecasting the impact of digital nomadism on workplaces. Moreover, digital nomadism gained significance, especially among intellectual workers, during the Covid-19 pandemic (Gupta et al., 2024).

Conversely, there is a dearth of focus in current tourist literature concerning longing. The separation, incompleteness, or absence from what you truly value leads to the emergence of longing (Køster, 2021). Køster (2021) defines longing as an emotional state marked by an intense desire for a cherished person, a feeling of purpose, or a specific location. In this study, longing is defined as a feeling of detachment from the true essence of existence. Longing signifies the loss of the authentic source of satisfaction and pleasure, akin to a bygone natural environment. Irrespective of affluence or contemporary employment settings, longing represents a yearning for something elusive within the surroundings. From a philosophical perspective, the Stoic philosophers Epictetus, Seneca, and Marcus Aurelius have contended that neither materialistic things, including fame, status, position, nor achievement-driven desires yield happiness, well-being, or pleasure (Seneca & Aurelius, 2024). Scholars also asserted that riches, pleasure, and tranquility are not contingent upon material possessions and accomplishments. They claimed that true happiness is in the expedition one undertakes (Aurelius & Moore, 2024). For them, happiness is all about aligning and being in harmony with nature, where one actually belongs. Moreover, wealth, prosperity, and tranquility ought to be regarded as a means rather than an end.

Research Problem

This chapter aims to clarify the key factors that affect the mobility decisions of digital nomads. Analyzing this link will allow destinations to develop, implement, and execute suitable strategies to meet the expectations and needs of digital nomads. Furthermore, technology is undeniably essential in appealing to most tourists, especially digital nomads who rely totally on it. Destinations may also emphasize the implementation of such technology systems or infrastructure. Nonetheless, as previously mentioned, even if destinations have the most sophisticated digital technologies, a failure to understand the essential motivations of digital nomads may jeopardize the entire growth plan. Moreover, locations are encountering challenges related to mass tourism. Unsustainable human practices exhaust the ecosystem. Local people are experiencing growing unhappiness and resentment against tourists at numerous sites. Moreover, it is unclear whether smart destinations can beneficially impact the environment, economy, and social values. This chapter seeks to delineate the many plans that destinations can develop to tackle the previously listed challenges. As a result, alternative tourism activities are more essential for locations.

Research Questions

The contemporary comprehension of tourism activities results from traditional tourism policies, which are guided by unsustainable human practices. Consequently, this reviewed study contends that tourism planners must establish innovative paradigms to transition their destinations toward more sustainable forms of tourism. Digital nomadism is one of the most intriguing, interesting, and expanding forms of tourism. This form of tourism is referred to as niche tourism, as it specifically caters to individuals who are educated, competent, and trained, not only in a particular field of knowledge but also in the stewardship of the environmental, sociocultural, and economic resources of the locations. Nevertheless, considering that this is a relatively recent occurrence, numerous inquiries remain unresolved. Consequently, this study seeks to elucidate several of the research inquiries enumerated below:

- What are the primary factors that compel digital nomads to leave their home countries or workplaces?
- Are local residents, officials, and company proprietors prepared to convert their destinations into smart ones?
- Will smart destinations mitigate the adverse impacts of tourism behaviors on the environment?
- Lastly, how will digital nomads impact the local economy, and to what extent?

Objectives of the Study

- To investigate the primary variables that compel digital nomads to depart from their home locations or employment environments.
- To assess the preparedness of local residents, authorities, and business proprietors for the transformation of their destinations.
- This study aims to determine if smart destinations mitigate the adverse environmental impacts of tourism behaviors.

- To examine the potential impact of digital nomads on the local economy and the degree of that influence.

Significance of the Study

This study diverges from the majority of existing literature in numerous ways. This study is one of the initial investigations aimed at understanding the motivations behind the mobility of digital nomads for remote work, despite the significant research conducted in this area. Secondly, this study distinguishes itself by examining the influence of digital nomadism on sustainability initiatives from sociocultural and environmental perspectives. Third, the strategies employed by local communities, authorities, and business proprietors to position their destination for sustained digital nomadism, in contrast to their competitors.

BACKGROUND AND CONTEXT

Digital nomadism represents both a novel notion for the public and an emerging phenomenon for scholars worldwide (Arslan, 2024; Jacobs & Gussekloo, 2016; Nash et al., 2018). Digital nomads are defined as those that engage in remote work and possess freedom in both time and location while traveling (Jacobs & Gussekloo, 2016; Zhou et al., 2024). These individuals are not merely working autonomously; they are existing outside the constraints of time, space, and lifestyle obligations. Digital nomads possess autonomy over their work schedules, enabling them to operate at their most productive and efficient hours (Woldoff et al., 2021). Digital nomads position their work assets, primarily a laptop, at any location conducive to completing their tasks, provided they have internet connectivity. These settings may range from the lobby to hotel rooms or from snack bars to the beach. In addition to temporal and spatial flexibility, they also experience the liberty to dress comfortably, free from the pressures of typical workplace formality. Ultimately, digital nomads are not obligated to endure the disingenuous and speculative conditions typically referred to as a toxic work environment, which can lead to various health complications, including burnout syndromes. Consequently, while digital nomadism is a nascent idea, it represents a potential and appealing postmodern paradigm that mirrors Paleolithic-era nomadism.

In contrast, tourism plays a significant role in national, international, regional, and local trade (Elmo, Arcese, Valeri, Poponi, & Pacchera, 2020; Yolal, 2016). Tourism creates substantial economic revenue and expenditure that propel both direct and indirect industries worldwide (Alipour, 1996). Destinations are the fundamental components that generate touristic activity in a specific region; this concept is commonly referred to as tourism geography. Tourism geography often features at least one tourism product that draws visitors. The appeal of tourism geography lies not only in the availability of touristic goods or services but also in the comprehensive management, promotion, and marketing of the destination. An innovative and creative approach that addresses the evolving requirements, expectations, and habits of consumers or visitors is a fundamental factor that affects the appeal of a destination's tourism offerings. Technology serves as a vital tool for all stakeholders in destinations to effectively attract the appropriate audience, irrespective of their geographical location. Conversely, a destination featuring state-of-the-art, secure, and sophisticated technologies appeals to a particular demographic seeking respite from their conventional job and living conditions. These individuals, termed digital nomads, seek not only a destination but also a locale that offers consistent, secure, and dependable networking and living conditions. Consequently, locations had to devise, execute, and embrace appropriate strategies—such as intuitive digital applications—to render their locale appealing and distinctive for digital nomads. Establishing a destination distinct from traditional locales can positively affect both conventional tourists, who visit for a limited duration, and individuals seeking to work remotely from their usual area, intending to remain for an extended period. Creating a location that caters to the requirements of digital nomads would also benefit local residents, enterprises, and governmental bodies.

The Origin of Nomadism or Prehistoric Nomadism and Digital Nomadism

Humans have been migrating since the prehistoric ages (Kiriatzi & Knappett, 2021). What were the historical reasons for the occurrence of nomadism? Archaeological and anthropological evidence suggest that archaic humans, our ancestors, were perpetually mobile to offset or evade potential threats to their physiological well-being (Kiriatzi & Knappett, 2021). They dedicated the majority of their time to satisfying their fundamental wants and needs corresponding to the lowest tier of Maslow's Hierarchy of Needs (Ehn, Jorge, & Marques-Pita, 2022; Noltemeyer, Bush, Patton, & Bergen, 2012). The foundational tier of Maslow's Hierarchy of Needs signifies that individuals must fulfill their hunger, satisfy their thirst, acquire enough shelter, and reproduce to perpetuate their lineage (Noltemeyer et al., 2012). The capacity to endure chaotic and adverse situations is the foremost priority for all living organisms, as evidenced in the foundational layer. These are the principal reasons why individuals in ancient times frequently migrated, thereby earning the designation of prehistoric nomads. Undoubtedly, numerous other criteria might be enumerated; however, this is beyond the scope of this chapter.

Individuals continue to be mobile in the 21st century, often referred to as the digital era. The nomadism of the digital age is indisputably different from that of the Paleolithic age in various respects. This time, people are being mobilized not only to satisfy their physiological demands but also to address their intrinsic needs, such as autonomy over their time and lifestyle, as well as flexibility about their optimal performance locations. Despite this layer being above basic necessities, many nevertheless desire to relocate from their customary locations. Mobility provides them with the capacity and chance to perform their tasks remotely without experiencing burnout or distress associated with traditional workplace settings (Gupta et al., 2024). Digital nomads choose locations that offer reliable high-speed internet, advanced technological resources, cost savings, an escape from detrimental and monotonous workplace settings, and opportunities to enhance interpersonal skills through engagement with diverse cultures, among other advantages (Arslan, 2024; Jiwasiddi et al., 2024). Digital nomads possess the capacity to acclimate to contemporary technological improvements in most global destinations. Despite the significant evolution of nomadism in the contemporary era compared to the archaic period, one constant remains: they continue to be mobile.

Smart Destinations

Continuous technological advancements have transformed nomadism into a modern lifestyle. Digitalization has impacted many aspects of our lives, leading to the evolution of destinations into smart ones (Xiang & Fesenmaier, 2017). Smart destinations offer numerous benefits for both communities and visitors. Destinations vigorously advertise and promote their unique tourism attractions to specific audiences, regardless of physical location. Simultaneously, tourists can apply advanced technologies that enable instant communication with relatives, ease transit challenges, and access online city assistants, chatbots, and translation software, among other tools. Current advanced technologies such as virtual reality, augmented reality, digital twins, artificial intelligence, cloud technologies, and machine learning provide numerous benefits not only for the accommodation industry but also for all involved in the tourism activities (Azis, Amin, Chan, & Aprilia, 2020; Yuce, 2023). Studies indicate that the advanced and newly developing technologies provide and offer significant opportunities and benefits to turn traditional-oriented tourism approaches into more sophisticated destinations. Destinations will increase their attractiveness as they adopt and adapt technologies and entities that enhance visitors' well-being. As mentioned above, technology and the tourism industry are interwoven elements. Hence, it is fundamentally important for the destinations to design their locations that will ease the digital nomads' lives.

The tourist sector is significantly reliant on technological advancements. Consequently, companies, institutions, and entities strive to adopt emerging technologies, unless hindered by budgetary constraints or factors such as reluctance or opposition, resulting in a digital divide. Nonetheless, choosing the appropriate technology for prolonged utilization is essential for sustainable tourism development. Yuce (2022) asserts that technology selection should be based on various criteria, including its appropriateness, user-friendly interface, and additional factors relevant to work requirements. Certain studies indicate that Earth is replete with a digital graveyard, attributed not only to the swift pace of digital innovation resulting in obsolescence but also to the aspiration to own the latest technologies for competitive advantage in the tourism sector. Both issues significantly contribute to unsustainable work behaviors. Consequently, destination management firms must guarantee that technology is utilized effectively to enhance productivity while designing destinations for digital nomads.

The Impact of Tourism: More Than Economic Outcome and Alternative Approach

Tourism has emerged as a vital industry regarded as a remedy for the economic challenges faced by numerous governments worldwide (Alipour, 1996). In industrialized countries with robust industries like automotive, electronics, and manufacturing, income from tourism substantially contributes to their Gross Domestic Product (GDP). In addition to GDP-related contributions, tourism generates several economic advantages for local, regional, national, and international economies. Prior to discussing the economic consequences of tourism, this study proposes arguments against the assessment of tourism's impact on local, regional, or national communities solely through economic outcomes, which are derived from faulty and biased data sets. Nevertheless, this study will also present evidence to demonstrate the contribution of classical tourism activities to economic growth.

Multiple studies indicate that tourism operations generate significant foreign exchange, categorized as both direct and indirect earnings (Katircioglu, Katircioğlu, & Altinay, 2018). Hotels, entertainment, shopping, and excursions at locations provide direct revenue, while suppliers typically obtain indirect revenue. Foreign exchange revenue advantages not only hotel owners and businesses but also allow local and national governments to distribute money in diverse ways. National governments necessitate foreign exchange for international trade, including imports and exports, which is crucial for nations whose own currency is not suitable for trade (Katircioglu et al., 2018; Yolal, 2016). Another benefit of earning foreign exchange is that it assists the national government in sustaining currency stability. Ensuring rate stability offers numerous benefits, such as preserving low inflation and attracting international investors to the nation's financial institutions. Foreign exchange aids governments in balancing or alleviating their trade deficits. Ultimately, if the local population is motivated, instructed, and educated, tourism operations can significantly help small and medium-sized firms and suppliers, while concurrently improving the local destination's infrastructure.

Moreover, tourism has the potential to generate economic possibilities, notwithstanding the seasonal nature of summer jobs (Aynalem, Birhanu, & Tesefay, 2016; Yolal, 2016). Employment opportunities provided by tourism expose local and other workers to foreign cultural and social values while offering temporary money. Students have the ability to participate in work at various facilities in the areas. Interacting with tourists provides seasonal employees and students with a unique opportunity to adapt to a practical experience. Several more economic benefits can be identified, including the tax money produced by tourists. Nonetheless, it exceeds the scope of this chapter.

However, it is essential to analyze and interrogate whether forms of tourism generate significant economic advantages and the associated costs of such benefits. A burgeoning corpus of scholarship on sustainable tourism development indicates that persistent tourism activities, often termed mass tourism, are the principal contributors to considerable ecological damage. Furthermore, mass tourism engenders significant socioeconomic concerns for local populations, including heightened crime rates, strained transportation systems, escalated living costs, and a sense of alienation from their own environment during peak seasons. From an environmental standpoint, overpopulation at destinations leads to substantial water usage and the generation of liquid and solid waste, necessitating the efficient organization of waste management systems and personnel during peak periods. Although the teams operate efficiently under a limited budget, rampant tourism activities cause significant damage to ecosystems, including the exhaustion of natural resources.

From a cultural perspective, mass tourism-oriented tourism activities also have numerous detrimental effects on cultural values. As more visitors arrive to the destinations, then cultural values such as sensitive natural assets, cultural identity in terms of local people's language, belief system and rituals might be prone to be faded in the long run. As a matter of fact, what makes a destination attractive is its unique authenticity. Moreover, mass tourism causes the destinations to turn into homogenous environment in which even global food and beverage chains are available. As a result current tourism activities cannot be continued and therefore they need to be evaluated and transformed into newer forms such as smart tourism destinations in which more elite, sophisticated, responsible visitors can be hosted.

The majority of the research indicates that tourism is one of the fastest growing and essential sectors driving economic growth from local to global markets (Akkemik, 2012; Aynalem et al., 2016; Harrill, 2004). It generates substantial money, fosters employment, and enables local economies to thrive within a highly competitive capitalist framework. Tourism presents several opportunities but also engenders significant sustainability issues, including environmental degradation, sociocultural deterioration, and heightened income inequality. Tourism is a comparatively more environmentally sustainable industry that generates fewer greenhouse gas emissions than numerous other sectors (Sun, 2016). Conversely, modern literature emphasizes the significance of digitalization in fostering more sustainable tourist sites through the implementation of new technology (Ruggerio, 2021). Technology possesses significant potential to transform traditional tourism destinations into intelligent locales. Tourism and technology are interconnected ideas that act as a catalyst for the evolution of destinations in response to the swiftly changing interests and intentions of travelers concerning specific locations (Buhalis & Law, 2008). The concept of a smart destination presents significant prospects for both supply and demand at the location. Recent studies characterize smart destinations as utilizing advanced technology to enhance production, efficiency, and tourist satisfaction while reducing resource use.

Smart destinations differ from the classical destinations in myriad ways. Classical destinations are designed to provide some basic services to visitors. Some of the services are accommodations that ranges from a small apart hotel to upscale hotels, transportation including charters and safaris and food and beverages, information centers that gives basic information at the information centers and, of course touristic products including Sea, Sand and Sun (3Ss) and other attractions such as antic cities, natural landscapes and more. Classical destinations provide most of these services by using the traditional approaches which require human participation in most cases. However, smart destinations ensure that instead of employing people, they prefer to implement advanced technologies to enhance visitors' experiences and satisfaction during their trips to the destination.

On the other hand, there is also a new trend that can be described as 'from tourists to nomads' (Arslan, 2024). There are different versions of definitions of digital nomads in the literature. According to Jacobs and Gussekloo (2016) digital nomads are 'location independent' individuals who work remotely using his/her digital component that are connected to the Internet through different versions of network and data storage tool. Another study defines digital nomads more simply: "globally travelling" digital worker (Jiwasiddi et al., 2024) due to showing rejection to classical work hours (9 to 5 obligations) or as Müller (2016) stated digital nomads are not "restricted to working 09:00 – 17:00 like in traditional office hours (Nash et al., 2018; Wang, Schlagwein, Cecez-Kecmanovic, & Cahalane, 2019).

Research studies also state that digital nomads are seeking for freedom to complete their work assignments without being in an office environment (Nash et al., 2018; Wang et al., 2019). Vagena (2021) defines digital nomads as global nomads who are working independently without being at a specific place to complete their given task using their digital device which have access to the internet. Lastly, Ji et al. (2024) explains digital nomads as technology based individuals who are "engaged in web design, programming, and online marketing but are not constrained by their workspace while freely choosing a workplace." Although studies define digital nomads in various ways, there are three common features of digital nomads: They need have a digital device to work remotely and internet access and being a traveler out of his/her regular hometown that is why digital nomads are called by Jiwasiddi et al. (2024) "globally travelling" digital worker(s). A conceptualized study (Arslan, 2024) which reviewed the current literature found that there are four key factors that drive the digital nomadism. These four key factors are 'freedom' (Hannonen, 2020; Müller, 2016; Reichenberger, 2018; Thompson, 2019), 'working style' (lifestyle) (Hannonen, 2020; Nash et al., 2018; Stickel, 2020; Thompson, 2019), employment (Müller, 2016) and 'travelling' (Nash et al., 2018; Reichenberger, 2018; Stickel, 2020; Thompson, 2019).

Upon synthesizing and examining the aforementioned research results using a hermeneutic approach, it becomes evident that the majority of these studies predominantly focus on occupational satisfaction, lifestyle, autonomy, and travel. This chapter, as previously said, diverges from other studies by examining the notion that various situations, motivations, or incentives lead individuals to reject standard employment settings. Herold's (2019) thesis investigation indicates that more significant components warrant examination. Key qualities include the younger population, especially population Z, physical and mental health, work-life balance, happiness and life satisfaction, and personal growth (Herold, 2019).

Digital nomads are a novel kind of visitors who have an environmentally aware and respectful disposition towards the natural resources and social values of their destinations. Digital nomads are typically well-educated, possess heightened awareness, and demonstrate respect for cultural and societal norms. Many have a propensity for caution to reduce their environmental impact while traveling. Furthermore, as environmentally conscious travelers, they favor places that not only offer a safe and secure lifestyle and technology but also have robust sustainability practices. Therefore, it is essential for destinations to adopt environmentally sustainable strategies that will reduce the adverse effects and enhance the beneficial impacts of tourism operations.

In addition to the environmentally friendly location, destinations should develop newer and unique strategies to make their location a 'digital nomadism friendly' destination. Numerous studies reveal a clear correlation between job happiness and factors such as the work environment, hours, workload, and traditional dress codes (Abubakar, Rezapouraghdam, Behravesh, & Megeirhi, 2022; Stickel, 2020). Furthermore, a causal relationship exists among independence, the aspiration to travel, the pursuit of physical and mental well-being, and digital nomadism. Digital nomads seek fulfillment in both their professional and personal lives (Woldoff et al., 2021). They prefer freedom over surveillance while on the sky decks. Ultimately, individuals would rather be in intelligent destinations than in intelligent structures (Reichenberger, 2018). All of these aspirations are inherently connected to their well-being, a vital component of a sustained and healthy life that fosters the development of a 'digital nomadism-friendly' place.

Conversely, there are fundamental differences between archaic and digital era nomadism, commonly termed "digital work" and "future of work" in numerous papers (Ahuja, 2023; Jiwasiddi et al., 2024; Wang et al., 2020). As previously indicated, prehistoric nomadism was not a voluntary decision; it was a necessity for survival among harsh living conditions. Digital nomadism is a lifestyle option characterized by moving to various locations to fulfill personal needs. Digital nomadism pertains to the pursuit of well-being while traversing the globe as a digital nomad, utilizing a computer, the primary digital tool for this lifestyle. Digital nomadism, often known as a mobile office, denotes the ability to operate from any location with internet connectivity. The lifestyle of digital nomadism has gained popularity among many, particularly tech-savvy individuals, as it allows them to fulfill their professional obligations while traveling globally. Consequently, the number of individuals traveling globally without a permanent residence has risen over the past decade (Jiwasiddi et al., 2024).

What advantages will locations get from digital nomadism? There are additional imperative inquiries: Are the locations prepared to deliver exceptional services utilizing advanced technology for digital travelers? The requirements, desires, and anticipations of digital nomads surpass the sheer availability of a technologically advanced place. Smart destinations do not necessarily include the implementation of the most advanced digitalization at the location. A smart destination entails recognizing the essential elements that influence the worldwide population of digital nomads. Upon comprehension, destinations can function as a refuge for digital nomads. While the exact number of digital nomads remains uncertain, Gupta et al. (2024) assert that "there are now 17.3 million digital nomads in the USA alone." It is anticipated that numerous additional workers will shift to this new tourist demographic. Consequently, digital nomadism has garnered interest from numerous countries, as it is increasingly favored by individuals who value life happiness and well-being over luxurious office settings. With the rise in 'knowledge workers', organizations are modifying their remote work rules to cater to those who like working from tourist locations (Gupta et al., 2024). Key elements that motivate places to undergo transformation include the attainment of sustainable goals that benefit local populations (Gupta et al., 2024).

METHODOLOGY

The phenomenon of digital nomadism has received increasing attention among experts. Despite the expanding literature on digital tourism, there remains limited knowledge regarding the primary causes that contribute to millions of digital nomads working remotely. It is anticipated that identifying the elements would lead to improved comprehension and approaches to appeal to the newly emerging tourist typologies, which vary in many ways, including longer stays, greater responsibility, and greater sensitivity to natural and cultural resources. Another goal of this study was to investigate the ways in which smart destinations differ from conventional ones.

The present investigation employed a qualitative methodology and literature analysis to identify the fundamental elements influencing the evolving preferences of digital nomads. Qualitative research is a basic paradigm that facilitates reliable, thorough, and in-depth analysis within the scientific environment. The basic structure of this study is derived from a conceptual analysis that gathers data from relevant literature. This study focused on scholarly resources including Web of Science, Google Scholar, and ResearchGate and critically and methodically analyzed secondary material using the keywords "digital nomadism" and "smart destinations" in the body of current literature.

CONCLUSION

This study utilized a hermeneutic approach to the existing literature to provide varied views that deepen the present understanding of the topic. Employing this critical hermeneutic hospitality sector utilizes advanced technologies. However, the adoption and alteration of such technologies do not fundamentally affect the motivations of travelers wishing to enjoy their work while traveling abroad. This study argued that the presence of advanced technology in offices fails to meet the desires, wants, and needs of employees. Research indicates that persons with advanced abilities, knowledge, and competence tend to seek remote employment options. Digital nomadism is a non-traditional work arrangement that enables individuals to use various areas as a base for remote employment. Destinations appealing to digital nomads may feature permanent personnel, locally generated income, and fewer environmental hazards. Ultimately, the probability of deterioration in homogenization and the erosion of sociocultural values and individuality decreases.

Classical tourism is often characterized as a temporary relocation from a regular location to another, where travelers can fulfill their fundamental needs, goals, and aspirations, including but not limited to exploring new destinations and experiencing the authentic sociocultural values of local hosts. This study contended that the swift advancement of technology has resulted in the emergence of new categories of tourists, differentiated from conventional mass tourism-oriented travelers. Digitalization has facilitated the development of unbiased, non-stereotypical perspectives and insights for prospective visitors regarding destinations, in contrast to iconic locations. In contrast to classical tourism, which primarily addresses the physiological needs of individuals, 'Digital Era Tourism' transcends this conventional definition by offering transformative travel experiences, including immersive journeys facilitated by virtual reality technologies.

In addition to the numerous unique characteristics and advantages of conventional destinations that attracted visitors, smart destinations provide more advanced yet authentic products and services that cater to the needs and preferences of digital nomads. Smart destinations aim to provide visitors with an environmentally sustainable, responsible, and digital nomad-friendly environment. The shift from a classical tourism model to a digital era has transformed traditional tourist attractions into smart tourist destinations. Smart destinations, an emerging form of tourism, primarily attract individuals looking to work remotely from their usual surroundings. The desire for the natural environment and the rejection of contemporary living and working conditions are significant elements propelling digital nomadism, notwithstanding varying motivations. Ultimately, several essential factors that propel digital nomadism include satisfying digital nomads' aspirations for personal development, seeking tranquility both internally and externally, as well as attaining success and self-actualization.

According to anthropological and archaeological data, our ancestors, the archaic humans, were constantly on the move to counteract or avoid any risks to their physical health until they started to settle down following the Neolithic Revolution. People are still mobile in the twenty-first century, which is sometimes called the "digital era". The nomadic lifestyle of the digital age is unquestionably distinct from that of the Paleolithic in several ways. In addition to meeting their physiological needs, people in the digital age are being mobilized to meet their intrinsic wants, which include flexibility over their ideal performance settings and autonomy over their time and lifestyle.

Digital nomads are those who perform remote work and enjoy flexibility in both time and location while traveling. In the literature, as aforementioned, digital nomads are referred to as "global travelers," "knowledge workers," or "extraterritorial elite." The primary distinction that differentiates digital nomads from traditional tourists is that digital nomads travel to work, whereas conventional tourists work to travel. Digital nomadism has emerged as a consequence of the persistent and swift advancement of technology, enabling individuals to work remotely. Digital nomads are disinclined to commit their knowledge, skills, and effort in an environment characterized by a monotonous daily routine.

Lastly, sustainability is an essential concept that transforms a conventionally oriented location into one that supports digital nomadism. Digital nomads typically display an increased awareness of environmental degradation, preferring destinations where local people, businesses, and governments show significant recognition and respect for natural, cultural, and social values. Protecting these resources is a crucial responsibility of the destination, given their closeness to human activities. Consequently, it is prudent to develop and refine sustainable human practices while creating a safe, secure, and reliable digital infrastructure at the location.

Recommendations and Practical Contributions

The primary objective of this study is to examine the fundamental factors influencing digital nomads' intent to labor outside their conventional living and working environments. Conversely, it is essential to examine how destinations have to be equipped to accommodate prospective digital nomads. Destinations ensure that they vary significantly from conventional and well-known locales frequented by digital nomads. Destinations ought to provide novel opportunities, including genuine settings where digital nomads can experience tranquility, comfort, and a laid-back atmosphere. Furthermore, it is essential to comprehend the cultural preferences and diversities among each group. It is essential to design measures that facilitate the mutual adoption of cultural and social values between digital nomads and local populations. Taking these factors into account can yield beneficial results for both ends of the spectrum: local individuals and communities. Host communities gain economic and social advantages, while digital nomads achieve work-life equilibrium, enhanced productivity, improved efficiency, and sustainable personal objectives. Last but not least, the rise of digital nomadism will promote alternative and sustainable travel, as opposed to traditional travel, which frequently results in environmental and sociocultural catastrophes in the majority of tourist locations.

REFERENCES

Abubakar, A. M., Rezapouraghdam, H., Behravesh, E., & Megeirhi, H. A. (2022). Burnout or boreout: A meta-analytic review and synthesis of burnout and boreout literature in hospitality and tourism. *Journal of Hospitality Marketing & Management, 31*(4), 458–503. DOI: 10.1080/19368623.2022.1996304

Akkemik, K. A. (2012). Assessing the importance of international tourism for the Turkish economy: A social accounting matrix analysis. *Tourism Management, 33*(4), 790–801. DOI: 10.1016/j.tourman.2011.09.002

Alipour, H. (1996). Tourism development within planning paradigms: The case of Turkey. *Tourism Management, 17*(5), 367–377. DOI: 10.1016/0261-5177(96)00036-2

Arslan, E. (2024). From tourists to nomads: Unveiling the transformative potential of digital nomads in travel and tourism. *Worldwide Hospitality and Tourism Themes, 16*(3), 269–281. DOI: 10.1108/WHATT-03-2024-0046

Aynalem, S., Birhanu, K., & Tesefay, S. (2016). Employment opportunities and challenges in tourism and hospitality sectors. *Journal of Tourism & Hospitality (Los Angeles, Calif.), 5*(6), 1–5. DOI: 10.4172/2167-0269.1000257

Azis, N., Amin, M., Chan, S., & Aprilia, C. (2020). How smart tourism technologies affect tourist destination loyalty. *Journal of Hospitality and Tourism Technology, 11*(4), 603–625. DOI: 10.1108/JHTT-01-2020-0005

Buhalis, D., & Law, R. (2008). Progress in information technology and tourism management: 20 years on and 10 years after the Internet—The state of eTourism research. *Tourism Management, 29*(4), 609–623. DOI: 10.1016/j.tourman.2008.01.005

Cook, D. (2023). What is a digital nomad? Definition and taxonomy in the era of mainstream remote work. *World Leisure Journal, 65*(2), 256–275. DOI: 10.1080/16078055.2023.2190608

Davenport, T. H. (2005). *Thinking for a living: how to get better performances and results from knowledge workers*. Harvard Business Press.

Dobrinskaya, D. E. (2016). Nomadic lifestyle in the network society: sociological aspect.

Ehn, K., Jorge, A., & Marques-Pita, M. (2022). Digital nomads and the COVID-19 pandemic: Narratives about relocation in a time of lockdowns and reduced mobility. *Social Media + Society, 8*(1), 20563051221084958. DOI: 10.1177/20563051221084958

Elmo, G. C., Arcese, G., Valeri, M., Poponi, S., & Pacchera, F. (2020). Sustainability in tourism as an innovation driver: An analysis of family business reality. *Sustainability (Basel), 12*(15), 6149. DOI: 10.3390/su12156149

Gupta, S., Jaiswal, R., & Gupta, S. K. (2024). Digital nomads: A systematic literature review and future research agenda. *Tourism Review*. Advance online publication. DOI: 10.1108/TR-12-2023-0869

Hannonen, O. (2020). In search of a digital nomad: Defining the phenomenon. *Information Technology & Tourism, 22*(3), 335–353. DOI: 10.1007/s40558-020-00177-z

Harrill, R. (2004). Residents' attitudes toward tourism development: A literature review with implications for tourism planning. *Journal of Planning Literature, 18*(3), 251–266. DOI: 10.1177/0885412203260306

Jacobs, E., & Gussekloo, A. (2016). *Digital nomads: How to live, work and play around the world*. Esther Jacobs & André Gussekloo.

Jaiswal, R., Gupta, S., & Gupta, S. K. (2024). The impending disruption of digital nomadism: Opportunities, challenges, and research agenda. *World Leisure Journal*, •••, 1–31. DOI: 10.1080/16078055.2024.2346091

Ji, Y., Kim, S.-M., & Kim, Y. (2024). A way to attract digital nomads to tourist destinations in the new normal era. *Sustainability (Basel), 16*(6), 2336. DOI: 10.3390/su16062336

Jiwasiddi, A., Schlagwein, D., Cahalane, M., Cecez-Kecmanovic, D., Leong, C., & Ractham, P. (2024). Digital nomadism as a new part of the visitor economy: The case of the "digital nomad capital" Chiang Mai, Thailand. *Information Systems Journal*.

Katircioglu, S., Katircioğlu, S., & Altinay, M. (2018). Interactions between tourism and financial sector development: Evidence from Turkey. *Service Industries Journal, 38*(9-10), 519–542. DOI: 10.1080/02642069.2017.1406479

Kiriatzi, E., & Knappett, C. (2021). *Human Mobility and Technological Transfer in the Prehistoric Mediterranean*. Cambridge University Press.

Mandić, A., & Garbin Praničević, D. (2019). Progress on the role of ICTs in establishing destination appeal: Implications for smart tourism destination development. *Journal of Hospitality and Tourism Technology, 10*(4), 791–813. DOI: 10.1108/JHTT-06-2018-0047

Müller, A. (2016). The digital nomad: Buzzword or research category? *Transnational Social Review, 6*(3), 344–348. DOI: 10.1080/21931674.2016.1229930

Nash, C., Jarrahi, M. H., Sutherland, W., & Phillips, G. (2018). *Digital nomads beyond the buzzword: Defining digital nomadic work and use of digital technologies.* Paper presented at the International conference on information. DOI: 10.1007/978-3-319-78105-1_25

Noltemeyer, A., Bush, K., Patton, J., & Bergen, D. (2012). The relationship among deficiency needs and growth needs: An empirical investigation of Maslow's theory. *Children and Youth Services Review, 34*(9), 1862–1867. DOI: 10.1016/j.childyouth.2012.05.021

Pencarelli, T. (2020). The digital revolution in the travel and tourism industry. *Information Technology & Tourism, 22*(3), 455–476. DOI: 10.1007/s40558-019-00160-3

Rainoldi, M. (2024). *Managing work and leisure in the digital age: A practice exploration of digital nomadism.* Bournemouth University, Reichenberger, I. (2018). Digital nomads–a quest for holistic freedom in work and leisure. *Annals of Leisure Research, 21*(3), 364–380.

Ruggerio, C. A. (2021). Sustainability and sustainable development: A review of principles and definitions. *The Science of the Total Environment, 786*, 147481. DOI: 10.1016/j.scitotenv.2021.147481 PMID: 33965820

Stickel, M. D. (2020). *Challenges and opportunities of digital nomadism and its implications for tomorrow's workforce.* Management from the NOVA–School of Business and Economics.

Sun, Y.-Y. (2016). Decomposition of tourism greenhouse gas emissions: Revealing the dynamics between tourism economic growth, technological efficiency, and carbon emissions. *Tourism Management, 55*, 326–336. DOI: 10.1016/j.tourman.2016.02.014

Thompson, B. Y. (2019). The digital nomad lifestyle:(remote) work/leisure balance, privilege, and constructed community. *International journal of the sociology of leisure, 2*(1), 27-42.

Vagena, A. (2021). Digital nomads and tourism industry. *Academia Letters, 765*, 1–6.

Wang, B., Schlagwein, D., Cecez-Kecmanovic, D., & Cahalane, M. (2019). *Digital Nomadism and the Market Economy: Resistance and Compliance.* Paper presented at the ICIS.

Wang, B., Schlagwein, D., Cecez-Kecmanovic, D., & Cahalane, M. C. (2020). Beyond the factory paradigm: Digital nomadism and the digital future (s) of knowledge work post-COVID-19. *Journal of the Association for Information Systems, 21*(6), 10. DOI: 10.17705/1jais.00641

Wang, B., Schlagwein, D., Cecez-Kecmanovic, D., & Cahalane, M. C. (2024). 'Emancipation' in Digital Nomadism vs in the Nation-State: A Comparative Analysis of Idealtypes. *Journal of Business Ethics*, •••, 1–34.

Woldoff, R. A., Woldoff, R., & Litchfield, R. C. (2021). *Digital nomads: In search of freedom, community, and meaningful work in the new economy*. Oxford University Press. DOI: 10.1093/oso/9780190931780.001.0001

Xiang, Z., & Fesenmaier, D. R. (2017). Big data analytics, tourism design and smart tourism. *Analytics in smart tourism design: concepts and methods*, 299-307.

Yolal, M. (2016). History of tourism development in Turkey. *Alternative Tourism in Turkey: Role, Potential Development and Sustainability*, 23-33.

Yuce, A. (2021). The Impact of Digital Transformation and Virtual Reality in Tourism Marketing: A Conceptualized Exploration. In *Handbook of Research on IoT, Digital Transformation, and the Future of Global Marketing* (pp. 1-14): IGI Global. DOI: 10.4018/978-1-7998-7192-7.ch001

Yuce, A. (2023). Digital twins and sustainable developments in the tourism and hospitality industry. In *Handbook of Research on Applications of AI, Digital Twin, and Internet of Things for Sustainable Development* (pp. 461-472): IGI Global. DOI: 10.4018/978-1-6684-6821-0.ch027

Zhou, L., Buhalis, D., Fan, D. X., Ladkin, A., & Lian, X. (2024). Attracting digital nomads: Smart destination strategies, innovation and competitiveness. *Journal of Destination Marketing & Management, 31*, 100850. DOI: 10.1016/j.jdmm.2023.100850

Chapter 5
Push and Pull Factors Making Istanbul an Attractive Destination for Digital Nomads

Nihan Uğur
Department of Tourism Management, Istanbul Nişantaşı University, Turkey

ABSTRACT

This study explores the factors that attract digital nomads to Istanbul, a dynamic city. Digital nomads use technology to work remotely, allowing them to travel freely and embrace a flexible lifestyle. They value independence, exploration, and balancing work with leisure, seeking to escape traditional office environments. While facing challenges such as visa procedures, reliable infrastructure, and time zone differences, digital nomads contribute to local economies and immerse themselves in new cultures, forming diverse identities. Push factors, like the desire for relaxation or adventure, and pull factors, such as a destination's attractions, climate, and culture, influence their travel decisions. Istanbul offers numerous attractions, including natural beauty, outdoor activities, and vibrant urban life, making it ideal for both work and leisure. This study examines how Istanbul can attract digital nomads and provides insights into destination marketing strategies tailored to their needs.

INTRODUCTION

Tourism movement refers to a form of temporary relocation, where tourists travel to and stay in a different destination for a short period. This type of temporary mobility involves a territorial shift that is not permanent (Bell & Ward, 2000).

DOI: 10.4018/979-8-3373-0076-4.ch005

There is a relationship between tourism and migration. Migration is typically defined as the permanent relocation of individuals to a different place (Boyle et al., 2014). Tourism can sometimes lead to migration. Initially, tourists may visit a destination, but over time, some choose to settle there permanently, becoming residents (Williams & Hall, 2000). Additionally, individuals seeking a new place to live often first explore potential destinations as tourists (Brown & Moore, 1970). The distinction between migration and tourism is becoming increasingly blurred, necessitating new conceptualizations of human mobility. According to Williams and Hall (2002), tourism-informed mobility can be conceptualized into five main forms: "entrepreneurial migration", where individuals move to start or manage businesses; "labor migration", involving the movement of individuals seeking employment opportunities; "return (labor) migration", which refers to individuals returning to their place of origin after working elsewhere; "economically active migration (consumption-led)", driven by lifestyle or consumption preferences; and "retirement migration", where individuals relocate to enjoy their retirement years in preferred destinations. Certain forms of movement, such as seasonal migration, can include owning a second home or using Airbnb rental properties, which may function as either tourism activities or lead to permanent migration. The tourism industry plays a significant role in promoting and facilitating these contemporary patterns of mobility (O'Reilly, 2003). Digital nomadism is a new form of tourist mobility, presenting both opportunities and challenges for destination management (Zhou et al., 2024). To attract this emerging type of tourist, destinations need to leverage both push and pull motivational factors.

Makimoto and Manners (1997) first used the term "digital nomad" to describe the effect of advancements in cutting-edge technologies on people's lifestyles. Digital nomads take advantage of mobility technologies to work remotely from any location with internet access. They use this flexibility to travel the world, embracing a lifestyle free from a fixed workplace. Preferring a freelance lifestyle, digital nomads explore new destinations and immerse themselves in diverse cultures while working (Mancinelli, 2020). This growing trend is connected to individualization, globalization, advanced technology, convenient transportation, and wireless communication. Emerging technologies create new opportunities, enabling more leisure time and a mobile lifestyle (Hannonen, 2020).

The digital nomad lifestyle is rapidly expanding. This way of life refers to mobile professionals working from locations worldwide. Especially following the COVID-19 pandemic, this lifestyle has gained momentum as the obligation to work from a fixed location has shifted toward location independence (Hannonen et al., 2023). As digital nomadism has become an important trend in tourism, destinations have begun developing new marketing strategies. They now offer co-working spaces as a key attraction, along with a variety of products and services such as co-living spaces, recreational activities, healthcare, and special visa regulations (Chevtaeva & Denizci-Guillet, 2021).

As with various lifestyles, scholars are increasingly interested in contemporary forms of living, including that of digital nomads. Several studies have focused on the lifestyle of digital nomads (Green, 2020; Mancinelli, 2020; Hall et al., 2019), while some have investigated the relationship between destination culture and nomads (Kannisto, 2016).

As digital nomads have become more prevalent in many destinations, destination managers are paying greater attention to attraction strategies. Several theoretical models are used to understand digital nomads' motivations in tourism, including the push and pull factors model (Crompton, 1979; Dann, 1981), which is applied to attract digital nomads. Push factors are the social and psychological reasons for travel, while pull factors are the attractions of a destination (Cifci et al., 2024).

Istanbul is an astonishing city located between Asia and Europe. It has been the center of different civilizations (Belge, 2018) and has been influenced by various cultures throughout history. The cultural traces of the Roman, Byzantine, and Ottoman Empires can be seen in Istanbul (Kubat, 1999). The city's panoramic view can be admired from the top of the Galata Tower. The Bosphorus Bridge provides a connection between Asia and Europe. Between the Black Sea and the Mediterranean Sea lies the Sea of Marmara, which serves as a link between them (Clark, 2012).

Greek leader Byzas took over İstanbul from pastoral Thracian tribes and named it Byzantium in 657 BCE. In 330 CE, Constantine the Great made it the capital city and referred to it as "New Rome." By the end of the first millennium, the city was commonly called *eis tēn polin* rather than Constantinople. In the 13th century, its name evolved into *Istinpolin*. Over the years, the name further changed to "Istanbul." Istanbul has seven hills—six of them are around the Golden Horn (Haliç), while the seventh is located in the southwest of the city. The Golden Horn separates the city (Ehrlich, 2025). Istanbul has a historic peninsula, surrounded by walls that were developed during the Byzantium and Constantinople periods. The city is home to unique architectural masterpieces, a heritage of Byzantine and Ottoman architects (UNESCO, 2025).

The purpose of this study is to identify the push and pull factors that attract digital nomads to Istanbul, a captivating destination. It utilizes a framework to explore how Istanbul can successfully appeal to digital nomads. This study offers a theoretical contribution to the literature on digital nomads. By using push and pull factors to provide insights into destinations, the study proposes supporting the development of more effective destination marketing strategies.

DIGITAL NOMADS

Globalization affects economic, technological, and demographic transformations while also influencing destinations. Additionally, globalization drives cultural transformation. Cutting-edge technologies and globalization enable the emergence of new lifestyles and promote multiculturalism. Increased mobility and globalization provide people with opportunities to adopt diverse lifestyles. Individuals who rely on mobile technologies in their daily lives may choose to migrate to other destinations (D'Andrea, 2013). Other destinations may offer an alternative lifestyle, providing new opportunities for work, leisure, and activities that enrich the human spirit. These new locations might also offer improved living conditions and a more fulfilling environment. Lifestyle motilities are shaped by individual preferences and specific contexts. People are often motivated by a desire to improve their quality of life. This means they need a certain level of financial stability and freedom to make such choices. The concept includes different types of movement across places and time, allowing for changes between these forms over a person's life (O'Reilly, 2003).

Pursuing the "good life" is often cited as a key motivating factor for digital nomads. They perceive the good life as fragmented and dispersed, with various quality-of-life elements available in different locations at different times. As a result, mobility becomes an essential resource and practice for digital nomads, enabling them to access and customize their version of the good life by moving between places as needed (Åkerlund, 2013). Personal desires evolve over time, influencing lifestyle, preferences, freedom of choice, and the pursuit of self-fulfillment. These changing desires manifest in various forms, such as seasonal second-home tourism, lifestyle migration, global nomadism, drifters, backpacking, and digital nomadism. While these categories sometimes overlap and are treated as similar, they differ in significant ways. Key differences include the duration of travel, frequency of revisiting destinations, and the likelihood of returning to one's hometown, the use of digital technologies, and the ability to work while traveling (Hannonen et al., 2023). The lifestyle of digital nomads is often associated with the freedom to balance leisure and work seamlessly. Digital nomads are mostly defined as young, career-focused professionals who reject traditional office jobs with fixed schedules. They prioritize autonomy, flexibility, and the freedom to travel and work from their preferred locations. The key difference between digital nomads and business travelers is that business travelers take trips for a limited period and return to their home base to continue their work. In contrast, digital nomads travel and work continuously, adapting their work to wherever they choose to go (Cook, 2020).

There are also differences between flashpackers and digital nomads. Flashpackers represent a new trend among backpackers. Unlike traditional backpackers, who primarily travel with minimal gear like a backpack and map, flashpackers incorporate digital equipment such as cameras, mobile phones, and laptops into their journeys. Flashpackers or backpackers may take up temporary jobs during their travels and stay abroad for short periods. However, if a flashpacker does not return home, they might settle permanently in one location. Similar to flashpackers, digital nomads rely on modern technologies during their travels. However, digital nomads go a step further by using these technologies to maintain their professional work life while being mobile (Müller, 2016).

Digital nomadism is gaining prominence in the tourism sector, leading researchers to explore and define the concept. According to Kannisto (2016), digital nomads are long-term travelers who prefer lifestyle mobility. Putra (2016) suggested that digital nomads engage in local experiences and have introduced new forms of creative tourism, such as slow tourism. Reichenberger (2018) described digital nomads as young professionals who work independently in online environments and travel to destinations where they can combine work and leisure. Wang et al. (2018) highlighted the relationship between digital nomadism and culture, economy, and technology. Orel (2019) argued that digital nomads represent a new form of the "knowmad" society—educated professionals whose lives merge leisure, travel, and work. Digital nomads engage in various types of work, including gig work, digital work, and nomadic work.

Gig Work

Gig work allows individuals to work as independent contractors on a short-term basis. Digital nomads arrange their work to be flexible. The gig economy provides flexibility for companies, as workers are paid only for the time they work. Workers in the gig economy often hold multiple contracts and work for several companies simultaneously (De Stefano, 2016). Freelancers or nomadic workers in the gig economy enjoy freedom and are not dependent on their employers. Conversely, employers may become dependent on these workers. However, workers in the gig economy often compete against one another. They may lower their wages to secure jobs (Sprague, 2015). Digital nomads can find gig work that matches their skills. Their salary depends on their skills and the time they spend working. However, they do not receive health insurance, sick leave, or retirement benefits (Donovan et al., 2016).

Digital Works

Digital nomads travel around the world while working at the same time. They use digital tools to create digital products (Durward et al., 2016). This working style suits them because it allows independent work. Nomads can visit different parts of the world while producing digital goods and services. Digital work conditions make travel easier for digital nomads, as they do not need to carry much equipment. Portable devices are essential for their work. Additionally, they use various technological platforms to create products. Many digital nomads also work on third-party websites (Nash et al., 2018). Access to the internet is crucial for digital nomads to connect with their customers.

Nomadic Work

Digital nomads not only move from one destination to another but also transition between different workplaces. Mobility itself is not the primary concern; the most critical factors are navigating local destinations and accessing mobilization resources (Nash et al., 2018). Flexible and knowledge-based jobs are integral to the nomadic lifestyle. Nomads can work anywhere as long as they have access to mobile resources (Davis, 2002). Cutting-edge technologies provide digital nomads with tools such as data storage, editing platforms, and real-time communication systems (De Carvalho et al., 2017). They typically communicate with colleagues via email or messaging to share updates about their work. Due to their frequent changes in location, digital nomads rely heavily on mobile devices and internet access to adapt quickly to new environments. The most critical aspect of their work is maintaining communication with colleagues, employers, or customers while traveling. Thus, laptops and internet connectivity are essential for enabling the flexibility required for their work (Su & Mark, 2008).

DIGITAL NOMADS: FREEDOM AND RULES IN DAILY LIFE

Digital nomads are individuals who travel while working, without settling permanently in the destinations they visit. They typically have flexible jobs, enjoy freedom, and rarely worry about burnout. Their motivations often stem from a desire to escape structured workplaces, excessive workloads, and fixed working hours (Cook, 2020). Reichenberger (2018) highlights that their primary motivation is to break free from traditional, location-dependent work and to have more time for leisure. Digital nomads can work from anywhere in the world, whether from a hotel room or a beach, while enjoying their time (Makimoto & Manners, 1997). This gig economy offers them flexibility, freedom, and autonomy (Thompson, 2018).

There are two types of freedom in nomadic life. The first is the freedom to change destinations, which exists at different levels. The first level includes individuals with mobile work opportunities who remain relatively stable. The second level includes those who have a home base but still travel frequently. The final level represents individuals who travel continuously without having a home base. The second type of freedom refers to the absence of boundaries between work and leisure (Reichenberger, 2018).

Although freedom is central to digital nomadism, various levels of rules and discipline are essential for managing nomadic daily life (Cook, 2020). While traveling, digital nomads prioritize their work (Müller, 2016), as productivity is a key aspect of their lifestyle (Nash et al., 2018). They take responsibility for their tasks and follow self-imposed rules to maintain a balance between work and leisure. Even though digital nomads reject traditional work structures, they still invest time and effort to achieve work-life balance (Cook, 2020).

WORK-LIFE BALANCE OF DIGITAL NOMADS

Digital nomads rely on technology to balance work and leisure. This lifestyle requires a destination-independent approach to living and working (Müller, 2016). While combining leisure and work is important for digital nomads, it differs from the pursuits of leisure-seeking tourists. Digital nomads blur the boundaries between work and leisure, often seeking new places and activities.

The primary motivation for becoming a digital nomad is geographical freedom, allowing them to choose where they live. Additionally, this way of living is less stressful, more productive, and fosters creativity (Orel, 2019). Digital nomads aim to balance work and leisure in their lifestyle. According to Sutherland & Jarrahi (2017), they often choose destinations with like-minded communities, enabling them to enjoy leisure activities and socialize with locals (Müller, 2016).

FINANCIAL EFFECTS OF DIGITAL NOMADS

Digital nomads, while living in a community and enjoying leisure time, also contribute to economic activity. They both produce and consume while working. However, their economic influence on the local economy is less significant than that of permanent residents. This is because digital nomads rely on digital technologies, and their clients or customers can be located anywhere in the world. As a result, they often do not pay taxes like local citizens. Additionally, their use of flexible accommodation options, such as Airbnb, makes it challenging for governments to track their activities (Wang et al., 2018). Furthermore, digital nomads frequently utilize cryptocurrencies for transactions (Sutherland & Jarrahi, 2017).

Nash et al. (2018) emphasize that digital nomads share similarities with freelancers in the gig economy. Digital nomads are both self-employed and entrepreneurial, managing their personal brand and maintaining connections with their clients (Wang et al., 2018). The gig economy facilitates the connection between consumers and providers for short-term jobs or gigs. Gig workers enter into formal agreements with companies to deliver services to the company's customers. These customers request services online, which gig workers then fulfill (Donovan et al., 2016). Some digital nomads work as bloggers, restaurant and food reviewers, or travel advisors. These gig-based jobs create both challenges and opportunities for governments and businesses. For instance, companies like Airbnb or cryptocurrency platforms can adapt to these emerging trends and capitalize on the growing digital nomad market to generate profits (Wang et al., 2018). However, such activities also raise concerns about regulatory oversight, tax compliance, and the integration of digital nomads into local economies.

On the other hand, digital nomads contribute to local economies in developing countries. Highly skilled gig workers bring their income into the local economy as they move to new destinations. They rent accommodations, which can influence rental prices—potentially driving up costs for local residents. When digital nomads bring capital into the market, it can stimulate investment in tourism. For instance, if digital nomads work as tourism bloggers, they can increase the visibility of a destination and boost its popularity (Hernández, 2023).

CULTURAL EFFECTS OF DIGITAL NOMADS

The digital nomadic lifestyle is driving a cultural shift in developed countries. Challenges such as the high cost of education, living expenses, and housing have led some young adults to move to other countries where they can maximize their income while benefiting from lower costs. However, the digital nomadic lifestyle also comes with its own set of challenges, including finding short-term rentals, accessing healthcare and education, and managing work-related issues. Additionally, nomadic life is often viewed as being outside the norms of local communities (Eckhardt & Atanasova, 2024).

Digital nomads also face various challenges, including navigating immigration and visa processes, managing logistics, ensuring access to reliable technological infrastructure, and addressing safety concerns. Additionally, they often struggle with work-life balance due to time zone differences. Despite these challenges, digital nomads contribute to local economies. However, their presence can also affect the environment, disrupt local customs, and present language barriers (Sekayi, 2024).

The digital nomad lifestyle also involves experiential learning and exploration of new cultures. Digital nomads continuously reshape their routines and friendships. Each time they arrive at a new destination, they strive to adapt to the local culture, resulting in multifaceted identities. By constantly changing locations, digital nomads learn and adopt new cultural norms, blending them with their own identities. They embrace new customs, learn local languages, and participate in cultural rituals, fostering connections with local communities. One significant effect of the nomadic movement is its ability to facilitate cultural exchange. When digital nomads settle in a destination, they bring ideas, experiences, habits, and practices that enrich the local culture (Mansour, 2024).

DELIGHTING DIGITAL NOMADS: CREATING IRRESISTIBLE DESTINATIONS

The digital nomad market has diverse characteristics, with various types of nomads traveling the world for different reasons. While some seek a quick break, others pursue spiritual fulfillment or explore new places while remaining dependent on technology (BecomeNomad, 2016). The different types of digital nomads are illustrated in Figure 1.

Figure 1. Type of Nomads

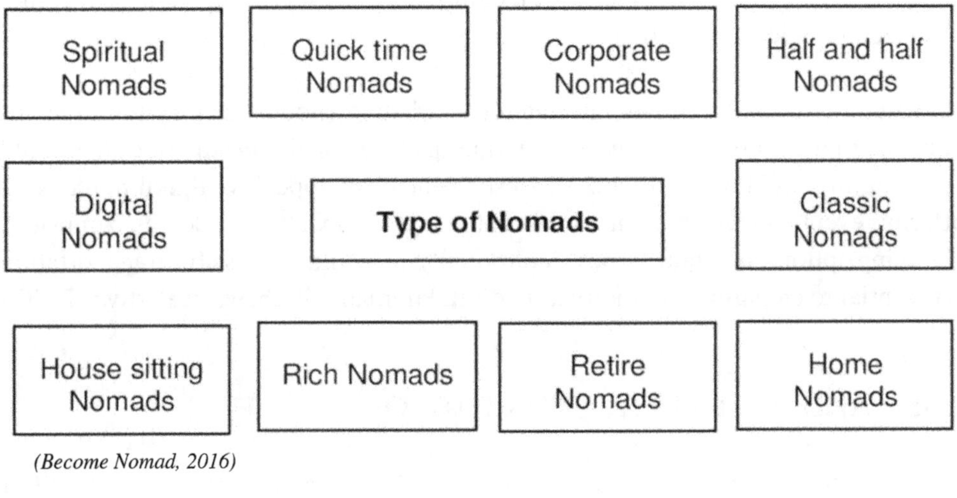

(Become Nomad, 2016)

According to Prabawa and Pertiwi (2020), there are various types of nomads, as shown in Figure 1:

- Spiritual Nomads: These individuals travel for spiritual purposes, seeking inspiration, meaning, and enlightenment.
- Quick-Time Nomads: Frequent travelers who take short breaks, often going on holiday every two months.
- Corporate Nomads: Employees of large companies who can work remotely, allowing them to work from any location they choose.
- Half-and-Half Nomads: Seasonal workers who spend part of the year working in a destination and then take a vacation in the same place.
- Classic Nomads: Also referred to as "offline nomads," this group includes freelancers, street performers, English teachers, cooks, and sports instructors. They move between destinations based on their field of work.
- House-Sitting Nomads: Travelers who stay in destinations as house sitters, avoiding accommodation and food expenses.
- Rich Nomads: Wealthy individuals who have the flexibility to travel freely. Their wealth may come from family inheritance, lottery winnings, or successful careers.
- Retired Nomads: Older adults who are drawn to the nomadic lifestyle, either inspired by stories of this way of living or fulfilling a long-held desire. Most are retired and do not work while traveling.
- Home Nomads: People who find meaning and adventure in their hometowns, feeling no need to travel.
- Digital Nomads: Individuals who combine work and travel, relying on digital technologies to maintain their lifestyle.

To attract digital nomads, destination marketers should identify the types of nomads, their motivations, and the unique qualities of the destination that could captivate those (Zhou et al., 2024). Destinations can appeal to digital nomads by offering events, entertainment, and suitable accommodations, such as campsites, glamping options, or rental homes. Additionally, providing accessible transportation is essential to engaging and motivating digital nomads (Prabawa & Pertiwi, 2020).

PUSH AND PULL MOTIVATION FACTORS

People travel for various reasons, and their purposes for traveling may differ significantly (Pektaş, 2022). Destination attraction is a key concern for destination marketers. To appeal to digital nomads, destinations offer unique values such as historical and technological features, as well as leisure and entertainment activities. Destination marketers adapt their offerings to meet the needs of digital nomads. During the pandemic, some hotels introduced innovative advertisements and products, such as "work from hotel" packages, to attract mobile workers (Zhou et al., 2024). Push and pull motivational factors play a significant role in tourism and are crucial for destination marketers (Crompton, 1979). Push factors are internal motivations, such as the desire for relaxation or adventure that drive individuals to travel. On the other hand, pull factors are external attributes of a destination, such as its attractions, climate, or cultural experiences, that draw travelers to a specific location (Dann, 1977). Understanding personal travel behaviors is vital, providing insight into individual motivations. Additionally, identifying these motivational factors is essential for effective market segmentation, allowing marketers to strategically target specific traveler groups (Cifci et al., 2024). Push factors refer to people's desire to travel, while pull factors are the characteristics of a destination that attract them. Some of the push and pull factors are presented in Table 1.

Table 1. Push & Pull Motivation Factors

Push Factors	Pull Factors
Desire for escape	Beaches
Rest and peace	Sports & Recreation facilities
Health and wellness	Historical sites
Adventure	Affordability
Prestige	Cultural resources
Social interaction	Pristine nature
Search for novelty	Ease of transportation
Exploration	Climate
Strengthening relationships	Safety and security
Learning new things	Scenery
Entertainment	Quality service
Daily working places	Digital infrastructure
Sports	Co-working space

Push factors driving digital nomads to seek different or better opportunities include the desire for new experiences and activities such as sports, entertainment, and leisure (Crompton, 1979). These factors may also involve a spiritual quest, the pursuit of a meaningful life, and the desire to connect with local inhabitants. Additionally, digital nomads are often motivated by the need to escape everyday routines and explore new environments (Dann, 1977). Digital nomads are also driven by emotional motivational factors. Their travels may involve seeking spiritual experiences, nostalgia, or romantic relationships (Heitmann, 2011). For those seeking entertainment, digital nomads often travel to destinations that enhance their social life, offer sea and sun, and allow them to balance leisure with their daily work (Hannonen et al., 2023).

Digital nomads are influenced by several push factors that motivate them to travel as tourists. The desire to escape often reflects a wish to leave their hometown due to personal reasons. This could include escaping a routine lifestyle, familiar environments, or the pressures of daily work (Alghamdi, 2007). Some individuals seek travel as a way to refresh themselves, rest, find peace, and alleviate daily life stress (Crompton, 1979). Health and wellness motivations may also play a role, as they are often linked to the desire for cleaner and healthier environments. Additionally, digital nomads may wish to avoid urban pollution, deteriorating living conditions, and instead seek destinations that offer better living and working conditions (Chen et al., 2008).

Prestige reflects a desire to maintain high standards in the eyes of others. Individuals with a strong ego (Mehmetoglu, 2005) may sometimes wish to showcase their social status and lifestyle to gain the respect of others (Alghamdi, 2007). Another motivation for travel is the opportunity to indulge in experiences and receive treatment that is not typically available in everyday life. Additionally, digital nomads often express a desire to socially interact with local residents. Digital nomads are also driven by interpersonal motivations, which sometimes involve developing new relationships and, at other times, strengthening existing ones. They may visit relatives or friends or seek opportunities to meet new people (Heitmann, 2011).

Digital nomads are often motivated by a desire to stay active and experience adventure during their travels. This can include participating in nature-based activities like hiking, kayaking, or other adventure sports (Ngondo et al., 2024). Sports also play a key role in their leisure pursuits. Some digital nomads engage directly by participating in sports activities, while others travel specifically to attend sporting events as spectators. Additionally, sports-related tourism may involve visiting iconic or historically significant venues, such as famous stadiums, which hold nostalgic value for travelers (Gibson, 2003).

Other push motivation factors for digital nomads include the search for novelty and a desire to learn new things. This encompasses a willingness to try different activities, explore new experiences, embrace diverse lifestyles, visit new places, meet new people, and immerse themselves in different cultures. It may also involve discovering natural resources, observing the local natural habitats of their destinations (Alghamdi, 2007), and exploring the cultural heritage and traditions of the places they visit (Heitmann, 2011).

Pull factors can be defined as the attributes and attractions of a destination that draw tourists to visit. These external factors motivate tourists to travel (Prabawa & Pertiwi, 2020). Destinations utilize pull factors to appeal to potential tourists. Such attractions may include natural environments, cultural heritage sites, and services like transportation, accommodation, and recreational activities (Dann, 1977). Potential tourists often gather information about destinations that interest them. They research appealing attractions and available services before deciding whether to visit. While push factors typically initiate the decision to travel, pull factors can play a significant role in the final decision-making process (Heitmann, 2011).

Historical sites, including ancient landmarks, buildings, ruins, castles, churches, mosques, works of art, and other artificial monuments, serve as significant pull factors that attract tourists to destinations. In addition to historical attractions, natural scenery and cultural resources are also essential elements for tourism appeal (Zhang et al., 2004).

Pristine nature, unspoiled habitats, favorable weather, and beautiful beaches draw digital nomads and other travelers to specific destinations (Alghamdi, 2007). While a destination may offer numerous attractions, factors such as accommodation quality and ease of accessibility are equally important pull factors for tourism (Kozak, 2002).

Digital nomads embrace an innovative lifestyle, and destinations that provide reliable infrastructure are particularly appealing to them (Zhou et al., 2024). Co-working spaces are essential for digital nomads, and destinations offering such spaces, along with recreational activities and sports facilities, tend to attract them (Hannonen, 2020). According to Jang and Cai (2002), safety is one of the most critical pull factors for digital nomads. Additionally, affordability, accessible transportation, and clean accommodation facilities also play a vital role in attracting them to a destination.

METHODOLOGY

This study employs a descriptive research methodology, primarily relying on secondary data sources. The research process involves several steps. Inıtially data collect on Digital Nomads. Initial information was gathered on the concept of digital nomads, including their characteristics, preferences, and lifestyles. Then explore of push and pull motivation factors. A detailed review of existing literature was conducted to identify the push factors (forces that drive individuals away from their current locations) and pull factors (attractions of specific destinations) influencing digital nomads' choices. Finally focus on Istanbul. The study then shifts focus to Istanbul, examining its historical sites, recreational facilities, and other factors that may attract digital nomads. This structured approach ensures a comprehensive understanding of the subject by combining theoretical insights with practical examples from Istanbul.

FINDINGS

Istanbul is a unique city that bridges two continents, Asia and Europe. It offers a stunning blend of nature and art, where the sea and land converge in harmony. Istanbul boasts numerous distinctive features and has served as the capital city during two successive empires: one Christian, the Byzantine Empire, and later the Islamic Ottoman Empire. As the former capital of the Ottoman Empire, Istanbul continues to be a significant commercial hub. It is a city rich in history and culture, embracing contradictions with ease. Modernity and antiquity, secularism and religion, reality and mysticism all coexist in Istanbul, creating a vibrant and multifaceted atmosphere. With 39 districts and countless attractions, Istanbul has much to offer, making it an appealing destination for digital nomads and travelers seeking diverse experiences (KTB, 2000).

ENVIRONMENT OF ISTANBUL FOR RECREATIONAL ACTIVITIES

Istanbul offers numerous attractions for digital nomads and other tourists. As a bustling megalopolis, the city caters to all types of digital nomads, whether visiting tourists or settling as residents. Istanbul is renowned for its natural beauty, which provides ample recreation opportunities. Visitors can enjoy daily excursions to scenic spots, engage in outdoor activities, or even find accommodations at locations suitable for extended stays or camping. The city's diverse environment perfectly balances urban vibrancy and natural tranquility, making it an ideal destination for work and leisure.

Natural Attractions in Istanbul

- Bosphorus: The Bosphorus is one of Istanbul's most iconic landmarks, located where the Marmara Sea and the Black Sea converge. It enhances the city's beauty with its stunning views. Visitors can enjoy Bosphorus tours organized by Şehir Hatları, available both during the day and at night under the moonlight. These tours stretch between Anadolu Hisarı and Rumeli Hisarı, offering breathtaking sights.
- Emirgan Grove: Decorated with vibrant tulips every spring, Emirgan Grove hosts the annual Tulip Festival in April. Visitors can enjoy picnics, explore the Yellow Pavilion (Sarı Köşk), Pink Pavilion (Pembe Köşk), and White Pavilion (Beyaz Köşk), and even have breakfast at these historical spots.

- Gülhane Park: Once the backyard of Topkapı Palace, Gülhane Park is steeped in history, having served as a private retreat for sultans. Today, it's a serene green space for visitors to enjoy.
- Belgrade Forest: Perfect for a day of recreation and exercise, the Belgrade Forest offers walking, running, and cycling trails. Visitors can picnic on tables set amidst nature while enjoying the sound of birds. The forest is also home to historical dams and fountains from the Byzantine and Ottoman periods.
- Atatürk Arboretum: Situated near the Belgrade Forest, Atatürk Arboretum is stunning year-round. Its lush greenery in spring and summer, autumn hues, and winter serenity make it a must-visit. The arboretum, also known as the "tree park," features over 1,500 tree species.
- Anadolu Kavağı: This charming fishing village is especially popular in summer. Visitors can explore Yoros Castle, located at the highest point of Anadolu Kavağı, which was built during the Eastern Roman Empire to control the strait. Nearby Poyrazköy is another great spot to spend the day.
- Elmasburnu Nature Park: Elmasburnu Nature Park boasts three beaches and a magnificent forest ecosystem, making it an ideal place to reconnect with nature.
- Inceğiz Caves: A favorite camping spot, the Inceğiz Caves have historical significance and have been used in Turkish cinema. Artifacts discovered here, believed to have been carved by human hands, are displayed at the Istanbul Archaeology Museum.
- Ağva: Ağva offers seaside cafes, seafood restaurants, and adult-friendly hotels. Visitors can enjoy a motorboat tour along the river or relax by the sea.
- Şile: Known for its beaches and natural beauty, Şile is perfect for picnics, breakfasts, and swimming. Popular spots include Şile Public Beach, Sahilköy Beach, Doğancılı Beach, and Sofular Beach (Torun, 2024). Şile have the white sandy beaches. The town rests on a clifftop, providing breathtaking views of the bay and its tiny island. Nearby stands a striking black-and-white striped lighthouse built by the French, along with a 14th-century Genoese castle situated on the neighboring island (KTB, 2000).
- Kilyos: Kilyos is the closest beach resort to Istanbul, located along the Black Sea coast on the European side of the Bosphorus.
- Polonezköy: Known as the "village of the Poles," this charming settlement has a remarkable history. It was founded in 1848 by Prince Czartoryski, a leader of the Polish nationals who sought refuge in the Ottoman Empire to escape Balkan oppression. During his exile, he established a Polish community on land purchased from a local monastery, and this community continues to thrive today. Since the 1970s, Polonezköy has become a favored destination

for both locals and visitors. Its vast greenery, designated as Istanbul's first national park, is perfect for forest walks along trails with streams and wooden bridges, offering a peaceful escape from the city.

- Prince's Islands: Located in the Marmara Sea, just an hour from the city, this group of eight islands is easily accessible by ferry, with more frequent services during the summer months. During the Byzantine era, these islands were home to monasteries and served as a favored summer retreat for palace officials. Today, the Prince's Islands remain a popular getaway from the city, offering a tranquil escape with rental summer homes available for those looking to stay longer.
- Golden Horn: This naturally horn-shaped estuary separates the European side of Istanbul. Recognized as one of the finest natural harbors globally, it once served as the hub for Byzantine and Ottoman naval fleets and commercial shipping. Today, the shores are adorned with charming parks and promenades, offering a scenic setting, particularly at sunset when the water reflects the golden hues of the sky. Perched atop a hill overlooking the shrine and the Golden Horn, the Pierre Loti Café provides a serene spot to take in the breathtaking view and enjoy a peaceful moment (KTB, 2000).

Istanbul's natural attractions offer a wide range of experiences, appealing to outdoor enthusiasts, history lovers, and those in search of relaxation. These areas might be particularly popular among digital nomads, who take advantage of Istanbul's natural beauty to unwind and work in inspiring surroundings. Digital nomads can explore these locations for a day trip or opt for longer stays, with various accommodation options available, including hotels, tents, campsites, caravans, and rental houses. The diverse facilities make Istanbul's natural areas ideal for both short-term visits and extended retreats.

Urban Recreation in Istanbul

Recreational activities, typically associated with "connecting with nature," also encompass socio-economic engagements within urban settings. Cafés, bistros, and bars serve as vibrant gathering spots for modern individuals. These venues act as hubs of urban recreation, offering spaces where people can socialize, meet friends, share meals and drinks, and enjoy their leisure time. For both locals and digital nomads, such experiences foster a sense of well-being. These establishments play a vital role in supporting social development, meeting the recreational needs of residents, travelers, and digital nomads, and contributing to their renewal, social connections, and psychological health (Uğur & Akova, 2021). For digital nomads, these moments provide a much-needed escape from daily challenges. Activities like listening to music, dancing, and engaging in casual conversations allow them to relax, experience joy, and enhance their mental well-being. In Istanbul, digital nomads immerse themselves in the city's dynamic entertainment scene, which blends freedom, happiness, and psychological well-being through recreational pursuits (Karaşah, 2017).

Digital nomads seek opportunities to unwind and socialize, stepping away from the monotony of their daily routines. Urban recreational options in Istanbul offer diverse experiences, including vibrant nightlife and cultural events such as open-air concerts at Cemil Topuzlu Amphitheater, Rumelihisarı (Rumelia Fortress), and Yedikule (The Seven Towers). With the rise of shopping malls, these spaces have become central to urban recreation. Digital nomads often gather at café-bars, bistro-style venues, and café-restaurants within malls, where they can socialize, enjoy their leisure time, and stay connected to the internet for work. The recreational focus of city life has increasingly shifted to these modern hubs, which host a variety of food and beverage establishments. In addition, Istanbul offers numerous small bars, cafés, pubs, and restaurants, providing ample opportunities for digital nomads to explore and move between venues during their free time (Uğur & Akova, 2021).

Digital nomads often seek alternatives to the typical vacation spots favored by the general public. Rather than visiting the popular tourist destinations in major cities, they tend to explore places that align with their personal interests. For digital nomads, discovering something new and unique, gaining meaningful experiences, and learning along the way are key priorities. Cities featuring restaurants that offer natural and locally sourced products, as well as museums, cultural centers, sports and entertainment facilities, art galleries, and vintage boutiques, are particularly appealing to digital nomads. These locations provide opportunities for both enrichment and enjoyment. With its authentic character and diverse offerings, Istanbul stands out as a destination that captivates digital nomads, offering them a unique blend of culture, history, and modern amenities (Uğur & Demirkol, 2021).

Cultural Heritage of Istanbul

Istanbul is one of Turkey's most significant cities, rich in archaeological, monumental, civil, modern, and industrial architectural heritage. It is home to numerous registered historical and cultural treasures (IBB, 2024).

Istanbul has a vast cultural heritage, with its historic peninsula recognized as a UNESCO World Heritage Site. Some landmarks, such as the Valens Aqueduct, date back to Roman times. However, the city is most known for its Byzantine and Ottoman architecture. The Hagia Sophia (AD 537) was once the largest cathedral in the world and is now a mosque. The Süleymaniye Mosque from the 16th century and the Blue Mosque from the 17th century are among the city's most significant historical sites. The Topkapi Palace, a key Ottoman landmark, served as the home and administrative center of the sultans for centuries (WCCF, 2024). There are some of the prominent historical landmarks in Istanbul (Sızan, 2024):

- Hagia Sophia Mosque (Ayasofya Mosque): A magnificent architectural wonder that has served as a church, mosque, and museum, now functioning as a mosque.
- Grand Bazaar (Kapalıçarşı): One of the oldest and largest covered markets in the world, known for its vibrant shops and cultural significance.
- Basilica Cistern (Yerebatan Sarnıcı): An ancient underground water reservoir featuring stunning columns and an eerie atmosphere.
- Column of Constantine (Çemberlitaş): A Roman monument commemorating Emperor Constantine the Great's establishment of Constantinople.
- Galata Tower (Galata Kulesi): A medieval stone tower offering panoramic views of the city.
- Ahrida Synagogue (Ahrida Sinagogu): One of the oldest synagogues in Istanbul, reflecting the city's rich Jewish heritage.
- Rumeli Fortress (Rumeli Hisarı): A historical fortress built by Sultan Mehmed II before the conquest of Constantinople.
- Yedikule Dungeons (Yedikule Zindanları): A historical fortress that once served as a prison and is now a museum.
- Hippodrome of Constantinople (At Meydanı): An ancient chariot-racing stadium that was the heart of social life in Byzantine times.
- German Fountain (Alman Çeşmesi): A gift from Kaiser Wilhelm II, this neo-Byzantine-style fountain symbolizes German-Ottoman friendship.
- St. George's Monastery (Ayayorgi Manastırı): A Greek Orthodox monastery located on Büyükada, part of the Princes' Islands.
- Ecumenical Patriarchate of Constantinople (Fener Rum Patrikhanesi): The spiritual center of the Eastern Orthodox Church.
- Halki Seminary (Heybeliada Ruhban Okulu): An Orthodox theological school located on Heybeliada, one of the Princes' Islands.
- Maiden's Tower (Kız Kulesi): A historical tower located on a small islet in the Bosphorus, surrounded by myths and legends.

Culture is one of the most important parts of Istanbul's tourism. The city has a rich history and culture spanning 8,500 years and attracts millions of visitors. Istanbul offers many cultural experiences for digital nomads and other visitors. It has modern art museums, galleries, streets filled with artists, concert venues, and vibrant festivals. These events bring the city's cultural energy to life. Digital nomads can also visit many museums in Istanbul during their leisure time. Here are some notable museums and historical sites in Istanbul (Istanbul Valiliği, 2021):

- Adam Mickiewicz Museum: A museum dedicated to the life and works of the Polish poet Adam Mickiewicz.
- Ahmet Hamdi Tanpınar Literature Museum Library: A museum and library honoring Turkish author Ahmet Hamdi Tanpınar.
- Military Museum (Askeri Müze): A museum showcasing Turkey's military history and artifacts.
- Aşiyan Museum: The former home of poet Tevfik Fikret, now a museum displaying his life and works.
- Atatürk Museum: A museum focusing on Mustafa Kemal Atatürk, the founder of modern Turkey.
- European Capital of Culture Exchange Museum: A museum highlighting cultural exchange during Istanbul's time as a European Capital of Culture.
- Press Museum (Basın Müzesi): A museum exploring the history of journalism in Turkey.
- Beşiktaş JK Museum: A museum dedicated to the history of Beşiktaş, one of Turkey's oldest sports clubs.
- Beyazıt Tower: An iconic fire-watch tower located in the Beyazıt area.
- Beylerbeyi Palace: A stunning Ottoman palace located on the Asian side of Istanbul.
- Glass and Crystal Museum (Billur ve Cam Müzesi): A museum featuring intricate glass and crystal works.
- Borusan Contemporary (Perili Köşk): A modern art museum housed in a historic mansion.
- Great Palace Mosaic Museum (Büyük Saray Mozaikleri Müzesi): A museum displaying mosaics from the Byzantine Great Palace.
- Tent Mansion (Çadır Köşkü): A historical pavilion located in the Emirgan Park.
- Tiled Pavilion (Çinili Köşk): A museum exhibiting Turkish and Islamic tiles and ceramics.
- Marine and Aquatic Products Museum (Deniz ve Su Ürünleri Müzesi): A museum about marine life and fishing.
- Doğançay Museum: A museum dedicated to Turkish contemporary artist Burhan Doğançay.
- 18. Dolmabahçe Clock Tower: A historic clock tower near Dolmabahçe Palace.
- Dolmabahçe Palace: A grand Ottoman palace on the Bosphorus.

- Museum of Ancient Oriental Works (Eski Şark Eserleri Müzesi): A museum displaying ancient artifacts from the Middle East.
- Galata Tower: A medieval stone tower offering stunning views of the city.
- Carpet Museum (Halı Müzesi): A museum showcasing Turkish carpets and their history.
- Aviation Museum (Havacılık Müzesi): A museum displaying the history of aviation in Turkey.
- Ihlamur Pavilions (Ihlamur Kasırları): Ottoman-era pavilions used as retreats for sultans.
- Istanbul Archaeological Museums (İstanbul Arkeoloji Müzeleri): A collection of museums with artifacts from ancient civilizations.
- Istanbul Naval Museum (İstanbul Deniz Müzesi): A museum focusing on the history of the Ottoman Navy.
- Istanbul Photography Museum (İstanbul Fotoğraf Müzesi): A museum dedicated to photography.
- Istanbul Modern Art Museum (İstanbul Modern Sanat Müzesi): A modern art museum showcasing Turkish and international art.
- Crystal Palace (Kristal Sarayı): A historic structure known for its elegant design.
- Pera Museum: A museum featuring a wide range of art, including the famous Orientalist paintings.
- Rahmi Koç Museum: A museum dedicated to industrial and transportation history.
- Sakıp Sabancı Museum: A museum featuring art collections and exhibitions in a beautiful mansion.
- Hanım Sultanlar Museum: A museum dedicated to the lives and contributions of Ottoman sultanas.

Each of these places provides unique insights into Istanbul's history, art, and culture. Some museums use advanced 3D technologies to enhance the visitor experience. Virtual reality (VR) experiences offer physical immersion, allowing digital nomads and visitors to view a scene in 360 degrees (Uğur & Akova, 2022).

These experiences are available at the Blue Mosque, Suleymaniye Mosque, Fatih Mosque, Yeni Mosque, Beyazıt Mosque, Mihrimah Sultan Mosque, and Büyük Selimiye Mosque. Museums such as the Archaeology Museum, Rahmi Koç Museum, Panorama 1453 History Museum, and Kariye Museum also incorporate VR technologies to provide an interactive and immersive experience.

Digital nomads are often driven by the desire to stay active and enjoy recreational activities while traveling (Ngondo et al., 2024). They look for destinations that provide good living standards and conducive working environments (Chen et al.,

2008). Many digital nomads choose places that improve their social lives, offer a mix of sun and sea, and help them balance relaxation with daily work (Hannonen et al., 2023). Istanbul and its surrounding areas provide what digital nomads are looking for. In their leisure time, they can explore historical landmarks. The city is also home to numerous museums, waiting to be discovered by digital nomads and tourists alike.

CONCLUSION

Digital nomads are individuals who use advanced technology to work remotely from any location. They have the freedom to live wherever they can access the internet. Their work does not require them to stay in one fixed place. Modern technologies provide new ways to live and work. The lifestyle of digital nomads is growing rapidly. They are often described as young, career-driven professionals who avoid traditional office jobs with fixed hours. They value independence, flexibility, and the ability to travel while working from places they choose. Digital nomads explore different countries while continuing to work. They rely on digital tools to produce online content and services. A desire for a better life is often seen as a key reason why people choose this lifestyle. Digital nomads enjoy the freedom to combine work and leisure without difficulty. The digital nomad lifestyle has become an important trend in tourism. Many destinations are now creating new marketing strategies to attract them.

Digital nomads do not just travel from one place to another; they also switch between various workspaces. Their main focus is not movement itself. The most important factors are exploring local areas and finding the resources they need to stay mobile. Digital nomads use technology to manage both work and leisure. Their lifestyle allows them to live and work without being tied to a specific location. They mix work and leisure, often looking for new experiences and places. The main reason people become digital nomads is the freedom to live wherever they choose. This lifestyle is also less stressful, boosts productivity, and encourages creativity.

The economic impact of digital nomads on local economies is smaller than that of permanent residents. However, they still contribute by spending money while living in a community and enjoying leisure activities. Digital nomads both create and consume as they work. This lifestyle also brings unique challenges. Digital nomads often struggle to find short-term housing, access healthcare, or handle work-related issues. They may face difficulties with visas, immigration rules, and managing logistics. Reliable technology and safety are also important concerns. At the same time, the digital nomad lifestyle offers opportunities to learn through experience and explore new cultures.

Destinations attract digital nomads by offering unique features like historical sites, modern technology, and leisure activities. Tourism marketers adjust their services to fit the needs of digital nomads. Push factors are personal reasons, like the need for rest or the search for adventure, that inspire people to travel. Digital nomads are encouraged to travel by several personal reasons, called push factors. Many want to escape their hometown because of personal issues. They may wish to leave behind routine, familiar surroundings, or the stress of daily work. Travel can be a way for them to relax, find peace, and reduce everyday stress. Health and wellness are also important, as some seek cleaner and healthier places to live temporarily. Traveling offers chances to enjoy unique experiences or treatments that are not available in their usual lives.

Digital nomads often want to connect with local people. Building new relationships is another reason they travel. Many are also motivated to stay active and try exciting activities. This could include nature-based experiences like hiking, kayaking, or adventure sports. Digital nomads are also motivated by the need for new experiences and learning. They enjoy trying new activities and exploring unfamiliar things. Many want to experience different ways of living, visit new locations, and meet new people. They are often eager to learn about and connect with different cultures.

Pull factors are external qualities of a destination, like its attractions, weather, or cultural experiences that encourage travelers to visit. Understanding these motivations is important for segmenting the market. This helps marketers focus on specific traveler groups, such as digital nomads, more effectively. Pull factors are the features of a destination that attract tourists to visit. Historical attractions, such as ancient landmarks, ruins, castles, churches, mosques, and art, are important reasons people travel to certain places. Natural beauty, including untouched landscapes, clean habitats, pleasant weather, and stunning beaches, also draws digital nomads and other travelers. Digital nomads enjoy a modern way of living, and they are especially interested in destinations with dependable infrastructure.

Istanbul is a captivating city that attracts digital nomads. It lies at the crossroads of Asia and Europe, offering a beautiful mix of nature and art, where land and sea meet in harmony. The city has many attractions for digital nomads and tourists. Visitors can explore scenic spots, enjoy outdoor activities, or find places to stay for longer visits or camping. Istanbul perfectly blends urban energy with peaceful nature, making it a great place for both work and relaxation. Istanbul's natural attractions offer various experiences for outdoor lovers, history enthusiasts, and those seeking rest. These spots are popular among digital nomads, who enjoy working in these inspiring surroundings.

Recreational activities, which often involve connecting with nature, also include social and economic activities in urban areas. Cafés, bistros, and bars are lively places where people gather. The city's urban activities offer vibrant nightlife and cultural events like open-air concerts. Istanbul is one of Turkey's most important cities, with a rich history in architecture, from ancient to modern styles. Many digital nomads choose destinations that enhance their social lives, offer a mix of sun and sea, and allow them to balance work with relaxation.

According to Hannonen et al. (2023), digital nomads have multiple identities and play different roles within a destination. They may seek leisure, social connections, and access to digital technology. When visiting new places, digital nomads also want to engage with local people. Istanbul is an ideal destination for digital nomads. The city offers reliable technical infrastructure and opportunities for social interaction. It is important for destination marketers and government agencies to support digital nomads, especially with visa issues, translation services, and healthcare. Istanbul's municipality could provide co-working spaces and co-living arrangements for digital nomads. This is crucial, as having accommodation and workspaces with reliable internet is a top priority for them. Destination marketers need to understand the needs of digital nomads and the push and pull factors that influence their decisions.

REFERENCES

Åkerlund, U. (2013). The best of both worlds: Aspirations, drivers and practices of Swedish lifestyle movers in Malta (Doctoral dissertation). Umeå universitet.

Alghamdi, A. (2007). Explicit and implicit motivation towards outbound tourism: A study of Saudi tourists. University of Glasgow. (Doctoral dissertation).

BecomeNomad. (2016, 05. 05.). Different Types of Nomads. BecomeNomad: https://becomenomad.com/different-nomadic-lifestyles/ (22.12.2024) adresinden alındı

Belge, M. (2018). *İstanbul gezi rehberi*. Tarih Vakfı Yayınları. İletişim Yayınları.

Bell, M., & Ward, G. (2000). Comparing temporary mobility with permanent migration. *Tourism Geographies*, *2*(1), 87–107. DOI: 10.1080/146166800363466

Boyle, P., Halfacree, K., & Robinson, V. (2014). *Exploring contemporary migration*. Routledge., DOI: 10.4324/9781315843100

Brown, L., & Moore, E. (1970). The intra-urban migration process: A perspective. *Geografiska Annaler. Series B, Human Geography*, *52*(1), 1–13. DOI: 10.1080/04353684.1970.11879340

Chen, J., Prebensen, N., & Huan, T. (2008). Determining the motivation of wellness travelers. *Anatolia*, *19*(1), 103–115. DOI: 10.1080/13032917.2008.9687056

Chevtaeva, E., & Denizci-Guillet, B. (2021). Digital nomads' lifestyles and coworkation. *Journal of Destination Marketing & Management*, *21*, 100633. DOI: 10.1016/j.jdmm.2021.100633

Cifci, I., Atsiz, O., Kahraman, O., & Istanbullu Dincer, F. (2024). Recreational fishers' motivations at wetland destinations: The push and pull theory approach. *Leisure Sciences*, *46*(5), 595–617. DOI: 10.1080/01490400.2021.2016520

Clark, P. (2012). Istanbul: a cultural history. Interlink Publishing.

Cook, D. (2020). The freedom trap: Digital nomads and the use of disciplining practices to manage work/leisure boundaries. *Information Technology & Tourism*, *22*(3), 355–390. DOI: 10.1007/s40558-020-00172-4

Crompton, J. L. (1979). Motivations of pleasure vacations. *Annals of Tourism Research*, *6*(4), 408–424. DOI: 10.1016/0160-7383(79)90004-5

D'Andrea, A. (2013). *Deciphering the Space and Scale of Global Nomadism: Subjectivity and Counterculture in a Global Ag. S. Sassen içinde, Deciphering the global: Its Scales, Spaces and Subjects*. Routledge.

Dann, G. (1977). Anomie, ego-enhancement and tourism. *Annals of Tourism Research, 4*(4), 184–194. DOI: 10.1016/0160-7383(77)90037-8

Dann, M. S. (1981). Tourist motivation an appraisal. *Annals of Tourism Research, 8*(2), 187–219. DOI: 10.1016/0160-7383(81)90082-7

Davis, G. (2002). Anytime/anyplace computing and the future of knowledge work. *Communications of the ACM, 45*(12), 67–73. DOI: 10.1145/585597.585617

De Carvalho, A., Ciolfi, L., & Gray, B. (2017). Detailing a Spectrum of motivational forces shaping nomadic practices. Proceedings of the 2017 ACM Conference on Computer Supported Cooperative Work and Social Computing (pp. 962-977). Sheffield Hallam University Research Archive. DOI: 10.1145/2998181.2998313

De Stefano, V. (2016). The rise of the 'just-in-time workforce': On-demand work, crowd work and labour protection in the 'gig-economy. *Comparative Labor Law & Policy Journal, 37*(3), 471–504.

Donovan, S., Bradley, D., & Shimabukuru, J. (2016). *What does the gig economy mean for workers?* Congressional Research Service.

Durward, D., Blohm, I., & Leimeister, J. (2016). Crowd work. *Business & Information Systems Engineering, 58*(4), 281–286. DOI: 10.1007/s12599-016-0438-0

Eckhardt, G., & Atanasova, A. (2024, 02. 05.). The New Reality of Digital Nomads. HBR: https://hbr.org/2024/02/the-new-reality-of-digital-nomads (21.12.2024) adresinden alındı

Ehrlich, B. (2025, 02. 28.). Istanbul. Britannica: https://www.britannica.com/place/Istanbul (07.03.2025) adresinden alındı

Gibson, H. J. (2003). Sport tourism: An introduction to the special issue. *Journal of Sport Management, 17*(3), 205–213. DOI: 10.1123/jsm.17.3.205

Green, P. (2020). Disruptions of self, place and mobility: Digital nomads in Chiang Mai, Thailand. *Mobilities, 15*(3), 431–445. DOI: 10.1080/17450101.2020.1723253

Hall, G., Sigala, M., Rentschler, R., & Boyle, S. (2019). Motivations, mobility and work practices; the conceptual realities of digital nomads. Information and Communication Technologies in Tourism 2019: Proceedings of the International Conference in Nicosia. Cyprus, January 30–February 1, 2019: Springer International Publishing. https://link.springer.com/chapter/10.1007/978-3-030-05940-8_34 adresinden alındı

Hannonen, O. (2020). In search of a digital nomad: Defining the phenomenon. *Information Technology & Tourism, 22*(3), 335–353. DOI: 10.1007/s40558-020-00177-z

Hannonen, O., Quintana, T., & Lehto, X. (2023). A supplier side view of digital nomadism: The case of destination Gran Canaria. *Tourism Management, 97*, 104744. DOI: 10.1016/j.tourman.2023.104744

Heitmann, S. (2011). Tourist behaviour and tourism motivation. Research themes for tourism (s. 31-44). içinde Wallingford UK: CABI.

Hernández, I. (2023, 10. 27.). Digital Nomadism: Transnational Economic Relations in the Emerging Economies. Harvard International Review: https://hir.harvard.edu/digital-nomadism-transnational-economic-relations-in-the-emerging-economies/ (21.12.2024) adresinden alındı

IBB. (2024). Kültürel Miras Koruma Müdürlüğü. Istanbul Metropolitan Municipality Directorate of Cultural Heritage. İstanbul Bütük Şehir Belediyesi: https://kulturelmiras.ibb.istanbul/english/ (26.12.2024) adresinden alındı

İstanbul Valiliği. (2021). Tarihi ve Turistik Mekânlar. T.C. İstanbul Valiliği: http://www.istanbul.gov.tr/tarihi-ve-turistik-mekanlar (27.12.2024) adresinden alındı

Jang, S., & Cai, L. (2002). Travel motivations and destination choice: A study of British outbound market. *Journal of Travel & Tourism Marketing, 13*(3), 111–133. DOI: 10.1300/J073v13n03_06

Kannisto, P. (2016). Extreme mobilities: Challenging the concept of 'travel'. *Annals of Tourism Research, 57*, 220–233. DOI: 10.1016/j.annals.2016.01.005

Karaşah, B. (2017). Kentsel ve kırsal rekreasyon alanlarına yönelik kullanıcı tercihlerinin belirlenmesi 'Artvin kenti örneği. *Bartin Orman Fakültesi Dergisi, 19*(1), 58–69.

Kozak, M. (2002). Comparative analysis of tourist motivations by nationality and destinations. *Tourism Management, 23*(3), 221–232. DOI: 10.1016/S0261-5177(01)00090-5

KTB. (2000). İstanbul. Republic of Türkiye Ministry of Culture and Toursim: https://www.ktb.gov.tr/EN-33048/istanbul.html adresinden alındı

Kubat, A. S. (1999). The morphological history of Istanbul. *Urban Morphology, 3*(1), 28–41. DOI: 10.51347/jum.v3i1.3883

Makimoto, T., & Manners, D. (1997). *Digital nomad.* Wiley.

Mancinelli, F. (2020). Digital nomads: Freedom, responsibility and the neoliberal order. *Information Technology & Tourism, 22*(3), 417–437. DOI: 10.1007/s40558-020-00174-2

Mansour, R. (2024). The Rise of Digital Nomadism: Reshaping Cultural Identity in a Globalised World. Rock & Art: https://www.rockandart.org/digital-nomadism-reshaping-cultural-identity/#:~:text=By%20embracing%20a%20global%20digital,diversity%2C%20independence%2C%20and%20flexibility. (21.12.2024) adresinden alındı

Mehmetoglu, M. (2005). A case study of nature-based tourists: Specialists versus generalists. *Journal of Vacation Marketing*, *11*(4), 357–369. DOI: 10.1177/1356766705056634

Müller, A. (2016). The digital nomad: Buzzword or research category? *Transnational Social Review*, *6*(3), 344–348. DOI: 10.1080/21931674.2016.1229930

Nash, C., Jarrahi, M., Sutherland, W., & Phillips, G. (2018). Digital nomads beyond the buzzword: Defining digital nomadic work and use of digital technologies. International conference on information (pp. 207-217). Cham: Springer International Publishing.

Ngondo, E., Hermann, U., & Venter, D. (2024). Push and pull factors affectıng domestıc tourism in the Erongo Region, Namibia. *Geo Journal of Tourism and Geosites*, *53*(2), 575–583. DOI: 10.30892/gtg.53221-1233

O'Reilly, K. (2003). When is a tourist?: The articulation of tourism and migration in Spain's Costa del Sol. *Tourist Studies*, *3*(3), 301–317. DOI: 10.1177/1468797603049661

Orel, M. (2019). Coworking environments and digital nomadism: Balancing work and leisure whilst on the move. *World Leisure Journal*, *61*(3), 215–227. DOI: 10.1080/16078055.2019.1639275

Pektaş, F. (2022). Destination as a brand: The impact of push and pull factors of travel motivation on customer-based destination equity. *Uluslararası Yönetim İktisat ve İşletme Dergisi*, *18*(3), 856–874. DOI: 10.17130/ijmeb.1002537

Prabawa, I., & Pertiwi, P. (2020). The Digital Nomad Tourist Motivation in Bali: Exploratory Research Based on Push and Pull Theory. Exploratory research based on push and pull theory. *Athens Journal of Tourism*, *7*(3), 161–174. DOI: 10.30958/ajt.7-3-3

Putra, G., & Agirachman, F. (2016). Urban coworking space: creative tourism in digital nomads perspective. *Proceedings of Arte-Polis 6 international conference* (pp. 169-178).

Reichenberger, I. (2018). Digital Nomads – A Quest for Holistic Freedom in Work and Leisure. *Annals of Leisure Research, 21*(3), 364–380. DOI: 10.1080/11745398.2017.1358098

Sekayi, M. (2024, 02. 21.). Digital Nomads and their Impact on Culture. London Intercultural Centre: https://londoninterculturalcenter.co.uk/blogs/f/digital-nomads-and-their-impact-on-culture (21.12.2024) adresinden alındı

Sızan, T. (2024). İstanbul'da Gezilecek Yerler, Görülmesi Gereken En Güzel 51 Yer. Etstur Let's Go: https://www.etstur.com/letsgo/istanbul-gezilecek-yerler/ (27.12.2024) adresinden alındı

Sprague, R. (2015). Worker (mis) classification in the sharing economy: Trying to fit square pegs into round holes. *ABA Journal of Labor & Employment Law, 31*(1), 53–76. DOI: 10.2139/ssrn.2606600

Su, N., & Mark, G. (2008). Designing for nomadic work. *Proceedings of the 7th ACM conference on Designing interactive systems* (pp. 305-314). Cape Town, South Africa. DOI: 10.1145/1394445.1394478

Sutherland, W., & Jarrahi, M. (2017). The gig economy and information infrastructure: The case of the digital nomad community. Proceedings of the ACM on human-computer interaction, 1(CSCW), 1-24. DOI: 10.1145/3134732

Thompson, B. (2018). Digital Nomads Employment in the Online Gig Economy. *Glocalism*, (1), 1–26. DOI: 10.12893/gjcpi.2018.1.11

Torun, G. (2024, 11. 27.). İstanbul'da gezilecek doğal yerler. Enuygun Blog: https://www.enuygun.com/bilgi/istanbul-da-gezilecek-yerler-mutlaka-gorulmesi-gereken-70-yer/doga/ (26.12.2024) adresinden alındı

Uğur, N., & Akova, O. (2021). The effect of Covid-19 pandemic on cafe-bar, bistro and night clubs. *Uluslararası Beşeri ve Sosyal Bilimler İnceleme Dergisi, 5*(2), 139–153.

Uğur, N., & Akova, O. (2022). *The Use of Virtual Reality and Augmented Reality in Cultural Heritage and Deep-Diving Destinations. L. Oliveira içinde, Handbook of Research on Digital Communications, Internet of Things, and the Future of Cultural Tourism.* IGI Global., DOI: 10.4018/978-1-7998-8528-3.ch008

Uğur, N., & Demirkol, Ş. (2021). Hipster Turist Arketipleri ve Hipster Turizminin Oluşumuna Katkısının Analizi. *Journal of New Tourism Trends, 2*(2), 125–137.

Unesco. (2025). Historic Areas of Istanbul. Unesco World Heritage Convention: https://whc.unesco.org/en/list/356/ adresinden alındı

Wang, B., Schlagwein, D., Cecez-Kecmanovic, D., & Cahalane, M. (2018). Digital work and high-tech wanderers: Three theoretical framings and a research agenda for digital nomadism. *Australasian Conference on Information Systems*. Sydney. DOI: 10.5130/acis2018.bl

WCCF. (2024, 08. 22.). Byzantine Wonders to Contemporary Culture: İstanbul's Tourist Appeal. World citiws culture forum: https://worldcitiescultureforum.com/city/istanbul/ (26.12.2024) adresinden alındı

Williams, A., & Hall, C. (2000). Tourism and migration: New relationships between production and consumption. *Tourism Geographies*, *2*(1), 5–27. DOI: 10.1080/146166800363420

Williams, A., & Hall, C. (2002). Tourism, migration, circulation and mobility: The contingencies of time and place. Tourism and migration: New relationships between production and consumption (s. 1-52). içinde Dordrecht: Springer Netherlands.

Zhang, H., Qu, H., & Tang, V. (2004). A case study of Hong Kong residents' outbound leisure travel. *Tourism Management*, *25*(2), 267–273. DOI: 10.1016/S0261-5177(03)00096-7

Zhou, L., Buhalis, D., Fan, D., Ladkin, A., & Lian, X. (2024). Attracting digital nomads: Smart destination strategies, innovation and competitiveness. *Journal of Destination Marketing & Management*, *31*, 100850. DOI: 10.1016/j.jdmm.2023.100850

Chapter 6
Digital Nomads on Tourism Destinations Economies by Mediation of Marketing of Destinations in Horn of Africa

Fikeralem Toma
https://orcid.org/0009-0006-5078-7763
Bule Hora University, Ethiopia

Shashi Kant
https://orcid.org/0000-0003-4722-5736
Bule Hora University, Ethiopia

Metasebia Adula
https://orcid.org/0000-0001-5732-2850
Bule Hora University, Ethiopia

ABSTRACT

This study investigates the interrelationships among Digital-Nomads, marketing of destination, and economies of tourism based destinations to comprehend the influence of digital nomadism on tourism based economies. Utilizing structural equation modeling with 302 sample size, output manifested that Digital-Nomads meaningfully enhance both the marketing influence of destinations and their economic performance. The outcomes manifest a strong direct influence of Digital-Nomads on economies

DOI: 10.4018/979-8-3373-0076-4.ch006

of tourism based destinations, as well as a substantial indirect influence mediated by marketing of destination. This proposes that influence marketing strategies are essential for maximizing the economic contributions of Digital-Nomads. Our research manifest the necessity for tourism stakeholders to adopt targeted marketing approaches that resonate with the unique preferences of Digital-Nomads, thereby fostering enhanced economic growth in tourism destinations. The implications extend to practical recommendations for emphasizing the need for infrastructure and services tailored to this demographic.

INTRODUCTION

The concept of digital nomadism, has gained a lot of currency in the world that seems to get smaller and more connected, so the notion of destination internationalization (Bozzi, 2024). The new generation of tourists could be divided into two categories: Digital-Nomads are tourists who work using Internet connections when traveling. It this regard, their mode of living not only determines the tourism attractions they prefer but also a greatly affect the economy of the areas they venture into. Understand the impacts on the tourism based economy especially in the region of Eastern part of Africa, because this way of life is getting popular with more working people around the world (Sztuk, 2024). Technology breakthroughs and the growth of the gig economy, which have freed workers from conventional office settings, are the roots of digital nomadism. As a result of this change, there is now more interest in travel locations that provide both cultural experiences and favorable working circumstances. With its varied landscapes and rich cultural legacy, the Eastern part of Africa offers unrealized potential for drawing in this kind of customer. Nonetheless, the marketing tactics used to advertise these locations have a crucial role in moderating the interaction between local economies and Digital-Nomads (Kiki, 2024).

The body of empirical research on digital nomadism is continually developing. Current research frequently ignores areas like the Eastern part of Africa in favor of concentrating on the experiences and motives of Digital-Nomads in popular tourist locations. Although research on the economic influences of tourism is expanding, little is known about the precise contributions made by Digital-Nomads to local economies. This disparity emphasizes the necessity of focused research that tackles the distinct traits and difficulties encountered by this group in unconventional locations (Miocevic, 2024). Practical difficulties are especially common in the Eastern part of Africa, where problems like poor internet access, insufficient infrastructure, and unstable political environments might impede the development of a long-lasting community of Digital-Nomads. These difficulties have an influence on local communities' potential economic gains in addition to the experience of Digital-Nomads. A sophisticated grasp of how marketing tactics interact with Digital-Nomads' expectations is necessary to overcome these obstacles (Liestiandre et al., 2024).

By offering a thorough examination of how Digital-Nomads influence tourism based economies in the Eastern part of Africa through efficient marketing techniques, this chapter aims to close the research gaps. The chapter will provide insights into influence practices for drawing in Digital-Nomads and encouraging collaborations among regional stakeholders by combining the body of current research with actual data. A roadmap for upcoming researchers and policymakers will also be provided, emphasizing the significance of creating policies and infrastructure that serve this population (Bahri, 2024). This study's main research question is: *"How can focused marketing techniques improve the financial influence of Digital-Nomads on Eastern part of Africa travel destinations, and what workable solutions can be put in place to get beyond current obstacles?"* In order to create a more inclusive and sustainable tourism model, this question highlights the TD Essay's investigation of the relationship between digital nomadism, marketing, and local tourist economics. By answering this query, the chapter will not only highlight the potential of Digital-Nomads as change agents in the economy, but it will also provide stakeholders with practical proposeions for efficiently using this trend (Ay et al., 2024).

BACKGROUND OF STUDY

People are looking for places where they may continue to pursue their careers while seeing different cultures as technology gives them more freedom. Tourism based economies are meaningfully influenced by this trend, especially in developing areas like the Eastern part of Africa. However, there are several obstacles to overcome before Digital-Nomads may be successfully included into these economies, necessitating significant thought and strategic planning (Gupta et al., 2024). A major obstacle that Eastern part of Africa destinations must deal with is the absence of proper infrastructure. Because they rely on connectivity to carry out their profession, Digital-Nomads must have dependable internet access. For example, whereas Ethiopian cities such as Addis Ababa are making progress in enhancing internet connectivity, rural regions frequently lack the TD infrastructure required to facilitate distant work (Adedoyin et al., 2023). The difficulty of drawing in Digital-Nomads because of erratic internet connectivity and a lack of co-working spaces is shown by a case study from an Addis Ababa co-working space. The city's rich history and culture notwithstanding, these pragmatic constraints turn off prospective tourists, demonstrating how inadequate infrastructure might jeopardize attempts to use the digital nomad movement (Bozzi, 2024).

Also, the scenario may get much more complicated due to political unrest and security issues in some Eastern part of Africa nations. For instance, Somalia, which has seen decades of strife, offers Digital-Nomads both potential and threats. Although the nation's historical landmarks and coasts draw daring tourists, many prospective tourists may be put off by the perceived security threats. According to a case study on Mogadishu, the capital of Somalia, local business owners have tried to provide a welcoming and secure atmosphere for Digital-Nomads, but they continue to encounter obstacles with regard to infrastructure support and global safety perceptions (Liu et al., 2022). The incorporation of Digital-Nomads into local economies is also meaningfully influenced by cultural variables. The way of life of Digital-Nomads may not align with traditional beliefs and community customs in many places of the Eastern part of Africa. For example, the temporary nature of Digital-Nomads might lead to miscommunications and conflicts in Ethiopia, where hospitality and community living are strongly embedded in the culture. An actual case study of nearby guesthouses serving Digital-Nomads in places like Lalibela shows how these businesses aim to address cultural divides but frequently have trouble striking a balance between local traditions and visitors' expectations (Morrison, 2023). Also, several governments in the Eastern part of Africa have not yet completely developed marketing strategies to draw in Digital-Nomads. Despite the fact that internet marketing has been successful in drawing tourists from all over the world, many local tourism boards lack the tools and know-how necessary to properly target Digital-Nomads. A case study of Kenya's marketing initiatives, for instance, shows how the nation influence positioned itself as a destination for Digital-Nomads by forming alliances with regional influencers and setting up co-working spaces. But neighboring nations have fallen behind, indicating a difference in marketing efficacy that may make it more difficult for them to compete for this group (Vanhove, N. 2022).

STATEMENT OF PROBLEM

The Eastern part of Africa could ideally become a top location for Digital-Nomads, with strong infrastructure, successful marketing plans, and welcoming locals. This ideal, however, is in sharp contrast to the existing situation (Bozzi, 2024). The region's attractiveness to Digital-Nomads is severely hampered by political unpredictability, poor co-working spaces, and unreliable internet access, despite its picturesque scenery and rich cultural legacy (Poulaki et al., 2023). The situation is made more difficult by contradicting evidence. Some studies point to the possible negative influences, such cultural displacement and economic inequality, while others manifest that Digital-Nomads boost local economies through spending and employment creation. This discrepancy emphasizes the necessity of a more sophisticated comprehension of the consequences of digital nomadism (Gupta et al., 2024). Also, the research now in publication frequently offers conflicting outcomes about the economic influence of Digital-Nomads in developing regions, especially in the Eastern part of Africa. There is a dearth of empirical data unique to this area because most research concentrate on well-known tourist destinations (Zerva et al., 2022).

Since the majority of frameworks on digital nomadism and tourism economics are derived mostly from research conducted in more developed environments, theoretical gaps still continue to exist. These frameworks' usefulness may be limited since they fail to take into account the distinct socioeconomic and cultural dynamics of the Eastern part of Africa. Additionally, there are clear information gaps about the relationship between local economies and Digital-Nomads in this area. Few studies have looked at their contributions, experiences, and motivations all of which are crucial for creating successful marketing and policy plans (Ji et al., 2024). Another level of intricacy is introduced by contextual gaps. Digital-Nomads' experiences are influenced by the different cultures, languages, and sociopolitical realities found in the Eastern part of Africa. However, the majority of research applies generalized outcomes from other locations without taking these contextual variables into consideration. The expansion of this population in the Eastern part of Africa is further hindered by practical issues including inadequate infrastructure, a lack of safety, and cultural misinterpretations (Bahri, 2024).

By offering a thorough examination of the function of Digital-Nomads in the Eastern part of Africa's tourism economy, this research aims to close these gaps. This study will provide insights into the particular possibilities and problems experienced by Digital-Nomads in the area by doing empirical research and synthesizing the body of previous literature. Along with addressing the existing practical issues, it will also examine how efficient marketing techniques might improve the integration of Digital-Nomads into local economies. By doing this, this study will provide a theoretical framework that is pertinent to the Eastern part of Africa and advance a more nuanced comprehending of digital nomadism within its unique setting. It will also offer practical propose ions for local stakeholders and legislators, directing future initiatives to establish a supportive atmosphere for Digital-Nomads. By filling up these gaps, the study will assist local communities and the population of Digital-Nomads by improving academic comprehending and guiding the development of sustainable tourism in the Eastern part of Africa.

THEORETICAL FOUNDATION

The dynamics of digital nomadism and its influences on tourism based economies, especially in the Eastern part of Africa, may be better understood using a number of theoretical frameworks. "*Social Exchange Theory*", which holds that social conduct results from an exchange process meant to maximize benefits and minimize costs, is one pertinent theory (Bahri, 2024). This theory may be used to comprehend how local communities and Digital-Nomads interact. The ideal setting for Digital-Nomads is one that provides both the necessary infrastructure for their jobs and stimulating cultural activities. In exchange, they make economic contributions through their expenditures. However, elements like cultural misinterpretations or subpar services might upset the equilibrium of this interaction, resulting in conflicts and unfulfilled expectations (Ay et al., 2024).

The "*Tourism Area Life Cycle (TALC) Theory*" is another significant paradigm that describes how tourist locations change over time through the following stages: discovery, participation, development, consolidation, and stagnation. According to this notion, the Eastern part of Africa may become a popular location for Digital-Nomads. Knowing the region's present tourist development stage can assist determine the necessary TDE measures, such as marketing and infrastructure expenditures, to draw in and keep Digital-Nomads. However, the linear development proposed by TALC may be challenged by the distinct sociopolitical setting of the Eastern part of Africa, and TDE is a more adaptable implementation of the theory (Zhou et al., 2024).

Geert Hofstede's "*Cultural Dimensions Theory*" also provides insightful information, especially when it comes to the cultural exchanges between local communities and Digital-Nomads. In an area with a wide range of cultural identities, this theory emphasizes how cultural variations may influence expectations and behavior. By being aware of these factors, local companies may better adapt their offerings to the demands of Digital-Nomads, leading to a more cordial working relationship (Özgen Çiğdemli, et al., 2024). Although each of these theories offers insightful viewpoints, *Social Exchange Theory* is the primary theoretical framework used in this investigation. Because it highlights the mutually beneficial interaction between local communities and Digital-Nomads, this decision is especially pertinent. A more sustainable integration of digital nomadism into the Eastern part of Africa's tourism industries can be facilitated by examining how both sides might optimize their gains from this connection.

DEFINITION AND ORIGIN OF TERMS

Digital Nomad: Those who spend their time working online while traveling or living in various locations are known as Digital-Nomads. They may go on to organize their working professional lives in a way that does not confine them to a particular geographical location. Digital-Nomads can be both independent contractors and full-fledged employees of a company they work for in various spheres, including technology, marketing, writing and consulting. They often type their work using computers, cellphones or other devices that would allow them to have internet access. This concept emerged only in the second half of the twentieth century, fundamentally, with the development of Internet and mobile technologies in the 2000s it started to spread. Digital nomadism, which is a larger pattern of flexibility at work, has become more desirable due to the widespread viability of working remotely, especially in the wake of the COVID-19 pandemic (Mancinelli, 2020).

Tourism Economy: Items and services associated with travel and leisure are among those produced and consumed as economic activities, which are captured under the tourist economy. This includes expenses incurred in accommodation, feeding, transport, entertainment and other services connected with tourism. It has widely been taken as a central factor in many nations' economic development, employment and foreign exchange earnings. The concept was developed in the period after the Second World War, and with the development of the travel facility all over the world the Tourism was recognized as an important sector of the economy. Tayler and Sonmez (2023) have noted that studies on impacts on domestic and international economic systems have expanded as tourist knowledge of economic effects has advanced (Poulaki et al., 2023).

Marketing of Destinations: Destination marketing is the term used to describe the deliberate attempts to market particular places as alluring travel destinations for prospective tourists. This involves showcasing a destination's distinctive features, such its natural beauty, cultural legacy, and recreational activities, using digital marketing, social media, public relations, and advertising. When travel firms and tourist boards started aggressively promoting vacation experiences in the early 20th century, destination marketing had its start. With the introduction of digital platforms, marketing methods have advanced more quickly, enabling more interactive and focused campaigns that speak directly to prospective tourists (Woldoff et al., 2021).

Social Exchange Theory: According to the sociological and psychological theory known as "social exchange theory," social conduct results from an exchange process. It implies that people want to reduce expenses and increase benefits while interacting with others. The writings of sociologists and economists like George Homans and Peter Blau had an influence on the development of this theory in the middle of the 20th century. The paradigm has been widely used to investigate interpersonal relationships, community dynamics, and even economic connections in a variety of domains, including organizational behavior, psychology, and sociology (Bahri, 2024).

EMPIRICAL LITERATURE REVIEW

Digital Nomad and Tourism Destination Economies

Digital-Nomads have a wide-ranging and growingly important influence on the economic environment of tourist locations. This group supports local economies by spending money on lodging, food, transportation, and recreational activities while traveling and working remotely. Digital-Nomads frequently spend longer lengths of time in one place than regular visitors, who might only be there for a short while. This results in a more long-lasting economic influence. Their existence can increase demand for services like cafés, coworking spaces, and community gatherings, which will help local companies expand (Bahri, 2024). Additionally, genuine cultural experiences are frequently sought after by Digital-Nomads, which can support community involvement and the preservation of regional customs. In addition to enhancing the destination's cultural richness, this interaction gives local service providers and craftspeople a platform to display their products. Also, especially in areas that can be strongly dependent on conventional tourism, the entry of Digital-Nomads might help diversify the local economy and offer a vital source of foreign cash (Gupta et al., 2024).

But there are other negative economic repercussions as well. Tensions between nomads and the local population may arise as a consequence of the increased demand for housing and facilities, which can occasionally raise living expenses for locals. Policymakers and destination managers must develop plans that strike a balance between the demands of the local population and the advantages of drawing in Digital-Nomads (Jiwasiddi et al., 2024). All things considered, promoting sustainable tourism development that benefits both tourists and host communities requires an awareness of the economic influences of digital nomadism.

H1: *Digital nomad has significant influence on tourism destination economies*

Digital-Nomads and Marketing of Destinations

Tourism locations' marketing methods are drastically altered by the existence of Digital-Nomads, forcing them to adjust to the particular requirements and tastes of this group (Bahri, 2024). Destinations need to highlight connection, flexibility, and genuine experiences in their marketing strategies since these qualities are important to Digital-Nomads (Arslan, 2024). This change frequently entails promoting dependable internet connection, co-working facilities, and neighborhood gatherings that encourage social contact amongst like-minded people. Also, the popularity of social media has increased the influence of Digital-Nomads, who serve as unofficial brand ambassadors by often sharing their experiences online. Their real-time material and genuine narrative can increase a destination's attractiveness and exposure, drawing in more visitors (Sztuk, 2024).

To reach this target group, destination marketing companies are also increasingly using collaborations with influencers and online communities of nomads. Destinations may get a competitive edge by focusing their marketing efforts on features that appeal to Digital-Nomads, such local culture, lifestyle, and cooperation possibilities. According to Xiao et al. (2023), marketers must provide content that speaks to the unique problems and goals of Digital-Nomads, which calls for a sophisticated grasp of their lifestyle and the difficulties they encounter. Digital-Nomads' influence on destination marketing, taken as a whole, promotes a more vibrant, participatory, and community-oriented strategy that can eventually improve the allure and sustainability of travel services.

H2: *Digital-Nomads has significant influence on marketing of destinations*

Marketing of destinations and tourism destination economies

Destination marketing has a significant and wide-ranging influence on tourist economies, influences everything from the number of visitors to the expansion of local businesses (Bahri, 2024). A destination's exposure may be greatly increased by using efficient marketing techniques, which will draw a wider range of visitors. Destinations may stand out in a crowded market and attract more tourists by emphasizing distinctive cultural, recreational, and historical features. This inflow encourages the establishment of jobs in the hotel and service industries in addition to increasing income from lodging, eating, and attractions (Hannonen et al., 2023). Additionally, by targeting particular groups like families, adventure tourists, or Digital-Nomads, customized marketing may encourage longer stays and higher spending. Marketing efforts that highlight cultural events or outdoor activities, for example, might draw specialized customers and have a longer-lasting economic influence. Also, influence marketing may encourage off-peak tourism, which helps local businesses maintain year-round revenue stability and lessen the demand on resources during peak seasons (Baptista et al., 2024).

But marketing has more than just beneficial benefits. Overzealous advertising may result in excessive tourism, putting a burden on the community's resources and infrastructure and perhaps lowering the standard of living for locals. Because local populations may feel overburdened by the flood of visitors, this can lead to dilution of culture and increased living expenses. Therefore, sustainable methods that take into account the demands of both tourists and local communities must be balanced with influence marketing, which is essential for promoting economic growth in tourist locations. In the end, the interaction between tourist economics and destination marketing emphasizes how crucial strategic planning is to promoting long-term gains for all parties (Bozzi, 2024). Digital-Nomads' economic contributions are meaningfully shaped by the mediation influence of destination marketing between them and tourism destination economies. Due to their spending habits, Digital-Nomads, who are motivated by the need for flexible work schedules and intensive cultural experiences, may have a big influence on local economies. However, the way that destinations promote themselves has a major role in mediating how successful this influence is (Sztuk, 2024).

H3: *Marketing of destinations has significant influence on tourism destination economies*

Mediation of destination Marketing, Digital-Nomads, Tourism Destination Economies

Digital-Nomads can be drawn to a place by means of efficient marketing methods that emphasize key features like dependable internet connectivity, co-working spaces, and lively local cultures. In addition to increasing exposure, venues that influence convey these advantages build an engaging story that speaks to the needs and ideals of Digital-Nomads the local economy may be stimulated by this focused strategy, which may result in more visitors, longer stays, and more money spent at nearby establishments (Miocevic, 2024) On the other hand, the potential financial gains could not be completely realized if marketing initiatives don't take into account the unique interests of Digital-Nomads. This group may become less involved as a consequence of inadequate advertising, which would reduce their financial contributions (Bahri, 2024). Additionally, by highlighting lesser-known locations and promoting eco-friendly travel methods, efficient marketing may aid in reducing issues like over tourism (Sztuk, 2024). In conclusion, destination marketing acts as a bridge to strengthen the connection between Digital-Nomads and travel destination economies. Destinations may optimize the economic advantages of digital nomadism by proactively positioning themselves to appeal to this demography, which promotes sustainable growth and community involvement (Ay et al., 2024).

> H4: *Digital-Nomads and tourism destination economies has meaningfully influence by mediation of marketing of destination*

CONCEPTUAL FRAMEWORK

Several essential elements make up a conceptual framework for comprehending the connection between Digital-Nomads, destination marketing, and tourist destination economies. The framework's central claim is that Digital-Nomads, who are distinguished by their preference for flexible work schedules and genuine cultural experiences, have a big influence on local economies through their purchasing habits. However, the success of destination marketing tactics acts as a mediator for this influence.

Figure 1. Conceptual Framework

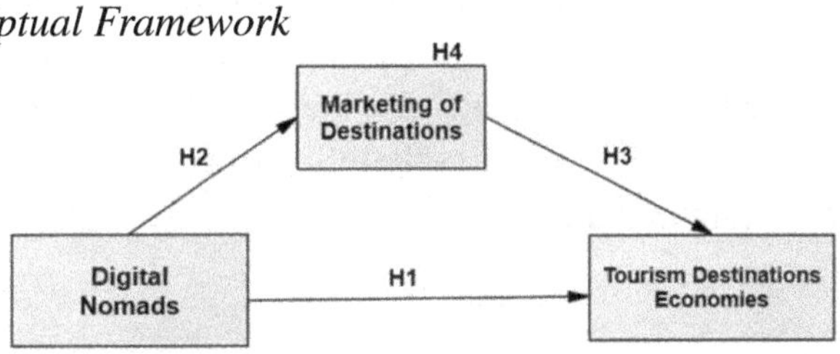

RESEARCH METHODOLOGY

With a sample size of 392 participants, the study methodology used a quantitative approach to investigate the connection between tourism destination economies, Digital-Nomads, and destination marketing. After a thorough analysis of pertinent literature, a structured questionnaire was created as the first step in the study. The development of scales assessing important constructs, such as Digital-Nomads' opinions on the efficacy of destination marketing and their economic influence on local communities, was guided by this research. The study initially evaluated the sample's suitability for factor analysis using the Kaiser-Meyer-Olkin (KMO) test to guarantee the validity and reliability of the scales. The sample was deemed appropriate for additional analysis if the KMO value was more than 0.6. Exploratory Factor Analysis (EFA) was then used to determine the constructs' underlying dimensions. Varimax rotation and factor extraction were used in this procedure to give the data a more lucid shape.

Following the establishment of the factor structure, the proposeed linkages within the conceptual framework were tested using Structural Equation Modeling (SEM) with AMOS software. SEM made it possible to investigate both the direct and indirect relationships between Digital-Nomads' economic contributions and destination marketing. To verify the model's sufficiency, the model fit indices such as the Chi-square, RMSEA, and CFI were assessed. By using this exacting approach, the study sought to add to the body of knowledge in tourism research by offering empirical insights into the mediation influence of marketing on the economic contributions of Digital-Nomads. The research carefully examined the body of literature on digital nomadism, destination marketing, and tourist economics in order to find pertinent concepts and elements for the scale. Important aspects including perceived value, destination appeal, and the economic influence of tourism were emphasized in earlier research. In order to ensure that the scale represented both theoretical underpinnings and practical issues, particular items were developed based on this literature to capture the subtleties of each construct. Pilot testing and input from subject-matter experts were part of the iterative scale development process, which further improved the items' relevance and clarity. This meticulous process guaranteed the final scale's validity and reliability, offering a strong instrument for the study's data collecting and analysis.

DATA ANALYSIS

Table 1. KMO and Bartlett's Test

Kaiser-Meyer-Olkin Measure of Sampling Adequacy.		**.850**
Bartlett's Test of Sphericity	Approx. Chi-Square	1419.736
	df	90
	Sig.	.000

Source: Authors

As shown in Table 1, the Kaiser-Meyer-Olkin (KMO) Measure of Sampling Adequacy and Bartlett's Test of Sphericity were evaluated before the data analysis got underway. A high degree of sampling adequacy is shown by the KMO score of 0.850, which implies that the data is appropriate for factor analysis. A KMO number around 1.0 manifests a significant correlation between variables, which improves the reliability of the factor analysis results. In general, KMO values above 0.6 are regarded as acceptable. The data's suitability for component analysis is further supported by Bartlett's Test of Sphericity, which produces an estimated Chi-Square of 1419.736 with 90 degrees of freedom and a significance level (Sig.) of 0.000. This outcome shows that there exist relationships between the variables since the correlation matrix differs greatly from an identity matrix. The conclusion that factor analysis may be successfully carried out to investigate the underlying structure of the data is supported by the significant p-value (less than 0.05), which manifests that the variables employed in the study are appropriate for factor analysis. When combined, these tests confirm that the data is ready for additional analysis, opening the door for exploratory factor analysis (EFA), which finds the important dimensions associated with the relevant constructs.

Table 2. Total Variance Explained

Component	Initial Eigenvalues			Extraction Sums of Squared Loadings			Rotation Sums of Squared Loadings		
	Total	% of Variance	Cumulative %	Total	% of Variance	Cumulative %	Total	% of Variance	Cumulative %
1	4.51	32.235	32.235	4.51	32.235	32.235	3.00	21.451	21.451
2	1.37	9.787	42.022	1.37	9.787	42.022	2.16	15.491	36.942
3	1.27	9.087	51.110	1.27	9.087	51.110	1.98	14.168	51.110
4	.949	6.782	57.892						
5	.871	6.223	64.115						
6	.773	5.519	69.634						

Extraction Method: PCA
Source: Authors

The outcomes of the Principal Component Analysis (PCA)-based Total Variance Explained from the Exploratory Factor Analysis (EFA) are shown in Table 2. Each component's eigenvalue and the proportion of variation it accounts for are shown in the table. With an eigenvalue of 4.51, the first component accounts for 32.235% of the variance, demonstrating that it captures a substantial amount of the data's underlying structure. The first component has a significant contribution to the entire variance, as seen by the cumulative percentage that reaches 32.235% following it. With eigenvalues of 1.37 and 1.27, respectively, the second and third components also show noteworthy contributions, explaining 9.787% and 9.087% of the variance. These three elements jointly account for 51.110% of the cumulative variance, indicating that they collectively constitute a significant fraction of the structure of the data. With eigenvalues less than 1.0, the following components exhibit declining returns and make up a smaller portion of the total variance. The integrity of the factor structure is further supported by the extraction sums of squared loadings for these components, which stay consistent with the original eigenvalues. According to the rotation sums of squared loadings, the top three components continue to contribute meaningfully to the variance following rotation, with the first factor alone accounting for 21.451% of the total. This analysis manifest the influence of the EFA in identifying key dimensions within the data, providing a solid foundation for further investigation into the relationships among the constructs related to Digital-Nomads and destination marketing.

Confirmatory principle component examination

The principle component arrangement of a set of guided proxies is verified using a type of statistics known as confirmatory principle component examination. Based on the underlying frame job and correlatives among observed proxies, investigations can evaluate hypotheses utilizing CFA. To evaluate the hypothesis that there is a association among the proxies that are being steered and the latent conceptions that underpin them, the inquiry employed CFA under table 3.

Table 3. Covariances

Covariance			Approximation	S.E.	C.R.	P	Hy.
MD	**<-->**	**DN**	**.241**	**.022**	**8.232**	***	**H2**
MD	<-->	TDE	.302	.033	7.693	***	**H3**
DN	<-->	TDE	.253	.25	7.832	***	**H1**

Source: Authors

The co-variances between the Economies of tourism based destinations (TDE), Digital-Nomads (DN), and Marketing of destination (MD) constructs are shown in Table 3. By showing the direction and intensity of the correlations between these constructs, the covariances shed light on how interrelated they are. With a standard error (S.E.) of 0.022 and a covariance of 0.241 between Marketing of destination and Digital-Nomads, the critical ratio (C.R.) is 8.232, indicating statistical significance ($p < 0.001$). This high covariance manifests a positive association, meaning that successful marketing tactics have a big influence on a destination's ability to draw in Digital-Nomads. Similar to this, there is statistical significance ($p < 0.001$) in the covariance between Marketing of destination and Economies of tourism based destinations, which is 0.302 with a S.E. of 0.033 and a C.R. of 7.693. This research emphasizes how crucial marketing is to boosting the financial gains that travel locations receive from Digital-Nomads. Finally, the correlation between the economies of tourism based destinations and Digital-Nomads is 0.253, with a C.R.

of 7.832 and a S.E. of 0.25, both of which are significant ($p < 0.001$). This positive correlation proposes that the economic influence on the destination rises in tandem with the number of Digital-Nomads. When taken as a whole, these outcomes demonstrate how interconnected these concepts are and support the idea that luring Digital-Nomads and promoting economic growth in travel locations depend heavily on destination marketing.

Table 4. Validity Concern

	CR	AVE	MSV	MaxR(H)	DN	MD	TDE
DN	0.732	0.643	0.219	0.852	**0.654**		
MD	0.758	0.657	0.132	0.763	0.171	**0.665**	
TDE	0.793	0.603	0.274	0.797	0.383	0.193	**0.684**

Note: DN= Digital Nomad; MD= Market destination; TDE=tourism destination economies
Source: Authors

Key indicators for the constructs of Digital-Nomads (DN), Marketing of destination (MD), and Economies of tourism based destinations (TDE) are presented in Table 4 to address validity problems. Maximum Shared Variance (MSV), Composite Reliability (CR), Average Variance Extracted (AVE), and Maximum Reliability (MaxR(H)) are included for every construct in the table. The CR values, which are DN at 0.732, MD at 0.758 and TDE at 0.793, all surpass the generally recognized cutoff point of 0.7, indicating excellent internal consistency. This implies that each construct's measuring items have high dependability. With DN at 0.643, MD at 0.657, and TDE at 0.603, the AVE values provide additional evidence for the validity of the constructs. Given that every AVE value is higher than the permissible cutoff point of 0.5, this proposes that each latent construct accounts for a substantial amount of the variance in the observable variables. The CR values, which are DN at 0.732, MD at 0.758, and TDE at 0.793, all surpass the generally recognized cutoff point of 0.7, indicating excellent internal consistency. This implies that each construct's measuring items have high dependability. With DN at 0.643, MD at 0.657, and TDE at 0.603, the AVE values provide additional evidence for the validity of the constructs. Given that every AVE value is higher than the permissible cutoff point of 0.5, this proposes that each latent construct accounts for a substantial amount of the variance in the observable variables.

Mediating role Examination

Figure 2. Structural Equation Model

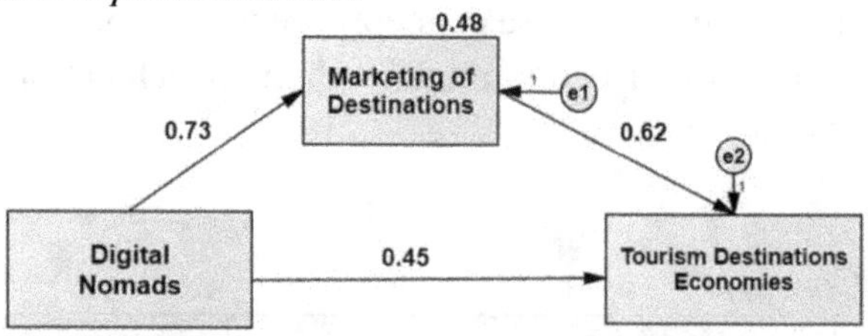

Model fit indices

Table 5. indices for Model Fit

Sig.	Chi-Sq	RMR	Fitness Goodness	Fitness Confirmatory	TLI	RMSEA
0.004	1.953	.035	0.931	0.913	0.912	.027

Source: Authors

The model fit indices for analyzing the mediating role in the structural equation model are shown in Table 5. The model fit is statistically significant, with a significance level (Sig.) of 0.004, indicating that the proposed model accurately depicts the data. The comparatively low Chi-Square score of 1.953 manifests a good match between the actual and predicted data, which is advantageous. The model's adequacy is further supported by the Root Mean Square Residual (RMR) value of 0.035, which shows that the average difference between the observed and predicted covariance matrices is small and falls below the acceptable threshold of 0.08. With corresponding values of 0.931 and 0.913, the Confirmatory Fit Index (CFI) and the Goodness of Fit Index (GFI) are both robust. Values above 0.90 are seen as propulsive of a good fit, and these indices are frequently used to evaluate the model's overall fit. The model's structural integrity and dependability are further supported by the Tucker-Lewis Index (TLI), which is likewise good at 0.912. Finally, a tight fit to the data is shown by the Root Mean Square Error of Approximation (RMSEA) of 0.027, which is meaningfully lower than the proposed threshold of 0.06 and proposes that the model well represents the underlying connections among the components. The analysis of the mediating function is strongly supported by these model fit indices, which collectively demonstrate that the structural equation model is a reliable depiction of the connections between Digital-Nomads, Marketing of destination, and Economies of tourism based destinations.

Table 6. Regression Examination

Relative			Approx.	S.E.	C.R.	P	Ass.
MD	**<---**	**DN**	**.863**	**.142**	**7.582**	***	**H2**
TDE	<---	MD	.327	.130	2.852	***	H3
TDE	<---	DN	.956	.191	7.957	***	H1

Source: Authors

The outcomes of the regression analysis that assesses the connections between the concepts of Digital-Nomads (DN), Marketing of destination (MD), and Economies of tourism based destinations (TDE) are shown in Table 6. With a critical ratio (C.R.) of 7.582, a standard error (S.E.) of 0.142, and a regression coefficient of 0.863, the association between Digital-Nomads and Marketing of destination is statistically significant ($p < 0.001$). This robust positive coefficient supports Hypothesis 2 (H2) by showing that a significant rise in the number of Digital-Nomads is linked to an improvement in the efficacy of marketing techniques. There is a substantial ($p < 0.001$) correlation between Marketing of destination and Economies of tourism based destinations, with a coefficient of 0.327, a S.E. of 0.130, and a C.R. of 2.852. This implies that a destination's economic success is positively influenced by its efficient marketing, supporting Hypothesis 3 (H3). Finally, the direct influence of Digital-Nomads on the economies of tourism based destinations has a regression value of 0.956, a statistically significant ($p < 0.001$) S.E. of 0.191, and a C.R. of 7.957.

The strong correlation manifested by this high coefficient supports Hypothesis 1 (H1), which states that Digital-Nomads have a direct influence on the financial sustainability of travel destinations. All things considered, these regression results show the important ways that Digital-Nomads influence marketing initiatives and financial results, highlighting the significance of focusing on this group for successful destination marketing tactics.

Table 7. Mediating role Influence

	Influence	worth	Path Influence
DN→TDE	Direct Influence	.45	Direct influence stated
DN→ MD→ TDE	Indirect Influence	.73*.62=.48	Indirect Influence Ensued
	Whole influence	.90	Partial mediation

Source: Authors

The link between Digital-Nomads (DN) and the Economies of tourism based destinations (TDE) is mediated by Marketing of destination (MD), as shown in Table 7. Digital-Nomads have a large direct influence on the economies of tourism based destinations, as manifested by their 0.45 quantification. This implies that when evaluated separately, Digital-Nomads have a discernible influence on the financial success of travel destinations. Multiplying the path influence of MD to TDE (0.62) by the path influence of DN to MD (0.73) yields an indirect influence of 0.48, which is the indirect influence through Marketing of destination. This proposes that marketing initiatives are essential to increasing the influence of Digital-Nomads on the financial results of travel destinations. When direct and indirect influences are included, the overall influence comes to 0.90. This significant cumulative influence implies that even if there is a strong direct correlation, marketing's mediating role cannot be disregarded. The results show partial mediation as the total influence of Digital-Nomads on the economy of tourist destinations is influenced by both direct and indirect factors. This emphasizes how crucial good marketing techniques are to maximizing the financial gains for travel locations by utilizing the presence of Digital-Nomads.

DISCUSSION

The study's conclusions shed light on the intricate interactions between Economies of tourism based destinations (TDE), Marketing of destination (MD), and Digital-Nomads (DN). The outcomes show that Digital-Nomads have a major influence on a destination's economic success as well as its marketing efficacy. Since DN and TDE have a strong direct correlation, the presence of Digital-Nomads may boost local economies in tourist destinations. Also, marketing's recognized mediating function demonstrates how influence marketing initiatives may magnify this influence and enable a larger economic contribution from Digital-Nomads. These outcomes highlight the need for travel destinations to implement focused marketing campaigns that cater especially to this expanding segment. This paper seeks to establish that the impacts of the DN/TDE nexus are both direct and indirect and thus both dimensional. As it emerged from the analysis, the direct effect of DN on TDE is estimated at 0.45 which implies that a great deal of the economic effects can be traced to direct effects of the DN in these tourism destinations. This finding absolves digital nomads as a strategic segment in travelers whose expenditure patterns and life choices help boost demand for services and commodities in tourism-related regions. However, the relationship between DN and TDE which was initially discussed is now expanded by the variable of Marketing of destination (MD) in which its effect is said to be indirectly linked to DN and TDE. Here, the analysis shows an indirect impact of 0.48 which was established by the impact of DN to MD 0.73 and MD to TDE 0.62. This mediation reveals how Destination Marketing Organizations grow the economic impacts of the segment through optimally marketing the destinations. This means that when the destinations promote themselves to target this segment, there is a potential to boost on the economic returns accruing from their presence. Communication of marketing campaigns that highlighted a destination's unique selling proposition and an appropriate image that appealed to the digital nomads greatly increased their likelihood of travelling and spending time in those destinations.

The total influence shows pro-eminence of the relationship with a score of 0.90 and therefore totals mediation with partial mediation. While this means that MD partially mediates the DN to TDE relationship suggesting that others variables exist that influence this relationship. This leads to a question on such factors, which are socio-cultural, the quality and availability of infrastructure and community participation, which may in turn determine the sojourning of digital nomads, as well of their economic impact. In particular, the results reveal that tactical marketing initiatives exist between the digital nomads and the tourism-dependent countries. It is not only underscoring the importance of the need for destinations to adopt suitable marketing strategies to appeal to this population and the need for more studies on the impacts that this population has on receivers locations. In this way, the stakeholders can clearly see how the presence of the digital nomads can be utilized in order to attain sustainable economic development in regions that greatly rely on tourism industry.

CONCLUSION

The results of this research increase understanding of the connection between Digital Nomads (DN), place promotion and tourist destination's economic performance. Through showing both the direct and indirect impacts, this research indicates that tourism organizations should pay close attention to the economic value of the DN segment in order to effectively incorporate them into their strategic planning. Directly, it demonstrates that several well-organized groups such as the Digital Nomads are important contributors to local economic circuits, thus affirming their place as one sub–segment of the tourism industry. Besides the support they give to local business people, they also help in creating market demand on nearly all sectors in their operations such as accommodation, sales among others. This direct influence demonstrates their capability to improve the economic coefficients of the countries and territories focused on developing tourism activity. Also and most importantly, the paper identifies destination marketing as a moderating factor that enhances such economic effects. By identifying the most suitable marketing approaches, Digital Nomads' attractions can be further boosted, by increasing the length of their stay and the amount spent within a destination. The results call for reframing the marketing strategies to focus on the specific characteristics that the discussed audience seeks, including co-working spaces, culture, and cultural activities, and community engagement platforms. In addition, the study recommends that tourism stakeholders should embrace a paradigm that incorporates not only the marketing of the destination but also the creation of the suitable environment that would be suitable for the Digital Nomads. This means that besides providing resources for internet access for example, one should also build appealing environments that people want and need to come out of their homes and interact, provision of basic needs and other amenities that people might require especially with the new advances in technology embracing remote working. Therefore, the study presents an argument for tourism marketing practitioners to consider and level lean marketing communication messages toward the Digital Nomads. In this way, their presence should be credited for contributions to the destination's economic standing, as well as their targeting by marketing strategies that correspond with their choice patterns in order to guarantee optimal financial returns and sustained economic development. The need to grasp and appreciate the interactions between Digital Nomads, destination marketing, and tourist economies will be pivotal to the various destinations success in the future considering the growing remote work trend. This paper extends the literature on tourism economics while providing an accessible reference for stakeholders who want to understand how the dynamics of global travel and remote work affect the industry.

MANAGERIAL IMPLICATIONS

Based on this study, the following are the managerial implications that will benefit tourism managers who plan to venture into the business of reaching out to Digital Nomads. First of all, it is possible to identify an obvious need for the consistent construction of marketer oriented strategies aimed at this segment. Digital Nomads are in constant search of stimulating and appealing conditions since they are required to be in a position that enables them to carry out their work and enjoy at the same time. Understanding their needs, including things like fast-speed internet, comfortable co-working spaces, and other recreational services, tourism managers can effectively create more detailed targeted promotional messages to this group. However, the promotion of business relationships with local businesses is crucial. Partnerships can complement the attractiveness of the economies by building packages, which would comprise work spaces, health and fitness facilities, and art. For example, collaboration with cafes, gyms, and local tour operators may create benefits for Digital Nomads that match work and fun. It is not only a way to enhance their camping experience but also a way that contributes to development of local economies due to increase in visits to the near by outlets. In addition, the specific actions that tourism managers should undertake include: promoting the improvements of the worlds that support remote work. The Digital Nomads' appreciation for technologies, ergonomics, silence and networking opportunities make their attraction contingent upon investments into reliable technological equipment and comfortable furniture, as well as mutually beneficial events for tourists and locals. Finally, constant communication and interaction with Digital Nomads can help in providing insights into temporal adjustments with relevant services and moreover marketing approaches. This is because when managing for tourism, it reaches out to this demographic in the development of offerings in efforts to keep them interested. Concisely, the analysis of the determinants of Digital Nomadism and targeting them indirectly helps tourism managers to market destinations as versatile places for professional and recreational activities simultaneously boosting the local economy and improving the visitors' satisfaction.

PRACTICAL IMPLICATIONS

From an applied approach, this study emphasizes the necessity of using the presence of Digital Nomads as a distinctive differentiator for locations. To effectively attract this generation, destination marketers should prioritize the construction of amenities and infrastructure that meet their demands. Consistent internet access, flexible accommodation alternatives, and well-designed coworking spaces are all essential. By investing in these facilities, destinations may create an atmosphere that not only appealing to Digital Nomads but also encourages longer stays and higher spending. Increased connection facilitates remote work, while flexible accommodations accommodates various periods of stay and personal preferences. Shared workplaces may help Digital Nomads connect and collaborate, improving their experiences and increasing community participation. Furthermore, advertising local companies that provide services relevant to this demographic, such as cafés with dependable Wi-Fi, fitness facilities, and cultural events, might help to increase a destination's appeal. Destinations that present themselves as Digital Nomad-friendly may tap into this increasing market, benefiting the local economy and generating long-term tourist growth. To summarize, tailoring destination services to the unique demands of Digital Nomads can result in major tangible advantages for both tourists and local communities.

THEORETICAL IMPLICATIONS

Theoretically, by clarifying the mediating function of marketing in the interaction between Digital-Nomads and tourism based economies, this study adds to the body of knowledge on tourism and marketing. By including the idea of digital nomadism into destination marketing frameworks, the outcomes expand on current models and imply that more study is necessary to examine the influence of these new demographics on other aspects of tourism. Future investigations into the subtleties of digital nomad choices and their consequences for destination marketing tactics are made possible by this study.

RECOMMENDATIONS

It is advised that those involved in the tourist industry give the incorporation of Digital-Nomads into their marketing plans first priority. To further comprehend the unique requirements and preferences of Digital-Nomads, market research may be necessary. Their experience may also be improved by developing community projects that accept Digital-Nomads and offer networking possibilities. Additionally, destinations have to think about creating adaptable pricing plans and special deals to appeal to this short-lived yet lucrative demographic.

FUTURE DIRECTIONS

To further improve marketing tactics, future studies should focus more on the unique traits and inclinations of Digital-Nomads. The changing character of digital nomadism and its long-term influences on travel economies might be investigated through longitudinal research. Comparative research across various locations may also shed light on the efficacy of different digital nomad-specific marketing tactics. Investigating the possible social and environmental influences of a rise of Digital-Nomads in tourist destinations may potentially provide insightful information.

REFERENCES

Adedoyin, F. F., Seetaram, N., Disegna, M., & Filis, G. (2023). The influence of tourism taxation on international arrivals to a small tourism-dependent economy. *Journal of Travel Research*, *62*(1), 135–153. DOI: 10.1177/00472875211053658

Arslan, E. (2024). From tourists to nomads: Unveiling the transformative potential of Digital-Nomads in travel and tourism. *Worldwide Hospitality and Tourism Themes*, *16*(3), 269–281. DOI: 10.1108/WHATT-03-2024-0046

Ay, E., & Güzel, M. O. (2024). Digital-Nomads in destination marketing. *Worldwide Hospitality and Tourism Themes*, *16*(3), 316–328. DOI: 10.1108/WHATT-03-2024-0050

Bahri, M. T. (2024). Evidence of the digital nomad phenomenon: From" Reinventing" migration theory to destination countries readiness. *Heliyon*, *10*(17), e36655. DOI: 10.1016/j.heliyon.2024.e36655 PMID: 39263067

Baptista, R. G. T. (2024). *Digital-Nomads in Peniche: Exploring the Relation between Remote Work and Surfing* (Master's thesis, Instituto Politecnico de Leiria (Portugal)).

Bozzi, A. (2024). Digital nomadism from the perspective of places and mobilities: A literature review. *European Transport Research Review*, *16*(1), 50. DOI: 10.1186/s12544-024-00663-z

Gupta, S., Jaiswal, R., & Gupta, S. K. (2024). Digital-Nomads: A systematic literature review and future research agenda. *Tourism Review*. Advance online publication. DOI: 10.1108/TR-12-2023-0869

Hannonen, O., Quintana, T. A., & Lehto, X. Y. (2023). A supplier side view of digital nomadism: The case of destination Gran Canaria. *Tourism Management*, *97*, 104744. DOI: 10.1016/j.tourman.2023.104744

Ji, Y., Kim, S. M., & Kim, Y. (2024). A way to attract Digital-Nomads to tourist destinations in the new normal era. *Sustainability (Basel)*, *16*(6), 2336. DOI: 10.3390/su16062336

Jiwasiddi, A., Schlagwein, D., Cahalane, M., Cecez-Kecmanovic, D., Leong, C., & Ractham, P. (2024). Digital nomadism as a new part of the visitor economy: The case of the "digital nomad capital" Chiang Mai, Thailand. *Information Systems Journal*.

Kiki, E. (2024). *The Influence of Location-Related Attributes to Portugal's Brand Image: Motivating Factors for Digital Nomad Relocation* (Master's thesis, Universidade NOVA de Lisboa (Portugal)).

Liestiandre, H. K., Morrison, A. M., Yasa, N. N. K., Sukawati, T. G. R., & Sukaatmadja, I. P. G. (2024). The influence of a local well-being philosophy on revisit intentions to Bali among Digital-Nomads. *Tourism and Hospitality*, *5*(4), 1099–1124. DOI: 10.3390/tourhosp5040062

Liu, A., Kim, Y. R., & Song, H. (2022). Toward an accurate assessment of tourism economic influence: A systematic literature review. *Annals of Tourism Research Empirical Insights*, *3*(2), 100054. DOI: 10.1016/j.annale.2022.100054

Mancinelli, F. (2020). Digital-Nomads: Freedom, responsibility and the neoliberal order. *Information Technology & Tourism*, *22*(3), 417–437. DOI: 10.1007/s40558-020-00174-2

Miocevic, D. (2024). Baby come back: Resident-digital nomad conflicts, destination identification, and revisit intention. *Journal of Travel Research*, ●●●, 00472875231220945.

Morrison, A. M. (2023). *Marketing and managing tourism destinations*. Routledge. DOI: 10.4324/9781003343356

Özgen Çiğdemli, A. Ö., Yayla, Ş., & Çiğdemli, B. S. (2024). The world from the perspective of Digital-Nomads: Exploring sentiments in destination reviews. *Worldwide Hospitality and Tourism Themes*, *16*(3), 303–315. DOI: 10.1108/WHATT-03-2024-0044

Poulaki, I., Mavragani, E., Kaziani, A., & Chatzimichali, E. (2023). Digital-Nomads: Advances in hospitality and destination attractiveness. *Tourism and Hospitality*, *4*(3), 483–498. DOI: 10.3390/tourhosp4030030

Sztuk, A. (2024). Digital-Nomads as Recipients and Users of the City's Offer. Status and Prospects of Research. *Zeszyty Naukowe Politechniki Śląskiej. Organizacja i Zarządzanie*, (193).

Vanhove, N. (2022). *The economics of tourism destinations: Theory and practice*. Routledge. DOI: 10.4324/9781003258186

Woldoff, R. A., Woldoff, R., & Litchfield, R. C. (2021). *Digital-Nomads: In search of freedom, community, and meaningful work in the new economy*. Oxford University Press. DOI: 10.1093/oso/9780190931780.001.0001

Xiao, Y., & Agrawal, B. (2023). *Becoming Mainstream: What Makes You a Digital Nomad?* (Master's thesis, Handelshøyskolen BI).

Zerva, K., Huete, R., & Segovia-Pérez, M. (2022, May). Digital nomad tourism: The experience of living at the destination. In *International Conference on Modern Trends in Business Hospitality and Tourism* (pp. 15-26). Cham: Springer International Publishing.

Zhou, L., Buhalis, D., Fan, D. X., Ladkin, A., & Lian, X. (2024). Attracting Digital-Nomads: Smart destination strategies, innovation and competitiveness. *Journal of Destination Marketing & Management*, *31*, 100850. DOI: 10.1016/j.jdmm.2023.100850

KEY TERMS AND DEFINITIONS

Digital-Nomads: Those who use technology to work from home while on the road or in other places, frequently in search of a work-life balance.

Marketing of destination: Techniques and initiatives used by travel agencies to advertise a destination and draw tourists, emphasizing its special qualities and attractions are called as Marketing of destination

Economies of tourism based destinations: It is the advantages and influences of tourism on the local economy, such as the development of jobs, income, and general economic expansion.

Mediation: A statistical concept that illustrates the indirect influences of connections by showing how one variable influences another through a third variable.

Composite Reliability: It higher numbers signifying more dependability, which is a measure of the internal consistency of a group of indicators or items designed to assess the same construct.

Chapter 7
Promoting Digital Nomads in Rural Japan

Keita Matsushita
https://orcid.org/0000-0002-5506-3303
Kansai University, Japan

ABSTRACT

This chapter explores strategies that rural destinations in Japan can adopt to attract digital nomads—a growing demographic of remote workers seeking new environments. It analyzes the potential impacts of this trend on local communities and the experiences of digital nomads. Through a case study from a rural area in Japan, the chapter outlines actionable strategies for attracting remote professionals. These include infrastructure improvements, the promotion of local culture, and the development of coworking spaces tailored to the needs of digital nomads. Furthermore, the chapter discusses the socio-economic contributions digital nomads can make to rural areas, such as stimulating local economies, fostering cultural exchange, and supporting sustainable community development. By providing a comprehensive analysis, the chapter offers valuable insights into how rural Japan can position itself as an appealing destination for digital nomads while benefiting local residents and preserving cultural and environmental heritage.

INTRODUCTION

The global spread of COVID-19 has dramatically accelerated the widespread adoption of remote work, resulting in a remarkable increase in the number of digital nomads across the globe. In the tourism sector, growing concerns over issues such as over-tourism, climate change, and the detrimental environmental impacts of mass tourism have led to a rising interest in slow travel. Digital nomads, who typically

DOI: 10.4018/979-8-3373-0076-4.ch007

choose to reside in a single location for extended periods, resonate strongly with this slow travel movement, presenting a more sustainable alternative to traditional short-term tourism practices. This evolving dynamic has brought to light the significant economic and social contributions that digital nomads can make to the regions they inhabit.

A survey from Nomad List (2025) indicated that the largest segment of digital nomads is full-time workers, representing 39% of the community, followed by freelancers at 18% and startup founders at 18%. Financially, this group showcases impressive earning potential, with an average income hovering around $120,000 and a median income of around $850,000. One notable example of this phenomenon is Nomad Fest, an event held in the picturesque town of Bansko, Bulgaria, in June 2023. This vibrant gathering symbolises the burgeoning community of digital nomads. What began in 2020 with a modest 100 participants has blossomed into a remarkable assembly of over 700 nomads from 40 countries by 2023. The demographics of the 2023 festival showcased a diverse international presence, with approximately 22% of attendees hailing from the USA, followed by 11% from Germany, 10% from Bulgaria, 9% from the UK, 17% from various EU nations, 8% from Israel, 5% from Canada, 3% from Japan, and 1.5% from Australia. While the USA hosted many participants, the event was truly international in scope, highlighting a rich tapestry of representation from across the globe.

The evolving narrative surrounding digital nomads has shifted dramatically as they transition from being perceived as 'heretics'—independent business owners akin to backpackers or retirees—into a recognised work style with a firm grounding in traditional employment. This transformation is exemplified by the increasing prevalence of 'digital nomadic employees (DNE),' now emerging as the dominant group within the digital nomad community. This trend also reflects a growing acceptance among companies, as more organisations are laying the groundwork to allow and support a digital nomadic work style.

Digital nomadism, as envisioned by Makimoto & Manners (1997), is a lifestyle and workstyle that has gained significant traction with the widespread adoption of the internet and mobile media in the 2010s. According to Bozzi (2024), digital nomads are professionals who leverage remote working capabilities and digital technology to live, travel, and work from various locations with reliable internet access. Since the late 2010s, digital nomadism has been increasingly examined in academic research, with efforts to elucidate its realities and theorize its implications (Cook, 2020; Müller, 2016; Reichenberger, 2018).

Digital nomadism can be characterized as a workstyle and lifestyle practice that integrates digital work and tourism (Cook, 2020; Hannonen, 2020). From a tourism perspective, digital nomads are considered long-term leisure travelers (Reichenberger, 2018) or culture-driven travelers attracted to the creative aspects of cities and regions

(Bertola et al., 2022). Conversely, from the perspective of workstyles, studies have examined how leisure elements and environments can be integrated into digital work (Orel, 2019; Prester et al., 2019), as well as the challenges posed by loneliness and overwork (Nash et al., 2018; Thompson, 2018). Beyond the realm of digital work, analyses have also focused on digital nomads' perceptions of space and time, as well as themes of flexibility, mobility, identity, and community (Hensellek & Puchala, 2021; Matsushita, 2021; Thompson, 2019).

The global spread of COVID-19 significantly expanded the prevalence of remote work, leading to a remarkable increase in the number of digital nomads. According to an insightful survey by MBO Partners (2024), the landscape of digital nomadism in the United States has shifted dramatically over recent years. In 2019, there were approximately 7.3 million digital nomads, but by 2024, this figure had more than doubled to an astonishing 18.1 million, constituting approximately 11% of the entire workforce. A closer examination of this burgeoning demographic reveals a distinct trend: the rise of employee workers among digital nomads has grown substantially (from 3.2% in 2019 to 10.2% in 2024), outpacing the increase of independent workers (from 4.1% in 2019 to 7.9% in 2024). This growth is attributed not only to independent freelancers and entrepreneurs but also to the increasing presence of "Digital Nomadic Employees (DNE)" (Matsushita, 2024), a new category of salaried workers who engage in remote work while adopting a nomadic lifestyle.

In response to the post-pandemic landscape, Cook (2023) proposed a refined classification of digital nomads into five categories: (1) Freelance digital nomads, (2) Digital nomad business owners, (3) Salaried digital nomads, (4) Experimental digital nomads—those who are exploring this lifestyle without a stable income, and (5) Armchair nomads—those planning to become digital nomads within the next few years. This classification reflects the growing acceptance of remote work beyond traditional office settings and highlights the diverse motivations and economic conditions that define digital nomadism (MBO partners, 2022).

At the same time, the COVID-19 pandemic imposed significant restrictions on mobility, particularly international travel, which severely impacted the tourism industry. As a countermeasure, many destinations turned to digital nomads as a means to mitigate the decline in tourism. Destinations experiencing slow tourism recovery actively implemented policies, services, and visa programs to attract digital nomads (Sánchez-Vergara et al., 2023). Locations such as Canggu in Bali and Chiang Mai in Thailand have strengthened their appeal to digital nomads, even surpassing pre-pandemic levels (Jiwasiddi et al., 2024; Pipin Oktapiani & Putu Mahyuni, 2025). Since 2020, not only Southeast Asian countries but also Japan, South Korea, and Taiwan have introduced digital nomad visa programs to encourage this new form of mobility.

A review of digital nomad research reveals an initial focus on digital nomads themselves, followed by studies on the impact and responses of host regions and policies for digital nomad attraction (Jiwasiddi et al., 2024). Particularly after the COVID-19 pandemic, research has increasingly examined digital nomads in relation to sustainable tourism and regional development. Specific regions that have been the focus of research include the Canary Islands in Spain (Hannonen et al., 2023), Lisbon in Portugal (Mariati et al., 2023), Madeira (Sardinha et al., 2023), and, in Asia, Bali in Indonesia (Rahayu et al., 2022; Wibowo, 2024) and Chiang Mai in Thailand (Choi & Qu, 2024; Lhakard, 2022). However, relatively few studies have examined Japan, South Korea, and Taiwan—regions that have been rapidly developing policies to attract digital nomads. As Bozzi (2024) notes, analysing the social, economic, and environmental impacts of both established and emerging digital nomad destinations is crucial.

Given this research background, this chapter addresses the following research question: How do local regions structure and implement strategies to attract and accommodate digital nomads? Using a case study approach, this research examines local efforts to establish reception frameworks, manage programs, and address emerging challenges. Specifically, the study focuses on Hyuga City in Miyazaki Prefecture, Japan, conducting interviews with local government officials and business operators and participant observations in planning meetings and digital nomad programs.

Digital nomadism represents a form of global mobility that extends beyond urban centers to regional and tourist areas. Unlike traditional migration, digital nomads often maintain employment while moving, simultaneously mitigating and exacerbating issues associated with the Global South. In Japan, where rapid aging and population decline are intensifying the concentration of people in Tokyo, sustaining regional communities has become a pressing issue (Nakazawa, 2023). In regions where aging populations have weakened the labor force and industries, the professional skills of digital nomads are seen as a potential driver of revitalization. At the same time, as tourism expands, overtourism has become a growing concern (Asahi, 2024). The attraction of digital nomads can thus be positioned as a strategic component of regional transformation and sustainable tourism development (Ji et al., 2024).

Can the attraction of digital nomads serve as a strategic approach to rethinking the sustainability of local communities and tourism in Japan? This study aims to provide significant insights into this question by examining how digital nomads are received and supported.

The remainder of this chapter is structured as follows. Section 2 reviews relevant literature. Section 3 discusses the research methodology, case study region, and organizations involved, followed by a detailed program management and operations analysis. Section 4 identifies key factors and challenges in managing digital nomad attraction in local communities. Section 5 presents theoretical and practical implications before concluding with a summary and future outlook.

LITERATURE REVIEW

What are digital nomads

Digital nomads are adventurous individuals who embrace a lifestyle that allows them to travel freely while working remotely through the power of digital technology. This unique way of life is defined by exceptional geographical mobility, made feasible by groundbreaking advancements in communication tools and a widespread shift away from traditional office settings (Litchfield & Woldoff, 2023; Mancinelli, 2022). Unlike merely working from home, digital nomadism embodies a philosophy that harmonises work with leisure, emphasising a commitment to personal freedom and minimalism, as well as challenging conventional ideas about stability and material wealth (Cook, 2023; Mancinelli, 2020; Reichenberger, 2018).

Often, freelancers or entrepreneurs, digital nomads prioritise independence and flexibility, actively seeking experiences that blend work with travel. They favour a lifestyle that allows them to roam freely rather than adhering to predictable career trajectories (Woldoff & Litchfield, 2021). The recent pandemic has underscored their remarkable adaptability as they navigated challenges posed by restricted movement while reaffirming their core values centred on self-fulfilment and personal freedom (Ehn et al., 2022; Hermann & Paris, 2020).

The concept of digital nomadism traces its roots back to the late 1990s when visionary thinkers predicted that portable technology would empower people to work from any corner of the globe (Mancinelli, 2022). This lifestyle has gained tremendous popularity in recent years, driven by the emergence of the collaborative economy, affordable travel options, and an increasing number of remote work opportunities (Ili & Büyükbaykal, 2022; Mancinelli, 2022). Destinations like Bali and Lisbon have become epicentres for digital nomads, fostering vibrant communities where like-minded individuals can connect, share experiences, and take advantage of lower living costs (Woldoff & Litchfield, 2021).

These communities serve as a vital support system, countering the loneliness accompanying a nomadic lifestyle and providing a sense of belonging among individuals with similar values and ambitions (Andino-Frydman, 2023). However, beneath the alluring perception of absolute freedom, digital nomadism operates within a framework shaped by global inequalities and neoliberal economic systems. Those with privileged backgrounds often find it easier to traverse these complexities, raising important questions about fairness and access (Mancinelli, 2020). This rise of digital nomadism signals a broader societal transformation towards flexible work arrangements and reflects a growing intertwining of mobility, technology, and daily life (Hannonen, 2020).

The lifestyle choices embraced by digital nomads are not merely personal whims but resonate with the evolving demands of the contemporary labor market, where non-traditional employment is increasingly prevalent (Rakhmetulina et al., 2024). As this nomadic way of life continues to flourish, it provokes profound discussions about the essence of work and community, challenging us to reconsider the future of urban living and the importance of place in our digital era (Woldoff & Litchfield, 2021). With their ability to navigate the global landscape with ease, digital nomads benefit from the infrastructure of modern technology and favorable visa policies, spotlighting significant issues surrounding privilege and freedom of movement (Edwards, 2021). Ultimately, digital nomadism represents a monumental shift in how work integrates with life, offering valuable insights into the larger cultural and economic transformations occurring in the age of digital connectivity (Pupavac et al., 2023).

As the phenomenon of digital nomadism evolves, pressing concerns have emerged regarding its sustainability, environmental footprints, and social equity. While many nomads cherish their mobility and remote work capabilities, their influx into popular tourist destinations can lead to overtourism, resulting in the depletion of local resources and disturbances in community dynamics. Additionally, recent research reveals that a reliance on technology not only influences personal identities but also creates a distinctive cultural landscape, where a unique subculture develops among nomads through shared experiences—sometimes marginalising local traditions and practices. This duality provides an essential opportunity for reflection on how digital nomads can engage more thoughtfully and responsibly with their host communities. It invites us to consider how their presence can enrich local culture and promote sustainable practices, ensuring that they contribute positively to the regions they inhabit, rather than undermine them.

Digital nomads and Local

The relationship between digital nomads and local communities is intricate and layered, involving a variety of economic, social, and cultural dimensions. Digital nomads, who possess the unique capability to work remotely from any location with internet access, are increasingly viewed as potential agents of change for rural revitalisation and economic growth across diverse regions.

In the charming village of Pécsdevecser in Hungary, for instance, digital nomads have become vital contributors to the community's rejuvenation. Their presence injects new streams of income into the economy and creates a dynamic environment for local businesses. However, the village continues to face certain challenges, particularly concerning infrastructure and housing, which must be addressed to fully capitalise on this influx of new residents (Kókai & Rétfalvi, 2024).

Similarly, the vibrant island of Bali has emerged as a hotspot for digital nomads, who form a distinctive market segment characterised by specific travel habits and consumption patterns. These nomads enrich the local digital ecosystem by engaging in knowledge transfer and entrepreneurial initiatives, thereby weaving themselves into the fabric of the community (Christiansen et al., 2023).

Nevertheless, the arrival of digital nomads is not without its challenges. Concerns regarding their legal status and the potential for cultural integration must be carefully navigated (Christiansen et al., 2023). In Gran Canaria, the interactions between nomads and local residents reveal both opportunities for collaboration and hurdles that need to be overcome. Stakeholders in the area emphasise the importance of developing better integration strategies that can maximise the positive impacts while mitigating potential conflicts (Hannonen et al., 2023).

The Tulsa Remote Program in Oklahoma serves as a compelling case study of how communities can harness local attributes to attract and retain digital nomads. This program has not only enhanced community engagement but has also brought about significant economic benefits (Teodorovicz et al., 2023).

Despite these promising developments, the relationship between digital nomads and local residents can sometimes lead to tensions. Social conflicts may emerge in various destinations where the identities of nomads and long-term residents intersect uneasily, manifesting as competing interests and differing lifestyles (Miočević, 2024).

Moreover, the transformative influence of digital nomadism on tourism is clear, as it fosters new perspectives on travel and cultural exchange. However, this shift necessitates regulatory changes to tackle issues such as taxation and gentrification, ensuring that the benefits of these interactions are equitably distributed (Arslan, 2024). In Bali, local sentiments toward digital nomads are complex and multifaceted, shaped significantly by economic factors and sociocultural impacts (Agniera et al., 2023).

In conclusion, while digital nomads hold the potential to make substantial contributions to local communities, achieving successful integration requires a concerted effort to address existing infrastructure gaps, legal hurdles, and cultural sensitivities. Only through these efforts can mutually beneficial relationships be fostered, paving the way for a harmonious coexistence between digital nomads and local residents.

Digital Nomadism in Japan

Digital nomadism in Japan is a rich and intricate phenomenon that intertwines with the country's cultural and economic landscape, particularly through the evolving concept of 'workation.' This innovative approach has gained substantial traction in Japan, especially in the aftermath of the COVID-19 pandemic, where it has been recognised as a strategic form of digital nomadism aimed at breathing new life into local communities and economies. The Japanese-style workation seeks to address pressing challenges such as the urban population's concentration, an aging demographic, and the downturn of the tourism industry. By encouraging remote workers to immerse themselves in rural settings, workation fosters meaningful interactions between digital nomads and local residents, bolstering community engagement and catalysing economic development (Matsushita, 2021a; 2021b; 2022).

Distinct from the conventional notion of digital nomadism—characterised by global mobility and a lifestyle detached from any permanent location—the Japanese model emphasises local involvement and sustainable tourism. In this setting, digital nomads are not just transient visitors; they are potential catalysts for revitalising depopulated areas, playing a crucial role in enhancing the socio-economic fabric of these communities (Horiuchi & Morishige, 2024). This localised approach resonates with the broader global trend of digital nomadism, which merges work, travel, and leisure due to advancements in digital technology and the growing decentralisation of the workplace (Edwards, 2021; Mancinelli, 2022).

However, the Japanese model also sheds light on the complexities of merging the typically individualistic lifestyles of digital nomads with the community-centric ethos associated with traditional work practices. This situation highlights the need for further exploration into how these two models can harmoniously coexist, ultimately benefiting both the nomads and the local communities they engage with (Matsushita, 2022). Thus, the discourse around digital nomadism in Japan presents a unique adaptation of global trends, meticulously tailored to tackle specific socio-economic challenges while leveraging the potential of digital technologies to cultivate new avenues for community and economic resilience (Kuzheleva-Sagan & Spicheva, 2020; Hannonen, 2022).

In Japan, the concept of workation is not merely a lifestyle choice for digital nomads; it is a multifaceted strategy that combines work, tourism, and community involvement to rejuvenate local economies while addressing pressing social issues. This strategic framework does more than redistribute labour; it actively contributes to human resource development within local businesses, all while strengthening key industries such as tourism and entrepreneurship (Matsushita, 2021b).

The Japanese government has long deliberated on workation as a vital policy tool aimed at preventing rural depopulation and sparking regional revitalisation efforts, particularly in less populated locales such as farming, mountain, and fishing villages (Kim & Kim, 2023). This initiative emerges as a promising response to the downturn in inbound tourism caused by the pandemic, encouraging interactions between urban professionals and rural communities to bridge economic gaps (Matsushita, 2022).

Typically, workation in Japan involves a delightful blend of staying at picturesque resorts while working from local coworking spaces. This harmonious combination of work and leisure not only supports personal and professional growth but also encourages exploration and development of regional tourism resources suitable for longer stays, inspiring both companies and employees to partake in local social projects (Matsushita, 2021b). Furthermore, this approach represents a groundbreaking fusion of tourism, work, and daily life, offering fresh and enriched long-term tourism experiences that stand apart from traditional travel methods (Lee & Kim, 2024).

The rapid digital transformation we are witnessing globally significantly amplifies the integration of work and leisure, paving the way for more flexible working arrangements (Shin et al., 2023). In Japan, the notable rise of 'workation' exemplifies this trend, emerging as a promising frontier for innovation. This movement is linked to new services and businesses catering to hybrid work models, which are pivotal in transforming local economies and community dynamics (Matsushita, 2022).

At its core, workation in Japan represents a strategic initiative that underpins not only local economies but also nurtures cultural exchange and personal growth, positioning it as a significant trend within the evolving landscapes of work and tourism (Kim & Kim, 2023; Lee & Kim, 2024; Matsushita, 2021a; 2021b; 2022; 2024; Shin et al., 2023).

In this context, the present study endeavours to illuminate the proactive measures being taken by rural areas, mainly those distant from urban hubs, to attract and accommodate digital nomads. We will investigate the specific strategies and initiatives undertaken by various regions in Japan, focusing intently on the administrative and managerial practices that underpin these efforts. Rather than spotlighting well-known destinations like Chiang Mai (Thailand) and Bali (Indonesia), this research will highlight Japan's distinct initiatives and projects designed to create an inviting environment for contemporary travellers embracing the digital nomad lifestyle.

CASE STUDY

Research Method

This research endeavours to provide a comprehensive understanding of how rural areas—distinct from traditional urban centres—successfully attract and cater to the needs of digital nomads. It seeks to investigate the strategies these regions implement to create conducive environments and systems that support the lifestyle and preferences of this emerging demographic. Prior studies focused on the outcomes of various initiatives to welcome digital nomads, concluding primarily from completed projects and their respective results. However, there has been a notable lack of focus on the underlying processes and methodologies that led to the development of these initiatives. Gaining insights into these processes is critical for informing and enhancing future efforts to attract digital nomads to rural settings.

To address this gap in knowledge, this research adopts a Participatory Action Research (PAR) approach, which emphasises collaboration and active involvement of various stakeholders in the research process. The researcher will monitor tours explicitly designed to attract digital nomads as part of this approach. These tours are scheduled for February, September, and November 2024, allowing in-depth exploration of the region's appeal during different times. Furthermore, the researcher will participate in monthly planning meetings beginning in June 2024. These sessions will be pivotal for conceptualising and refining the project plan, facilitating collaboration among local stakeholders, and aligning community efforts with the needs of digital nomads.

The qualitative data collection will be robust and multifaceted, primarily relying on in-depth interviews with diverse participants. This will include local government officials who shape policy, business owners who provide services and amenities, community managers who facilitate local engagement, and digital nomads who experience the region firsthand. These interviews aim to capture a wide range of perspectives and insights. In addition to interviews, the analysis will encompass relevant program documents and reports associated with the initiative, further enriching the data context.

To ensure a comprehensive evaluation of both the region's offerings and the effectiveness of the programs in place, triangulation will be employed. This process will synthesise information from various sources, paying careful attention to the viewpoints of both the host community and the digital nomads who participate. By integrating these perspectives, the research aims to develop a nuanced understanding of how rural areas can effectively attract and serve the unique needs of digital nomads, ultimately contributing to the sustainable development of these regions.

The Research Site: Hyuga, Miyazaki - From Workation to Digital Nomads

Digital nomads are primarily engaged in high-value sectors, including artificial intelligence (AI), software development, and digital design. In addition to their role as consumers contributing to local tourism economies, they act as potent catalysts for regional economic development, facilitating knowledge exchange and entrepreneurial activities. Recognising these valuable contributions, numerous countries have implemented targeted initiatives—such as digital nomad visas and attractive fiscal incentives—to draw this demographic. Estonia, for instance, took the lead by launching its Digital Nomad Visa in 2020, permitting remote workers to reside for up to a year. Following suit, countries like Portugal and Croatia have developed comprehensive programs aimed at seamlessly integrating digital nomads into their local economies.

In a significant move, Japan introduced the "Special Activity Visa for Digital Nomads and Their Spouses" in April 2024, enabling international remote workers to stay for periods of up to six months. This initiative reflects Japan's growing recognition of the pivotal role digital nomads play in both its tourism strategy and broader economic revitalisation efforts. To further this agenda, the Japan Tourism Agency selected five pilot regions—including Hyuga City in Miyazaki Prefecture in July 2024—to develop models conducive to attracting digital nomads. These efforts entail substantial enhancements in regional infrastructure to accommodate nomads, promote long-term business development, and stimulate regional revitalisation through tailored support programs.

Japan faces significant structural challenges, such as an ageing population, the centralisation of urban life in Tokyo, and depopulation issues in rural areas. In response to these pressing realities, local governments are turning their attention to expanding what is known as "related populations" (kankeijinkō)—individuals who maintain sustainable connections with a region through repeated visits or active participation in local engagements without establishing permanent residency. Within this context, digital nomads emerge as a novel and prominent form of related population, known for fostering strong relationships with local communities during their extended stays. Their economic participation and social engagement play a crucial role in sustaining critical infrastructure in areas grappling with depopulation.

Moreover, the presence of digital nomads is instrumental in addressing fundamental challenges faced by Japan's regional development, particularly in regions where generating permanent population growth proves difficult. Digital nomads offer innovative solutions to revitalise rural areas, encouraging community involvement and enhancing interregional collaboration. This unique potential positions them as key players in reshaping Japan's approach to sustainable regional development, paving the way for a more integrated and vibrant future.

Hyuga City, nestled in the southern part of Kyushu, is a charming city with approximately 60,000 residents. Like many areas in Japan, it faces the challenge of a declining population, having experienced a reduction of about 2,000 people, or roughly 13.5%, between 2015 and 2020. Renowned for its fertile agricultural land, the city benefits from a warm climate, making it a vital agricultural hub. Additionally, Hyuga is a key logistics centre, with its operations centred around the bustling Hososhima Port. The city's picturesque coastal region, designated as a national park, is celebrated for its breathtaking scenery and as a revered surfing destination, attracting enthusiasts from near and far.

Despite its alluring natural surroundings, Hyuga City is relatively distant from major metropolitan areas like Tokyo and Kyoto, historically limiting the influx of international tourists. However, the city is actively working to change this by positioning itself as a prime destination for digital nomads. This initiative is rooted in an existing workation acceptance project that Hyuga launched in response to the shifts brought about by the COVID-19 pandemic in 2020.

Since then, Hyuga City has made significant strides in promoting workation opportunities. In 2021, the city received a grant to revitalise the region through telework initiatives. The following year, it hosted the 'Workation Collective Impact 2022' event, coordinated by the Workation Local Government Council and the Ministry of Internal Affairs and Communications. Moreover, Hyuga was selected as a model demonstration area for the Japan Tourism Agency's 'Workation Promotion Project' in 2022 and earned certification as a model area for the 'Workation Dissemination Promotion Project' in 2023. These accolades underscore the city's commitment to innovative approaches that foster workation, garnering support from the national government.

The tangible impact of Hyuga's workation initiative is evident in its user statistics. The number of workation participants skyrocketed from 76 in 2020 to 270 in 2021—a staggering increase of 355.3%. In 2022, participation surged again to 727, representing a notable growth of 269.3% compared to the previous year. By mid-2023, there were already 500 users, bringing the total number of participants over four years to an impressive 1,600 individuals from 110 different companies.

From an economic perspective, the influence of the workation program is quite significant. According to the 2021 Miyazaki Prefecture Tourism Visitor Survey, out-of-prefecture day-trippers spent an average of 6,500 yen daily. However, participants in the 2022 Japan Tourism Agency model project exhibited a much higher daily expenditure of 21,300 yen—an astonishing 327.7% increase. These figures reflect the positive ripple effect of the workation project on the local economy.

Central to promoting workation in Hyuga is the 'Hyuga City Workation Promotion Council.' This organisation has been instrumental in establishing a framework for workation since its predecessor, the 'Hyuga City Workation Registration Cooperation Facilities and Groups,' was founded in 2021. The council currently boasts 23 diverse members, including accommodation providers, restaurants, coworking spaces, and organisations offering experiential programs throughout Hyuga City. Together, they collaborate with public and private sectors to elevate the workation experience, illustrating Hyuga's dedication to innovation and economic revitalisation.

In 2020, Hyuga City embarked on an innovative journey by launching workation initiatives to integrate work and leisure. By 2023, these efforts had expanded to welcome inbound digital nomads, marking a significant development in the city's approach to remote working. In February 2024, Hyuga hosted a unique monitor tour that brought together five digital nomads from four diverse countries: Italy, Ukraine, Indonesia, and Korea. This four-day event showcased the city's potential as a haven for remote workers.

Participants in this immersive experience included international digital nomads, regional coordinators, university staff, and representatives from the Japan Digital Nomad Association and the Japan Workation Association. Despite its brevity, the tour offered a rich tapestry of activities that allowed attendees to explore the vibrant culture of Hyuga City. They enjoyed surfing at a renowned local surf spot, experienced the thrill of fishing, and stayed in cosy local accommodations. Using a coworking space enabled them to blend productivity with their penchant for exploration, while interactions with locals provided a deeper understanding of the community.

One of the tour's highlights was the carefully curated cultural experiences that went beyond the typical workation offerings. Participants could don traditional kimono and wander through the picturesque streets of a district recognised as an Important Preservation District for Groups of Historic Buildings. They immersed themselves in Japanese arts by participating in calligraphy sessions and crafting shimenawa (sacred rope) at a locally revered temple designated for its scenic beauty. To ensure that these valuable experiences could be showcased to future visitors, all activities were documented and published on Hyuga City's official website for promotional purposes.

In preparation for future initiatives, the Hyuga City Workation Promotion Council members engaged in the JDNA Community Manager Academy (CMA), hosted by the Japan Digital Nomad Association. This involvement aimed to enhance their knowledge and expand professional networks, laying the groundwork for future digital nomad hosting.

While overall, the monitor tour was a success, participants reported a few challenges that reflected common issues faced by travellers. Language barriers and currency conversion did not pose significant hurdles, but concerns related to safety were paramount. Through feedback from the digital nomads, several key areas for improvement were identified.

Firstly, the coworking spaces were described as somewhat cramped, and there was a noticeable scarcity of authentic Japanese cuisine in the nearby commercial areas. This highlighted a distinct need tailored to the preferences of international workationers. Secondly, participants expressed concerns regarding accommodation options. Issues around security and privacy in shared living spaces and a lack of incentives for long-term stays emerged as significant points of contention. There was a need for accommodation plans that catered specifically to the unique lifestyle of digital nomads.

Another critical enhancement area was the tour schedule's clarity and flexibility. Participants found that insufficient advance information limited their freedom to explore leisurely. Given the potential need to prioritise work due to time zone differences, a clear and flexible stay plan was deemed essential for future iterations. Furthermore, challenges in rural areas surfaced, such as the necessity for accessible domestic transport from international airports, effective safety management, and English-language support for legal compliance. There was a strong call for the development of local coordinators proficient in multiple languages to address these challenges.

In conclusion, this monitor tour represented a pivotal moment for Hyuga City. It provided a wealth of insights into how the city could leverage its domestic workation experiences to attract and cater to the growing demographic of digital nomads. The feedback received will serve as a foundation for evolving and enhancing their offerings, ensuring a welcoming and enriching environment for future visitors.

Digital Nomads Promotion and Monitor Tour in 2024

Leveraging its extensive experience, Hyuga City has been chosen as one of five model projects nationwide for an innovative demonstration initiative to attract digital nomads. This initiative is part of Japan's broader effort to promote remote work, encapsulated by the 'Digital Nomad Visa' launch in April 2024. A key focus of Hyuga City's model project is the local digital nomad workation monitor tour. This tour is designed to explore the unique business potential of local workation opportunities, which significantly differ from the bustling urban workation scenes typically found near international airports and large-scale facilities. This project aims to understand the specific needs and challenges faced by digital nomads residing in this charming locale.

To achieve this aims, the project aspires to foster the idea of a 'second home' in Hyuga City, facilitating interactions between local communities and visiting digital nomads. By aligning the needs of these nomads with the unique offerings of the area—also tied to local cultural content—the project aims to create a welcoming environment that encourages a sense of belonging and return. Additionally, it seeks to enhance domestic tourism by promoting collaboration across broader regions and encouraging exchanges among digital nomads. The initiative targets explicitly surfers, digital nomads, and local residents, with a strategic emphasis on improving the overall experience and infrastructure available to them.

A unique feature of this monitor tour is its full subsidisation of costs during the stay, including accommodations and coworking facilities. This initiative is not just about economic growth; it sets measurable goals, outlined through four key performance indicators (KPIs): (1) a participant satisfaction rate of 90%, (2) an average local consumption of 200,000 yen per person over 14 days, (3) the involvement of 40 local businesses in exchange events, and (4) training participation of 50 individuals in coordinator seminars.

An essential element for the success of this project is the involvement of digital nomad influencers in the monitor tour. These influencers, known for actively sharing their travel experiences on platforms such as Instagram and Facebook, play a pivotal role in raising awareness about Japan's embracing of digital nomads. They often belong to or influence communities seeking cost-effective destinations that still offer a conducive environment for work and leisure. By showcasing the hidden gems of Hyuga City, these influencers can effectively promote its unique appeal to prospective digital nomads.

The project includes two carefully planned monitor tours. Participants include surfers based in Bali and influencers from South Korea, all drawn to the allure of Hyuga City. The primary facilities utilised during these tours consist of one coliving space and two coworking environments, providing visitors with a comfortable and productive atmosphere.

The Hyuga City Workation Promotion Council leads the organisation and facilitates preparations for digital nomads arriving in the area. This organisation has developed a robust network to connect experts in international exchange and community management with those experienced in hosting workation participants.

The first monitor tour took place from September 16th to September 29th, 2024, welcoming five digital nomads, including three influencers, primarily drawn from the local surfing cohort. The second tour, held from November 25th to December 9th, 2024, catered to 12 digital nomads from South Korea, including two influencers, with one individual participating throughout the entire duration.

A diverse array of programs enriched each monitor tour. Of the 14-day itinerary, certain activities were mandatory, fostering deeper connections through resident exchanges and business networking events. Other programming options, such as fishing and surfing, were available for participants based on their interests, work commitments, or fluctuating weather conditions.

Below is some supplementary information about the content and aims of the programme.

- Night Culture

One key factor for attracting digital nomads is the availability of "night culture," a feature highly valued by many digital nomads. As part of the monitoring tour, participants will experience Japan's unique "snack" bars, a concept unfamiliar to many foreigners and considered a distinct aspect of Japanese culture. Miyazaki Prefecture is known for having the highest density of snack bars in Japan, and these establishments are deeply embedded in the culture of Hyuga City. This program will include business networking events in collaboration with economic organizations, where participants will connect with local businesses and startups. By integrating the night culture experience into these events, the program aims to deepen interactions and enhance the potential for successful business matching.

- Surfing

As "surfer digital nomads" represent a primary target group for this initiative, many participants are expected to engage in daily surfing activities independently, even if not included in the monitoring tour. A beginner-friendly surfing school will be offered for beginners or non-surfer digital nomads. This initiative seeks to familiarize participants with Hyuga City and foster opportunities for interaction between local surfers and digital nomads. Surf shop operators and local surfers will be involved in the program, creating a platform for meaningful exchanges. This connection, facilitated by beginner participants, will enhance satisfaction among surfer digital nomads and establish stronger ties with the local community, encouraging future visits.

- Symposium

A "Local Digital Nomad Symposium" will be held to promote digital nomad initiatives domestically. The role of government in such efforts is significant, and similar to the spread of workation practices, municipalities strongly demand foundational information and guidance. The symposium, accessible to municipalities nationwide via a hybrid format, will feature easily understandable content for beginners. The program includes panel discussions by domestic digital nomad experts and municipal staff and discussions by participating digital nomads about their workation experiences in Hyuga City.

- Village Visit Tour / Tour

In collaboration with the Shiiha Village Tourism Association, part of one of Japan's "Three Great Remote Areas" and a recognized "World Agricultural Heritage" site, the program will explore the potential for regional tourism centred around Hyuga City as a base camp. This initiative aims to create a success story of regional tourism collaboration triggered by digital nomad attraction. By fostering broader cooperation between Hyuga City, Shiiha Village, and the Hyuga and Higashi Usuki regions, the program aspires to establish a "Regional Collaboration DMO" to address tourism challenges. Additionally, a collaborative tour with Beppu City, Japan's largest hot spring destination and a leader in workation practices, will evaluate the potential for digital nomads to explore a "Golden Route" across East Kyushu, combining tourism and business programming.

- Business Exchange

In partnership with economic organizations, business exchange events will address local companies' digital challenges and foster new community formation through interactions. In Hyuga City, participating companies will present their businesses and challenges, while digital nomads will share their initiatives, exploring potential business opportunities. Selection criteria for participating companies will emphasize elements unique to Hyuga City, such as the use of marine and forest resources, to enhance regional problem-solving efforts and business opportunities. As part of a broader evaluation of domestic digital nomad mobility, collaboration with Beppu City and B-biz LINK will facilitate business exchanges with local companies and higher education institutions in the Beppu area. This partnership aims to create business opportunities with startups and other organizations in Beppu, a leading region for innovation while building momentum for mutual visitor exchanges and attraction efforts in the fields of workation and digital nomadism.

Throughout the tours, dedicated staff from Hyuga City and the Hyuga City Workation Promotion Council provided seamless transportation to and from accommodations, coworking spaces, and various program venues, ensuring a smooth and enjoyable experience for all participants.

Table 1. Objectives in the Hyuga City model project

second home	Interaction between local communities and digital nomads.
Creating an awareness of revisiting	Matching through content discovery and creation and potential research in Hyuga City.
Domestic excursions	Wide-area cooperation in domestic workcations and reciprocal sending of digital nomads.
Surfer/local digital nomad	Clarification of targets and use of local resources (coast and city size) in Hyuga

Table 2. Digital nomad influencers participating in the monitoring tour

		nationality	occupation	role	length of one's stay
A	1st.	Indonesia	Coliving Community Manager	Surfing Digital Nomads.	14 days
B	1st.	Italy	programmer	Surfing Digital Nomads.	14 days
C	1st.	Ukraine	Marketer	Surfing Digital Nomads.	14 days
D	2nd.	Korea	Coliving manager	Korean Digital Nomads.	14 days
E	2nd.	Korea	Coliving Manager	Korean Companies	14 days

Table 3. Acceptance environment

<table>
<tr><td rowspan="2">Work Place</td><td>Surf Office</td><td>A central working space in the country's workcation, located next to one of the country's best surf spots and beaches. It uses smart locks for entry and exit and is available 24 hours a day.</td></tr>
<tr><td>STAIRS OF THE SEA</td><td>This is one of the city's most popular commercial facilities adjacent to the Surf Office. It has a café, a burger shop that originated in Hawaii, an Italian restaurant that uses a lot of local ingredients, a gelateria and other restaurants, as well as a souvenir shop and a mini-supermarket, making it a work-cation complex. Although there are restrictions on opening hours, the facility can be used as a workspace for up to 50 people by making use of the rental space and food court within the facility.</td></tr>
<tr><td>Coliving Space</td><td>PUMPING SURF</td><td>Surfers' guesthouse with a strong following among surfers. The owner has lived abroad as a surfer himself and can communicate in English. Kitchen space and co-working space available on site.</td></tr>
</table>

Table 4. Structure of the Hyuga City Workcation Promotion Council

	role	Profile
A	Interpreter and regional coordinator	Accurate interpretation services based on extensive study abroad experience
B	Foreign coordinator	Ambassador in the city's co-working spaces. Canadian businessman with extensive experience as a digital nomad himself. He is also active as a community manager, organising cross-industrial exchange events at the facility.
C	Accommodation support Experience programme provision	Official concierge of the Japan Workers' Association. Refining the attractions of Hyuga City from an 'outside' perspective as an immigrant.
D	Accommodation support Experience programme provision	Certified concierge of the Japan Workers' Association. Owner-chef of an Italian restaurant and representative of a satoyama conservation organisation. Connection with local human resources.
E	Accommodation support Experience programme provision	Former systems engineer and current fisherman; provides DX fishing experience. Organises and provides social events based on the concept of interaction with the local community.

Table 5. Schedule of the monitor tour

Day	First Tour	Second Tour
1	welcome party	welcome party
2	*city tour	supermarket shopping experience *city tour
3	local exchange *trekking	local exchange
4	business exchange(Hyuga) night culture tour *fishing experience/fishers market	*cafe tour
5	*beach stretch/beach clean	*beach walk
6	*surfing	*international exchange *night culture tour
7	*village visit tour (Shiiha)	tour
8	*international exchange	*fishing experience
9	business exchange(Beppu)	business exchange
10	tour(Beppu)	*Japanese calligraphy
11	※local cooking	*local cooking
12	symposium	*local festival
13	farewell party *tea ceremony *Japanese calligraphy	farewell party *kimono experience

Day	First Tour	Second Tour
14	closing session	closing session
	*optional	

Establish self-driven system

At a review meeting for the monitor tour held in February 2024, the author pointed out the three Ss (Surfing, Sushi, Snack) that are the city of Hyuga's strengths in attracting digital nomads.

Hyuga City, a coastal gem in Miyazaki Prefecture, is celebrated for its stunning surf spots that attract both seasoned surfers and beginners alike. The region is well-prepared to welcome travellers, offering a variety of accommodations, including charming guesthouses equipped for long-term stays, making it an ideal destination for those seeking a blend of adventure and comfort. Here, surfing is not merely a sport; it forms an integral part of the community's lifestyle, with locals often seen gliding over the waves at dawn or catching swells just as the sun sets, embracing the soothing rhythm of the ocean before or after a day at work.

Among the diverse group of digital nomads, many are drawn to the idyllic beaches and the chance to catch some waves. Hyuga is a particularly appealing choice, offering a surf culture that differs significantly from more crowded hotspots like Canggu in Bali, where surfers often contend for space in the water. The waves in Hyuga are less congested, providing a serene surfing experience ideal for those just starting. Local surfers are known for their camaraderie, often encouraging newcomers by yielding their turns, fostering an inclusive and supportive environment that makes learning to surf enjoyable and stress-free. This welcoming vibe is particularly evident at Okuragahama, where the beach comes alive with surfers of varying skill levels, creating a lively yet relaxed atmosphere.

Culinary delights are another major draw of Hyuga, with a food culture that proudly showcases the region's specialities, particularly its exquisite sushi. While Miyazaki is famous for its succulent local chicken, the culinary landscape is rich with a wide array of seafood that reflects the ocean's bounty. What truly enhances the dining experience for digital nomads is the opportunity to engage directly with the vibrant fishing culture. They can participate in fishing excursions and experience the thrill of catching fresh fish, not to mention the exhilaration of visiting local fish markets where lively auctions occur. This direct interaction with the sea adds depth to their culinary journey, as they enjoy fresh sushi prepared from their own catches. Furthermore, for those with dietary restrictions, such as a need for halal options, Hyuga accommodates diverse palates with a range of choices, including delicious local chicken, premium beef, and wild boar, ensuring that all visitors find something delectable to enjoy.

Another unique aspect of Hyuga is its vibrant snack bar scene, highlighting the region's bustling nightlife. Miyazaki Prefecture boasts the highest concentration of snack bars in Japan, making it an excellent place for nightlife enthusiasts. These bars offer a distinct experience, diverging from the more commonly known izakaya and traditional bars. Digital nomads often venture into these inviting spaces after dinner, where they can indulge in local delicacies and forge connections with the friendly locals. The atmosphere in snack bars is infused with energy as patrons participate in lively conversations, share stories, and enjoy a variety of snacks and drinks. The music, laughter, and chatter create a unique ambience reminiscent of a neighbourhood gathering.

Being attuned to the local night culture is essential for those planning an extended stay. Engaging with the community means understanding its rhythms, which may include everything from dance parties to live DJ events. This cultural exchange enriches the experience for digital nomads, allowing them to connect with the local way of life and forge meaningful relationships. As they immerse themselves in surfing, savour the local cuisine, and partake in the spirited nightlife, digital nomads find that Hyuga City offers a beautiful place to work remotely and a vibrant culture that fosters a sense of belonging and adventure. Hyuga City is a vibrant haven for surfing enthusiasts in Miyazaki Prefecture, renowned for its picturesque coastline and inviting surf spots. The area is well-equipped to cater to the needs of surfers, boasting a range of accommodations, including cosy guesthouses perfect for extended stays. This coastal paradise attracts many surfers and embodies a culture where the waves are woven into the rhythm of daily life, with locals often catching morning swells before or after their work commitments.

Among the diverse tribe of digital nomads, many seek a beachside sanctuary, and Hyuga uniquely appeals to this crowd. Surfers have noted that the waters here are relatively uncrowded compared to hotspots like Canggu in Bali, which often swells with fellow surf seekers. This tranquil environment fosters a welcoming atmosphere where even beginners can thrive, as the local surfers readily share the waves. On any given day, the picturesque Okuragahama beach is alive, with riders enjoying the gentle surf.

The culinary scene in Miyazaki adds yet another layer of allure to this coastal destination, with sushi taking centre stage. While Miyazaki is celebrated for its delectable local chicken, the seafood offers a bountiful variety that delights the senses. The appeal goes beyond simply savouring fresh dishes; digital nomads have the unique opportunity to immerse themselves in the local fishing culture, experiencing market auctions and enjoying the fruits of their labour. This rich connection to the sea offers a captivating glimpse into life on the coast, ensuring that even those with dietary restrictions—such as halal—can relish the flavours of the region. Fresh local chicken, prime cuts of beef, and wild boar provide satisfying alternatives for those not inclined towards seafood.

Adding to the charm of Hyuga is its vibrant snack culture, which serves as a cornerstone of nighttime entertainment. Miyazaki Prefecture boasts Japan's highest concentration of snack bars per capita, turning evenings into lively social outings. Digital nomads often find themselves stepping into these unique establishments after dinner, mingling with locals in an inviting atmosphere that distinguishes them from traditional izakaya or nightlife spots. The snack bar experience offers an enigmatic blend of culinary delights and local camaraderie, where the interplay of music and movement flourishes.

Engaging with the local community and understanding the dynamics of night culture—including dancing and live DJ performances—becomes essential for those considering a long stay. As digital nomads navigate their adventure in this captivating locale, the vibrant culture around them promises to enrich their experience beyond surfing and dining, creating lasting connections with the sea and its people.

The common theme among all these points is 'community.' The integration of the local community with the digital nomad community will enable the project to take root and potentially develop into a world-class advanced region. Other experts have noted several important factors regarding the attraction of digital nomads:

(1) The most crucial aspect is establishing a system that the local community can sustainably, rather than solely aiming for the social impact typically targeted in urban areas.
(2) Regions that have successfully attracted digital nomads usually have a mature community that facilitates this acceptance; however, it is essential to recognise that the goals of workations and digital nomads differ.
(3) Lastly, it was emphasised that remote areas hold the key to success, focusing more on the unique experiences and connections made rather than simply the destination itself.

This project and the accompanying monitor tour are designed to establish a self-sustaining system in each region for future operations. To achieve this, the city of Hyuga proactively engages in both the application and implementation phases, orchestrating efforts to develop a comprehensive system, as depicted in Figure 1. Central to this initiative are the city of Hyuga and the Hyuga City Workation Promotion Council, which are expected to lead the charge.

In the realm of business, several key organisations will collaborate closely to ensure effective coordination. These include the Hyuga Chamber of Commerce and Industry, the Hyuga City Small and Medium Enterprise Support Organization, and the Hyuga City Industrial Support Center, Himuka-Biz. Together, they will foster a thriving business environment.

On the tourism front, the general incorporated association Hyuga City Tourism Association will serve as a pivotal hub, facilitating various tourism-related activities. Furthermore, the Hyuga City Commerce and Industry Department will be instrumental in promoting collaboration within Hyuga and with neighbouring regions. This collaboration will extend to organisations like the Shiibamura Tourism Association, Beppu City, the Beppu City Industry Collaboration and Cooperation Platform, and B-biz LINK.

The Hyuga City Commerce, Industry and Harbor Division will also act as a crucial bridge, connecting diverse government departments responsible for immigration, agriculture, forestry, fisheries, culture, tourism, and exchange. This integration will involve close partnerships with private sector entities, particularly those centred around the Hyuga City Workation Promotion Council.

Additionally, the city will engage with external organisations dedicated to promoting and increasing awareness of digital nomad lifestyles. Key partnerships will include collaborations with the Japan Workation Association and the Japan Digital Nomad Association. Recognising the growing trend of workationers, efforts will also focus on welcoming overseas professionals, with Digital Nomad Korea positioned as a central hub for these activities. Through these multifaceted initiatives, Hyuga aims to create a vibrant, interconnected environment supporting local and global workation communities.

Figure 1. Structure for Attracting Digital Nomads in Hyuga City

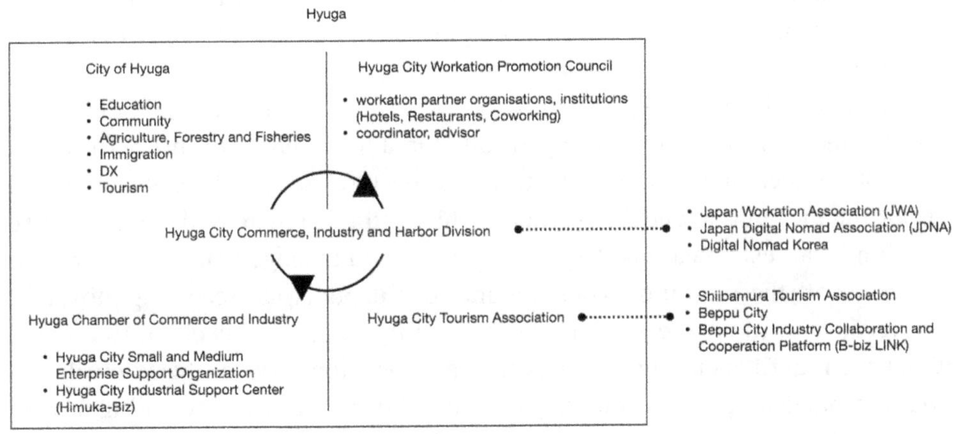

EMPIRICAL FINDINGS

The digital nomad attraction project, including the monitor tour in Hyuga City, has provided much knowledge about the administrative and operational side, which was lacking in the past when local areas in Japan tried to attract digital nomads. Hyuga City has accumulated experience and various tourism resources. For example, the shopping experience at the supermarket in the programme shows that even everyday life in Japan can be content for digital nomads. This was born from the observations of the staff who accompanied the monitor tour, and it shows the importance of carefully interacting with them from a different perspective to that of conventional domestic workation and tourism.

From the results of the interviews and observations, we can point out three issues in the acceptance of digital nomads in rural areas of Japan: (1)' secondary transportation measures' unique to regional cities, (2) issues arising from daily life, and (3) the literacy of the receiving side (human resource development).

(1) Mobility Challenges for Digital Nomads and Workation Participants

One of the key issues identified for international digital nomads and local participants in domestic workations is the challenge of obtaining and using an international driver's license. This challenge is particularly evident for those traveling from overseas, but it also affects individuals from urban areas engaged in domestic workations. In previous pilot tours, the reliance on staff to transport participants was critical in facilitating mobility. While participants did not incur any costs for transportation or face the burden of arranging their own travel, their freedom to move about the area was significantly constrained.

For instance, during the second pilot tour, a particular family brought their four-year-old child, who was successfully enrolled in a local nursery school. However, this situation necessitated that city staff take on the additional responsibility of transporting the child to and from school, which led to an increased administrative burden on local resources. The local government and management are better positioned to absorb these additional burdens and costs in pilot tours receiving subsidies.

Nevertheless, to ensure the long-term viability of such projects in the region without external financial support, it is critical to develop services that allow digital nomads to navigate their surroundings easily. This could involve creating a more compact living environment that caters specifically to the needs of these travellers. Multiple participants expressed that the limitations around mobility hindered their ability to balance work with leisure activities, highlighting the need for better communication about existing transportation options and the possibility of enhancing mobility solutions in the area.

(2) Language Barriers and Communication in Japan

Language presents a significant barrier in Japan, particularly for digital nomads seeking to integrate into local communities and professional environments. Despite the increasing frequency of translation devices and the use of body language to facilitate basic communication in day-to-day interactions, there is a demand for more proficient English skills in business contexts and cross-cultural understanding scenarios. Securing the necessary technology and human resources to bridge this gap remains a formidable challenge.

Moreover, the issue of time differences complicates matters further. Many digital nomads work for companies based in Western countries, resulting in a misalignment of working hours that can hinder productivity and collaboration. Thus, it is crucial to ensure the availability of office spaces and accommodations that support constant connectivity and allow for meetings with clients at all hours.

Existing accommodation facilities in the area currently face capacity constraints, which exacerbates the challenges digital nomads experience. Participants highlighted the need for co-living spaces that accommodate long-term stays and facilitate community engagement, explicitly tailored to their unique lifestyle requirements.

One of the most pressing needs identified among participants was the establishment of facilities designed to foster community building. Creating opportunities for meaningful interactions between digital nomads and local residents and developing cultural experience programs could significantly enhance the understanding of local culture and customs. However, it is also vital to consider the financial sustainability of coworking spaces and community engagement initiatives, which may require initial governmental support to establish a solid foundation.

(3) Enhancing Host Community Literacy and Integration

Addressing issues related to mobility and language, a third significant area of concern is the improvement of literacy and human resource development within the host community. While recruiting interpreters and coordinators is beneficial, the more pressing objective is to cultivate awareness among local residents regarding how they can create meaningful connections with digital nomads.

The monitoring tour conducted in Hyuga City served as a model for facilitating these connections, mainly through interactions with the local surfing community and business professionals. This approach resulted in noteworthy outcomes, such as the establishment of individual exchanges outside of the official tour schedule and fostering an environment conducive to networking and collaboration.

To enhance these community engagement efforts further, it is essential to develop targeted programs and facilities and train digital nomad coordinators who can effectively orchestrate activities that encourage interactions between digital nomads and locals. The experiences in Hyuga City, which is recognised as a pioneering region in this endeavour, have highlighted these emerging issues and underscored the importance of a structured approach to community integration.

One significant challenge facing the promotion of the workation project is identifying suitable successors for the organisations that have been driving this initiative. Since 2020, the city has actively engaged in developing a robust system to foster workation opportunities, yielding substantial progress. To capitalise on this foundation and ensure sustainable growth, uncovering and nurturing new stakeholders within the region is crucial. This includes cultivating a diverse pool of human resources to support the ongoing operations and strategic development of a comprehensive program that attracts digital nomads. This initiative should extend beyond merely assisting individual businesses or governmental entities to foster a cohesive regional impetus that benefits the community as a whole.

Additionally, establishing clear impact and Key Performance Indicator (KPI) targets for the workation project presents another pivotal challenge. There exists a delicate balance to maintain: on the one hand, an excessive influx of digital nomads can overwhelm the existing local infrastructure and strain staff resources, potentially diminishing service quality and overall experience. Conversely, if the intake of digital nomads is insufficient, the potential benefits to the local economy and community engagement may fall short, hindering the project's intended impact. Therefore, it is essential to strike a harmonious balance that maximises benefits without overextending resources.

Moreover, ensuring the quality of outsourced services poses another critical issue within the project framework. Attracting and accommodating digital nomads encompasses a broad range of tasks, necessitating a significant degree of outsourcing, particularly in regions lacking in-house management capacity. In the specific case of this survey, it was observed that several selected regions scheduled their monitoring tours simultaneously, which led to a concentration of requests for human resource development and influencer recruitment directed at a limited number of companies and organisations. This bottleneck occasionally resulted in subpar outcomes, where the delivered services did not meet the anticipated initial standards of quality and timeliness.

To address these concerns moving forward, assessing and determining the appropriate level of service supply that each region can realistically provide is imperative. Additionally, there should be an emphasis on expanding and diversifying the range of entities involved in the project, ensuring that a broader spectrum of capabilities and resources is available to meet the varying demands associated with attracting and supporting digital nomads. This strategic approach is vital for fostering resiliency and adaptability within the workation initiative, ultimately enhancing its potential for success.

DISCUSSION AND IMPLICATION

The implications of this research indicate several key points worth considering regarding the interplay between digital nomads and local communities in Japan.

Local communities across Japan are optimistic about the potential economic benefits that digital nomads can bring. They anticipate that these individuals will contribute to the local economy by spending, engaging with and enriching the social fabric of their communities. However, it is essential to recognise that digital nomads often prioritise their professional activities and unique lifestyles, placing a premium on flexibility and independence.

A clear and tangible context must be established to foster meaningful relationships between digital nomads and local communities. This context should demonstrate how collaboration and social engagement can yield mutual benefits, specifically in reducing environmental impacts and generating social value. Additionally, it is crucial to highlight the opportunities for digital nomads to participate in local business ventures, emphasising the value they could add.

The Japanese digital nomad visa currently includes restrictions on engaging in direct business activities within the country. To address this limitation, it will be important to devise strategies that involve collaboration with relevant government ministries, local authorities, and businesses. A synergistic approach that integrates visa requirements with startup visas could pave the way for more fruitful engagements.

Looking ahead to 2025, as Japan, South Korea, and Taiwan introduce new visa programs aimed at attracting digital nomads, it is anticipated that the competition to lure these individuals will intensify across the East Asian region. However, emerging challenges have also been noted in areas that have successfully attracted digital nomads. To avert such challenges and ensure harmonious coexistence, it is crucial to develop a comprehensive long-term strategy that promotes the attraction of digital nomads and fosters inter-regional cooperation.

Key strategies include sharing best practices among regions, standardising services offered to nomads, and facilitating mobility across multiple destinations for a seamless experience. Such measures are expected to significantly enhance the overall quality of the tourism and business environment in the region.

Furthermore, as this study underscores, the role of community managers—individuals who deeply understand both the digital nomad lifestyle and local community needs—is vital for nurturing sustainable relationships. However, there is currently a lack of structured training for these community managers. Addressing this gap will require sharing insights and expertise from leading regions and establishing a comprehensive training program. This program should aim to standardise training content to ensure quality and effectiveness.

Since developing human resources is time-intensive, an immediate and practical approach would involve designing and disseminating frameworks for exchange programs. For example, while local events that facilitate interaction between digital nomads and residents have been organised, they have often lacked a strategic design and have been overly reliant on the facilitators' individual skills. To optimise these exchanges, creating and sharing structured scenarios and formats that encourage engagement is essential, thereby alleviating the burden on facilitators and enhancing the likelihood of positive outcomes in each community.

CONCLUSION

This study presents significant findings on promoting and integrating digital nomads into rural areas of Japan, offering a thorough empirical examination of the dynamic relationship between these remote workers and the local communities they inhabit. It delves into the various types of resources and forms of capital that can be harnessed to facilitate the transition from temporary workation options to sustained attraction and acceptance of digital nomads within Japan's rural landscapes.

The context of this research is intertwined with the ongoing efforts related to regional revitalisation, which frequently target workation initiatives in Japan. These initiatives aim to cater to the desires of digital nomads seeking an environment that starkly contrasts the over-commercialised and congested tourism hotspots prevalent in many Japanese cities. It highlights how rural regions may offer tranquillity, natural beauty, and unique cultural experiences typically attractive to this demographic.

However, the study also emphasises that while concepts such as mobility, community, and human resource development are promoted in domestic workation strategies in Japan, there are critical distinctions that necessitate careful consideration. This nuanced approach ensures that digital nomads' specific needs and expectations are adequately addressed while fostering meaningful interactions with the local populace.

Furthermore, this research contributes a fresh perspective to the field of digital nomad studies, which has traditionally focused on the nomads themselves. By engaging with the administrative and management frameworks that support these rural areas, the study uncovers new dimensions in the dialogue surrounding digital nomadism, advocating for a more holistic understanding of the phenomenon.

The case study of Hyuga City yielded particularly insightful findings, demonstrating the potential benefits and challenges faced when integrating digital nomads into local communities. However, to derive conclusions that have broader applicability, it is crucial to conduct comprehensive research across various regions, including urban environments. Additionally, the investigation into how Japan's unique sociocultural factors influence the success or failure of these integration initiatives is essential. Such an analysis promises to provide critical insights into how digital nomads can be effectively integrated into varied local contexts, ultimately leading to more prosperous and more sustainable communities.

REFERENCES

Agniera, I. G. A. A., Pella, F. A., & Halim, E. (2023). *Local Perceptions Towards Foreigners Digital Nomads in Bali*. DOI: 10.1109/ICoSNIKOM60230.2023.10364406

Andino-Frydman, A. (2023). *Who is a Digital Nomad?* The Evolving Identities of the New Nomadic Workforce., DOI: 10.1108/S0277-283320230000035005

Arslan, E. (2024). From tourists to nomads: Unveiling the transformative potential of digital nomads in travel and tourism. *Worldwide Hospitality and Tourism Themes*, *16*(3), 269–281. Advance online publication. DOI: 10.1108/WHATT-03-2024-0046

Asahi, S. (2024). Analysis of the Impact of Overtourism in Japan: The Effects of Congestion Phenomena. In *Econometric Analysis of Regional Economy*. Springer., DOI: 10.1007/978-981-99-8707-8_3

Bozzi, A. D. (2024). Digital nomadism from the perspective of places and mobilities: A literature review. *European Transport Research Review*, *16*(1), 50. Advance online publication. DOI: 10.1186/s12544-024-00663-z

Choi, J. W., & Qu, J. (2024). *An Empirical Study on the Rise of Digital Nomad and Workcation Ecosystems: Focusing on the Case of Thailand*. DOI: 10.17086/JTS.2024.48.8.121.150

Christiansen, R. A., Ihalauw, J. J. O. I., Kriestian, A. N.A.N., Purwati, Y. SE. (2023). Developing Digital Nomads as a New Market Segment and Their Role in the Local Digital Ecosystem. *Journal of System and Management Sciences*. DOI: 10.33168/JSMS.2023.0201

Cook, D. (2020). The freedom trap: Digital nomads and the use of disciplining practices to manage work/leisure boundaries. *Information Technology & Tourism*, *22*(3), 355–390. DOI: 10.1007/s40558-020-00172-4

Cook, D. (2023). What is a digital nomad? Definition and taxonomy in the era of mainstream remote work. *World Leisure Journal*, *65*(2), 256–275. DOI: 10.1080/16078055.2023.2190608

Edwards, S. E. (2021). *"If you can work from anywhere, why work anywhere else?": flexible citizenship, regimes of mobility, and the discourse of digital nomadism*. DOI: 10.5210/spir.v2021i0.11906

Ehn, K., Jorge, A., & Marques-Pita, M. (2022). Digital Nomads and the Covid-19 Pandemic: Narratives About Relocation in a Time of Lockdowns and Reduced Mobility. *Social Media + Society*, *8*(1), 20563051221084958. Advance online publication. DOI: 10.1177/20563051221084958

Hannonen, O. (2020). In search of a digital nomad: Defining the phenomenon. *Information Technology & Tourism*, *22*(3), 335–353. Advance online publication. DOI: 10.1007/s40558-020-00177-z

Hannonen, O. (2022).*Towards an Understanding of Digital Nomadic Mobilities*. DOI: 10.3167/TRANS.2022.120310

Hannonen, O., Quintana, T. A., & Lehto, X. Y. (2023). A supplier side view of digital nomadism: The case of destination Gran Canaria. *Tourism Management*, *97*, 104744. DOI: 10.1016/j.tourman.2023.104744

Hermann, I., & Paris, C. M. (2020). Digital Nomadism: The nexus of remote working and travel mobility. *Information Technology & Tourism*, *22*(3), 329–334. Advance online publication. DOI: 10.1007/s40558-020-00188-w

Horiuchi, S., & Morishige, M. (2024).*Affiliative nomads in Japan: potential sustainable tourism stakeholders in depopulated rural areas*. DOI: 10.3389/frsut.2024.1329856

Ili, B., & Büyükbaykal, G. (2022). *Di ji tal göçebe araştirmalarinin bi bli yometri k anali zi*. Nevşehir Hacı Bektaş Veli Üniversitesi SBE Dergisi., DOI: 10.30783/nevsosbilen.1121236

Ji, Y., Kim, S.-M., & Kim, Y. (2024). A Way to Attract Digital Nomads to Tourist Destinations in the New Normal Era. *Sustainability (Basel)*, *16*(6), 2336. DOI: 10.3390/su16062336

Jiwasiddi, A., Schlagwein, D., Cahalane, M., Cecez-Kecmanovic, D., Leong, C., & Ractham, P. (2024). Digital nomadism as a new part of the visitor economy: The case of the "digital nomad capital" Chiang Mai, Thailand. *Information Systems Journal*, *34*(5), 1493–1535. DOI: 10.1111/isj.12496

Kim, H.-J., & Kim, S.-Y. (2023).*A Study on the Operation Direction of Workation in Japan for the Development of Local Areas and the Expansion of Related Populations*. DOI: 10.46396/Kjem..101.7

Kókai, N., & Rétfalvi, D. (2024). Digital Nomads as Engines for Rural Revitalization: The Development Strategy of Pécsdevecser, Hungary (pp. 143–149). https://doi.org/DOI: 10.18485/arh_pt.2024.8.ch16

Kuzheleva-Sagan, I. P., & Spicheva, D. I. (2020).*The Phenomenon of Digital Nomadism in the Modern Interdisciplinary Discourse*. DOI: 10.17223/15617793/454/9

Lee, J.-H., & Kim, N.-J. (2024). *Examining the tourism experiences of Workation travelers*. https://doi.org/DOI: 10.17086/JTS.2024.48.1.13.34

Lhakard, P. (2022). Destination city for digital nomad's in Thailand: A case study of digital nomad community in Chiang Mai. [JHSSS]. *Journal of Humanities and Social Sciences Studies*, *4*(1), 178–188. https://ssrn.com/abstract=4053619. DOI: 10.32996/jhsss.2022.4.1.18

Litchfield, R. C., & Woldoff, R. A. (2023). Digital nomads: Curiosity or trend? *Handbook of Virtual Work*, 186–196. DOI: 10.4337/9781802200508.00018

Makimoto, T., & Manners, D. (1997). *Digital Nomad*. Willey.

Mancinelli, F. (2020). Digital nomads: Freedom, responsibility and the neoliberal order. *Information Technology & Tourism*, *22*(3), 417–437. Advance online publication. DOI: 10.1007/s40558-020-00174-2

Mancinelli, F. (2022).*Digital Nomads*. https://doi.org/DOI: 10.4337/9781800377486.digital.nomads

Mariati, S., Rahmanita, M., Djati, S. P., & Adawiyah, R. (2023). Analysis of Sustainable Tourism Destination Development for Digital Nomads (Comparative Study: Lisbon-Portugal and Canggu, Bali-Indonesia). *Technium Social Sciences Journal*. DOI: 10.47577/tssj.v43i1.8773

Matsushita, K. (2021a). *Workation and the Doubling of Time and Place*. DOI: 10.1007/978-981-16-2425-4_7

Matsushita, K. (2021b). *Workations and Their Impact on the Local Area in Japan*. DOI: 10.1007/978-3-030-62167-4_12

Matsushita, K. (2022). How does the Japanese workcation embrace digital nomadic work style employees? *World Leisure Journal*. Advance online publication. DOI: 10.1080/16078055.2022.2156594

Matsushita, K. (2024). Social problem-solving workation through collaboration between local regions and urban companies: the case of Kamaishi in Japan.*Frontiers in Sustainable Tourism*. DOI: 10.3389/frsut.2024.1337097

Miočević, D. (2024). Baby Come Back: Resident-Digital Nomad Conflicts, Destination Identification, and Revisit Intention. *Journal of Travel Research*. Advance online publication. DOI: 10.1177/00472875231220945

Nakazawa, T. (2023). Toward a Politico-Economic Population Geography: A Critique of *The Shock of a Shrinking Japan*. In Ishikawa, Y. (Ed.), *Japanese Population Geographies II. SpringerBriefs in Population Studies*. Springer., DOI: 10.1007/978-981-99-2076-1_5

Nash, C., Jarrahi, M. H., Sutherland, W., & Phillips, G. (2018). Digital nomads beyond the buzzword: Defining digital nomadic work and Use of digital technologies. In Chowdhury, G., McLeod, J., Gillet, V., & Willett, P. (Eds.), *Transforming digital worlds* (pp. 207–2017). Springer International Publishing. DOI: 10.1007/978-3-319-78105-1_25

Nomad List. (2025) The 2025 State of Digital Nomads https://nomadlist.com/digital-nomad-statistics

Orel, M. (2019). Coworking environments and digital nomadism: Balancing work and leisure whilst on the move. *World Leisure Journal*, *61*(3), 215–227. DOI: 10.1080/16078055.2019.1639275

Partners, M. B. O. (2022). Working from the Road: The Aspirations and Reality for Digital Nomads. https://www.mbopartners.com/state-of-independence/digital-nomads/

Partners, M. B. O. (2024). Digital Nomads - Nomading Normalizes in 2024-www.mbopartners.com/state-of-independence/digital-nomads/

Pipin Oktapiani, N. M., & Putu Mahyuni, L. (2025). Exploring the Canggu-Bali Magnet as a Choice for Digital Nomads. *Dinasti International Journal of Economics, Finance &Amp. Accounting*, *5*(6), 6180–6188. DOI: 10.38035/dijefa.v5i6.3252

Prester, J., Cecez-Kecmanovic, D., & Schlagwein, D. (2019). Becoming a Digital Nomad: Identity Emergence in the Flow of Practice. In *ICIS*.

Pupavac, D., Malbašić, A., & Ivaniš, M. (2023).*Digital Nomads: Croatian Experience*. DOI: 10.31410/ITEMA.2023.249

Rahayu, D. P., Kusumastuti, A., & Puspitosari, W. A. (2022). Sentiment Analysis of Digital Nomad in Indonesia: A Case Study in Bali. *Masyarakat: Jurnal Sosiologi*. DOI: 10.7454/MJS.v26i2.13685

Rakhmetulina, Z., Suleimenova, A. O., & Abylaykhanova, T. A. (2024). «Digital nomads» in the modern labour market.*Central Asian Economic Review*. DOI: 10.52821/2789-4401-2024-2-89-101

Reichenberger, I. (2018). Digital nomads – a quest for holistic freedom in work and leisure. *Annals of Leisure Research*, *21*(3), 364–380. Advance online publication. DOI: 10.1080/11745398.2017.1358098

Sánchez-Vergara, J. I., Orel, M., & Capdevila, I. (2023). "Home office is the here and now." Digital nomad visa systems and remote work-focused leisure policies. *World Leisure Journal*, *65*(2), 236–255. DOI: 10.1080/16078055.2023.2165142

Sardinha, L., Vieira, M., de Sousa, Á. S., & Leite, E. (2023). DIGITAL NOMADS—THE CASE OF THE AUTONOMOUS REGION OF MADEIRA. *Journal of Entrepreneurial Researchers*, *1*(2), 55–69. DOI: 10.29073/jer.v1i2.14

Shin, H., Lee, J., & Kim, N. (2024, May). Hwui., & Kim, N.-J. (2023). Workcation (Workation) Travel Experiences, Satisfaction and Revisit Intentions: Focusing on Conceptualization, Scale Development, and Nomological Network. *Journal of Travel Research*, *63*(5), 1150–1168. Advance online publication. DOI: 10.1177/00472875231188717

Teodorovicz, T., & Choudhury, P. (Raj), & Starr, E. (2023). Location Specificity and Geographic Competition for Remote Workers.*Social Science Research Network*. https://doi.org/DOI: 10.2139/ssrn.4467579

Thompson, B. Y. (2018). Digital nomads: Employment in the online gig economy. *Glocalism: Journal Of Culture. Politics and Innovation*, *1*(1). Advance online publication. DOI: 10.12893/gjcpi.2018.1.11

Thompson, B. Y. (2019). The digital nomad lifestyle: (remote) work/leisure balance, privilege, and constructed community. *International Journal of the Sociology of Leisure*, *2*(1-2), 27–42. DOI: 10.1007/s41978-018-00030-y

Voll, K., Gauger, F., & Pfnür, A. (2022). Work from anywhere: traditional workation, coworkation and workation retreats: a conceptual review. *World Leisure Journal*, *65*(2), 150–174. DOI: 10.1080/16078055.2022.2134199

Wibowo, T. O. (2024). Dynamic of Migration lifestyle and settlement of nomad in Bali, Indonesia. *The Indonesian Journal of Geography*, *56*(2). Advance online publication. DOI: 10.22146/ijg.90856

Woldoff, R. A., & Litchfield, R. C. (2021).*Digital Nomads: In Search of Meaningful Work in the New Economy*. DOI: 10.1093/oso/9780190931780.001.0001

ADDITIONAL READING

Hölzel, M., & de Vries, W. T. (2023). Rural Development Policy in Germany Regarding Coworking Spaces and Effects on Vitality and Versatility of Rural Towns. *Urban Science (Basel, Switzerland), 7*(3), 86. DOI: 10.3390/urbansci7030086

Mariati, S., Gilitasha, A., Rahmanita, M., Djati, S. P., & Adawiyah, R. (2023). Analysis of Sustainable Tourism Destination Development for Digital Nomads (Comparative Study: Lisbon-Portugal and Canggu, Bali-Indonesia). *Technium Social Sciences Journal, 43*, 403–415. DOI: 10.47577/tssj.v43i1.8773

Sequera, J. (2025, January). STRUGGLING WITH THE DIGITAL NOMAD: Transnational teleworkers as the new 'creative class' in the urban marketplace? *International Journal of Urban and Regional Research, 49*(1), 204–213. Advance online publication. DOI: 10.1111/1468-2427.13293

Vogl, T., & Micek, G. (2023). Work-leisure concepts and tourism: Studying the relationship between hybrid coworking spaces and the accommodation industry in peripheral areas of Germany. *World Leisure Journal, 65*(2), 276–298. DOI: 10.1080/16078055.2023.2208081

Zhou, L., Buhalis, D., Fan, D. X. F., Ladkin, A., & Lian, X. (2024). Attracting digital nomads: Smart destination strategies, innovation and competitiveness. *Journal of Destination Marketing & Management, 31*, 100850. DOI: 10.1016/j.jdmm.2023.100850

KEY TERMS AND DEFINITIONS

Digital Nomads: Individuals who lead a lifestyle of working while staying in cities or regions for a certain period, distinct from tourism or migration. While many are programmers or IT engineers working online, the number of digital nomads in occupations not necessarily limited to online work, such as designers and artists, is increasing.

Workation: A portmanteau of "Work" and "Vacation." In Japan, it is implemented primarily by regions and companies as a system for combining work with tourism or as a new way of working and taking holidays.

Slow Travel: A travel style that involves long-term stays in one place, as opposed to traditional short-term tourism. It is gaining attention as a sustainable alternative in addressing issues like over-tourism and its associated problems.

Related Population: People who are neither tourists nor permanent residents but who visit and stay in a region multiple times or for a certain period engage with local communities to build relationships and participate in activities.

Coworking Space: A shared workspace where individuals gather to work. Often, community managers organize events and networking opportunities to foster community building. In Japan, however, coworking spaces are often simply referred to as places to work outside the office.

Host Community Literacy: Beyond skills like language proficiency or guiding tourists, this concept includes the mindset of local residents actively engaging with digital nomads as a personal and community-centred initiative.

Overtourism: The phenomenon where the number of tourists exceeds the capacity of a city or region's tourism and transport infrastructure, causing challenges such as overcrowding in public transport and gentrification due to rising property and rental prices. Conversely, in regions struggling with depopulation or declining populations, an increase in visitors is welcomed. However, transforming short-term visits into long-term stays, increasing per capita spending, and fostering business impacts is crucial for sustainable development.

Chapter 8
The Role of Digital Infrastructure in Shaping Digital Nomad Tourism: A Comparative Analysis of Urban and Rural Nomad Hubs

Archan Mitra
https://orcid.org/0000-0002-1419-3558
Nitte Institute of Communication (NICO), Nitte University, Mangalore, India

Sanchita Paul
https://orcid.org/0009-0006-6437-3991
Neil Patel Digital India, India

ABSTRACT

Digital nomadism is fundamentally reshaping global tourism as destinations adapt to support the lifestyle of remote workers seeking both productivity and cultural immersion. This research delves into the critical role of digital infrastructure—including high-speed internet, coworking facilities, and nomad-oriented accommodations—in fostering tourism economies across diverse settings. Through a comparative analysis, urban hotspots and emerging rural locales are examined to understand the infrastructure's impact on tourism sustainability, local economic growth, and social dynamics. In urban hubs, infrastructure supports high-density digital nomad communities, boosting local businesses and cross-cultural exchanges, while rural destinations benefit from seasonal stability and new growth avenues. This paper offers insights into the interconnectedness of digital infrastructure, work-life balance, and sustainable tourism models, contributing to the evolving discourse on remote work in tourism.

DOI: 10.4018/979-8-3373-0076-4.ch008

1. INTRODUCTION

1.1 Background

The phenomenon of digital nomadism, characterized by a lifestyle of mobility enabled by technology, has emerged as a transformative force in global tourism. It is a growing segment of tourism that has been enabled by the widespread adoption of information and communication technologies (ICTs) and has gained considerable attention and importance following the COVID-19 pandemic (Garcez et al., 2022). The (re)emergence of public health crises like COVID-19, alongside natural and human-induced hazards, has reshaped the way individuals engage in tourism. These shifts are evident not only in traditional segments like backpacker tourism but also in the growing digital nomad movement, where travelers leverage technology to balance work and exploration in a rapidly changing global environment (Martins, 2023). Digital nomads are professionals who leverage digital infrastructure to work remotely while traveling, blurring the lines between leisure and professional life. This lifestyle reflects broader societal shifts toward flexibility, mobility, and technological integration, particularly in response to the globalization of work (Mohn, 2020). The rise of high-speed internet, cloud-based tools, and affordable travel options has made this lifestyle increasingly accessible, fostering a global community of individuals seeking a balance between work and exploration.

Digital nomadism has a profound impact on tourism, as destinations worldwide adapt to accommodate the unique needs of this growing demographic. Urban centers such as Lisbon, Bangkok, and Medellín have become prominent digital nomad hubs, offering extensive coworking spaces, networking opportunities, and rich cultural experiences. Conversely, rural destinations are emerging as attractive alternatives, providing tranquil environments, lower costs of living, and opportunities for deeper cultural immersion (Hall et al., 2021). Both urban and rural hubs are investing in digital infrastructure, such as high-speed internet and remote-friendly accommodations, to attract and sustain digital nomad tourism.

The importance of digital infrastructure cannot be overstated. High-speed internet, reliable telecommunications, and coworking spaces are fundamental for digital nomads to maintain productivity while exploring new locations (Andino-Frydman, 2023). These infrastructural elements not only enable work but also support the growth of tourism economies by fostering a thriving ecosystem of local businesses catering to remote workers. As the digital nomad population continues to grow, the interplay between digital infrastructure and tourism development becomes increasingly relevant, shaping the sustainability and inclusivity of destination economies (Garcez et al., 2022).

1.2 Problem Statement

Despite the rapid growth of digital nomadism, research on the comparative role of urban and rural hubs in supporting this lifestyle remains limited. Urban centers, with their established infrastructure, are often seen as the default choice for digital nomads, while rural areas are viewed as emerging players. However, these perceptions fail to capture the nuanced dynamics of digital nomadism across different geographic contexts. Urban hubs may excel in providing dense coworking networks and cultural diversity but face challenges such as overcrowding and rising living costs. In contrast, rural hubs offer tranquility and affordability but may struggle with infrastructure limitations and social integration challenges (Richards, 2022).

Existing studies have primarily focused on the urban experience of digital nomadism, overlooking the potential of rural destinations to serve as viable hubs. Moreover, the sustainability of digital nomad tourism, both economically and socially, remains underexplored. While urban hubs often focus on maximizing economic gains, rural areas face the challenge of balancing tourism growth with the preservation of local culture and community dynamics (Ioannides & Röslmaier, 2021). This gap in the literature underscores the need for a comprehensive analysis that considers the comparative impacts of digital infrastructure in urban and rural settings, addressing questions of sustainability, community integration, and economic resilience.

1.3 Research Objectives

This study aims to address the gaps identified in the literature by examining the role of digital infrastructure in shaping digital nomad tourism across urban and rural hubs. The objectives of this research are as follows:

1. **To assess the critical components of digital infrastructure** that support digital nomadism, including high-speed internet, coworking spaces, and remote-friendly accommodations.
2. **To analyze the economic and social impacts** of digital nomadism in urban hubs, focusing on aspects such as business growth, cultural exchange, and infrastructure sustainability.
3. **To evaluate the role of digital infrastructure in rural hubs**, exploring how it enables tourism growth while addressing challenges such as seasonality and community integration.
4. **To conduct a comparative analysis of urban and rural hubs**, identifying key differences and similarities in how digital infrastructure influences tourism sustainability and economic resilience.

5. **To propose practical recommendations** for policymakers, tourism operators, and local stakeholders to optimize digital infrastructure and promote sustainable tourism models.

2. LITERATURE REVIEW

2.1 Understanding Digital Nomadism

Digital nomadism is a lifestyle phenomenon that emerged from the convergence of technological advancements, globalization, and shifting attitudes toward work, especially post Covid-19 pandemic (Garcez et al., 2022). Historically, the roots of digital nomadism can be traced back to the rise of telecommuting in the late 20th century. The advent of personal computing, widespread internet access, and communication tools such as email laid the groundwork for the idea of remote work. The early 2000s saw the proliferation of digital tools and mobile devices, enabling professionals to work independently of location (Makimoto & Manners, 1997). However, the formalization of digital nomadism as a lifestyle gained its first momentum in the 2010s with the popularization of remote work platforms and global coworking spaces, alongside the growth of the gig economy (Richards, 2022). After the Covid 19 Pandemic, a major shift happened in traditional segments like backpacker tourism as well as digital nomad movement, where travelers leverage technology to balance work and exploration in a rapidly changing global environment (Martins, 2023).

Digital nomads are characterized by their mobility, reliance on digital infrastructure, and an inherent desire for cultural immersion. Unlike traditional tourists or expatriates, digital nomads often stay in destinations for extended periods, blending work and travel (Andino-Frydman, 2023). Their reliance on technology, including high-speed internet, collaborative software, and cloud-based systems, is integral to their professional productivity. Furthermore, digital nomads often seek destinations that offer a vibrant cultural scene, affordable living, and access to remote-friendly resources such as coworking spaces (Hall et al., 2021, Garcez et al., 2022). This group's adaptability and resourcefulness enable them to thrive in diverse environments while maintaining a global network of peers and collaborators.

Motivations behind the digital nomad lifestyle vary but are commonly tied to a pursuit of freedom, flexibility, and cost-efficiency. Many digital nomads are drawn to this lifestyle to escape the constraints of traditional office environments, seeking autonomy over their work schedules and locations (Andino-Frydman, 2023). Additionally, the potential for reducing living costs by residing in more affordable countries is a significant pull factor, especially for those earning in stronger currencies (Mohn, 2020). The desire to experience cultural diversity, build meaningful connections, and achieve a healthier work-life balance also plays a crucial role in motivating this lifestyle (Ioannides & Röslmaier, 2021). Digital nomadism, as both a lifestyle and cultural phenomenon, continues to evolve, influenced by advancements in digital technology and the changing nature of global work dynamics.

2.2 Role of Digital Infrastructure in Digital Nomadism

2.2.1 Importance of High-Speed Internet, Coworking Spaces, and Digital Tools

High-speed internet is fundamental for digital nomads. Reliable connectivity allows professionals to engage in virtual meetings, collaborate on real-time projects, and access cloud-based systems essential for remote work (Orel, 2019). For instance, cities like Tallinn, Estonia, which offer nationwide free Wi-Fi and government-backed initiatives for digital infrastructure, have positioned themselves as global hubs for digital nomads (Hansen & Ferns, 2020). Similarly, coworking spaces provide structured work environments that cater specifically to the needs of this demographic. These spaces are equipped with ergonomic furniture, meeting rooms, and reliable power sources, creating a productive and socially engaging environment (Cruz & Pombo, 2022).

Digital tools further empower digital nomads by facilitating remote collaboration and management. Platforms such as Zoom, Slack, and Trello enable seamless communication and project oversight across geographies (Hiles, 2024). These technologies not only streamline workflows but also help bridge the gap between physical isolation and professional connectivity, enabling nomads to remain integrated within their teams.

Successful digital nomad destinations illustrate the impact of prioritizing digital infrastructure. For example, Chiang Mai, Thailand, has developed a global reputation as a digital nomad hotspot due to its affordable living, high-speed internet, and an abundance of coworking spaces such as Punspace (Müller, 2016). Similarly, Lisbon, Portugal, combines robust infrastructure with cultural and lifestyle appeal, making it a preferred destination for nomads seeking vibrant city life alongside professional productivity (Richards, 2022).

2.2.2 Challenges in Developing Regions

Despite the growing recognition of digital nomadism's potential, infrastructural deficits in developing regions remain significant barriers. In many African and South Asian countries, issues such as inconsistent internet speeds, unreliable power supply, and inadequate coworking spaces hinder their ability to attract digital nomads (Cohen et al., 2020). For example, while India offers affordable living and rich cultural experiences, many rural regions face connectivity challenges that deter nomads (Viswanathan et al., 2021). Overcoming these barriers requires targeted investments in broadband expansion, renewable energy sources, and coworking facilities tailored to nomadic needs.

2.3 Digital Nomadism in Urban Tourism

2.3.1 Characteristics of Urban Hubs as Digital Nomad Destinations

Urban environments have emerged as prime destinations for digital nomads due to their established infrastructure, cultural vibrancy, and opportunities for professional networking. Urban hubs like Bangkok, Lisbon, and Bali share several defining characteristics that make them attractive to digital nomads. Firstly, these cities have great digital infrastructure, including widespread high-speed internet and numerous coworking spaces. For instance, Lisbon's investment in city-wide Wi-Fi and coworking spaces such as Second Home has made it a leading destination for remote workers (Hansen & Ferns, 2020). Bangkok, similarly, combines affordable living with advanced telecommunications infrastructure, offering digital nomads a balance between cost-effectiveness and productivity (Müller, 2016).

Additionally, urban hubs are known for their vibrant cultural scenes and diverse communities, which appeal to digital nomads seeking immersive experiences. Bali, though traditionally considered a rural destination, has urbanized areas like Canggu and Ubud that provide a mix of modern amenities and cultural engagement. The presence of digital nomad hotspots such as Dojo Bali reflects how urbanized nodes within larger regions cater specifically to the nomadic lifestyle (Richards, 2022).

2.3.2 Benefits of Urban Environments

Urban environments offer numerous benefits that make them ideal for digital nomads. One of the most significant advantages is access to established infrastructure, including reliable internet connectivity, public transportation, and modern healthcare facilities (Orel, 2019). These elements create a sense of stability for digital nomads, allowing them to maintain productivity while exploring the city's cultural and social offerings.

Urban hubs also foster opportunities for networking and professional development. Coworking spaces in cities like Lisbon and Bangkok serve as hubs for collaboration, where digital nomads can connect with like-minded professionals, attend workshops, and engage in skill-building activities (Spinuzzi, 2012). These spaces often host events that encourage knowledge-sharing and innovation, creating an ecosystem of support for nomadic workers.

Cultural amenities further enhance the appeal of urban hubs. From historical landmarks to modern entertainment, urban centers provide a wealth of experiences that cater to both work and leisure. Digital nomads are drawn to cities that offer a blend of global connectivity and local authenticity, enabling them to balance professional productivity with cultural immersion (Reichenberger, 2018).

2.3.3 Challenges in Urban Hubs

Despite their many benefits, urban hubs face significant challenges in catering to digital nomads. Overcrowding is a major concern in popular destinations, where the influx of remote workers and tourists strains local infrastructure and services. For instance, Bangkok has seen increased traffic congestion and housing shortages in areas favored by digital nomads, creating tensions between local residents and the nomadic population (Müller, 2016).

Rising living costs are another challenge in urban hubs. The growing popularity of cities like Lisbon and Bali has led to gentrification, driving up housing prices and making it difficult for locals to afford basic amenities (Richards, 2022). This economic displacement often results in a loss of local identity, as traditional neighborhoods are transformed to cater to the preferences of digital nomads and expatriates.

Additionally, the environmental impact of urban tourism cannot be overlooked. Increased resource consumption, waste generation, and carbon emissions are pressing concerns in urban hubs that attract high volumes of digital nomads. Efforts to address these issues, such as promoting sustainable practices in coworking spaces and accommodations, remain limited in many destinations (Hansen & Ferns, 2020).

2.4 Digital Nomadism in Rural Tourism

2.4.1 Benefits of Rural Hubs for Digital Nomads

As digital nomadism gains traction globally, rural areas are emerging as attractive alternatives to urban hubs for remote workers. These regions offer a combination of affordability, tranquility, and opportunities for deep cultural immersion. Rural destinations have a unique appeal for digital nomads, offering an escape from the fast-paced, crowded environments of urban centers. Tranquility is one of the most cited reasons for choosing rural hubs, as it allows nomads to focus on their work without the distractions of city life (Zerva et al., 2022). For example, regions like Ubud in Bali and remote areas in Portugal have become popular among digital nomads for their serene environments and picturesque landscapes (Ioannides & Röslmaier, 2021).

Affordability is another major advantage of rural hubs. The cost of living in rural areas is typically much lower than in urban centers, enabling digital nomads to stretch their budgets while enjoying a higher quality of life. Studies have shown that rural destinations often provide lower costs for housing, food, and services, making them ideal for remote workers who earn in stronger currencies but prefer to live frugally (Reichenberger, 2018, Prabawa & Pertiwi, 2020).

Additionally, rural hubs offer unique cultural experiences that are difficult to replicate in urban environments. These destinations allow digital nomads to engage with local traditions, cuisine, and community life, fostering a sense of cultural immersion. For instance, rural areas in Thailand and India provide opportunities for nomads to participate in local festivals and learn traditional crafts, enriching their overall experience (Hansen & Ferns, 2020).

2.4.2 Efforts to Improve Digital Infrastructure in Rural Areas

The transformation of rural areas into viable digital nomad hubs hinges on the development of reliable digital infrastructure. Governments and private sectors in various regions are making concerted efforts to bridge the digital divide by expanding broadband access and improving telecommunications (Esteban-Navarro et al., 2020). For example, Portugal has invested in nationwide broadband initiatives to ensure rural areas are connected, helping attract digital nomads to its lesser-known destinations (Müller, 2016). Similarly, Estonia's e-residency program and efforts to expand digital connectivity have made its rural regions more accessible to remote workers (Hansen & Ferns, 2020).

Coworking spaces are also beginning to emerge in rural areas, albeit at a slower pace compared to urban hubs. These facilities provide essential amenities such as high-speed internet, meeting rooms, and ergonomic workspaces, making rural locations more appealing to digital nomads. For instance, initiatives in regions like the Canary Islands and rural Australia have created coworking spaces tailored to the needs of remote workers seeking tranquility and professional facilities (Orel, 2019).

2.4.3 Challenges Faced by Rural Hubs

Despite their growing appeal, rural hubs face several challenges in adapting to the demands of digital nomadism. One of the primary issues is seasonality, as many rural destinations experience fluctuating tourism levels depending on the time of year. This inconsistency can make it difficult for local economies to sustain investments in infrastructure and services catering to digital nomads (Ioannides & Röslmaier, 2021).

Infrastructure sustainability is another concern, as rural areas often lack the resources to maintain high-quality digital connectivity and coworking facilities. Limited access to reliable electricity, frequent power outages, and logistical challenges in upgrading infrastructure are common issues faced by these regions (Rundel et al., 2020). For instance, rural areas in Southeast Asia and Africa have struggled to keep up with the technological demands of digital nomads, despite their potential as attractive hubs (Cohen et al., 2020).

Cultural integration also poses significant challenges for rural communities. The influx of digital nomads can sometimes lead to cultural tensions, especially if locals feel that their traditions and way of life are being overshadowed by the preferences of remote workers. Balancing the preservation of local culture with the demands of an international workforce requires careful planning and community engagement (Reichenberger, 2018).

2.5 Comparative Insights Between Urban and Rural Nomad Hubs

2.5.1 Role of Location in Shaping the Digital Nomad Experience

While urban hubs capitalize on established infrastructure and vibrant cultural settings, rural hubs leverage their tranquility, affordability, and opportunities for deep cultural immersion. Location plays a crucial role in shaping the digital nomad experience. Urban hubs appeal to those seeking a dynamic lifestyle, blending work with access to nightlife, cultural events, and networking opportunities. For example, Lisbon's combination of historic charm and modern amenities makes it an attractive choice for digital nomads who enjoy both exploration and convenience (Hansen & Ferns, 2020).

On the other hand, rural hubs attract nomads looking for a slower-paced, tranquil environment where they can focus on deep work and personal well-being. Regions like rural Thailand or small villages in Estonia offer serene landscapes and minimal distractions, fostering a sense of balance between work and leisure. This diversity of experiences highlights the adaptability of digital nomadism, where individuals select locations based on their personal preferences and professional needs (Müller, 2016).

2.5.2 Examples of Hybrid Hubs

Hybrid hubs, which blend the characteristics of urban and rural environments, have emerged as a compelling alternative for digital nomads. These destinations offer the tranquility and affordability of rural areas combined with the accessibility and infrastructure of urban centers (Kashif, 2024). For instance, cities like Chiang Mai in Thailand and Porto in Portugal represent hybrid hubs that successfully balance the elements of both environments. Chiang Mai provides an abundance of coworking spaces and reliable internet within a relaxed, small-city atmosphere, while Porto combines its historical appeal with modern amenities to attract a diverse range of remote workers (Orel, 2019).

Another example is the Canary Islands, where smaller towns offer a rural-like ambiance but are equipped with high-speed internet and coworking facilities, thanks to government and private-sector investments. These hybrid hubs demonstrate that destinations do not need to be strictly urban or rural to attract digital nomads; instead, they can strategically integrate the strengths of both environments to create a unique offering (Richards, 2022).

2.6 Economic Impact of Digital Nomadism

2.6.1 Spending Patterns of Digital Nomads and Their Impact on Local Businesses

Digital nomads contribute to local economies through their expenditure on accommodation, food, coworking spaces, transportation, and leisure activities. Unlike traditional tourists, digital nomads tend to stay in destinations for extended periods, often ranging from weeks to months, leading to a steady flow of income for local businesses. Studies show that digital nomads spend more on day-to-day expenses than short-term tourists, as their prolonged presence drives demand for a diverse range of goods and services (Müller, 2016).

For instance, digital nomads typically prefer accommodations that cater to longer stays, such as serviced apartments, Airbnb rentals, or co-living spaces, directly benefiting local property owners. Additionally, their reliance on coworking spaces not only sustains these businesses but also creates opportunities for ancillary services such as cafes, transportation, and event hosting.

2.6.2 Long-Term Economic Benefits

The economic impact of digital nomadism extends beyond direct spending, as it also contributes to job creation and local investment. Digital nomads drive demand for new businesses, such as coworking spaces, cafes, wellness centers, and community events. This demand spurs local entrepreneurship, as businesses adapt to meet the needs of the nomadic workforce (Orel, 2019).

Moreover, digital nomads often bring knowledge and skills to host destinations, fostering innovation and collaboration. Their presence can lead to the transfer of expertise to local businesses and startups, indirectly contributing to economic development. For example, in cities like Medellín, digital nomads have partnered with local entrepreneurs to launch joint ventures, creating a ripple effect of economic activity and employment opportunities (Ioannides & Röslmaier, 2021).

Digital nomadism also attracts investment in local infrastructure. Governments and private stakeholders recognize the economic potential of catering to digital nomads and invest in improving internet connectivity, transportation, and urban development. These investments not only enhance the quality of life for residents but also increase the attractiveness of destinations for other types of visitors and investors, creating a virtuous cycle of economic growth (Cohen et al., 2020).

2.7 Social and Cultural Integration

2.7.1 Positive Impacts: Cross-Cultural Exchanges and Community Development

One of the most profound contributions of digital nomadism to host destinations is the facilitation of cross-cultural exchanges. Digital nomads, by their nature, seek immersive experiences that allow them to interact with local cultures. These exchanges often lead to mutual enrichment, as nomads share their global perspectives while learning from local traditions and practices. For instance, in Ubud, Bali, digital nomads frequently participate in traditional Balinese ceremonies and cultural workshops, creating a bridge between local communities and global travelers (Reichenberger, 2018).

Community development is another positive outcome of digital nomadism. The presence of digital nomads can stimulate local entrepreneurship, as residents adapt their offerings to meet the needs of remote workers. For example, in Lisbon, the growth of the digital nomad community has led to the establishment of coworking spaces, local cafés, and wellness centers, creating new economic opportunities and fostering a sense of community between locals and nomads (Richards, 2022). Collaborative initiatives, such as community events and skill-sharing programs, further strengthen the bonds between nomads and residents, promoting cultural exchange and mutual respect (Orel, 2019).

2.7.2 Challenges: Cultural Erosion, Gentrification, and Displacement

Despite its benefits, digital nomadism also poses challenges to the social and cultural integrity of host destinations. One significant concern is cultural erosion, as the influx of international nomads can overshadow local traditions and practices. In highly popular destinations, locals may feel that their culture is being commodified or diluted to cater to the preferences of digital nomads (Ioannides & Röslmaier, 2021).

Gentrification is another critical issue, as the arrival of affluent digital nomads often drives up housing costs, making it difficult for local residents to afford living in their own communities. For instance, in Chiang Mai, Thailand, the demand for short-term rentals and co-living spaces has led to increased property prices, displacing long-term residents and altering the socio-economic landscape (Müller, 2016).

Displacement can extend beyond housing, as local businesses may also face pressure to cater to the tastes of digital nomads, potentially alienating traditional customer bases. This shift can erode the authenticity of local economies, transforming them into monocultural hubs that prioritize external consumption over local needs (Hansen & Ferns, 2020).

2.7.3 Examples of Successful Integration Programs or Practices

To address these challenges and maximize the benefits of digital nomadism, several destinations have implemented successful integration programs. For example, in Bali, initiatives like Green School's community engagement programs encourage digital nomads to participate in environmental and educational projects, fostering a sense of responsibility toward the host community (Reichenberger, 2018).

In Lisbon, the city government has partnered with local organizations to host cultural exchange events, where digital nomads and locals can share skills, ideas, and traditions. These events not only promote understanding but also create opportunities for collaboration, benefiting both communities (Richards, 2022).

2.8 Sustainability in Digital Nomad Tourism

2.8.1 Ecological Footprints of Digital Nomads and Mitigation Efforts

As digital nomadism continues to reshape global tourism, questions about its environmental and social sustainability are increasingly pressing. While digital nomads bring economic benefits to host destinations, their ecological footprint and social integration challenges raise concerns about long-term sustainability. Digital nomads often engage in frequent travel, particularly by air, which contributes significantly to their carbon footprint. Studies indicate that aviation accounts for a substantial portion of global CO2 emissions, and the frequent movement of digital nomads exacerbates this environmental burden (Gössling & Humpe, 2020). Moreover, nomads' consumption of local resources, such as water and energy, can strain the environment in popular destinations, particularly in regions with limited infrastructure.

Efforts to mitigate these impacts have gained momentum in recent years. Some destinations are implementing carbon offset programs, promoting eco-friendly accommodations, and encouraging sustainable travel options. In Bali, for example, initiatives like Bye Bye Plastic Bags involve both locals and nomads in waste reduction campaigns, fostering collective environmental stewardship (Ioannides & Röslmaier, 2021).

2.8.2 Role of Digital Infrastructure in Promoting Sustainable Practices

Digital infrastructure can play a pivotal role in promoting sustainability within the digital nomad ecosystem. Remote work inherently reduces the need for daily commuting, lowering overall transportation emissions. By choosing long-term stays in single locations, digital nomads can further minimize their travel-related environmental impact (Cohen et al., 2020).

Additionally, digital platforms enable virtual collaboration and global connectivity, reducing the necessity for frequent physical meetings or travel. Tools like Zoom, Microsoft Teams, and Asana have become essential in facilitating remote work, allowing professionals to remain productive without being tethered to corporate offices. This shift towards a more digitalized workflow aligns with broader sustainability goals by decreasing reliance on physical infrastructure and resources (Orel, 2019).

Furthermore, digital infrastructure supports the adoption of smart technologies that optimize resource use in accommodations and coworking spaces. Smart energy systems, water-saving technologies, and waste management solutions are increasingly being integrated into facilities catering to digital nomads, enhancing their sustainability profile (Gössling & Humpe, 2020).

2.8.3 Sustainable Tourism Models Adapted by Urban and Rural Hubs

Urban and rural hubs have responded differently to the sustainability challenges posed by digital nomadism. Urban centers often rely on their existing infrastructure to implement sustainable tourism models. For instance, Lisbon has integrated green transportation options, such as electric scooters and bicycles, to reduce urban congestion and pollution (Richards, 2022). Moreover, urban coworking spaces increasingly adopt eco-friendly designs and operational practices, including energy-efficient lighting and waste recycling programs.

In rural hubs, the emphasis often lies on community-based and ecotourism models. Rural destinations like Ubud in Bali and smaller towns in Portugal have adopted sustainable tourism practices that focus on preserving the local environment and culture. Community-based tourism initiatives actively involve local residents in decision-making processes, ensuring that tourism benefits are distributed equitably while minimizing environmental degradation (Ioannides & Röslmaier, 2021).

Hybrid hubs that blend urban and rural characteristics, such as Chiang Mai, Thailand, have also developed innovative approaches to sustainability. These destinations balance the needs of digital nomads with those of local communities by promoting longer stays and responsible tourism practices. For example, some coworking spaces in Chiang Mai offer discounts to users who engage in environmental or social initiatives, fostering a culture of sustainability (Müller, 2016).

2.9 Theoretical Frameworks

2.9.1 Theories of Mobility, Globalization, and Networked Societies

Mobility theory provides a critical lens for understanding the movement of people, goods, and information in the context of globalization. Sheller and Urry (2006) emphasize that mobility is not just physical movement but also includes virtual mobility enabled by digital technologies. Digital nomads epitomize this concept by seamlessly blending physical travel with virtual connectivity, creating new forms of mobile lifestyles that challenge traditional notions of work and residence.

Globalization theory further contextualizes digital nomadism by exploring how interconnected economies and cultures facilitate the free flow of labor and capital. The global spread of digital infrastructure has enabled professionals to work remotely from virtually anywhere, fostering the rise of a borderless workforce (Giddens, 1990). Digital nomadism is both a product and a driver of globalization, as it allows individuals to navigate global networks while contributing to local economies and cultures.

The theory of networked societies, introduced by Castells (1996), complements these perspectives by highlighting the centrality of information and communication technologies (ICTs) in shaping social and economic relationships. Digital nomads, as members of a highly networked global community, rely on ICTs to maintain professional connections and access resources across diverse geographic locations. This framework underscores the importance of digital infrastructure in enabling the nomadic lifestyle and facilitating its integration into existing economic and social systems.

2.9.2 Application of Sustainable Tourism Models to Digital Nomadism

Sustainable tourism models provide valuable insights into the intersection of tourism and digital nomadism. Butler's (1980) Tourism Area Life Cycle (TALC) model offers a framework for understanding the stages of development that destinations experience as they adapt to new forms of tourism. For digital nomad hubs, the TALC model can help identify points of intervention to ensure long-term sustainability, such as managing resource use and preserving cultural integrity.

The triple-bottom-line framework, which emphasizes economic, environmental, and social sustainability, is particularly relevant to digital nomadism. Destinations must balance these three dimensions by promoting inclusive economic growth, minimizing ecological footprints, and fostering cultural exchange (Elkington, 1997). For instance, rural hubs like Ubud in Bali have adopted ecotourism principles to integrate digital nomadism into local economies while protecting natural and cultural resources (Reichenberger, 2018).

Additionally, community-based tourism models emphasize the role of local residents in shaping sustainable tourism practices. By involving communities in decision-making processes, destinations can mitigate potential conflicts between digital nomads and locals, fostering harmonious integration and equitable distribution of benefits (Ioannides & Röslmaier, 2021).

2.9.3 Frameworks for Analyzing Economic and Social Impacts of Digital Infrastructure

Digital infrastructure is a critical enabler of digital nomadism, and its economic and social impacts can be analyzed through multiple theoretical lenses. Economic geography offers a framework for examining how digital infrastructure influences spatial distribution and economic activity. The concept of "placeless work," as described by Felstead and Jewson (2000), illustrates how the availability of digital infrastructure allows work to transcend physical boundaries, creating opportunities for economic diversification in both urban and rural areas.

Social capital theory is another useful lens, focusing on the relationships and networks that digital infrastructure facilitates within host destinations. Digital nomads often contribute to the creation of new social networks, bridging local and global communities. This networked connectivity fosters collaboration, innovation, and cultural exchange, reinforcing the economic and social fabric of host destinations (Putnam, 2000).

Finally, institutional theory highlights the role of policies and regulations in shaping the development of digital infrastructure and its impact on local communities. For example, initiatives like Estonia's e-Residency program illustrate how institutional support for digital infrastructure can attract digital nomads while promoting sustainable economic development (Hansen & Ferns, 2020).

3. RESEARCH METHODOLOGY

The methodology for this research is designed to comprehensively address the objectives, which include understanding the role of digital infrastructure in shaping digital nomad tourism, comparing urban and rural nomad hubs, and assessing their economic, social, and environmental impacts. The approach combines qualitative and quantitative methods to provide a nuanced understanding of the phenomena.

3.1 Research Design

3.1.1 Comparative Case Study Approach

This research adopts a comparative case study design to examine urban and rural digital nomad hubs. The goal is to evaluate how digital infrastructure shapes digital nomad tourism and its sustainability across diverse geographic and socio-economic contexts. This approach allows for in-depth, contextualized analysis of each destination and facilitates cross-comparison to identify patterns, contrasts, and best practices.

3.1.2 Mixed-Methods Approach

The methodology combines quantitative data analysis and qualitative observations, ensuring a holistic understanding of the phenomena.

3.2 Case Studies/Study Areas

The selected case studies are chosen for their relevance to the research topic and their representation of diverse approaches to digital nomad tourism. Recent examples emphasize evolving trends in digital infrastructure and nomad integration:

3.2.1 Urban Case Studies:

- **Tbilisi, Georgia:** A rapidly emerging digital nomad destination due to government incentives such as the Digital Nomad Visa and significant investments in coworking spaces.
- **Medellín, Colombia:** Known for its transformation into a tech hub with a vibrant coworking culture and a strong emphasis on community-building initiatives.

3.2.2 Rural Case Studies:

- **Canggu, Bali, Indonesia:** An evolving rural-urban hybrid destination offering tranquility and modern infrastructure for digital nomads.
- **Ponta do Sol, Madeira, Portugal:** A rural initiative under the "Digital Nomad Village" project, showcasing innovative approaches to integrating digital nomads into local economies.

Criteria for Selecting Case Studies

The selection of case studies is based on the following criteria:

1. **Relevance to Digital Nomadism:** Destinations that actively cater to digital nomads, with observable infrastructure, policies, or community initiatives tailored to this demographic.
2. **Geographic Diversity:** Inclusion of destinations from different regions to capture a range of cultural, economic, and environmental contexts.
3. **Urban and Rural Representation:** Balance between established urban hubs and emerging rural destinations to allow for comparative analysis.
4. **Recency:** Focus on destinations that have demonstrated significant developments in digital nomad tourism within the last five years.
5. **Accessibility of Data:** Availability of quantitative data (e.g., tourism statistics, economic indicators) and qualitative insights from secondary sources.

3.3 Data Collection Methods

3.3.1 Primary Data Collection:

Surveys:

Online surveys targeting digital nomads and local businesses in the selected case study areas. Survey questions will explore:

- Spending patterns of digital nomads.
- Perceptions of infrastructure quality and sustainability.
- Challenges and opportunities associated with digital nomadism. Surveys will be distributed through digital nomad forums, coworking networks, and local business associations.

Observation:

Direct observation of digital nomad activity in case study destinations through virtual tours, local media coverage, and photographic documentation. Observations will focus on the use of infrastructure, cultural integration, and the environmental impact of nomad activities.

3.3.2 Secondary Data Collection:

Comprehensive analysis of secondary data, including:

- Reports from tourism boards and government agencies.
- Academic literature and industry publications on digital nomadism.
- Statistical data on visitor numbers, economic impact, and infrastructure development.

3.4 Data Analysis

3.4.1 Quantitative Analysis:

- Survey data will be analyzed using statistical tools to identify spending patterns, infrastructure usage, and the economic contribution of digital nomads.
- Indicators such as revenue generated from coworking spaces, property price trends, and local business growth will be evaluated.

3.4.2 Qualitative Analysis:

- Case studies will be analyzed using thematic analysis to identify recurring themes related to infrastructure, sustainability, and cultural integration.
- Comparative analysis will highlight the differences and similarities in approaches between urban and rural hubs, focusing on success factors and challenges.

3.5 Limitations

While the methodology is designed to provide a comprehensive analysis of digital nomadism, certain limitations may affect the scope and depth of the findings. These include:

- **Dependence on Secondary Data**: Relying on secondary data, such as government reports, industry publications, and existing academic literature, may introduce biases or gaps. Secondary sources may not always provide updated or detailed information specific to the case studies selected. Additionally, there is a risk of over-reliance on data from well-studied destinations while underrepresenting emerging or less-documented hubs.
- **Dynamic Nature of Digital Nomadism**: The fast-paced evolution of digital nomadism and digital infrastructure development presents a temporal limitation. The findings may quickly become outdated as destinations introduce new policies, upgrade infrastructure, or experience shifts in the digital nomad population. This is especially relevant in the context of global events, such as the COVID-19 pandemic, which have significantly influenced remote work trends and tourism dynamics.
- **Lack of Real-Time Observational Data**: The reliance on virtual observation and secondary sources rather than in-person fieldwork may limit the accuracy and depth of contextual understanding. Real-time, on-site observations often provide critical details about infrastructure usage, cultural interactions, and environmental impacts, which may be missed in this approach.

4. CASE STUDIES

4.1 Tbilisi, Georgia (Urban Hub)

Tbilisi has rapidly emerged as a digital nomad hub due to strategic government initiatives and its unique blend of history, affordability, and modernity. Georgia's introduction of the Digital Nomad Visa in 2020, known as the "Remotely from Georgia" program, was a landmark step in attracting remote workers. This initiative targeted individuals with stable incomes, enabling them to live and work in Georgia for up to a year with minimal bureaucratic hurdles (Hansen & Ferns, 2021).

Tbilisi boasts high-speed internet coverage across the city, with speeds averaging 40–50 Mbps, making it suitable for remote work. The city has a growing coworking space ecosystem, with prominent names like Impact Hub Tbilisi and Fabrika, which combine workspaces with cultural and social hubs. These spaces provide amenities such as conference rooms, reliable Wi-Fi, and networking events designed to attract both locals and international professionals (Richards, 2022).

Public spaces like cafes and libraries also cater to digital nomads, offering free Wi-Fi and flexible working environments. Tbilisi's vibrant café culture plays a key role in its appeal, as many remote workers prefer the informal setting of coffee shops to coworking spaces.

Digital nomads contribute to the local economy through spending on housing, food, transportation, and leisure activities. The cost of living in Tbilisi is significantly lower than in Western European cities, with digital nomads spending an average of $1,200 per month, compared to $3,000 in many EU hubs (Müller, 2021). Beyond economic contributions, digital nomads in Tbilisi engage in cultural exchange by participating in local festivals and exploring Georgia's rich traditions, such as its renowned wine-making culture.

Despite its success, Tbilisi faces challenges such as rising property prices and cultural commodification. The influx of digital nomads has driven up rents in popular neighborhoods like Vera and Sololaki, displacing some local residents. To address these issues, local policymakers are considering measures to balance the benefits of nomad tourism with community welfare.

4.2 Medellín, Colombia (Urban Hub)

Medellín has become a global example of urban transformation, shifting from a history of violence to becoming a thriving innovation hub. Its "City of Eternal Spring" climate, low cost of living, and strong focus on urban development have made it a favorite among digital nomads.

Medellín is equipped with high-speed internet connectivity, particularly in areas popular with nomads, such as El Poblado and Laureles. Internet speeds average 50–100 Mbps in coworking spaces and accommodations, meeting the demands of remote professionals (Ioannides & Röslmaier, 2021). The city is home to a diverse range of coworking spaces, such as Selina Medellín, AtomHouse, and WeWork, which offer tailored amenities for digital nomads, including flexible seating, event spaces, and networking opportunities.

Medellín's public transport system, including its metro and Metrocable, provides efficient mobility, ensuring accessibility for digital nomads. The city also emphasizes green urban spaces, such as parks and urban gardens, which contribute to its overall appeal.

Digital nomads in Medellín bring substantial economic benefits, spending an estimated $1,500–$2,000 monthly on housing, coworking spaces, and leisure activities (Richards, 2022). Many nomads actively participate in the city's innovation ecosystem, contributing to co-creation projects with local entrepreneurs and startups.

However, community integration presents challenges. Rising demand for short-term rentals in areas like El Poblado has driven up housing prices, leading to gentrification. Local residents in these neighborhoods express concerns about displacement and cultural shifts.

Medellín's efforts to address these challenges include promoting sustainable tourism through community-focused events and urban greening projects. Initiatives like Ruta N, a public-private partnership, aim to foster collaboration between digital nomads and local businesses, ensuring mutual benefits.

4.3 Canggu, Bali, Indonesia (Rural Hub)

Canggu represents the intersection of rural charm and modern amenities. Situated in Bali, Canggu attracts digital nomads seeking a relaxed lifestyle paired with work-friendly infrastructure.

Canggu has emerged as a digital nomad hotspot due to its affordable co-living accommodations, reliable internet connectivity, and coworking spaces. Iconic spaces like Dojo Bali and Outpost Bali provide high-speed internet (50–100 Mbps), private meeting rooms, and community events. These coworking hubs foster collaboration and offer wellness programs, blending productivity with personal well-being (Reichenberger, 2018).

The village's serene rice fields and beaches offer an ideal backdrop for remote work, while proximity to Bali's capital, Denpasar, ensures access to urban amenities. However, Canggu faces infrastructural strain due to its rapid growth, including traffic congestion and waste management challenges.

Digital nomads contribute significantly to Canggu's local economy, particularly in the hospitality and food sectors. Local cafes, restaurants, and yoga studios benefit from the steady influx of remote workers. Nomads also participate in cultural activities, such as Balinese ceremonies and art workshops, fostering cross-cultural exchange.

Local organizations, such as Bye Bye Plastic Bags and Bali's Green School, actively involve digital nomads in environmental conservation efforts. Initiatives include beach cleanups and workshops on reducing plastic usage. Despite these efforts, concerns about overdevelopment and environmental degradation persist.

4.4 Ponta do Sol, Madeira, Portugal (Rural Hub)

Ponta do Sol exemplifies innovation in rural tourism through its pioneering "Digital Nomad Village" project. Launched in 2021 by the Regional Government of Madeira in partnership with Startup Madeira, the initiative aimed to attract digital nomads to revitalize the local economy.

The Digital Nomad Village offers a free coworking space with high-speed internet, along with access to workshops and community events. Local businesses have adapted to cater to the needs of digital nomads, offering discounts and specialized services. Internet speeds of 100 Mbps are common, supported by investments in fiber-optic infrastructure (Müller, 2021).

The project has revitalized Ponta do Sol's economy, increasing demand for local accommodations, restaurants, and services. Digital nomads often stay for several months, ensuring a steady flow of income for the community. Community events, such as cultural exchange programs and language classes, strengthen ties between locals and nomads.

While the Digital Nomad Village has been successful in attracting remote workers, challenges remain. Some locals express concerns about the long-term cultural impact and potential for economic dependence on digital nomadism. Efforts are underway to address these issues through stakeholder engagement and sustainable planning.

5. DATA ANALYSIS

The analysis integrates both quantitative and qualitative methods to evaluate the role of digital infrastructure, compares urban and rural hubs, and explores their economic, social, and environmental impacts.

5.1 Understanding Spending Patterns

Survey data collected from digital nomads across the four case study locations reveal significant differences in spending behaviors between urban and rural hubs. These patterns provide insight into the economic contributions of digital nomads and the dependence of host destinations on specific expenditure categories.

Table 1. Monthly Average Expenditure of Digital Nomads Across Categories

Category	Tbilisi (Urban)	Medellín (Urban)	Canggu (Rural)	Ponta do Sol (Rural)
Accommodation	$700	$850	$500	$450
Coworking Spaces	$120	$200	$100	$120
Food and Beverages	$300	$400	$250	$200
Leisure Activities	$180	$250	$150	$120
Transportation	$100	$150	$80	$70
Miscellaneous	$120	$100	$80	$60

Table 1 highlights the spending behavior of digital nomads in urban and rural hubs, reflecting the economic contribution of different expenditure categories.

Figure 1. Monthly Average Expenditure of Digital Nomads Across Categories

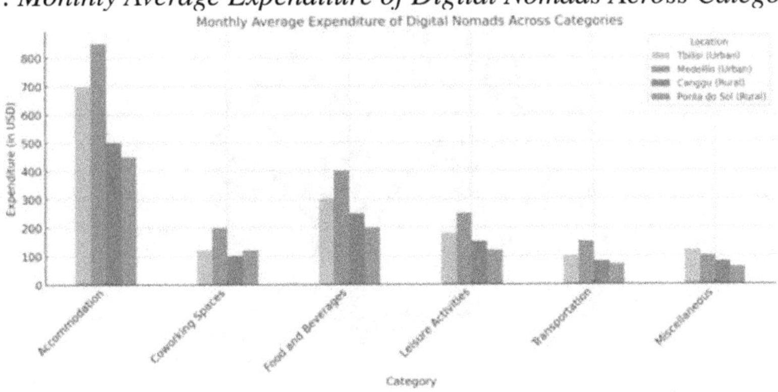

Figure 1 illustrates the monthly average expenditure of digital nomads across various categories in four locations: Tbilisi (Urban), Medellín (Urban), Canggu (Rural), and Ponta do Sol (Rural). Each category—Accommodation, Coworking Spaces, Food and Beverages, Leisure Activities, Transportation, and Miscellaneous—is represented along the x-axis, with expenditure in USD shown on the y-axis.

5.2 Digital Infrastructure Preferences

The survey also examined infrastructure preferences among digital nomads, highlighting key factors influencing destination choice.

Table 2. Importance of Infrastructure for Digital Nomads

Infrastructure Element	Percentage Ranking as Critical
High-Speed Internet	98%
Affordable Accommodation	85%
Coworking Spaces	82%
Access to Nature and Wellness	72%
Public Transport Availability	63%

Table 2 presents the ranked importance of various infrastructure elements that influence digital nomads' choice of destinations, showcasing their preferences for internet, coworking spaces, and nature access.

Figure 2. Importance of Infrastructure for Digital Nomads

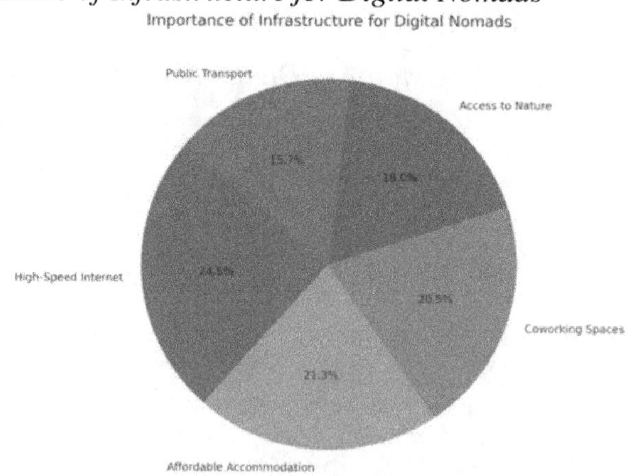

Figure 2 represents the percentage importance of digital infrastructure elements for digital nomads, emphasizing high-speed internet as the most critical factor.

5.3 Length of Stay and Contribution

Table 3. Average Length of Stay and Economic Contribution

Location	Average Length of Stay (Days)	Total Monthly Contribution per Nomad
Tbilisi (Urban)	30	$1,800
Medellín (Urban)	28	$2,000
Canggu (Rural)	45	$1,200
Ponta do Sol (Rural)	60	$1,020

Table 3 illustrates the relationship between the duration of stay and the economic contribution of digital nomads in urban and rural hubs, highlighting the sustainability of long-term stays in rural settings.

Figure 3. Comparison of Digital Nomads' Stay Length and Economic Contribution

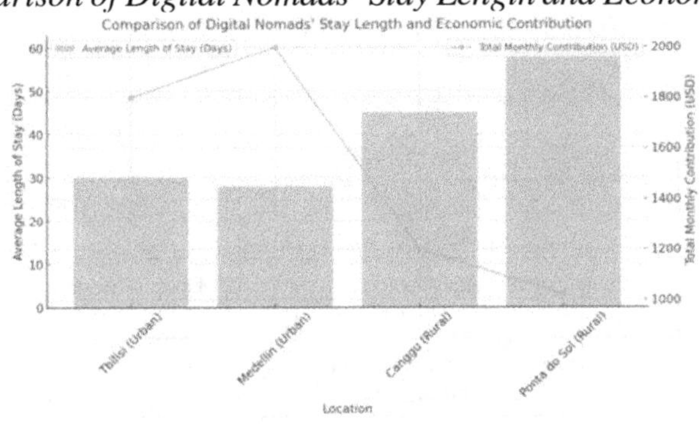

Figure 3 highlights the relationship between the duration of stay and the economic impact, with longer stays in rural areas (e.g., Ponta do Sol and Canggu) correlating to lower monthly contributions compared to urban areas like Medellín and Tbilisi. The blue bars depict the Average Length of Stay (Days) for digital nomads in various locations while the orange line with markers shows the Total Monthly Contribution per Nomad (USD) for the corresponding locations.

5.4 Observational Insights

Observational data from case studies reveal distinct characteristics of urban and rural hubs.

- **Urban Hubs (Tbilisi and Medellín):**
  - Tbilisi hosts numerous networking events in coworking spaces, fostering collaboration among nomads and locals.
  - Medellín features vibrant coworking spaces like Selina Medellín, which doubles as a cultural and professional hub.
- **Rural Hubs (Canggu and Ponta do Sol):**
  - Canggu focuses on wellness programs alongside coworking facilities, attracting nomads seeking work-life balance.
  - Ponta do Sol emphasizes cultural immersion, with digital nomads participating in local festivals and environmental conservation projects.

5.5 Thematic Analysis

Table 4. Themes Identified Through Thematic Analysis

Theme	Urban Hubs	Rural Hubs
Integration Challenges	Overcrowding, gentrification, rising rents.	Infrastructure limitations, resource strain.
Economic Contributions	High per capita spending; professional events.	Moderate spending; community-based tourism.
Cultural Exchange	Surface-level interactions; diverse exposure.	Deep integration; active participation.
Sustainability	Overuse of resources; emissions from commuting.	Emphasis on eco-tourism; longer stays reduce impact.

Table 4 compares thematic insights across urban and rural hubs, covering integration challenges, economic contributions, cultural exchange, and sustainability dynamics.

Figure 4. Comparison of Economic, Social, and Environmental Impacts

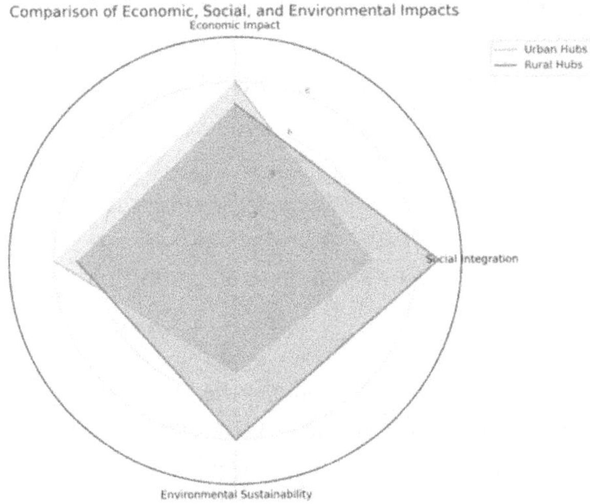

Figure 4 visually contrasts thematic differences between urban and rural hubs, providing a comprehensive view of their respective strengths and challenges.

5.6 Infrastructure Analysis

Table 5. Comparison of Infrastructure in Urban and Rural Hubs

Infrastructure Element	Urban Hubs (Tbilisi, Medellín)	Rural Hubs (Canggu, Ponta do Sol)
High-Speed Internet	Ubiquitous; fiber-optic networks.	Available; reliant on private providers.
Coworking Spaces	Plentiful, professionally managed.	Limited but community-focused.
Accommodation	Premium options, higher costs.	Affordable, co-living spaces common.

Table 5 provides a side-by-side comparison of key infrastructure features in urban and rural hubs, illustrating their strengths and gaps in catering to digital nomads.

5.7 Sustainability Assessment

5.7.1 Environmental Impact

Survey and observational data highlight the environmental pressures associated with digital nomadism:

- Urban hubs, such as Medellín, face challenges with waste management and transportation emissions due to higher densities.
- Rural hubs, such as Ponta do Sol, exhibit better environmental practices through initiatives like eco-friendly coworking spaces and community-led conservation projects.

5.7.2 Social Impact

Rural hubs foster stronger cultural integration through localized initiatives. For instance:

- In Canggu, digital nomads participate in beach cleanups and cultural workshops, contributing positively to the community.
- In urban hubs, the emphasis on professional networking often limits deeper cultural engagement, as seen in Tbilisi.

6. FINDINGS

The findings from the data analysis align with the research objectives, providing insights into the role of digital infrastructure in shaping digital nomad tourism, the dynamics of urban and rural hubs, and the associated economic, social, and environmental impacts.

6.1 Role of Digital Infrastructure in Digital Nomad Tourism

The analysis underscores the centrality of digital infrastructure in enabling and sustaining digital nomadism. High-speed internet was ranked as essential by 98% of survey respondents, confirming its non-negotiable role in destination selection (Richards, 2022). Urban hubs such as Tbilisi and Medellín offer robust infrastructure, including widespread fiber-optic internet and well-equipped coworking spaces, making them ideal for nomads seeking professional environments.

Rural hubs, such as Canggu and Ponta do Sol, have improved connectivity through targeted initiatives, like the "Digital Nomad Village" in Madeira. However, these hubs still lag in coworking infrastructure and reliable public transport. This disparity highlights the need for continued investment to enhance the competitiveness of rural destinations.

6.2 Comparative Dynamics Between Urban and Rural Hubs

The comparison of urban and rural hubs reveals distinct dynamics in their ability to attract and sustain digital nomads:

- **Urban Hubs (Tbilisi, Medellín):**
  - o Urban hubs provide superior infrastructure and extensive coworking facilities, which cater to nomads prioritizing professional networks and convenience.
  - o Higher per-capita spending on accommodation, coworking spaces, and leisure activities drives immediate economic contributions.
  - o Challenges include overcrowding, gentrification, and limited cultural integration, as interactions with locals tend to remain surface-level (Ioannides & Röslmaier, 2021).
- **Rural Hubs (Canggu, Ponta do Sol):**
  - o Rural hubs attract nomads with affordability, tranquility, and opportunities for cultural immersion.
  - o Longer average stays (e.g., 45–60 days) ensure steady economic contributions, albeit at lower spending levels.
  - o Integration programs, such as cultural exchange events and community-based initiatives, promote deeper connections with local communities.

6.3 Economic Contributions

Economic contributions differ significantly between urban and rural hubs:

- Urban hubs benefit from higher short-term spending due to premium infrastructure and amenities. For example, digital nomads in Medellín spend approximately $2,000 monthly, primarily on accommodation and coworking spaces (Müller, 2021).
- Rural hubs derive long-term economic benefits from longer stays, with digital nomads in Ponta do Sol contributing consistently to local businesses in hospitality and cultural tourism.

6.4 Social and Cultural Integration

Urban hubs emphasize professional networking over cultural immersion, with nomads engaging in coworking spaces and innovation ecosystems but seldom in local traditions. Conversely, rural hubs foster meaningful cultural exchanges. In Canggu, nomads actively participate in wellness programs, local festivals, and environmental conservation initiatives, building strong ties with host communities (Reichenberger, 2018).

6.5 Environmental Sustainability

Environmental impacts vary between urban and rural hubs:

- Urban hubs face resource strain due to high population densities and frequent short stays, leading to overcrowding and waste management challenges.
- Rural hubs demonstrate better environmental sustainability. For instance, Ponta do Sol incorporates digital nomads into eco-tourism projects, while Canggu emphasizes waste reduction campaigns and environmental education (Ioannides & Röslmaier, 2021).

7. PRACTICAL RECOMMENDATIONS FOR OPTIMIZING DIGITAL INFRASTRUCTURE AND PROMOTING SUSTAINABLE TOURISM MODELS

The findings of this research emphasize the importance of robust digital infrastructure, balanced economic strategies, cultural integration, and environmental sustainability in creating effective digital nomad tourism models. The following consolidated recommendations are designed for policymakers, tourism operators, and local stakeholders, integrating all previously discussed and additional actionable suggestions.

7.1 Enhancing Digital Infrastructure

- **Expand High-Speed Internet Access:** Governments and private telecom providers must collaborate to extend high-speed internet coverage, particularly in rural areas. Estonia's nationwide broadband initiative and Madeira's investment in high-speed internet for its Digital Nomad Village are examples of success in this area (Hansen & Ferns, 2020). Satellite internet solutions like Starlink can also connect remote destinations.
- **Develop Coworking Spaces:** Invest in coworking hubs tailored to digital nomads' needs. In urban hubs, facilities like Selina Medellín provide professional amenities with cultural integration. Rural hubs can create smaller, community-oriented coworking spaces similar to Dojo Bali, blending functionality with local culture (Richards, 2022).

- **Leverage Smart Technology:** Integrate IoT solutions, AI, and Machine Learning in coworking spaces and accommodations to optimize resource usage, such as energy-saving systems and water management (Correia et al., 2024). For example, energy-efficient coworking hubs in Madeira help reduce environmental impact while maintaining operational efficiency (Müller, 2021).

7.2 Promoting Economic Sustainability

- **Create Diversified Revenue Streams:** Encourage local businesses to diversify offerings by developing packages that integrate cultural and leisure activities, such as guided tours, cooking classes, and artisanal workshops (Jimenez et al., 2024). This approach has succeeded in rural hubs like Ponta do Sol, where locals benefit directly from tourism revenues (Ioannides & Röslmaier, 2021).
- **Regulate Housing Markets:** Implement rental caps or prioritize long-term leases to avoid displacement caused by short-term rentals (Glaeser, 2022). Lisbon's rental cap initiative is an effective example of balancing local housing needs with tourism demands (Reichenberger, 2018).
- **Offer Financial Incentives:** Provide tax breaks or grants to businesses that cater to digital nomads, such as coworking operators and local cafes. These incentives encourage innovation while ensuring tourism revenue benefits local communities (Ji et al., 2024).

7.3 Encouraging Social and Cultural Integration

- **Host Cultural Exchange Programs:** Organize cultural events, such as traditional dance workshops, cooking classes, or language exchanges, to foster interaction between nomads and locals. Green School Bali successfully integrates nomads into the local community through environmental education programs (Richards, 2022).
- **Promote Community-Based Tourism Models:** Involve local residents in tourism planning and decision-making to ensure equitable benefits. Canary Islands' eco-tourism initiatives engage nomads in conservation projects, strengthening community bonds while supporting sustainability (Hansen & Ferns, 2020).
- **Facilitate Nomad-Led Workshops:** Encourage nomads to share skills with local entrepreneurs, such as digital marketing or web development. Medellín's coworking spaces regularly host workshops, boosting local innovation through knowledge exchange (Ioannides & Röslmaier, 2021).

7.4 Emphasizing Environmental Sustainability

- **Introduce Eco-Tourism Activities:** Promote activities like beach cleanups, reforestation projects, or wildlife conservation programs to involve nomads in sustainable practices (Ji et al., 2024). Canggu's "Bye Bye Plastic Bags" initiative is a strong example of integrating environmental stewardship with tourism (Müller, 2021).
- **Establish Carbon Offset Programs:** Encourage nomads to offset travel-related emissions by participating in local tree-planting or renewable energy projects. Medellín's urban reforestation programs effectively engage both tourists and locals in reducing carbon footprints (Dogan et al., 2023).
- **Adopt Sustainable Building Practices:** Develop coworking spaces and accommodations using eco-friendly materials and renewable energy. Madeira's Digital Nomad Village uses sustainable construction methods to reduce its environmental impact while maintaining functionality.

7.5 Developing Hybrid Models for Urban and Rural Integration

- **Small Cities with Rural Characteristics:** Foster the development of hybrid hubs like Chiang Mai, Thailand, which combine urban infrastructure with rural charm to attract nomads seeking a balance between productivity and tranquility (Reichenberger, 2018).
- **Rural Destinations with Urban Amenities:** Enhance rural hubs by introducing select urban amenities like coworking spaces and reliable internet while preserving cultural authenticity. For instance, Ponta do Sol's coworking hubs blend modern workspaces with eco-tourism activities.

7.6 Leveraging Technology for Smart Tourism Management

- **Digital Platforms for Nomads:** Create centralized portals that provide comprehensive information on coworking spaces, accommodation, events, and transportation (Torabi et al., 2022). Madeira's online nomad portal serves as a model for simplifying travel planning for nomads. To create more advanced portals of digital platforms, authorities should prioritize the integration of AI and Machine learning.
- **Real-Time Feedback Systems:** Use digital tools and utilize the power of AI to collect feedback from nomads about infrastructure, cultural integration, and sustainability. This allows for continuous policy refinement based on real-world data.

- **AI for Predictive Analysis:** Employ AI tools to forecast seasonal demand, optimize resource allocation, and plan infrastructure upgrades (Correia et al., 2024).

7.7 Tailoring Visa and Residency Policies

- **Flexible Visa Programs:** Introduce tiered digital nomad visas with benefits like tax exemptions, longer stays, or access to local healthcare. Croatia's digital nomad visa effectively combines these elements (Ioannides & Röslmaier, 2021).
- **Residency Linked to Community Contributions:** Grant long-term visas to nomads who participate in volunteer activities, such as teaching local skills or mentoring startups.

7.8 Strengthening Community Partnerships

- **Collaboration Platforms:** Develop AI-integrated digital platforms that connect nomads with local businesses offering tailored services. Tallinn's e-Residency program promotes such interaction by listing local service providers but the need of the hour is to utilize AI and advanced ICT (Hansen & Ferns, 2020).
- **Nomad-Focused Events:** Host annual summits or hackathons to engage nomads with local entrepreneurs and policymakers. Chiang Mai's Nomad Summit has set a strong precedent in this regard.

8. CONCLUSION

This research highlights the transformative impact of digital infrastructure on the rise of digital nomadism and its influence on urban and rural tourism hubs. High-speed internet, coworking spaces, and community integration are essential elements for destinations aiming to attract digital nomads. Urban hubs, such as Tbilisi and Medellín, excel in offering robust infrastructure and professional networks, making them appealing for short-term stays. Conversely, rural hubs like Canggu and Ponta do Sol leverage tranquility, affordability, and cultural immersion to attract nomads for longer durations.

However, the challenges of gentrification, cultural erosion, and environmental strain in urban hubs, and infrastructure gaps in rural hubs, underscore the need for targeted strategies. Promoting community-based tourism models, sustainable practices, and tailored policies, such as flexible visa programs and incentives for local businesses, are critical for fostering mutually beneficial relationships between digital nomads and host communities.

Practical recommendations, including the development of hybrid hubs, smart tourism solutions, and innovative coworking and co-living models, can ensure destinations cater to the unique needs of digital nomads while safeguarding local interests. By embracing a holistic approach that balances economic, social, and environmental priorities, stakeholders can enhance the resilience, inclusivity, and sustainability of digital nomad tourism, positioning their destinations as thriving hubs for the future of remote work and travel.

REFERENCES

Andino-Frydman, A. (2023). Who is a digital nomad? The evolving identities of the new nomadic workforce. In *Ethnographies of Work* (Vol. 35, pp. 95–137). Emerald Publishing Limited. DOI: 10.1108/S0277-283320230000035005

Cohen, S. A., Duncan, T., & Thulemark, M. (2020). Lifestyle mobilities: The crossroads of travel, leisure, and migration. *Mobilities, 15*(1), 53–69.

Correia, R., Martins, M., & Fontes, R. (Eds.). (2024). *AI Innovations for Travel and Tourism*. IGI Global. DOI: 10.4018/979-8-3693-2137-9

Cruz, R., & Pombo, F. (2022, June). Designing Furniture for Versatile Spaces of Collaborative Work. Covid-19 Accelerating the Change. In *Meeting of Research in Music, Arts and Design* (pp. 456–471). Springer International Publishing.

Dogan, E., Cuomo, F., & Battisti, L. (2023). Reviving urban greening in post-industrial landscapes: The case of Turin. *Sustainability (Basel), 15*(17), 12760. DOI: 10.3390/su151712760

Esteban-Navarro, M. Á., García-Madurga, M. Á., Morte-Nadal, T., & Nogales-Bocio, A. I. (2020, December). The rural digital divide in the face of the COVID-19 pandemic in Europe—recommendations from a scoping review. In Informatics (Vol. 7, No. 4, p. 54). MDPI.

Garcez, A., Correia, R., & Carvalho, A. (2022). Digital nomadism an opportunity for low-density territories: Trás-os-Montes lands case. In *Advances in Tourism, Technology and Systems: Selected Papers from ICOTTS 2021* (Vol. 1, pp. 91–102). Springer Nature Singapore. DOI: 10.1007/978-981-19-1040-1_8

Garcez, A., Correia, R., & Carvalho, A. (2022, December). Digital Nomads: Who They Are and What They Want from the Destinations? In International Conference on Marketing and Technologies (pp. 483-495). Singapore: Springer Nature Singapore.

Glaeser, J. (2022). The effects of digital nomads on housing affordability for local populations in Ericeira (Master's thesis, ISCTE-Instituto Universitario de Lisboa (Portugal)).

Gössling, S., & Humpe, A. (2020). The global scale, distribution and growth of aviation: Implications for climate change. *Global Environmental Change, 65*, 102–120. DOI: 10.1016/j.gloenvcha.2020.102194 PMID: 36777089

Hall, C. M., Scott, D., & Gössling, S. (2021). Tourism and global environmental change: Ecological, social, economic, and political interrelationships. *Journal of Sustainable Tourism*, *29*(4), 556–570.

Hansen, L., & Ferns, B. (2020). Digital nomadism and place attachment: The case of Tallinn, Estonia. *Journal of Tourism Futures*, *6*(3), 193–207.
Hansen, L., & Ferns, B. (2020). Digital nomadism and place attachment: The case of Tallinn, Estonia. *Journal of Tourism Futures*, *6*(3), 193–207.
Hiles, R. E. (2024). Exploring Virtual Team Project Success With Knowledge Management (Doctoral dissertation, National University).

Ioannides, D., & Röslmaier, M. (2021). Remote work in tourism: Impacts and opportunities in rural areas. *Tourism Geographies*, *23*(2), 300–317.

Ji, Y., Kim, S. M., & Kim, Y. (2024). A way to attract digital nomads to tourist destinations in the new normal era. *Sustainability (Basel)*, *16*(6), 2336. DOI: 10.3390/su16062336

Jimenez Ruiz, A. E., Bhartiya, S., & Bhatt, V. (Eds.). (2024). *Promoting Sustainable Gastronomy Tourism and Community Development*. IGI Global. DOI: 10.4018/979-8-3693-1814-0

Kashif, M. (2024). Enhancing the Digital Nomads Experience: A Service Design Approach to Address Challenges and Expectations, Developing a Tailored Solution.

Kolko, B. (2010). Writing in digital environments: Workplaces as multimodal texts. *Technical Communication Quarterly*, *19*(3), 275–302.

Makimoto, T., & Manners, D. (1997). *Digital Nomad*. John Wiley & Sons.

Martins, Márcio Ribeiro (2023). Backpacking culture and mobilities: Independent and nomadic travel. Journal of Hospitality and Tourism Management. eISSN 1839-5260. 55, p. 200-201

Mohn, T. (2020). The digital nomad revolution. *Forbes*. Retrieved from https://www.forbes.com

Müller, A. (2016). The emergence of the digital nomad: A new model of work and travel. *Global Nomad Research*, *3*(4), 45–60.

Müller, A. (2021). Digital nomad villages: The next wave in rural tourism development. *Tourism Innovation Journal*, *5*(1), 12–19.

Orel, M. (2019). Coworking spaces and the localized dynamics of innovation. *Environment and Planning A. Economy and Space*, *51*(4), 803–818.

Prabawa, I. W. S. W., & Pertiwi, P. R. (2020). The digital nomad tourist motivation in Bali: Exploratory research based on push and pull theory. *Athens Journal of Tourism, 7*(3), 161–174. DOI: 10.30958/ajt.7-3-3

Reichenberger, I. (2018). Digital nomads: A quest for lifestyle values. *Annals of Tourism Research, 73*, 98–107.

Richards, G. (2022). Cultural tourism in the age of remote work. *Current Issues in Tourism, 25*(7), 891–907.

Rundel, C. T., Salemink, K., & Strijker, D. (2020). Exploring rural digital hubs and their possible contribution to communities in Europe. *Journal of Rural and Community Development, 15*(3).

Spinuzzi, C. (2012). Working alone together: Coworking as emergent collaborative activity. *Journal of Business and Technical Communication, 26*(4), 399–441. DOI: 10.1177/1050651912444070

Torabi, Z. A., Shalbafian, A. A., Allam, Z., Ghaderi, Z., Murgante, B., & Khavarian-Garmsir, A. R. (2022). Enhancing memorable experiences, tourist satisfaction, and revisit intention through smart tourism technologies. *Sustainability (Basel), 14*(5), 2721. DOI: 10.3390/su14052721

Viswanathan, S., Anbazhagan, A., & Kannan, R. (2021). Bridging the digital divide in rural tourism destinations: A case for India. *Journal of Rural Studies, 87*, 12–21.

Zerva, K., Huete, R., & Segovia-Pérez, M. (2022, May). Digital nomad tourism: The experience of living at the destination. In *International Conference on Modern Trends in Business Hospitality and Tourism* (pp. 15-26). Cham: Springer International Publishing.

Chapter 9
The Role of Host–Guest Interactions in Remote Work–Driven Tourism Development

Dora Gomes
https://orcid.org/0009-0009-3712-8140
GOVCOPP, Universidade de Aveiro, Portugal

Elisabeth Kastenholz
https://orcid.org/0000-0003-4700-0326
GOVCOPP, Universidade de Aveiro, Portugal

Alcina Gaspar Ferreira
https://orcid.org/0000-0002-5119-5827
CARME, School of Technology and Management, Politécnico de Leiria, Portugal

João Almeida
https://orcid.org/0000-0003-1047-6515
GOVCOPP, Universidade de Aveiro, Portugal

ABSTRACT

Digital nomadism, characterised by location-independent work and enabled by digital technologies, represents a promising path for destinations seeking to revitalise their economies and attract new residents, associated to their quality of life, welcoming communities and interesting leisure and tourism proposals. This study examines the interplay between digital nomads and local communities by examining host-guest interactions, their influence on perceived quality of life, and the evolving attitudes of residents towards tourism development. In-depth interviews with resi-

DOI: 10.4018/979-8-3373-0076-4.ch009

dents from a low-population density rural area and representatives from the local Destination Management Organization (DMO) were conducted. The findings from this case study provide valuable insights into how rural communities can manage and benefit from the growing trend of 'remote working tourism', while also addressing potential challenges related to cultural integration, economic disparities, and community cohesion.

INTRODUCTION

The rise of digitalisation has significantly transformed the tourism sector reshaping how experiences are designed, communicated and consumed while additionally enabling new forms of mobility and work while travelling (Solvoll et al., 2015). Digital technologies have not only transformed the tourism experience but also facilitated the rise of digital nomadism, as well as residential tourism associated with remote work purposes, by permitting location-independent work (Chevtaeva et al. 2023; Popova & Malcheva, 2020). Remote work, made possible by digital technologies, allows professionals to work independently of location, leading to the emergence of new forms of tourism, often referred to as "workation tourism" (Popova & Malcheva, 2020) or 'remote work trips/ travel' (Chevtaeva et al. 2023). This phenomenon, where individuals combine work and leisure while temporarily residing in tourist destinations, has altered the way tourists and local residents interact, reshaping community dynamics in areas heavily affected by this trend (Solvoll et al., 2015; Almeida & Belezas, 2022). In this sense, remote work can be seen as a chance for destinations to develop a new strategy to attract visitors and stimulate both local economy and community life (Almeida & Belezas, 2022), with a direct impact on potentially enhancing these places' appeal also for residents, particularly interesting for rural areas (Mão & Xu, 2024).

The phenomenon of digital nomadism thus offers significant opportunities for places seeking to revitalise their economies and attract new residents. By leveraging the flexibility of remote work, these localities can position themselves as appealing options for individuals seeking to balance work and quality of life. This trend is particularly evident in regions where the cost of living is lower compared to the urban centres in the global north where many digital nomads come from, prompting relocation to destinations that offer affordability and better living standards (Kozak et al., 2024). Today, initiatives like digital nomad visas, infrastructure improvements, cultural and recreational incentives, are especially targeted to this increasing group of travellers, whose consumption and lifestyle patterns contribute directly to local economy, particularly its tourism sector (Arslan, 2024; Bednorz, 2024).

Digital nomadism may also foster a shift towards sustainability and responsible tourism practices, depending on the type (Todt & Kastenholz, 2010) and quantity of incoming nomads, but also on the way the phenomenon is managed locally, particularly regarding this group's integration into local community and culture (Teodoroviccz et al, 2023) and other regulatory measures (Arslan, 2024). As a matter of fact, environmentally, socially and culturally conscious tourists increasingly seek rural destinations that align with their values, prioritising sustainable travel and authentic cultural experiences (Leco et al, 2013). Mão and Xu (2024) found that digital nomads may enhance sustainable development of rural areas by bringing new skills, creativity, and cultural exchange, as also found by Yang for urban areas (2024). According to Vagena et al (2023), digital nomads in Greece often engage in local cultural activities, which not only enriches their experience but also supports local communities and cultural preservation. This is in line with Kastenholz and Carvalho's (2024) call for locally embedded co-creative rural tourist experiences responding to new market trends while contributing to sustainable rural development. There is evidence of this group's relevant economic impact through additional and new types of consumption and associated multiplier effects (Arslan, 2024; Bednorz, 2024; Vagena et al, 2023), which are particularly relevant for rural areas (Mão & Xu, 2024). Here, also transference of knowledge and skills from digital nomads to local community members presents a powerful means of enhancing rural development (Mão & Xu, 2024).

On the other hand, Teodoroviccz et al (2023) identified possible negative impacts of digital nomadism, such as the risk of commercialisation of local cultures, with possible dilution of local identity as communities adapt to the preferences of transient populations. Other issues relate to price pressure on housing and consequent issues of gentrification and unequal taxation. Teodoroviccz et al (2023) stress, in this context, the positive effects of community engagement and entrepreneurship among remote workers, whose attachment to the place, its culture and community may be decisive for more sustainable development. Such engagement however, is only possible, if both nomads and residents interact positively. To fully capitalise on the potential of host-guest interactions, it is essential to encourage meaningful exchanges between visitors and locals, enhancing the perceived authenticity of the experience and meaningful immersion in local culture (Carvalho et al 2021).

Despite the importance of positive and trustful host-guest interaction, the interaction between digital nomads and local communities remains underexplored in academic literature. While there is some evidence that these interactions can enhance the tourist experience and foster a sense of place attachment, further research is needed to understand the perceived effects of such interaction on both residents and visitors (Carvalho et al, 2021; Hunt & Stronza, 2014). Particularly the community's perspective less well understood, despite its crucial role in keeping local culture alive and providing a welcoming atmosphere to visitors (Kastenholz et al, 2013). Gupta et al. (2024) emphasise the need to evaluate initiatives that support local businesses, promote civic engagement, and contribute to community vitality, while analysing the health and well-being of digital nomad communities, so as to understand how these factors influence positive social interaction and community cohesion, both critical elements of sustainable tourism. To address these gaps, further investigation is needed into the role of host-guest interaction in shaping quality of life, residents' attitudes towards tourism, and the sustainability of lifestyle migration, particularly in the rural context.

This chapter seeks to explore the interplay between digital nomadism and local communities by examining host-guest interactions, their influence on residents' quality of life, and the evolving attitudes of residents towards tourism development. It aims to assess how lifestyle migration contributes to the economic, social, and cultural vitality of rural destinations, with a particular focus on digital nomads, remote working tourists and residential tourists. By addressing these themes, this research contributes to the broader discourse on sustainable tourism and the transformative potential of digital nomadism and remote work for local communities, specifically in low-population-density, rural areas.

Therefore, this chapter explores the role of host-guest interactions in affecting local residents' quality of life, their attitude towards tourism development and lifestyle migration as well as their views on these migrants' role for their community's development, particularly in the context of digital nomads, remote working and residential tourists.

It will, specifically, focus on how local residents perceive the arrival of these new types of visitors and the impact of their interactions on community life, exploring several key questions, from the perspective of local residents:

- What role can digital nomads and remote working tourists play in the economic and social development of rural communities?
- How do residents perceive interactions with remote workers and digital nomads?
- In what ways do interactions between residents and digital nomads contribute to social well-being and community cohesion?
- What challenges may negatively affect interaction and relations between local residents and new migrants, perceived as 'half-tourists'?
- How can rural communities capitalise on these interactions to revitalise the local economy and develop sustainable tourism?

LITERATURE REVIEW

The literature review examines the intersection of digital nomadism, remote-work tourism, host-guest interaction, and the socio-economic dynamics of rural communities. It contextualises the growing phenomenon of remote work tourism and new lifestyle mobilities within broader trends in rural development and tourism studies, identifying key theoretical insights and research gaps.

Evolution of Digital Nomadism and Remote Work Tourism

Digital nomadism, characterised by location-independent work, undertaken in distinct and changing locations, outside the usual place of residence and work, enabled by digital technologies, has emerged as a significant trend in global mobility. Defined as highly mobile professionals who work remotely, digital nomads often seek destinations where they can combine work with travel experiences and leisure (Chevtaeva et al. 2023; Kozak et al., 2024; Mancinelli, 2020). The concept has been suggested to fall into the sometimes-used term of "half-tourists", individuals who split their time between professional and leisure pursuits, often establishing semi-permanent ties to destinations and correspondingly perceived as a hybrid category (Cambridge Dictionary, 2021; Almeida & Belezas, 2022). In any case, digital nomads can be qualified as tourists, since they travel to and stay, usually for less than a year, at different destinations than the one they live in (Kozak et al., 2024). Digital nomad travel can take various forms, such as short trips, monthly retreats, or extended weekends where individuals incorporate a few extra days of remote work to explore a destination (Chevtaeva et al., 2023). After his systematic review study that focuses on the supply side of digital nomadism, particularly examining government responses to this emerging class of mobile workers, Bednorz (2024) pointed out the following definition of the digital nomad from the host country perspective: "a foreign professional who stays at the destination for a fixed period of time (defined by visa rules), sustained by their income from work or entrepreneurial activity based abroad and performed digitally" (p.11).

Digital nomads are conceptually close to, however distinct from the concept of 'remote-working tourists', with the latter travelling to a destination (for different periods of time), for the purpose of working there remotely, while also enjoying the place's quality of life, leisure and tourism amenities. Remote working tourists may or not change their location for remote working, with the first case corresponding to 'digital nomadism', so that the latter could actually be defined as a sub-category of remote-working tourists.

The COVID-19 pandemic catalysed this movement, reshaping work-life dynamics and encouraging lifestyle migration to less densely populated areas (Ehn et al., 2022; Eimermann & Carson, 2023). Prior to 2020, remote work was predominantly the domain of freelancers and technology professionals, but the pandemic highlighted its viability across diverse sectors. For example, the WYSE Travel Confederation estimated that by 2035, there could be over one billion digital nomads globally. This shift reflects a redefinition of tourism, work and migration, merging individuals' and social groups' professional and leisure pursuits, while offering unique opportunities for rural destinations to attract lifestyle migrants seeking sustainable and immersive experiences (Mao & Xu, 2024; Vagena et al, 2023). Unlike traditional tourists, who typically engage in short-term visits, remote working tourists and digital nomads often opt for extended stays that foster deeper immersion in local environments, allowing them to have a better understanding of the local culture (Chevtaeva et al. 2023; Shin et al., 2024; Vagena et al, 2023). Besides, travel activities undertaken during remote work trips have the potential to enhance subjective well-being (Chevtaeva et al. 2023).

Nevertheless, digital nomads also often face social challenges related to isolation and lack of belonging, if the previously mentioned integration in local community fails. While the flexibility of their lifestyle offers unparalleled freedom, many report feelings of loneliness and disconnection from both local communities and their home networks (Von Zumbusch & Lalicic, 2020). This has led to an increasing reliance on online platforms, social media, and co-living spaces as means of fostering community and support as well as the very identity of digital nomads (Aroles et al., 2020; Thompson, 2019). To overcome such negative feelings, these travellers often seek authentic and meaningful interactions with both the digital nomad community (Thompson, 2019) and the local community, enriching their experience and contributing to the socio-cultural fabric of their chosen destinations (Kastenholz et al., 2013; Carvalho et al., 2021). Such interactions, when well-managed, additionally benefit local residents by reducing social isolation, enhancing cultural exchange, and fostering community pride (Eusébio et al, 2014; Kastenholz et al, 2013; Stylidis, 2022). In certain contexts there may therefore be a common need and interest in social contacts and community building, in both the digital nomad and local community, requiring better understanding of its dynamics, conditioning factors and outcomes to guarantee socially sustainable place development.

Impacts of Digital Nomadism and Remote Work Tourism in Rural Areas

Digital nomads have a tendency to choose cozy, warm, picturesque and budget-friendly destinations (Arslan, 2024), with a variety of leisure activities, more authentic and immersive, and with a culturally diverse population (Thompson, 2019), rather than mass tourism destinations (Kelly & Arelano, 2021), making rural destinations a potentially attractive place to stay for longer periods (Mao & Xu, 2024). Moreover, this type of tourists often seek meaningful connections with other people, that may not only be to likeminded digital nomads (Kelly & Arelano, 2021), but also to those residing in that place and build a small-scale local community. The particular, more personalized, social structure of rural local community is, for some, another factor that attracts to less crowded, low-density regions.

Following this line of thought, some tourism destinations have already invested in promoting themselves as perfect places for digital nomads (Ehn et al., 2022; Rainoldi et al., 2022; Vagena et al, 2023). In fact, Portugal and Bulgaria are becoming increasingly popular among European digital nomads due to their high quality of life, affordability, and convenient time zone alignment with the rest of Europe (Kozak et al., 2024). In rural areas, remote work opportunities, increasing digital connectivity and new movements of digital nomads presents an opportunity to address major structural challenges such as depopulation, ageing demographics, limited economic opportunities, and social isolation (Mao & Xu, 2024), permitting chances for economic regeneration and social revitalisation (Almeida & Daniel, 2022). Besides, the changes in the perceptions of work-life balance have affected the geography of work and living preferences (Akhavan et al. 2021; Chevtaeva et al. 2023). Thus, digital nomadism and remote working represent a promising avenue for rural regions to attract new residents and visitors, leveraging their natural appeal as quiet, authentic and healthy lifestyle environments.

The influx of digital nomads offers significant economic potential for rural communities. By spending on local goods, services, and accommodations, nomads contribute to the revitalisation of economies suffering from population decline and unemployment (Almeida & Daniel, 2022; Mao & Xu, 2024; Zhou et al., 2024). Unlike short-term tourists, remote workers and digital nomads foster longer-term economic activity, such as creating demand for coworking spaces and knowledge-based services (Arslan, 2024; Bednorz, 2024; Günay et al., 2024). Additionally, their presence can attract businesses and stimulate entrepreneurship in peripheral regions. Socially, the presence of remote workers can reduce isolation among residents and foster cultural exchange (Kastenholz et al., 2013; Vagena et al, 2023). Knowledge sharing between digital nomads and local communities can inspire innovative projects and collaborations, enhancing the creative and intellectual capital of the region (Teodoroviccz et al, 2023). Yet, these benefits are contingent on the successful integration of nomads into local social networks, which requires intentional strategies to manage cultural differences and prevent potential tensions. On that account, apart from careful regulatory initiatives taking community interests into account (Arslan, 2024; Teodoroviccz et al, 2023), encouraging positive social interactions, inclusivity, and mutual understanding between digital nomads and the communities they join is highly recommended (Gupta, et al., 2024).

The Role of Local Communities and Host-Guest Interactions in Tourism

Cultural exchange and local engagement are vital aspects of digital nomadism, as these individuals typically seek authentic experiences, fostering a deeper connection with the local culture and positive impact on local communities (Kozak et al., 2024; Mancinelli, 2020; Teodoroviccz et al, 2023). Besides, digital nomads integrate into local communities as neighbours rather than mere tourists, fostering closer interactions with local residents. These frequent and meaningful interpersonal exchanges have the potential to bridge cultures and promote mutual understanding (Kozak et al., 2024; Vagena et al, 2023), often acting as 'cultural brokers' particularly in rural tourism context (Kastenholz & Sparrer, 2009). On the other hand, particularly the better integrated remote workers, as a specific type of amenity migrants, potentially staying longer and even investing in the visited locations (Teodoroviccz et al, 2023), may also play the role of 'cultural brokers' to new visitors of the revitalized rural destinations, with interesting dynamics permitting the renovation of declining rural areas (Membretti & Iancu, 2017).

Thus, the role of local communities as stakeholders in tourism cannot be overstated. Communities are central to the tourism ecosystem, serving as custodians of cultural identity and as key drivers of the destination's appeal (Roxas et al., 2020). In rural contexts, the interactions between people and institutions are unique and different from urban areas, fundamentally shaping and narrating rural places (Bosworth et al. 2023). The smaller size of networks and density in rural areas lead to higher levels of social isolation and exclusion of rural workers, especially if self-employed (Abreu et al. 2019). On the other hand, the network ties are usually stronger and with older connections, which can foster community cohesion but hinder change or integration of new residents (Roundy, 2017), posing challenges to amenity migrants (Membretti & Iancu, 2017). However, literature remains scarce on the socio-economic impacts of digital nomads on host communities and the analysis of governmental motivations behind implementing such policies (Wang et al., 2018; Sánchez-Vergara et al., 2023).

As pointed out, the local communities (hosts) are a key element of a tourist destination, being intrinsically tied to the destination's culture and way of life (Hong, 2009; Kastenholz & Sparrer, 2009; Kastenholz & Carvalho, 2024), which substantially enriches the place experience. This is particularly important for remote workers and digital nomads, who are often looking for more than just a place to work—they seek communities where they can build connections and feel a sense of belonging (Almeida & Belezas, 2022). These interactions also benefit the community by fostering social exchange, reducing isolation, and enhancing community pride (Kastenholz et al., 2013). In rural areas, where tourism tends to be less massified, the interactions between visitors and residents are often more personalised and meaningful, creating stronger bonds and fostering a sense of place attachment among visitors (Carvalho et al, 2021; Eusébio et al., 2014; Kastenholz et al., 2020). Moreover, the value of "community" in this context is bidimensional, encompassing both local residents and the network of remote workers who temporarily settle in these areas. Both communities, though distinct lenses, share overlapping interests and goals, such as fostering an inclusive and vibrant local environment. Collaboration between these groups is therefore critical for the success of tourism-driven development initiatives (Merrell et al., 2021; Bosworth et al., 2023; Teodoroviccz et al, 2023).

Consequently, efforts to create opportunities for positive social interaction would enhance an inclusive and dynamic local community, enriched through inputs from diverse backgrounds and cultures come together within remote working tourists and digital nomad communities. This convergence could foster meaningful cross-cultural exchange and collaboration, enriching the local cultural fabric with unique perspectives, traditions, and new practices (Gupta, et al., 2024; Teodoroviccz et al, 2023).

METHODOLOGY

Research Design

This study adopts a case study approach, in the village Figueiró dos Vinhos, with the goal of understanding residents' perceptions regarding interactions with remote workers and digital nomads, specifically yielding responses to the previously posed research questions.

In-depth interviews with Figueiró dos Vinhos residents and members of the local Destination Management Organization (DMO) – namely, of the municipal council and of the municipality's Business and Innovation Center 'Centro Investe' - were undertaken to comprehend the role of these interactions in enhancing the understanding of potential impacts of lifestyle migration and digital nomadism on quality of life and development perspective of local communities.

These interviews were conducted through the participation in the 'Rural experience' initiative. 'Rural Experience' is an initiative promoted by *Rural Move* (www.ruralmove.org), a non-profit organisation founded in 2020, which aims to create, develop, and promote activities and initiatives that enhance investment and repopulation in Portuguese rural areas. This organisation has been recognised both nationally and at European level as best practice for rural development through social innovation (Mariotti & Sasso, 2024). The idea for Rural Move was inspired by a broader view on rural areas, beyond agriculture, which helped to uncover opportunities to promote social and economic development of these areas, including remote working, green and social economies, and new perceptions about rural life. In that sense, Rural Experiences are short-term coworking and coliving experiences which aim to showcase a rural area to a group of remote workers who, for a short period of time, experience living and working there. The goals are to promote the territory as an attractive place for remote workers, but also to gather feedback from participants on the challenges, potential and points for improvement in the area, as well as, to encourage the involvement of local actors in strategies and initiatives to attract and retain new residents. Together with the Municipality of Figueiró dos Vinhos and partnering with the European Rural Coworking Project, Rural Move organised a one-week rural experience in May 2024.

CASE STUDY CONTEXT: FIGUEIRÓ DOS VINHOS

Figueiró dos Vinhos, a village in central Portugal, district of Leiria (figure 1), offers a compelling case study for understanding the dynamics of digital nomadism and host-guest interactions. Figueiró dos Vinhos is the headquarters of the municipality of Figueiró dos Vinhos, which has three other parishes – Aguda, Arega and Campelo.

Figure 1. Figueiró dos Vinhos map

Source: Own elaboration

Figueiró dos Vinhos county has a population density (No./km^2) of 30,1 (data from 2022). Like many rural areas in Portugal, Figueiró dos Vinhos has experienced economic challenges, including population decline, aging residents, and a lack of viable employment opportunities. The population of Figueiró dos Vinhos has fluctuated over the years, reflecting the demographic trends of Portugal's interior regions. Last statistics on Figueiró dos Vinhos (2023) reported that the municipality has 5270 residents, 57 more than in 2022. As seen in figure 2, Figueiró dos Vinhos has an ageing population, with older age ranges, particularly 70-74 years and 75-79 years, showing a larger share, especially on the female side. In fact, the percentage of population with 65 years and older has been increasing over the years. While in 2017 the population with 65 years and older was 33%, in 2023 it corresponded to 35,7%.

Figure 2. Figueiró dos Vinhos age range population

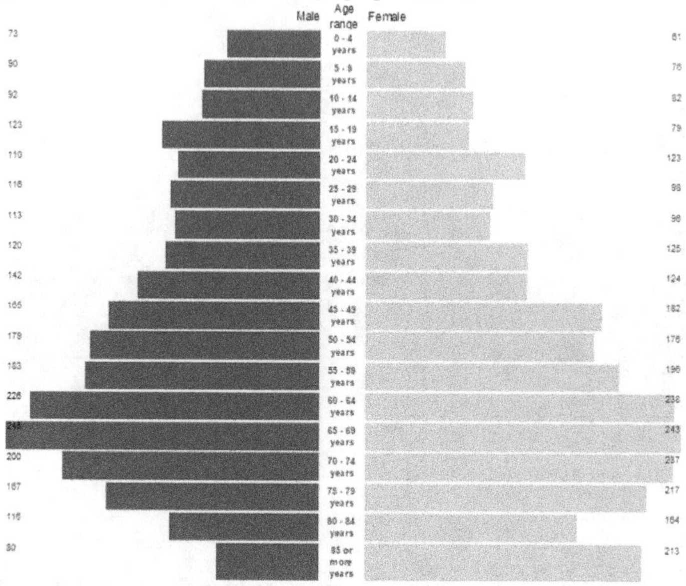

Source: Own elaboration based on INE – statistic Portugal data

The ageing index of Figueiró dos Vinhos increased from 391,1 in 2022 to 397 in 2023. This indicator, which reflects the ratio between the elderly population (aged 65 and over) and the young population (under 15 years), reveals a trend of progressive ageing within the local population, as also reflected in the natural growth rate of -1,20% in 2023. During the 20th century, the town experienced significant emigration, as residents sought better living conditions elsewhere, contributing to an ageing population, a reality shared by many rural areas in Portugal.

The effective growth rate was of 1,09%, driven primarily by a migration growth rate of 2,29%, partially as a result of the municipality's efforts in stimulating migration towards the locality as crucial in offsetting the natural population decline. These data underscore the importance of attracting and retaining new residents as a key factor for sustaining the region's population growth and vitality.

Regarding the number of people employed in companies and the average earnings between 2017 and 2022 in Figueiró dos Vinhos, data reveals a positive, although moderate, evolution in the local labour market (table 1). The number of workers experienced some fluctuations but remained stable over the years. This trend suggests a slight recovery in employment, with a relatively stable capacity to retain jobs in the region. Additionally, the average earnings showed consistent growth. This upward trend in wages highlights a steady improvement in workers' income, reflecting possible enhancements in working conditions and the economic performance of local businesses.

Table 1. Employment data

	2017	2018	2019	2020	2021	2022
People working in companies	1108	1072	1125	1116	1158	1156
Average gain (€)	814	875,4	871,6	913	948,7	1004,85

Source: INE – statistic Portugal

Figueiró dos Vinhos is surrounded by nature and has significant historical and cultural value. Huddled in the Serra da Lousã, it lies within an area of forests and rivers, making it a popular destination for outdoor enthusiasts. It is also part of the Rota das Aldeias do Xisto, a network that includes several traditional villages in the interior of Portugal, where the houses are built from schist stone. These locations preserve a simple and authentic way of life, while also offering opportunities for outdoor activities such as hiking and cycling. In the 19th century, Figueiró dos Vinhos became known for the naturalist movement in Portugal, with a particular focus on the painter José Malhoa, who found inspiration for some of his works there. The village was also a centre for cultural and artistic activities, which continue to be promoted today.

Among its attractions (table 2) are:

Table 2. Figueiró dos Vinhos attractions

Attraction	Description
Fragas de São Simão	One of the most famous tourist spots, with a river beach nestled between impressive rock formations. Fragas de São Simão are the village's most significant natural attraction. **Serving as a source of leisure for both local residents and visitors.**
Aldeia de Xisto da Casal de São Simão	A traditional village that preserves the typical architecture of the region, with houses made of schist, creating a picturesque and welcoming atmosphere, within appealing natural scenery.
José Malhoa Museum and Art	The village has a strong connection with this important Portuguese naturalist painter, and the Casa da Cultura may feature works or references to his life and work. Although the José Malhoa Museum is primarily located in Caldas da Rainha, the painter's presence in the region is quite evident in Figueiró dos Vinhos. The local cultural heritage is widely promoted through various art exhibitions and cultural events held throughout the year, celebrating the village's history and artistic traditions.
Churches and Religious Heritage	The Matriz Church of Figueiró dos Vinhos and other historic buildings in the region stand witness to its long history.

Source: Figueiró dos Vinhos council (https://www.cm-figueirodosvinhos.pt/)

In terms of infrastructures (table 3), Figueiró dos Vinhos has a decent range of infrastructure and services:

Table 3. Figueiró dos Vinhos infrastructure and services

Infrastructure and services	Description
Accommodation and Restaurants	There is a good range of accommodation options, including rural tourism houses, guesthouses, and small lodging units that respect the traditional style of the region. Local cuisine is a major attraction, with restaurants serving typical Portuguese dishes such as roasted kid, fish stews, and conventual sweets.
Health	Figueiró dos Vinhos has a health centre that provides primary medical care to both residents and visitors; however, it is limited on his services, which forces residents to go to nearby hospitals when needed, being the closest one 40kms of distance.
Transportation	The village is connected to other localities in the region by the A13, one of the main highways in Central Portugal, facilitating access to cities such as Leiria and Coimbra. The Figueiró dos Vinhos bus station links the village to other areas, although with reduced schedules.
Education	Figueiró dos Vinhos has primary and secondary schools, offering education from pre-school to high school.

Source: Figueiró dos Vinhos council (https://www.cm-figueirodosvinhos.pt/)

Despite demographic challenges, the local community has demonstrated resilience. Traditional events, including religious festivals, markets, and cultural activities, play a vital role in fostering community bonds and preserving local identity. Tourism, particularly centred on the area's natural heritage and the Schist Villages, has supported economic revitalisation and attracted new visitors to the region (table 4).

Table 4. Tourism data

	2017	2021	2023
Guests capacity in tourist accommodation establishment	94	72	80
Nights spent in tourist accommodation establishments (No.)	6774	7446	11973
Guests hosted in tourist accommodation establishments (No.)	3697	3710	6702
Average stay in tourist accommodation establishments ((No.)	1,8	2	1,8
Total income in of tourist accommodation establishments (10^3 €)	152	190	382

Source: Own elaboration based on INE – statistic Portugal data

The tourism data for Figueiró dos Vinhos from 2017 to 2023 reveals a significant growth and recovery in the sector. Although lodging capacity has decreased, there was a substantial increase in the number of guests and overnight stays, which highlights Figueró's growing appeal. In 2023, 9.862 overnight stays were by Portuguese tourists (82,4%) and 2.111 by foreigners (17,6%), reflecting a strong domestic presence. However, the average length of stay remained stable, fluctuating between 1,8 and 2 nights, suggesting the need to promote longer stays. Total income generated by accommodation establishments saw a remarkable rise.

In recent years, Figueiró dos Vinhos has invested in the revitalisation of its Schist Villages and the development of rural and sustainable tourism, aiming to draw visitors and provide new impetus to the local economy, according to the Municipal Master Plan (2015). While demographic issues, such as a declining resident population due to emigration, persist, the town has focused on creating quality living conditions and enhancing its appeal to young people, tourists, and entrepreneurs alike. In fact, in recent years, the village has started to attract digital nomads and remote workers, drawn by its natural beauty, affordable cost of living, and relative isolation—ideal for individuals seeking quiet environments for work. Figueiró dos Vinhos, with the primary goal of diversifying spaces for business activities and attracting a wide range of audiences, has developed a project to establish the SONUMA Business Complex Coworking Space. This complex offers an innovative coworking space designed for companies and individuals seeking a professional environment to carry out their work. This facility caters to remote work, telecommuting, and other flexible work modalities that were accelerated by the COVID-19 pandemic and have since become standard across various sectors. It is equipped with suitable furniture, internet access, a comfortable, welcoming and informal atmosphere, with a dedicated meeting area, and access to service zones such as a cafeteria and canteen. This facility proves the village's commitment to attracting new tourists and residents.

Data Collection

Data collection occurred during the fourth week of May 2024. During the Rural Experience, residents and DMOs who had contact with the Rural Experience participants were asked to contribute in this study, by answering questions in a semi-structured interview. To address the research objectives, five in-depth interviews were conducted: three with local residents and two with DMO representatives (one is the head of the office of the mayor of Figueiró dos Vinhos and the other is the operational manager of the investment support office at Centro Investe). For residents, the interviews began by exploring their motivations for living in a rural area. This was followed by an examination of their perceptions of rural life, including its advantages and disadvantages. Finally, the discussions addressed the impacts of the Rural Experience initiative, particularly regarding the attraction of new tourists and potential future residents. For DMOs, the focus was on the impacts of the Rural Experience initiative and the community's engagement with tourism and tourists. This was followed by an exploration of the activities developed to promote and enhance the tourist destination, as well as their perceptions of community satisfaction with these initiatives. Each interview lasted approximately 20 minutes. The interviews took place in the context of the before-mentioned Rural Experience that attracted 12 remote workers, aged between 25 and 65, representing a wide range of professions, from Portuguese urban and other rural areas for a one-week work stay, which also integrated social and cultural activities promoted by the municipality. The workers engaged with the local community not only at the coworking space, SONUMA, but also through various activities scheduled throughout the week. These activities included a walk around the village, a joint session for participants and residents, on the "Potential of Remote Work in a Rural Context", participation in the rehearsals for the São João Marches, a visit to the Fragas de São Simão, attendance at TEDx Figueiró dos Vinhos, as well as lunches and dinners at local restaurants in Figueiró dos Vinhos.

The interviews were designed to explore residents' perceptions regarding their interactions with the remote workers and to understand the perceived impacts of this interaction on residents' quality of life and local development. They also explored the reasons for living in a rural area, as well as some of the needs and difficulties faced by the residents. Comments on digital nomadism trends, along with associated benefits and challenges, were also discussed, providing a deeper understanding of residents' views on the impacts welcoming this new type of visitor on their lives.

All interviews were recorded with the consent of the participants. The one-on-one format provided a safe and informal space for interviewees to express their opinions freely, particularly on sensitive issues such as development needs and attitudes towards tourism. The relaxed atmosphere encouraged candid responses, enhancing the authenticity and depth of the data collected.

Data Analysis

Following data collection, the interviews were transcribed using the TurboScribe platform and subjected to thematic analysis. This approach involved identifying, analysing, and interpreting thematic patterns within the qualitative data. This methodology specifically addressed the following themes: (1) Community perceptions, understanding how residents perceive the presence and interactions with digital nomads and remote workers; (2) benefits of attracting tourists, identifying the impacts of digital nomadism and remote work on the local economy and community life; (3) tourism development perspectives, exploring how residents and DMOs view the potential for tourism development driven by remote work; (4) the community's openness to new types of tourists and residents within the context of lifestyle migration and community development; and, finally (5) identification of challenges and needs, highlighting the difficulties faced by rural communities and the investment required to support sustainable tourism.

RESULTS

After transcribing a total of 9333 words, corresponding to one hour and twenty-six minutes of recordings, the interviews' answers on the previously mentioned topic, centred on the local residents' view on the presence and possible increase of remote workers and digital nomads, were meticulously analysed, in order to understand the phenomenon under study, in the context of this rural destination.

By agglomerating all interviews discourses, taking in account the 5 main themes ((1) community perceptions; (2) benefits of attracting tourists; (3) tourism development perspectives; (4) the community's openness to new types of tourists and residents; and (5) identification of challenges and needs), it was possible, to create a word cloud, using the software *venngage*, (figure 3), visualizing the most common insights mentioned in the interviews, thus managing to identify some concerns of the population of Figueiró dos Vinhos.

Figure 3. Word Cloud

Source: own elaboration

The word cloud shows a clear focus on tourism and development, with frequent references to its role in improving both the economic and social landscape of the region and, particularly, its community. Keywords like "*tourism*" "*development*" and "*infrastructures*" underline the need for strategic planning and investment in tourism and infrastructure to cater to both visitors and residents. Rural regions as tourist destinations are often associated with terms like "quite", "identity" and "quality of life" as they offer authentic and healthy living environments (da Silva et al, 2016; Thompson, 2019), which is understood by local residents and DMO representatives. With the presence of digital nomads and remote workers, these regions may foster entrepreneurship, "innovation" and "investment", as expressed by most interviewees. Figueiró dos Vinhos stands out from other rural areas due to its strong connection to "culture" and "community", often associated to "events" which have been highlighted as key elements for the place's "sustainability" and its tourism potential, while "accomodation", "transport" and "accessibility" remains a particular challenge.

For a more holistic analysis, discourses were combined thematically, as follows (table 5).

Table 5. Impacts from attraction of digital nomads and remote workers

Impacts	Theme	Number of references
Benefits Perceived	Tourism stimulation	4
	Stimulation and preservation of culture	5
	Quality of life	6
	Population growth and revitalisation through new (young) residents	7
Challenges Perceived	Lack of public transport	4
	Healthcare limitations	2
	Language barriers	4
	Need for more services initiatives	4

Interviewees showed very positive reactions towards the arrival of these new tourists, reporting benefits for them and contributions to the social and economic revitalisation of the region, as highlighted by a DMO member - "*I believe the population views it positively... they can see the benefits of bringing all these activities and infrastructure*". However, there were also some challenges identified, for both tourists and residents. And, for many, the influx of these longer staying tourists represents an opportunity to meet these challenges by introducing new services, develop infrastructure, and enhance the community's overall quality of life. These perceptions are detailed next.

A. Benefits perceived

Among the many perceived benefits resident's underline: stimulation of tourism development and of culture, heritage preservation, and, last but not least, population growth through new (young) residents and enhanced quality of life.

Stimulation of Tourism development

There is a clear positive perception of the community on the impacts of local tourism development and attraction of new visitors. Not only is the local community noticing the arrival of a new type of tourist, but it is also showing receptiveness toward them – "*The population is, quite naturally, incorporating this change and internalising this new reality in a peaceful manner*". The willingness of residents to embrace these changes reflects not only their adaptability but also their recognition of tourism as a tool for community development. This readiness to welcome new types of tourists, particularly digital nomads, positions Figueiró dos Vinhos as a promising destination for work-driven tourism. Residents see the potential for tourism to contribute to local revitalisation, while DMOs view it as an opportunity to integrate visitors and residents in a way that benefits both groups.

Nevertheless, the development of tourism in rural areas, particularly in Figueiró dos Vinhos, is guided by a niche-oriented approach, as highlighted by the local DMOs – "*When we are talking about territories of our size, we operate within a niche logic*". This perspective underscores the importance of tailoring tourism initiatives to the unique characteristics and opportunities of the region, matching the needs of residents with those of visitors.

Tourism development in Figueiró dos Vinhos relies heavily on the creation of structured products, such as cultural and nature-based tourism. These initiatives attract visitors and generate a positive economic impact while encouraging private investment in services such as accommodation and dining. However, this growth demands careful planning to ensure infrastructure keeps up with the rising demand.

Efforts to improve the region's infrastructure reflect a dual-purpose strategy that benefits both residents and tourists. As noted by a DMO representative, "*The conditions we, as a council, create for residents are also extended to tourists*". This approach fosters a sense of shared development, ensuring that tourism-related investments align with local priorities while enhancing the visitor experience. By focusing on quality infrastructure, the council aims to create a welcoming environment: "*Our goal is to create quality conditions for welcoming* [visitors]". In addition, while tourism is recognised for its economic and social benefits, the integration of the local community into tourism development requires strategic planning, with DMO members underlining the importance of considering residents as central stakeholders – "*When we think about tourism, we must not forget what is also good for the resident*".

The potential for tourism to attract repeat visitors is another critical factor mentioned. Activities that integrate work and leisure, such as remote work retreats, are seen as opportunities to introduce visitors to the region's cultural and natural offerings, as explained by a resident - "*Sometimes people come just for a holiday and end up making friends. Many of them bring more people for a holiday, tourism, or visits. Friends bring friends, and sometimes they want to revisit to explore further and see more*". This dynamic is reinforced by organised events that encourage experiences beyond professional obligations, creating opportunities for visitors to immerse in local traditions and culture. Such interactions can transform one-time visitors into regular patrons, residential tourists or even long-term residents.

Residents also emphasised the virtuous circle created by this strategy, pointing out that increased tourism can drive population growth, which in turn improves infrastructure – "*With more population, more infrastructure is created. I believe those already in place are improved, and new ones are built, which I believe also helps tourism*". This virtuous cycle connects the well-being of the community with sustainable tourism growth, creating an environment where residents and tourists benefit equally.

Stimulation and preservation of Culture

The stimulation and preservation of culture emerged as one of the most prominent perceived benefits, with respondents underscoring the positive impacts on local culture. Events and cultural activities were specifically noted as ways to revitalise traditions, support community engagement, and promote the region's identity. As one participant stated: "*The presence of tourists helps to enrich local culture, and the interaction with visitors creates opportunities to enhance everyone's experience*".

The preservation of cultural heritage and historical monuments, although mentioned less frequently, was seen as integral to maintaining the authenticity of the area while attracting visitors – "*We have worked to preserve our heritage, such as the Aldeias do Xisto (Schist villages) and other historic buildings, while also promoting sustainable tourism*".

Moreover, "*sustainability*" was identified as a key factor for ensuring that tourism development aligns with the long-term needs of both the local community and the natural environment. It was acknowledged that preserving resources while fostering growth is essential for balanced and responsible development.

Increased quality of life

One of the defining characteristics of rural territories, including Figueiró dos Vinhos, is their slower pace of life, which is perceived in two distinct ways by local residents. For some, this tranquillity is cherished as a source of peace and community spirit – "*I've always loved the peace, quiet,... the sense of community*". For others, however, the lack of activity and socialising can lead to a feeling of isolation – "*I like being in a calmer area, but I miss the socialising and movement*". These dual perspectives highlight the need to strike a balance between preserving the region's quiet charm and fostering a more dynamic social environment.

Despite their differing views, residents share a common desire for more active social interactions – "*I often miss the noise and confusion of people. We need to be able to strike a balance*". This sentiment underscores the potential for digital nomads and other long-term visitors to enhance local community life. The integration of technology and a more socially active environment is seen as a viable solution – "*We need to stay in tune with modern technology and social life*".

DMO representatives echoed these perspectives, recognising the residents' interest in welcoming newcomers. They emphasised that the community enjoys engaging with visitors – "*People here like to see tourists, they like to see people from abroad come here*". Importantly, they reassured that this increased interaction does not compromise the peaceful essence of Figueiró dos Vinhos – "*The arrival of tourists doesn't create [excessive] noise or confusion*", instead, the presence of visitors enriches the community by fostering social encounters with people from diverse backgrounds, thereby enhancing the quality of life in the region.

Population growth and revitalisation through new (young) residents

The influx of digital nomads and long-term visitors is increasingly seen as a transformative opportunity for rural regions, particularly those that were not traditionally considered tourist destinations. This phenomenon, driven by the rise of remote work, has allowed rural areas to attract not only temporary visitors but also new residents seeking improved quality of life and a tranquil environment. As stated in the interviews the public organisations are "*responsible for territorial management*" and need to change their perspective, "*not just towards tourists, but also [new] residents*".

Tourism, when strategically positioned, can serve as a catalyst for lifestyle migration, as decisions regarding both tourism and lifestyle migration often overlap (Benson & O'Reilly, 2009; Gosnell & Arams, 2011). Some rural residents initially discovered these regions as tourists, drawn by their natural beauty and peaceful surroundings, falling into the category of 'lifestyle or amenity migration'. Their positive experiences often led them to make the transition to becoming full-time residents. Therefore, destinations "*can, at some point, position and achieve a certain level of notoriety through tourism activities, that can be the first step for a tourist to become, in a second phase, a future resident*". These dynamic highlights the role of tourism not merely as a leisure activity but as a possible strategy for promoting sustainable community growth. By boosting the reputation of a destination, tourism enhances its visibility and appeal, encouraging individuals – both from national urban areas and abroad – to consider rural regions as potential places to live and work.

Innovative projects, such as Rural Move, were cited for their role in attracting new residents and stimulating regional development – "*These types of projects* (like Rural Move*) are innovative for the region, helping attract not just tourists but also new residents and families*"; "*When we talk about innovation, Figueiró has done a good job over the years, aiming to attract tourists and new residents*". Interviewees expressed optimism that tourism and remote work could reverse demographic decline, thus revitalising the community.

In fact, the arrival of young, active residents is particularly valuable for rural development in the Portuguese hinterland, suffering population ageing. The phenomenon of teleworking has enabled individuals from urban areas to relocate to Figueiró dos Vinhos, recognising the advantages of living in such a setting. Simultaneously, there is a growing interest from international citizens - "*We are starting to see young people from Portuguese society who lived in urban areas relocating here because of remote work opportunities, but also foreign citizens looking to settle here*". These active residents not only bring economic vitality but also contribute to a more dynamic and diverse social fabric. Encouraging individuals to create businesses and generate employment locally is considered essential for the sustainability of the rural economy. Organised activities aimed at attracting such residents are integral to this strategy, fostering a virtuous cycle of community dynamism, tourism, and economic growth.

Hence, tourism in Figueiró dos Vinhos is not merely a single business, however important to some agents, but a pivotal economic strategy. By attracting digital nomads and remote workers who can establish businesses or bring remote employment to the region, tourism becomes intertwined with local development goals. This approach is particularly impactful in sectors like hospitality and services, which are central to the region's economy and quality of life – "*Boosting not just the community but also tourism by attracting people to work remotely, create businesses, or engage in traditional work here is a way to increase the municipality's dynamism. In this regard, tourism is fundamental*" emphasised a DMO representative.

The combination of tourism and initiatives that integrate visitors and local communities stands out as a key strength of the region's strategy. By addressing both the needs of residents and visitors, this approach ensures that tourism contributes to long-term regional sustainability. An important consideration in this strategy is ensuring that tourism benefits align with local residents' needs – "*It is essential, when thinking about tourism, not to forget what is also good for the resident*". This alignment is critical to avoiding potential resistance from the community and ensuring that tourism-driven changes enhance rather than disrupt local life.

By attracting individuals who actively contribute to the local economy and integrate into the community, lifestyle migration reinforces the sustainability of rural development. The growing population stimulates further infrastructure improvements, enhances the region's services, and creates opportunities for deeper cultural and social integration between long-term residents and newcomers (Teodorovicz et al, 2023).

B. Challenges perceived

The development of rural destinations such as Figueiró dos Vinhos, while promising, is not without its challenges. Despite the positive reception of tourists and the opportunities they bring, several structural and linguistic barriers delay the region's ability to fully capitalise on its potential as a tourism destination. The most cited challenges were lack of public transport, healthcare limitations, language barriers and the need for more services. Residents also expressed concerns about the aging population issue on rural areas and the area's limited appeal to younger generations, mentioning a lack of employment opportunities, reduce healthcare services, and need for development in the education system.

Lack of public transport

One of the most pressing issues identified by residents is the lack of adequate transportation options – "*Public transport is often raised as an issue in the region. Although there are solutions, the lack of frequent and accessible transportation remains a significant challenge*". While the region has good road infrastructure, the absence of reliable public transport limits mobility for those without private vehicles – "*I cannot live a rural life without a car*", said a local resident." However, the statements show that the interviewees' perspective is not limited to Figueiró dos Vinhos but reflects a common situation and perception of living conditions in rural areas (see also da Silva et al, 2016). This dependency on personal vehicles not only affects residents but also impacts the accessibility of the region for tourists, particularly those seeking sustainable travel options. The absence of efficient and regular transport options is as impactful for residents as for tourists, because, as one resident puts it, "*(...) if you don't have a car, you can't get around*".

Healthcare limitations

The insufficiency of immediate healthcare services was also understood, posing a significant challenge for both residents and visitors – "*Although healthcare services exist, we still need to improve capacity and infrastructure to ensure adequate services for all residents*", said a resident. The lack of local facilities capable of addressing urgent medical needs creates a sense of insecurity among residents, especially the elderly. Addressing these gaps is critical to ensure a baseline quality of life for the community and a positive experience for tourists.

Language barriers

The poor multilingual communication tools and skills available presents another challenge, particularly for international tourists. For example, a resident highlighted the absence of English translations on event posters: "*There is no communication in English on the event posters. How are foreigners supposed to know?*". This issue extends beyond simple logistics, reflecting broader difficulties in bridging the cultural divide between locals and visitors. The limited fluency in foreign languages among residents contributes to superficial interactions and, at times, a perception of visitors as outsiders – "*There is a strong foreign community here... but there is no point of communication between foreigners and locals. There are language and cultural barriers*". This lack of connection makes the formation of deeper relationships difficult, however essential for fostering a sense of belonging and mutual understanding.

Need for more services and initiatives

Despite the region's openness to visitors, efforts to integrate tourists and residents into shared activities remain underdeveloped. The absence of structured initiatives aimed at fostering interaction, such as cultural forums or joint events, has been identified as a missed opportunity by the local community – "*I think there is a lack of connection... perhaps forums or events to bring locals and visitors together*". Without intentional strategies to address these gaps, the integration of visitors, particularly digital nomads and long-term tourists, risks being superficial. In this sense, and as pointed out by the DMO representatives, destinations "*must provide conditions for tourists who come here, beyond just visiting*". This highlights the need for comprehensive planning to ensure that tourism initiatives address infrastructure, accessibility, and community integration, creating an environment that supports both residents and visitors.

Respondents also identified significant infrastructure needs as essential for supporting the community's development and accommodating a growing number of visitors. The most frequently mentioned area was the need for more services. Interviewees stressed the importance of expanding services to better serve both residents and tourists – "*We have many events and tourism activities, but we need more infrastructure to accommodate this increase in visitors*". The need for better access to shopping was also highlighted. While essential services such as supermarkets and pharmacies are available, respondents noted the absence of more diverse retail options, including cinemas and shopping centres – "*Sometimes I miss being able to go shopping or to the cinema... I feel the lack of infrastructure*".

In summary, the arrival of digital nomads to rural destinations and their interactions with the local community can serve as a powerful tool and strategy for tourism development and population revitalisation. This dynamic, as pointed out by the interviewees, not only enhances the quality of life for residents but also improves local services and infrastructure. As a matter of fact, the destination strives to develop new and improved services and infrastructure for both new and existing residents, also benefitting tourism development. This, in turn, enriches the overall tourism experience, additionally through cultural exchange within a more vital social context, which finally may attract not only transitory visitors, but lifestyle migrants rejuvenating an ageing and declining rural community and making young local residents decide to stay, as previously mentioned – "*Sometimes people come just for a holiday and end up making friends. Many of them bring more people for a holiday, tourism, or visits.*", which helps to boost tourism in the region and potentially attract new residents. Consequently, such initiatives may contribute, through a set of intertwined effects and dynamics, to the development of a more sustainable, inclusive, dynamic, appealing and resilient destination, has highlighted by the following model (figure 4).

Figure 4. A conceptual model of the dynamics between host-guest interactions, tourism development and local quality of life

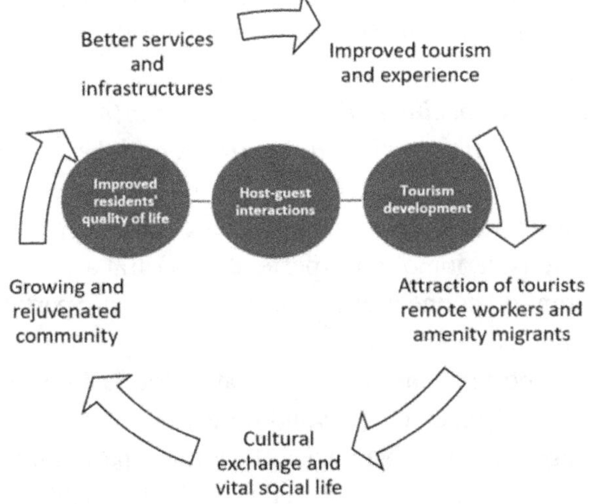

Source: own elaboration

The conceptual model (figure 4) illustrates the interconnected processes and overall dynamics through which digital nomads and remote workers contribute to tourism development and broader socio-economic transformations in rural communities. This model, which may be understood as a 'virtuous circle', underscores the importance of host-guest interactions in facilitating a cycle of economic revitalization, social enrichment, and improvements in local quality of life. Drawing on empirical evidence from Figueiró dos Vinhos, this section explains each component of the model, providing concrete examples from the here presented empirical study.

The attraction of digital nomads and amenity migrants to rural destinations has emerged as a transformative strategy for tourism development and community revitalization. As one interviewee noted, *"We are starting to see young people in Portuguese society who were previously living in other, more urban areas of the country moving here due to their remote work opportunities. They have realised that this place offers certain advantages. However, there is also another reality: the growing interest from foreign citizens."* This influx has driven investments in infrastructure and services, as highlighted by another respondent: *"We have strongly invested in the idea of offering a structurally distinctive [digital nomad] product."* The development of such a tourism product has required the creation of new infrastructure and services, such as new restaurants, more cultural activities and expansion of transportation routes, for example, which not only cater to tourists but also to local residents, significantly improving their quality of life. However, also challenges were noted: *"We are aware that there are certain months of the year when the existing infrastructure cannot support the number of visitors. We are already making adjustments to accommodate the growing demand."*

Cultural exchange and community engagement have also been key outcomes of this dynamic. The *Fazunchar* festival exemplifies the symbiotic relationship between visitors and locals, as described by an interviewee: *"It is very interesting to see, for example, in the specific activity of Fazunchar (artistic festival), which is a week where suddenly we have artists in the streets, and the local population joins the artists, getting involved in the activities. There is a very interesting symbiosis between them."* This interaction not only enriches community life but also reduces the social and cultural isolation often experienced in rural areas, creating more opportunities for meaningful connections. These initiatives are particularly important for retaining the young population.

In brief, the here reported benefits of co-creative tourism development, actively involving locals and tourists, extend beyond immediate economic gains. The local population has recognized the advantages of tourism, particularly in the form of improved infrastructure, but also social and cultural living dynamics, which enhances their daily lives and encourages young residents to stay.

CONCLUSIONS AND IMPLICATIONS

The findings from this case study provide valuable insights into how rural communities can develop strategies to benefit from the growing trend of remote work tourism, while also addressing potential challenges related to cultural integration and preservation, economic disparities, and community cohesion. While the arrival of these visitors has been positively received by residents and seen as a driver of social and economic revitalisation, several barriers, such as limited infrastructure, accessibility, and (cross-) cultural integration, need to be addressed.

This study revealed that digital nomads play a crucial role in revitalizing rural economies by contributing to local tourism, fostering entrepreneurship, and increasing consumption, thereby generating new income streams for small businesses and service providers in these areas. Additionally, the interactions between digital nomads and local residents facilitate cultural exchange, enriching both parties through shared experiences, traditions, and knowledge, ultimately reinforcing local identities and fostering a sense of community (Kastenholz et all., 2013).

Furthermore, when effectively managed through strategic policies and infrastructure development, the presence of digital nomads can serve as a viable solution to counteract rural depopulation, attracting younger, skilled individuals who contribute to the social and economic fabric of these regions (Kastenholz et al., 2013; Yang, 2024). Despite these benefits, the study also highlights significant challenges that must be addressed, including the rising cost of housing driven by increased demand, potential difficulties in cultural integration as different lifestyles and expectations converge, and the strain on existing infrastructure, such as internet connectivity, transportation, and public services, which may not be equipped to handle a sudden influx of remote workers. Addressing these challenges through proactive planning, community engagement, and investment in sustainable development strategies is essential to ensure that digital nomadism remains a mutually beneficial phenomenon for both visiting professionals and the rural communities that host them. To build a harmonious community, acceptance and tolerance from locals is required, which can lead to a more integrated social structure (Yang, 2024).

Digital nomads bring opportunities for economic growth, cultural exchange, and community revitalisation. Digital nomads and remote workers often seek comfort, tranquillity, and privacy (Benson & O'Reilly, 2009; Gosnell & Arams, 2011; Nash et al., 2018), making rural destinations an appealing option. However, much like traditional tourists, digital nomads choose their destinations based on factors such as accessibility, attractions, entertainment, infrastructure, and quality of life (Günay et al., 2024). In this context, rural destinations face certain challenges, particularly in terms of accessibility, availability of certain services and infrastructure.

Results align with previous research (e.g., Almeida & Daniel, 2022; Kastenholz et al., 2013; Mao & Xu, 2024; Teodorovicz et al, 2023), reinforcing the notion that longer staying tourists, remote workers and digital nomads can play a crucial role in revitalising rural destinations. Their presence and interactions with the community contribute to encourage social exchange, attracting a younger population, fostering economic growth, and addressing social isolation.

Despite the positive impact of digital nomads, their presence can also bring some inconveniences. The rise of digital nomads in a place can drive up prices for goods and services, making them less affordable for long-term residents (Yang, 2024). This economic pressure, coupled with the demand for infrastructure and services, often leads to gentrification, altering the character of communities and displacing long-term residents (Bozzi, 2024). Additionally, the spatial needs of digital nomads, particularly in popular hotspots, can result in the destruction of natural environments to build co-working spaces and other dedicated infrastructures, further straining local resources (Bozzi, 2024). These dynamics can create tensions between nomads and residents, especially if locals feel marginalized or economically disadvantaged (Jaiswal et al., 2024).

Social conflicts may also arise due to differing lifestyles and values between digital nomads and local residents. The influx of digital nomads and tourists can disrupt local traditions and everyday habits, leading to social tensions (Yang et al., 2013). Therefore, balancing the benefits of digital nomadism with the needs and well-being of local communities remains a critical challenge for sustainable development in host destinations.

The findings of the study suggest that fostering deeper connections between residents and digital nomads, improving local infrastructure, and leveraging the region's tranquillity and authenticity are essential steps for creating a sustainable and harmonious rural tourism ecosystem. It is then essential to develop integrated tourism infrastructure and services tailored to the needs of digital nomads and remote workers (Abbas et al., 2021), and empower communities to take an active role in tourism development and management. A close cooperation between local governments, private institutions, and the community must be fostered to create an ecosystem that supports both the needs of these new 'half-tourists', the preservation of local identity, resources and culture, as well as a fair distribution of the benefits of tourism (Alhadi et al., 2023; Almeida & Belezas, 2022; Suriyankietkaew et al., 2022).

To address the challenges and maximise the opportunities associated with digital nomadism and remote work tourism, a holistic and evidence-based approach is required, as well as the engagement and cooperation between all stakeholders involved.

Implications for Policymakers

One of the primary recommendations for stakeholders, in particular, policemakers, is to foster integration through cultural exchange. Events such as cultural forums, festivals, and community projects can provide structured opportunities for residents and digital nomads to interact and share experiences, building mutual understanding and strengthening community ties. By creating platforms for dialogue and collaboration, these initiatives can overcome cultural barriers and encourage long-term relationships between locals and visitors. Additionally, the provision of multilingual resources, such as signage, digital platforms, and event announcements, would make rural destinations more accessible to international visitors and facilitate greater participation in local activities (Alhadi et al., 2023).

Policymakers should also prioritise enhancing public transportation and multilingual communication, especially English, to support both residents and visitors, ensuring the inclusivity and attractiveness of rural destinations, like Figueiró dos Vinhos. This is not a one-time investment but rather an ongoing task. Therefore, as a way to complement other services, policymakers could create free language courses for their residents to learn English, as well as for new foreign residents to easily learn the country's language. Investments in transportation and healthcare infrastructure and services are critical for improving residents' and visitors' quality of life, through reliable access to essential services. Investments in public transport systems, particularly connecting rural areas to urban hubs, would enhance mobility for both residents and tourists.

Collaborative workspaces and all-inclusive co-living have emerged as essential infrastructure for digital nomads, offering not only professional facilities but also a social environment conducive to reducing isolation (Akhavan et al., 2021; Ciccarelli, 2023; Thompson, 2019). Repurposing public buildings, such as libraries or inactive schools, into co-working and co-living spaces, also accessible to local residents, can provide digital nomads with essential facilities while fostering community interaction and cultural exchange (Ciccarelli, 2023; Fuzi, 2015). These spaces can also play a vital role in supporting local entrepreneurs and fostering synergies between residents and digital nomads (Fuzi, 2015).

As Kelly & Arelano (2021) highlight, digital nomads increasingly prioritise destinations that align with their environmental and social values, therefore policymakers and stakeholders should integrate conservation efforts, support local businesses, and promote slow tourism models that emphasise authentic and meaningful travel experiences (Suriyankietkaew et al., 2022). Such initiatives ensure that tourism growth does not compromise the natural and cultural heritage of rural areas while enhancing their appeal to environmentally conscious travellers.

Embracing technological innovation can further support the digital nomad market. The development of digital platforms to promote rural destinations and connect digital nomads with local services and communities is essential (Kozak et al., 2024). These platforms can enhance the visibility of rural areas, showcasing them as ideal locations for remote work and slow tourism while facilitating knowledge exchange and collaboration between visitors and residents.

To mitigate the challenges associated with the growing presence of digital nomads and remote workers in rural areas while ensuring long-term socio-economic benefits for host communities, policymakers must adopt a multifaceted approach that prioritizes sustainable and inclusive development. A key strategy involves strengthening housing affordability measures to prevent gentrification, which can displace local residents due to rising rental costs; implementing rental caps and offering incentives for long-term stays can help maintain balanced housing markets while ensuring that both locals and digital nomads coexist harmoniously. Additionally, fostering cultural integration is essential, as it can enhance mutual understanding and social cohesion—community-led tourism initiatives and language-learning programs can serve as effective tools to bridge cultural gaps and encourage meaningful exchanges between visitors and residents. Furthermore, improving infrastructure and public services is crucial to accommodate the needs of an increasingly mobile workforce; investments in digital connectivity, healthcare access, and transportation networks will not only enhance the experience for digital nomads but also improve the quality of life for permanent residents. Another important consideration is the development of sustainable tourism models that emphasize slow tourism and community-driven initiatives, ensuring that economic gains from digital nomadism do not come at the expense of environmental degradation or the erosion of local culture. Finally, rural areas must be strategically positioned as attractive destinations for global talent, requiring targeted marketing campaigns that highlight their unique advantages as ideal workation hubs, leveraging scenic landscapes, lower costs of living, and opportunities for deep cultural immersion. By implementing these comprehensive measures, policymakers can maximize the positive contributions of digital nomads while safeguarding local communities against potential drawbacks, ultimately fostering a more resilient and prosperous rural economy.

Implications for the Local Community

The local community plays a central role in shaping the success of tourism development. Their active participation in planning and management ensures that initiatives align with local needs and aspirations. Collaborative forums and cultural events can facilitate meaningful interactions between residents and digital nomads, promoting mutual understanding and creating long-term relationship (Akhavan et al. 2021).

While tourism development can bring significant benefits, such as improved infrastructure, cultural life and economic growth, it must also address the risk of social isolation for digital nomads (Arslan, 2024). By fostering inclusive social spaces and shared activities, communities can mitigate this issue and create environments where residents and visitors thrive together, enhancing quality of life for all involved.

Implications for Tourists

Digital nomads and remote workers are attracted to rural destinations for their tranquillity, privacy, and cultural richness (Nash et al., 2018). However, to fully realise their potential as visitors, these destinations must address their expectations for modern infrastructure, cultural engagement, and accessible information (Günay et al., 2024).

Providing co-working spaces tailored to their needs can reduce isolation and foster connections with locals, enhancing their overall experience (Akhavan et al., 2021; Ciccarelli, 2023). Additionally, offering multilingual resources and promoting events that allow digital nomads to immerse in local traditions and their own motivation to engage in meaningful relationships with local residents will strengthen their connection to the destination, with possible long-term benefits for rural communities (Teodorovicz et al, 2023)

LIMITATIONS AND FUTURE RESEARCH

Despite the valuable contributions of this research, the study was limited to a single rural destination, including inputs from three residents and two DMO representatives. To strengthen the findings and provide a broader perspective, future research should involve a greater number of rural destinations, enabling the benefits from a multiple-case-study design (e.g. permitting the identification of patterns despite geographically distinct context) (Carvalho et. al, 2024) and the collection of more comprehensive data on the digital nomads topic and their impact on tourism development and population revitalisation, additionally using a survey approach.

Comparative studies examining the survey area alongside other regions in Portugal or internationally, with varying demographics and population densities, would provide deeper insights into the significance of interactions across different destinations. Such research could highlight how diverse contexts influence the dynamics between digital nomads, local communities, and tourism development, offering a more comprehensive understanding of the challenges and opportunities associated with these interactions. By analysing these variations, policymakers and stakeholders could identify best practices and tailor strategies to enhance the sustainability and inclusivity of rural and urban destinations alike.

Moreover, while this study identified several relevant issues and highlighted shared viewpoints, these findings serve as a foundation for further research. A deeper understanding of how host-guest interactions are formed and how they lead to positive outcomes should be approached, in order to highlight on how the interactions between these two groups contribute to the formation of a community and, consequently, produce a basis for destination management strategies aimed at enhancing the success and sustainable development of rural destinations, generating economic and social impacts.

Finally, longitudinal studies represent a critical area for further research. While this study provides a brief explanation of the impacts of digital nomadism on rural communities, long-term monitoring is needed to understand how these changes evolve over time. As Kozak et al. (2024) note, digital nomadism is a dynamic phenomenon influenced by technological advancements and global mobility trends, which is also true for remote work and lifestyle or amenity migration (Benson & O'Reilly, 2009; Gosnell & Arams, 2011). Longitudinal studies could assess how these trends evolve over time as well as how residents' attitudes, well-being and community dynamics change in response to such tourism and migration patterns."

REFERENCES

Abbas, J., Mubeen, R., Iorember, P. T., Raza, S., & Mamirkulova, G. (2021). Exploring the impact of COVID-19 on tourism: Transformational potential and implications for a sustainable recovery of the travel and leisure industry. *Current Research in Behavioral Sciences*, *2*, 100033. DOI: 10.1016/j.crbeha.2021.100033 PMID: 38620720

Abreu, M., Oner, O., Brouwer, A., & Leeuwen, E. (2018). Well-being effects of self-employment: A spatial inquiry. Journal of Business Venturing, 34, Article .DOI: 10.1016/j.jbusvent.2018.11.001

Akhavan, M., Mariotti, I., & Rossi, F. (2022). The rise of coworking spaces in peripheral and rural areas in Italy. *Territorio*, *97*, 35–42. DOI: 10.3280/tr2021-097-Supplementooa12925

Algassim, A. A., Saufi, A., & Scott, N. (2023). Residents' emotional responses to tourism development in Saudi Arabia. *Tourism Review*, *78*(4), 1078–1091. DOI: 10.1108/TR-10-2021-0457

Alhadi, Z., Zefnihan, M., Muchtar, B., & Evanita, S. (2023). Developing a community-based tourism model for sustainable tourism in the Mandeh area, West Sumatra Province, Indonesia. *International Journal of Sustainable Development and Planning*, *18*(11), 3491–3503. DOI: 10.18280/ijsdp.181114

Almeida, J., & Belezas, F. (2022). The rise of half-tourists and their impact on the tourism strategies of peripheral territories. In J. Leitão, V. Ratten, & V. Braga (Eds.), Tourism entrepreneurship in Portugal and Spain: Tourism, hospitality & event management (pp. 113–130). Springer. DOI: 10.1007/978-3-030-89232-6_9

Almeida, J., & Daniel, A. D. (2022). Post-pandemic opportunities for low-density territories: Insights and implications from Portuguese case studies. *European Planning Studies*, *31*(10), 2034–2057. DOI: 10.1080/09654313.2022.2074785

Aroles, J., Granter, E., & Vaujany, F. (2020). 'Becoming mainstream': The professionalisation and corporatisation of digital nomadism. *New Technology, Work and Employment*, *35*(1), 114–129. DOI: 10.1111/ntwe.12158

Arslan, E. (2024). From tourists to nomads: Unveiling the transformative potential of digital nomads in travel and tourism. *Worldwide Hospitality and Tourism Themes*, *16*(3), 269–281. DOI: 10.1108/WHATT-03-2024-0046

Bednorz, J. (2024). Working from anywhere? Work from here! Approaches to attract digital nomads. *Annals of Tourism Research, 105*, 103715. DOI: 10.1016/j.annals.2023.103715

Benson, M., & O'Reilly, K. (2009). Migration and the search for a better way of life: A critical exploration of lifestyle migration. *The Sociological Review, 57*(4), 608–625. DOI: 10.1111/j.1467-954X.2009.01864.x

Betre, H. K. (2022). Reconceptualizing the potential of digital nomads to transform community-based and sustainable tourism (Master's thesis). University of Girona.

Bosworth, G., Whalley, J., Fuzi, A., Merrell, I., Chapman, P., & Russell, E. (2023). Rural co-working: New network spaces and new opportunities for a smart countryside. *Journal of Rural Studies, 97*, 550–559. DOI: 10.1016/j.jrurstud.2023.01.003

Bozzi, A. (2024). Digital nomadism from the perspective of places and mobilities: A literature review. *European Transport Research Review, 16*(1), 50. Advance online publication. DOI: 10.1186/s12544-024-00663-z

Braun, E., Kavaratzis, M., & Zenker, S. (2013). My city – my brand: The different roles of residents in place branding. *Journal of Place Management and Development, 6*(1), 18–28. DOI: 10.1108/17538331311306087

Carvalho, M., Kastenholz, E., & Carneiro, M. J. (2021). Interaction as a central element of co-creative wine tourism experiences—Evidence from Bairrada, a Portuguese wine-producing region. *Sustainability (Basel), 13*(16), 9374. Advance online publication. DOI: 10.3390/su13169374

Carvalho, M., Kastenholz, E., Carneiro, M. J., & Souza, L. (2024). Dimensions of Co-Creative Food & Wine Tourism Experiences – Findings from A Multiple-Case Study. [AHTR]. *Advances in Hospitality and Tourism Research, 12*(4), 337–367. Advance online publication. DOI: 10.30519/ahtr.1287676

Chevtaeva, E., Neuhofer, B., Egger, R., & Rainoldi, M. (2023). Travel while working remotely: A topological data analysis of well-being in remote work trip experiences. *Journal of Travel Research, 63*(2), 466–480. DOI: 10.1177/00472875231151923

Ciccarelli, F. C. (2023). Exploring the potential of coworking spaces for quality of working life and wellbeing: A systematic review of academic literature. CIDADES. *Comunidades e Territórios, 46*(46). Advance online publication. DOI: 10.15847/cct.30874

Dictionary, C. (2021, January 18). Digital nomad definition. Retrieved from https://dictionaryblog.cambridge.org/2021/01/18/new-words-18-january-2021/

Ehn, K., Jorge, A., & Marques-Pita, M. (2022). Digital nomads and the Covid-19 pandemic: Narratives about relocation in a time of lockdowns and reduced mobility. *Social Media + Society*, *8*(1), 20563051221084958. Advance online publication. DOI: 10.1177/20563051221084958

Eusébio, C., Kastenholz, E., & Breda, Z. (2014). Tourism and sustainable development of rural destinations: A stakeholders' view. Revista Portuguesa de Estudos Regionais, 13–21.

Figueiró dos Vinhos council. (n.d.). Retrieved in December 26, 2024 from https://www.cm-figueirodosvinhos.pt/

Fuzi, A. (2015). Co-working spaces for promoting entrepreneurship in sparse regions: The case of South Wales. *Regional Studies, Regional Science*, *2*(1), 461–468. DOI: 10.1080/21681376.2015.1072053

Gosnell, H., & Abrams, J. (2011). Amenity migration: Diverse conceptualizations of drivers, socioeconomic dimensions, and emerging challenges. *GeoJournal*, *76*(4), 303–322. DOI: 10.1007/s10708-009-9295-4

Günay, F., Toksöz, D., & Aslan, Z. (2024). The causes, process, and result of becoming a digital nomad family: A phenomenological case study. *Worldwide Hospitality and Tourism Themes*, *16*(3), 294–302. DOI: 10.1108/WHATT-03-2024-0042

Gupta, S., Jaiswal, R., & Gupta, S. K. (2024). Digital nomads: A systematic literature review and future research agenda. *Tourism Review*. Advance online publication. DOI: 10.1108/TR-12-2023-0869

Hong, W. C. (2009). Global competitiveness measurement for the tourism sector. *Current Issues in Tourism*, *12*(2), 105–132. DOI: 10.1080/13683500802596359

Hunt, C., & Stronza, A. (2013). Stage-based tourism models and resident attitudes towards tourism in an emerging destination in the developing world. *Journal of Sustainable Tourism*, *22*(2), 279–298. DOI: 10.1080/09669582.2013.815761

Ienczak, L., Maines, L., & Silva, P. (2024). Environmentally responsible consumption by rural tourists in Rio Grande do Sul—Brazil. Smart Tourism, 4, Article .DOI: 10.54517/st.v4i1.2296

Instituto Nacional de Estatística. (n.d.). Recenseamentos gerais da população. Retrieved from https://www.ine.pt/xportal/xmain?xpid=INE&xpgid=ine_publicacoes

Jaiswal, R., Gupta, S., & Gupta, S. K. (2024). The impending disruption of digital nomadism: Opportunities, challenges, and research agenda. *World Leisure Journal*, 1–31. Advance online publication. DOI: 10.1080/16078055.2024.2346091

Kastenholz, E., Carneiro, M. J., Eusébio, C., & Figueiredo, E. (2013). Host–guest relationships in rural tourism: Evidence from two Portuguese villages. *Anatolia, 24*(3), 367–380. DOI: 10.1080/13032917.2013.769016

Kastenholz, E., & Carvalho, M. (2024). Co-creating Locally Embedded Rural Tourist Experiences Using Coopetition Strategies: Insights from Village Tourism in Portugal. In *Fumi Chim-Miki, A. & R.A. da Costa. Value Proposition to Tourism Coopetition- Building the Future of Tourism Series* (pp. 219–234). Emerald Publishing. DOI: 10.1108/978-1-83797-827-420241015

Kastenholz, E., Marques, C. P., & Carneiro, M. J. (2020). Place attachment through sensory-rich, emotion-generating place experiences in rural tourism. *Journal of Destination Marketing & Management, 17*, 100455. DOI: 10.1016/j.jdmm.2020.100455

Kastenholz, E., & Sparrer, M. (2009). Rural Dimensions of the Commercial Home. In Lynch, P., MacIntosh, A., & Tucker, H. (Eds.), *Commercial Homes in Tourism: An international perspective* (pp. 138–149). Routledge., DOI: 10.4324/9780203880319

Kelly, H., & Arelano, D. (2021). Work and wander: Meet today's digital nomads. Retrieved January 2, 2024, from https://www.adventuretravel.biz/research/work-and-wander-meet-todays-digitalnomads

Kozak, M., Cetin, G., & Alrawadieh, Z. (2024). Repositioning work and leisure: Digital nomads versus tourists. *International Journal of Tourism Research, 26*(4), e2732. Advance online publication. DOI: 10.1002/jtr.2732

Leco, F. (2013). Rural tourist and their attitudes and motivations towards the practice of environmental activities such as agrotourism. *International Journal of Environmental Research, 7*, 255–264.

Mancinelli, F. (2020). Digital nomads: Freedom, responsibility and the neoliberal order. *Information Technology & Tourism, 22*(3), 417–437. DOI: 10.1007/s40558-020-00174-2

Mao, Q., & Xu, S. (2024). *How Digital Nomad Communities Can Empower Rural Revitalisation*. Advances in Economics, Management and Political Sciences., DOI: 10.54254/2754-1169/105/20241997

Marco, E., & Carson, D. A. (2023). Towards a cordial dialogue between lifestyle migration/mobilities and rural tourism geographies. *Geografiska Annaler. Series B, Human Geography, 105*(4), 341–355. DOI: 10.1080/04353684.2023.2197921

Mariotti, I., & Sasso, S. (2024). *Revitalizing rural areas through innovation and entrepreneurship: Public and private initiatives to train, attract and retain human capital. Joint Research Centre*. European Commission., DOI: 10.2760/4727653

Membretti, A., & Iancu, B. (2017). From Peasant Workers to Amenity Migrants. Socialist Heritage and the Future of Mountain Rurality in Romania. Revue de géographie alpine. 105-1 | 2017. .DOI: 10.4000/rga.3567

Merrell, I., Füzi, A., Russell, E., & Bosworth, G. (2021). How rural coworking hubs can facilitate well-being through the satisfaction of key psychological needs. *Local Economy*, *36*(7-8), 606–626. DOI: 10.1177/02690942221075598

Nash, C., Jarrahi, M. H., & Sutherland, W. (2021). Nomadic work and location independence: The role of space in shaping the work of digital nomads. *Human Behavior and Emerging Technologies*, *3*(2), 271–282. DOI: 10.1002/hbe2.234

Popova, K., & Malcheva, M. (2020). Assessment of the potential of Varna City as a smart tourist destination. *Tourism (Zagreb)*, *68*(3), 308–321. DOI: 10.37741/t.68.3.5

Rainoldi, M., Ladkin, A., & Buhalis, D. (2022). Blending work and leisure: A future digital worker hybrid lifestyle perspective. *Annals of Leisure Research*, *27*(2), 215–235. Advance online publication. DOI: 10.1080/11745398.2022.2070513

Reynolds, L., Koenig-Lewis, N., Doering, H., & Peattie, K. (2022). Competing for legitimacy in the place branding process: (Re)negotiating the stakes. *Tourism Management*, *91*, 104532. DOI: 10.1016/j.tourman.2022.104532

Roundy, P. (2017). Social entrepreneurship and entrepreneurial ecosystems: Complementary or disjointed phenomena? *International Journal of Social Economics*, *44*(9), 1252–1267. Advance online publication. DOI: 10.1108/IJSE-02-2016-0045

Roxas, F. M. Y., Rivera, J. P. R., & Gutierrez, E. L. M. (2020). Framework for creating sustainable tourism using systems thinking. *Current Issues in Tourism*, *23*(3), 280–296. DOI: 10.1080/13683500.2018.1534805

Sánchez-Vergara, J. I., Orel, M., & Capdevila, I. (2023). "Home office is the here and now." Digital nomad visa systems and remote work-focused leisure policies. *World Leisure Journal*, *65*(2), 236–255. Advance online publication. DOI: 10.1080/16078055.2023.2165142

Shin, H., Lee, J., & Kim, N. (2023). Workcation (Workation) travel experiences, satisfaction and revisit intentions: Focusing on conceptualization, scale development, and nomological network. *Journal of Travel Research*, *63*(5), 1150–1168. Advance online publication. DOI: 10.1177/00472875231188717

Soares da Silva, D., Figueiredo, E., Eusébio, C., & Carneiro, M. J.Soares da Silva. (2016). The countryside is worth a thousand words - Portuguese representations on rural areas. *Journal of Rural Studies*, *44*, 77–88. DOI: 10.1016/j.jrurstud.2016.01.012

Solvoll, S., Alsos, G. A., & Bulanova, O. (2015). Tourism entrepreneurship: Review and future directions. *Scandinavian Journal of Hospitality and Tourism, 15*(sup1, Suppl. 1), 120–137. DOI: 10.1080/15022250.2015.1065592

Stylidis, D., & Dominguez Quintero, A. (2022). Understanding the effect of place image and knowledge of tourism on residents' attitudes towards tourism and their word-of-mouth intentions: Evidence from Seville, Spain. *Tourism Planning & Development, 19*(5), 1–18. DOI: 10.1080/21568316.2022.2049859

Suriyankietkaew, S., Krittayaruangroj, K., & Iamsawan, N. (2022). Sustainable leadership practices and competencies of SMEs for sustainability and resilience: A community-based social enterprise study. *Sustainability (Basel), 14*(10), 5762. DOI: 10.3390/su14105762

Sutherland, W., & Jarrahi, M. H. (2017). The gig economy and information infrastructure: The case of the digital nomad community. *Proceedings of the ACM on HumanComputer Interaction (CSCW)*, 1. DOI: 10.1145/3134732

Tan, G., & Hsu, C. H. C. (2024). Can host–tourist interaction pull the plug on tourist stereotypes? Exploring the power of emotional solidarity. *Tourism Management Perspectives, 50*, 101211. Advance online publication. DOI: 10.1016/j.tmp.2023.101211

Teodorovicz, T., Choudhury, P., & Starr, E. (2023). Location Specificity and Geographic Competition for Remote Workers. SSRN Electronic Journal. DOI: 10.2139/ssrn.4467579

Thompson, B. Y. (2019). The digital nomad lifestyle: (Remote) work/leisure balance, privilege, and constructed community. *International Journal of the Sociology of Leisure*, 2(1), 27–42. DOI: 10.1007/s41978-018-00030-y

Todt, A., & Kastenholz, E. (2010). Tourists as a driving force for sustainable rural development – a research framework. Atas do IV Congresso de Estudos Rurais – Mundos Rurais em Portugal: Múltiplos Olhares, Múltiplos Futuros, Universidade de Aveiro/ SPER, Aveiro, 4-6 Fevereiro (pp. 633-645). https://bdigital.ipg.pt/dspace/bitstream/10314/3265/1/%C3%8Dndice-%20LivroActasFinal-%20Aveiro-2010.pdf

Vagena, A., Yurevich, O., Leonidas, L., & Papakonstantinidis, A. (2023). *Greece as an Organic Space for the Development of Digital Nomadistry*. Qeios., DOI: 10.32388/D7NX7L

Von Zumbusch, J. S. H., & Lalicic, L. (2020). The role of co-living spaces in digital nomads' well-being. *Information Technology & Tourism, 22*(3), 439–453. Advance online publication. DOI: 10.1007/s40558-020-00182-2

Wang, B., Schlagwein, D., Cecez-Kecmanovic, D., & Cahalane, M. C. (2018). Digital work and high-tech wanderers: Three theoretical framings and a research agenda for digital nomadism (pp. 1-12). In *Proceedings of the Australian conference on information systems 2018*. DOI: 10.5130/acis2018.bl

Yang, J., Ryan, C., & Zhang, L. (2013). Social conflict in communities impacted by tourism. *Tourism Management, 35*, 82–93. DOI: 10.1016/j.tourman.2012.06.002

Yang, Y. (2024). Urban Sustainability in the Age of Digital Nomads - Diverse Group Impacts. Advances in Economics. *Management and Political Sciences, 112*, 70–74.

Yu, Y. (2024). Urban Sustainability in the Age of Digital Nomads - Diverse Group Impacts. Advances in Economics. *Management and Political Sciences, 112*(1), 70–74. DOI: 10.54254/2754-1169/112/20242277

Zhou, L., Buhalis, D., Fan, D. X., Ladkin, A., & Lian, X. (2024). Attracting digital nomads: Smart destination strategies, innovation and competitiveness. *Journal of Destination Marketing & Management, 31*, 100850. DOI: 10.1016/j.jdmm.2023.100850

ADDITIONAL READING

Chen, W., & Wu, M. (2024). Exploring the role of psychological ownership in tourists' shift toward sustainable behaviour in cultural tourism. *Tourism Management*.

Cohen, S. A., Duncan, T., & Thulemark, M. (2015). Lifestyle mobilities: The crossroads of travel, leisure and migration. *Mobilities, 10*(1), 155–172. DOI: 10.1080/17450101.2013.826481

Olga, H. (2020). In search of a digital nomad: Defining the phenomenon. *Information Technology & Tourism, 22*(3), 335–353. DOI: 10.1007/s40558-020-00177-z

Yıldırım, M., & Kaya, A. (2024). Experiences, expectations and suggestions of digital nomads towards an intangible cultural heritage. *Worldwide Hospitality and Tourism Themes, 16*(3), 396–409. DOI: 10.1108/WHATT-03-2024-0055

Chapter 10
Digital Nomads as Catalysts for Change: Enhancing Ethical Travel and Sustainability in Indian Tourism

Mehraj Din Wani
https://orcid.org/0000-0001-5034-1207
University of Kashmir, India

Sabreena Nawaz Baba
University of Kashmir, India

Shamim Ahmad Shah
University of Kashmir, India

Zubair Ahmad Dada
University of Kashmir, India

ABSTRACT

This chapter critically examines digital nomadism and its transformative impact on the ethical dimensions and sustainability of tourism in India. With remote work transcending geographic constraints, digital nomads are reshaping tourism in regions like Goa, Bangalore, and Rishikesh, where cultural richness, ecological diversity, and conducive work environments converge. Using secondary data from academic literature, industry reports, and case studies, the chapter explores digital nomads' nuanced impacts on local socio-economic structures, environmental sustainability, and cultural integrity. While benefiting local economies and fostering community-driven initiatives, they risk overtourism, cultural commodification, and ecological strain. The chapter proposes actionable strategies, including region-specific policies,

DOI: 10.4018/979-8-3373-0076-4.ch010

digital nomad visas, and eco-conscious travel behaviors, to sustainably integrate digital nomads into India's tourism ecosystem, ensuring a balance between economic growth, cultural preservation, and environmental protection.

INTRODUCTION

In the wake of globalization and technological advancements, the traditional boundaries of work and leisure are becoming increasingly blurred (Lirio, 2017; Standing, 2009). One of the most compelling outcomes of this shift is the rise of digital nomadism—a lifestyle that combines remote work with the ability to travel freely across the globe (Spracklen, 2015). This growing phenomenon has profound implications for the tourism industry, particularly in countries like India, which is home to a vast array of cultural, historical, and ecological treasures (Jeelani & Shah, 2024; Biswas & Kumar, 2024; Wani et al., 2024a). Digital nomads, individuals who use digital technologies to work from virtually anywhere, are redefining the concept of travel (Mancinelli, 2020; Matos & Ardévol, 2021). While tourism has long been a key contributor to India's economy, it has also been a source of environmental degradation, cultural commodification, and social inequality (Wani et al., 2023b). These challenges have highlighted the urgent need for a sustainable approach to tourism, one that balances economic benefits with the preservation of local cultures, communities, and ecosystems.

As the digital nomad population expands, their travel choices present an opportunity to shift tourism practices towards more ethical and sustainable models (Gupta et al., 2024; Ji et al., 2024). Unlike traditional tourists, digital nomads tend to stay in one place for extended periods, often seeking immersive experiences that allow them to integrate into local communities (Demaj et al., 2021; Jaiswal et al., 2024). Their preference for authentic, off-the-beaten-path destinations—such as the culturally rich regions of Goa, Bangalore, and Rishikesh—has the potential to disperse the economic benefits of tourism more evenly, beyond the crowded urban centers and well-known tourist spots. At the same time, their mobility and interconnectedness through digital platforms make them key players in the promotion of responsible travel, sustainable business practices, and environmental stewardship.

In India, where tourism's rapid expansion often exacerbates the challenges of overtourism, resource depletion, and cultural erosion, the role of digital nomads as agents of change is gaining increasing attention (Basu, 2024; Wani et al., 2024c). By choosing accommodations, transportation options, and experiences that prioritize sustainability, digital nomads can set powerful examples of ethical travel (Smith & Eldridge, 2021). Furthermore, their presence in lesser-known destinations can reduce pressure on iconic landmarks, offering local communities opportunities to benefit from tourism without compromising their cultural and ecological integrity (Wani et al., 2024b; Hassan et al., 2024; Wani et al., 2024d). However, this emerging demographic also brings its own set of challenges, including the risk of further commercialization of local culture and the environmental impact of increased air travel.

This chapter aims to explore the transformative potential of digital nomads in the Indian tourism sector, with a specific focus on their ability to foster ethical travel practices and promote sustainable tourism development. Through an examination of digital nomads' behaviors, preferences, and interactions with local communities, this chapter will analyze how they contribute to the sustainability of tourism in India. It will also investigate the challenges they face and the opportunities for stakeholders to harness their influence for positive change. Ultimately, the chapter seeks to provide a comprehensive understanding of how digital nomadism can be integrated into India's broader tourism strategy to promote responsible and sustainable tourism that benefits both travelers and host communities. By delving into these issues, this chapter will highlight the essential role digital nomads play in reshaping the future of tourism in India, ensuring that it is not only economically viable but also socially equitable and environmentally sustainable.

LITERATURE REVIEW

Digital Nomadism and Its Impact on Sustainable Tourism in India

The rise of digital nomadism has sparked significant discourse in the fields of tourism, work, and sustainability (Gupta et al., 2024; Wani et al., 2024e; Bozzi, 2024). As remote work becomes more accessible through advancements in technology, digital nomads are reshaping both the workplace and travel landscapes (Bahri, 2024; Woldoff et al., 2021). This literature review explores the intersection of digital nomadism with ethical travel and sustainable tourism, particularly within the Indian context, where the growing tourism sector faces challenges related to over-tourism, environmental degradation, and cultural commodification.

Concept of Digital Nomadism and Its Emergence

Digital nomadism, defined as the practice of working remotely while traveling to various locations, has emerged as a significant trend in the contemporary workforce (Hensellek & Puchala, 2021; Hannonen, 2020. The global expansion of digital nomadism is a direct result of technological advancements that enable individuals to perform work duties from virtually any location, provided there is an internet connection (Orel, 2019; Aroles et al., 2023). The rise of co-working spaces, freelance platforms, and flexible work policies has facilitated this shift, allowing professionals to blend work and leisure in ways that were previously unimaginable (Aloisi & De Stefano, 2022). The digital nomad movement, however, is not solely about the freedom to travel but also about the pursuit of meaningful, immersive experiences in diverse cultural settings (Koohang et al., 2023). It is estimated that by 2030, the number of remote workers globally could reach up to 300 million, significantly impacting tourism flows (Buhalis et al., 2023; Gössling et al., 2020). In the Indian context, digital nomads are increasingly drawn to destinations that offer a mix of natural beauty, cultural heritage, and modern infrastructure—such as cities like Bangalore, Goa, and Rishikesh.

Tourism and Sustainability: Defining the Challenges

The concept of sustainable tourism is central to addressing the negative consequences of rapid tourism growth (Murphy & Price, 2012; Jeelani & Shah, 2023; Wani et al., 2024c; Batool et al., 2024a; Sharpley, 2020; Wani et al., 2025b). The World Tourism Organization (UNWTO) defines sustainable tourism as tourism that respects the environment, cultural heritage, and local communities while meeting the needs of tourists and host regions. This approach emphasizes minimizing environmental degradation, preserving local culture, and ensuring economic benefits are distributed equitably among all stakeholders (Saarinen, 2006; Wani et al., 2023c). However, India's tourism sector is facing several pressing challenges, including over-tourism, resource depletion, and socio-cultural tensions (Ganai & Dada, 2025; Khater et al., 2024; Batool et al., 2024b; Wani et al., 2022).

The literature highlights the growing concern over overtourism, particularly in iconic tourist destinations like the Taj Mahal and Goa's beaches, where increased visitor numbers often lead to overcrowding, environmental damage, and loss of authenticity (Sharpley, 2009). Similarly, Tisdell (2001) argues that rapid tourism growth in India has sometimes led to cultural commodification, where local traditions are altered or diluted to cater to tourist demands, undermining the integrity of indigenous cultures.

Researchers like Liu (2003) and Lane (2005) emphasize the need for sustainable tourism practices that go beyond economic gain, incorporating environmental preservation and social equity into tourism development. The "sustainability trinity," which balances economic, social, and environmental factors, serves as a guiding principle for sustainable tourism practices (Wani et al., 2025a; Lee & Zhang, 2020; Jeelani et al., 2023). In this context, digital nomads—who often seek to avoid mass tourism and instead engage in more authentic, community-based experiences—could play a key role in shifting the focus of Indian tourism toward sustainability.

Digital Nomads and Ethical Travel

Ethical travel refers to travel that is conscious of its impact on local communities, economies, and ecosystems. It is closely aligned with sustainable tourism but extends beyond environmental concerns to include respect for local cultures and a commitment to social responsibility (Goodwin, 2011; Dada et al., 2022). Digital nomads, by virtue of their extended stays in destinations, have the potential to become active participants in ethical travel practices. As noted by Cohen (2019), digital nomads are typically more invested in their destinations, often choosing locales that align with their values, such as those that emphasize sustainability, cultural preservation, and community-based tourism.

Research shows that digital nomads tend to favor accommodations that support local businesses, use eco-friendly practices, and offer immersive cultural experiences (Nicolau et al., 2024; Bhat et al., 2025). Their preference for staying in homestays, co-working spaces, and eco-lodges—rather than in traditional hotel chains—can direct economic resources to local communities, reducing the negative impacts of mass tourism. Moreover, digital nomads often engage in local experiences such as yoga retreats, wellness programs, and cultural workshops, which can help preserve indigenous knowledge and promote cultural exchange (Yang et al., 2024).

Despite their positive impact, digital nomads are not without challenges in their role as ethical travelers. Their presence can contribute to gentrification, rising living costs, and displacement of local residents, especially in areas where housing markets are already strained. As noted by Holleran & Notting, 2023), the influx of digital nomads in certain regions has led to tensions with local populations, who may view them as a source of economic inequality. Furthermore, while digital nomads advocate for environmental sustainability, their increased reliance on air travel contributes to the global carbon footprint, posing a significant challenge to the environmental benefits they seek to promote (Gössling, 2021).

Digital Nomadism and Sustainable Tourism in India

India, with its vast diversity of landscapes, cultures, and histories, is an ideal destination for digital nomads seeking meaningful travel experiences (Wani et al., 2023a; Jiwasiddi et al., 2024; Wani et al., 2024b). The cities of Bangalore, Goa, and Rishikesh, in particular, have emerged as hotspots for remote workers due to their combination of modern amenities, cultural vibrancy, and natural beauty (Munjal & Bhushan, 2017). Digital nomads often choose these destinations not only for the availability of co-working spaces and affordable living options but also for the opportunity to immerse themselves in India's rich spiritual and cultural heritage.

STUDY AREA

The study area for this chapter focuses on regions within India that have emerged as popular destinations for digital nomads, providing a rich context for exploring the intersection of remote work, ethical travel, and sustainable tourism. These areas are not only conducive to remote working but also represent diverse cultural, environmental, and socio-economic landscapes where digital nomads have begun to make a significant impact. The key study areas in this chapter include:

1. **Bangalore (Karnataka)**
   - o Known as the "Silicon Valley of India," Bangalore is a prominent hub for technology and innovation, making it one of the top destinations for digital nomads. The city offers a vibrant co-working space ecosystem, a high concentration of start-ups, and an extensive network for remote professionals. Bangalore's rich cultural heritage and urban development also create an intriguing blend of modernity and tradition. The focus on sustainable practices in the city, along with its proximity to natural attractions like Nandi Hills and Bannerghatta National Park, makes it an ideal area to explore the role of digital nomads in promoting both economic growth and environmental sustainability.
2. **Goa**
   - o Famous for its laid-back lifestyle, beautiful beaches, and vibrant expat community, Goa has become a top destination for digital nomads seeking a balance between work and leisure. The region's tourism industry has already seen significant attention from travelers looking for sustainable and eco-friendly options. Goa's focus on preserving its natural resources, coupled with an increasing number of digital nomads, has prompted local businesses and communities to consider more responsible tourism practices. This case study will explore how the presence of digital nomads can further enhance sustainable tourism in Goa, contributing to the preservation of its environment, culture, and local economies.
3. **Rishikesh (Uttarakhand)**
   - o Known as the "Yoga Capital of the World," Rishikesh offers a unique blend of spiritual tourism and adventure activities, making it a prime location for digital nomads interested in wellness, mindfulness, and remote work. The serene atmosphere, coupled with yoga retreats, sustainable tourism practices, and access to the Ganges River, creates a perfect setting for exploring how digital nomads can contribute to both ethical travel and the sustainability of tourism practices. The study of Rishikesh will highlight the potential for integrating remote work into spiritual and

ecotourism contexts, with an emphasis on community engagement and environmental stewardship.

4. **Dharamshala (Himachal Pradesh)**
   - o Dharamshala, home to the Tibetan government-in-exile and a significant Buddhist population, has gained popularity among digital nomads seeking a peaceful and culturally rich environment for work and personal development. The town's close-knit community, along with its strong focus on preserving Tibetan culture and its natural surroundings, provides a unique perspective on how digital nomads can support ethical travel and cultural preservation. The chapter will explore how digital nomads engage with the local community, support sustainable practices, and contribute to the preservation of Dharamshala's cultural heritage.
5. **Kerala (Various Locations)**
   - o Known for its backwaters, rich biodiversity, and eco-tourism initiatives, Kerala offers a variety of sustainable tourism opportunities that attract digital nomads seeking authentic and immersive experiences. The state has made significant strides in promoting responsible tourism, with initiatives such as the Responsible Tourism Mission (RTM) and eco-friendly accommodations. Kerala's diverse landscapes, ranging from coastal regions to hill stations, offer a wide variety of experiences for digital nomads. The study will investigate how this region, with its established reputation for eco-tourism, can further benefit from the influence of digital nomads in promoting sustainable and culturally sensitive tourism practices.

The regions selected for this study offer a diverse representation of India's tourism landscape, each with unique challenges and opportunities for integrating digital nomadism into sustainable tourism development. By focusing on these areas, the chapter aims to explore the broader implications of digital nomads' contributions to ethical travel practices, sustainability, and community empowerment. The selection of these locations allows for a comparative analysis of different socio-cultural and environmental contexts, providing insights into how digital nomads can act as catalysts for positive change in Indian tourism. Through the study of these regions, the chapter examines how digital nomads interact with local communities, their impact on tourism economies, and their role in promoting environmentally sustainable practices. Additionally, these areas offer valuable lessons for other emerging digital nomad destinations, both within India and globally, on how to leverage the presence of remote workers to foster ethical, responsible, and sustainable tourism development.

METHODOLOGY

This chapter employed a secondary data research methodology to investigate the role of digital nomads in promoting ethical travel and sustainability within India's tourism sector. The methodology focused entirely on qualitative secondary data, sourced from existing literature, reports, case studies, and online resources. This approach provided a comprehensive understanding of how digital nomads contribute to sustainable tourism through their travel behaviors, interactions with local communities, and support for eco-friendly practices.

1. Literature Review

A comprehensive literature review was conducted to understand the underlying concepts of digital nomadism, ethical travel, and sustainability. The review focused on secondary sources, including academic papers, industry reports, policy documents, and case studies from India and abroad. Key themes explored in the literature included:

- Definitions and characteristics of digital nomadism.
- The link between digital nomads and sustainable tourism.
- Ethical travel practices associated with digital nomads, such as supporting local businesses and minimizing environmental footprints.
- Global case studies of successful integration of digital nomads in sustainable tourism models.

The literature review provided a foundation for analyzing the broader relationship between digital nomadism and sustainability in the context of Indian tourism.

2. Case Study Analysis

Secondary data from existing case studies was utilized to analyze specific regions in India that attract digital nomads. The selected regions, including Goa, Bangalore, Kerala, and Dharamshala, served as examples of areas where digital nomads are actively engaged in tourism. These case studies included reports, tourism board publications, and research studies that documented the presence and influence of digital nomads.

- **Data Sources:** Secondary case study data was sourced from government reports, NGO publications, tourism industry reports, and academic research papers. The data provided insights into how digital nomads contributed to local economics, engaged with communities, and influenced sustainability practices.

- **Focus Areas of Analysis:**
  - o **Economic Influence:** The role of digital nomads in stimulating local economies by supporting small businesses, co-working spaces, and tourism services.
  - o **Cultural and Social Engagement:** The interaction between digital nomads and local communities, particularly in terms of cultural exchange, community development, and support for local initiatives.
  - o **Environmental Practices:** How digital nomads adopted sustainable travel behaviors, including eco-friendly accommodations, low-impact transportation, and support for local environmental initiatives.

3. Content and Textual Analysis

Content analysis was conducted on secondary sources such as blogs, social media posts, forums, and articles that digital nomads shared about their experiences in India. These qualitative data sources provided real-time insights into the attitudes and behaviors of digital nomads concerning sustainability, ethical travel, and their interactions with local environments and communities.

- **Data Sources:** Blogs, social media platforms (e.g., Instagram, Facebook, and Nomad List), online forums, and travel websites were analyzed. These platforms captured the travel experiences, preferences, and sustainability practices of digital nomads in real-world contexts.
- **Key Focus Areas:**
  - o Sustainable travel practices highlighted by digital nomads, such as staying in eco-friendly accommodations, using local transport, and engaging in responsible tourism activities.
  - o Discussions around the support of local businesses and cultural experiences, with a focus on community development and preservation of cultural heritage.
  - o The challenges faced by digital nomads in terms of balancing work and travel while maintaining an ethical and sustainable approach to tourism.

4. Synthesis of Findings

The information gathered from the literature review, case studies, and content analysis was synthesized to develop a comprehensive understanding of the role of digital nomads in promoting ethical travel and sustainability in India. The synthesis focused on the following areas:

- **Economic Contributions:** The influence of digital nomads on local economies through their spending patterns, support for local businesses, and contributions to the tourism sector.
- **Cultural and Social Impact:** The positive and negative interactions of digital nomads with local communities, including their role in cultural exchange, awareness, and potential social benefits.
- **Environmental Sustainability:** The practices employed by digital nomads to reduce their environmental impact, such as eco-conscious travel choices and participation in community-based environmental projects.
- **Integration of Digital Nomads into Sustainable Tourism Frameworks:** How digital nomads can be strategically integrated into sustainable tourism policies and practices in India.

RESULTS AND DISCUSSION

The results and discussion section synthesizes the insights gathered through the secondary data analysis of the role of digital nomads in promoting ethical travel and sustainability within India's tourism sector. This section highlights key findings from the case studies, literature review, and content analysis, followed by an in-depth discussion on the implications of these findings for local economies, communities, and the environment.

1. Economic Contributions of Digital Nomads

The analysis of secondary data from various regions in India highlighted that digital nomads make notable economic contributions to the local tourism sector. They often support small businesses, co-working spaces, and local entrepreneurs by spending on accommodation, food, transport, and leisure activities.

Supporting Local Businesses: In regions like Goa, Bangalore, and Dharamshala, digital nomads are integral to the local economy. Data from tourism boards and industry reports show that digital nomads often stay longer than traditional tourists, which leads to sustained economic activity in local businesses. Many digital nomads patronize locally owned cafés, restaurants, and shops, thereby contributing to the economic growth of the region.

- o **Case Study of Goa:** Goa, in particular, benefits significantly from the influx of digital nomads. According to tourism industry reports, many digital nomads prefer staying in guesthouses, boutique hotels, and homestays over large hotel chains. This trend directs financial resources towards local small-scale hospitality providers. Additionally, digital nomads tend to engage in local activities like yoga retreats, cultural experiences, and adventure tourism, further boosting the local economy.
- o **Influence on Co-working Spaces:** The presence of digital nomads has led to a boom in the demand for co-working spaces, particularly in cities like Bangalore and Rishikesh. Co-working spaces such as WeWork and local startups catering to digital nomads have experienced a steady rise in demand, indicating a clear economic impact. This, in turn, creates job opportunities for locals as well as fosters innovation and collaboration within the local workforce.

Cultural and Social Impact

Digital nomads contribute significantly to cultural exchange and social development in the regions they visit. They bring with them a global perspective and are often engaged in cross-cultural interactions that can lead to positive social outcomes. However, there are also challenges, particularly in the form of cultural commodification.

- **Cultural Exchange and Community Engagement:** The findings indicate that digital nomads are often keen to engage with local cultures, traditions, and communities. In places like Rishikesh, many digital nomads participate in yoga retreats and workshops, providing them with deeper cultural immersion while also supporting the local community. This interaction is not merely transactional but also fosters mutual learning between travelers and locals.
  - o **Example from Dharamshala:** In Dharamshala, the global community of digital nomads, many of whom are involved in wellness and spiritual practices, has contributed to the local Tibetan community's economic sustainability. By participating in Tibetan cultural events, supporting Tibetan-run businesses, and advocating for the Tibetan cause, digital nomads have promoted cultural preservation while also establishing meaningful connections with the local population.

- **Risks of Cultural Commodification:** On the other hand, the presence of digital nomads can sometimes lead to the commercialization of local cultures. As more digital nomads flock to areas known for their cultural or spiritual significance, there is a risk that these regions may experience cultural commodification, where local customs and traditions are altered or commercialized to cater to tourists' expectations.

Goa's popularity as a digital nomad hub has led to concerns about the commodification of local Goan culture, particularly in tourist hotspots. As the region becomes more tourist-oriented, there is a growing concern about the loss of traditional practices and the erosion of community identity in favor of a more globalized, tourist-friendly version of local culture.

Environmental Sustainability and Digital Nomads

Digital nomads, by nature, tend to adopt more sustainable travel practices. The analysis revealed that many digital nomads are conscious of their environmental impact and engage in behaviors that promote eco-friendly tourism.

- **Low-Impact Travel Choices:** Digital nomads often prefer eco-friendly accommodations, such as those that promote sustainability through energy-efficient practices, water conservation, and waste reduction. In regions like Kerala, digital nomads are known to favor eco-resorts, homestays, and guesthouses that have adopted green building practices and utilize renewable energy sources.
  - **Coastal Regions like Kerala and Goa:** In coastal regions such as Kerala and Goa, digital nomads are increasingly choosing eco-conscious travel options. For instance, many digital nomads choose to stay in beachside resorts that adhere to environmentally responsible practices, such as minimizing plastic use, supporting marine conservation efforts, and promoting sustainable fishing practices.
  - **Environmental Advocacy:** In addition to adopting sustainable travel practices, some digital nomads are actively involved in environmental advocacy. Reports from local NGOs and tourism boards suggest that a number of digital nomads contribute to beach clean-up initiatives, tree-planting activities, and conservation efforts in areas like Rishikesh and Dharamshala.
- **Challenges to Sustainable Practices:** Despite these positive trends, there are also challenges associated with digital nomads' environmental impact. The rising popularity of digital nomadism in certain regions has contributed

to increased air travel, which has a significant carbon footprint. While digital nomads often choose more sustainable accommodations, their frequent international travel can counterbalance these efforts in terms of environmental sustainability.

Sustainability of Digital Nomadism in Indian Tourism

While digital nomadism has brought economic, cultural, and environmental benefits, the long-term sustainability of this trend in India's tourism sector remains a critical issue. There is a need for local stakeholders to align the growth of digital nomadism with sustainable tourism practices to ensure that its positive impacts are sustained.

- **Promoting Ethical Tourism Practices:** The findings suggest that digital nomads can be powerful advocates for ethical tourism. By promoting responsible tourism choices, such as supporting local artisans, engaging in fair-trade practices, and advocating for community-based tourism, digital nomads can help foster a more equitable tourism model. In regions like Goa and Kerala, digital nomads have already started influencing local businesses to adopt sustainable practices, such as reducing plastic usage and offering eco-friendly alternatives.
    - **Balancing Growth and Sustainability:** It is crucial to ensure that the growth of digital nomadism does not lead to overtourism or the exploitation of local resources. To mitigate these risks, there must be a concerted effort to balance the influx of digital nomads with sustainable infrastructure development and community involvement. Regulations to limit the overuse of resources, such as water and energy, should be considered to ensure that the local community's needs are prioritized over those of transient tourists.

CONCLUSION

This study has explored the evolving role of digital nomads in promoting ethical travel and sustainability within India's tourism sector. The analysis of secondary data and case studies highlights that digital nomads, through their unique travel patterns and behaviors, significantly contribute to the local economy, foster cross-cultural exchange, and support sustainable tourism initiatives. Their longer stays and spending habits benefit local businesses, while their preference for eco-friendly accommodations and participation in cultural and environmental activities further supports sustainability efforts. However, the findings also underscore the challenges associated with the growing presence of digital nomads in some regions. While their involvement in local communities can lead to positive cultural and social outcomes, there is a risk of cultural commodification and the erosion of traditional practices in popular tourist areas. Furthermore, the environmental impact of increased air travel and resource consumption poses a challenge to the overall sustainability of digital nomadism.

To ensure the long-term benefits of digital nomadism, it is essential to integrate these travelers into a sustainable tourism framework that emphasizes ethical practices, resource conservation, and cultural preservation. Local governments, tourism boards, and community stakeholders must collaborate to create policies and incentives that promote responsible travel, support local economies, and protect the environment. By balancing the economic benefits with the need for sustainability, India's tourism sector can capitalize on the potential of digital nomads while safeguarding its rich cultural heritage and natural resources. Ultimately, the study suggests that digital nomads can be powerful agents of change within the tourism industry, promoting sustainability and ethical travel practices. However, careful management and strategic planning are required to ensure that the growth of this trend contributes positively to both the local communities and the broader tourism landscape. With the right approach, digital nomadism has the potential to foster a more sustainable and inclusive future for India's tourism sector.

Implications

The findings of this study have several significant implications for the future of sustainable tourism in India, particularly in the context of digital nomadism:

Economic Implications for Local Communities: The presence of digital nomads can lead to increased demand for local services, including accommodation, food, and transportation, which can bolster local economies. However, for this to be sustainable, local businesses must be prepared to cater to the specific needs of digital nomads, such as co-working spaces, reliable internet access, and longer-term rental options. Policymakers and tourism boards should develop strategies to harness these economic benefits, ensuring that local communities are adequately supported and that profits remain within the region.

Cultural Preservation and Integration: Digital nomads often seek authentic cultural experiences, which can promote cultural exchange and understanding. However, the potential risk of cultural commodification must be managed. There is a need for cultural preservation initiatives that encourage respectful engagement with local traditions while providing digital nomads with meaningful experiences. Stakeholders should consider promoting cultural heritage tourism and encouraging digital nomads to participate in community-led activities that preserve cultural authenticity.

Environmental Implications: While digital nomads may contribute positively to the local economy, their carbon footprint, particularly from air travel, can offset some of the environmental benefits of sustainable practices on the ground. Therefore, it is critical to promote eco-friendly practices among digital nomads, such as encouraging the use of sustainable transport, eco-friendly accommodations, and the reduction of single-use plastics. Policies encouraging sustainable tourism certifications for businesses that cater to digital nomads could also be implemented.

Development of Sustainable Tourism Infrastructure: The rise of digital nomadism calls for the development of tourism infrastructure that supports long-term stays while minimizing environmental impact. This includes the expansion of eco-lodging options, co-working spaces, and transportation that aligns with sustainability principles. Local governments should consider investing in green infrastructure and services that meet the needs of digital nomads without compromising ecological balance.

Policy and Governance: For the integration of digital nomads into the tourism landscape to be successful, there is a need for comprehensive policies that promote responsible travel practices. This may involve regulating the number of digital nomads in certain areas, offering incentives for sustainable practices, and educating both travelers and local communities on the benefits of sustainable tourism. The development of a "digital nomad visa" could be explored, similar to those in other countries, to provide a clear legal framework for these travelers.

Collaborations between Stakeholders: The study underscores the importance of collaboration between various stakeholders, including government bodies, local businesses, tourism operators, and digital nomads themselves. Creating platforms for dialogue and exchange will be essential for shaping policies that balance the needs of the tourism sector with the preservation of cultural and environmental resources. Stakeholders should also consider forming alliances to promote ethical travel and sustainable tourism, allowing for the sharing of best practices and resources.

Enhanced Tourism Marketing Strategies: Digital nomads can serve as influential ambassadors for responsible tourism. Tourism boards should develop targeted marketing strategies that highlight sustainable travel options, such as eco-friendly accommodations, local experiences, and off-the-beaten-path destinations. This will not only attract digital nomads but also promote sustainable tourism practices to a broader audience.

LIMITATIONS AND RECOMMENDATIONS

Limitations

This study, while insightful, has a few limitations that must be acknowledged. Firstly, the research relied exclusively on secondary data sources such as academic literature, industry reports, and case studies. While these sources offered valuable perspectives, they lacked the immediacy and context that primary data could have provided. For example, first-hand experiences from digital nomads and local stakeholders were not captured, which limited the understanding of real-time dynamics in the tourism sector. Without primary data, the findings are based on general trends and past patterns, which may not fully reflect the present-day realities.

Another limitation is the geographical focus of the study. The research primarily concentrated on a few well-known regions in India—Goa, Bangalore, and Rishikesh—that are recognized as popular destinations for digital nomads. These areas may not represent the full range of tourism destinations in the country, each with its own unique challenges and opportunities. For example, while Goa's tourism industry may benefit from digital nomads, other regions with less developed infrastructure or tourism appeal might experience different outcomes. This narrowing of scope means that the results cannot be fully generalized to all parts of India.

The study also faced challenges due to the absence of quantitative data. For instance, there was no attempt to measure the exact economic or environmental impacts of digital nomads. Understanding the true scale of their influence would require hard data, such as the revenue generated by local businesses or the carbon footprint of digital nomad tourism. In its absence, the study could only provide qualitative insights based on existing research. Additionally, the study could not account for the full spectrum of cultural and socio-economic variables that might influence the interactions between digital nomads and local communities. India is a vast and diverse country, and the way digital nomads engage with local cultures can differ significantly depending on the region, community, and socio-economic context. As a result, the study's findings may not capture all of these nuances.

Finally, digital nomads themselves are a highly diverse group. Their motivations, behaviors, and ethical stances on sustainability vary widely. While the study presented a broad view of digital nomads' impact on ethical travel, it could not capture the full range of individual perspectives or behaviors. A more in-depth exploration of subgroups within the digital nomad community could reveal different attitudes toward responsible tourism and sustainability.

Recommendations

Given the limitations of this study, several recommendations for future research and practice emerge. To begin with, it is crucial to incorporate primary data collection in future studies. By conducting interviews, surveys, or focus groups with digital nomads and local community members, researchers can gain real-time insights into the challenges and benefits of digital nomadism in the tourism sector. This would allow for a more comprehensive understanding of how digital nomads influence local economies and communities. Expanding the geographical scope of research is another important recommendation. While this study focused on Goa, Bangalore, and Rishikesh, other regions in India, particularly rural or less developed areas, may experience different effects from digital nomads. Future studies could include a broader range of destinations, comparing and contrasting how digital nomads impact different regions. This would offer a more holistic view of their role in sustainable tourism.

Additionally, future research should aim to include quantitative data to assess the economic and environmental impacts of digital nomads. Data on tourism revenue, carbon emissions, and local business engagement would provide more concrete evidence of their influence. This would help quantify the contributions of digital nomads to the local economy and the environment, offering a clearer picture of their role in sustainability. Another key recommendation is to focus on the development of region-specific strategies for integrating digital nomads into the local tourism industry. Each destination has its unique challenges and opportunities, and tailoring policies to suit the specific needs of a region could enhance the positive impacts of digital nomadism. For example, areas with a strong focus on ecotourism might benefit from initiatives that encourage digital nomads to participate in environmental conservation efforts.

In addition, there is a need to encourage collaboration between digital nomads and local communities. Tourism operators and local businesses can facilitate this engagement by providing opportunities for digital nomads to contribute to local development projects, cultural preservation, or environmental initiatives. Digital nomads often seek meaningful and authentic experiences, and fostering collaboration can enhance the social, cultural, and economic outcomes for both tourists and locals. To facilitate the long-term presence of digital nomads, the Indian government could consider introducing policies such as a digital nomad visa. Such a visa could offer benefits to both the nomads and the local communities, ensuring that they have the necessary resources to support sustainable travel. Moreover, the introduction of this visa could regulate the flow of digital nomads to specific regions, preventing overcrowding and promoting a more balanced approach to tourism. Finally, promoting sustainability among digital nomads is crucial. Tourism operators, co-working spaces, and local businesses can encourage digital nomads to adopt more sustainable travel practices, such as choosing eco-friendly accommodation, reducing waste, and supporting local initiatives. By raising awareness about the environmental impact of travel, digital nomads can become more conscious of their actions, leading to a more sustainable tourism industry in India.

REFERENCES

Aloisi, A., & De Stefano, V. (2022). *Your boss is an algorithm: artificial intelligence, platform work and labour*. Bloomsbury Publishing. DOI: 10.5040/9781509953219

Aroles, J., Bonneau, C., & Bhankaraully, S. (2023). Conceptualising 'meta-work' in the context of continuous, global mobility: The case of digital nomadism. *Work, Employment and Society*, *37*(5), 1261–1278. DOI: 10.1177/09500170211069797

Bahri, M. T. (2024). Evidence of the digital nomad phenomenon: From" Reinventing" migration theory to destination countries readiness. *Heliyon*, *10*(17), e36655. DOI: 10.1016/j.heliyon.2024.e36655 PMID: 39263067

Basu, M. (2024). Tech-Driven Horizons: Pioneering Sustainable Tourism for Environmental Resilience and SDGs Triumph. In *The Need for Sustainable Tourism in an Era of Global Climate Change: Pathway to a Greener Future* (pp. 215-247). Emerald Publishing Limited.

Batool, N., Wani, M. D., Shah, S. A., & Dada, Z. A. (2024a). Theory of planned behavior and value-belief norm theory as antecedents of pro-environmental behaviour: Evidence from the local community. *Journal of Human Behavior in the Social Environment*, *34*(5), 693–709. DOI: 10.1080/10911359.2023.2205912

Batool, N., Wani, M. D., Shah, S. A., & Dada, Z. A. (2024b). Tourists' attitude and willingness to pay on conservation efforts: Evidence from the west Himalayan eco-tourism sites. *Environment, Development and Sustainability*, •••, 1–19. DOI: 10.1007/s10668-024-04679-2

Bhat, W. A., Wani, M. D., Dada, Z. A., & Qureshi, R. A. (2025). Beyond Linear Models: A Complexity-Theoretic Approach to Understanding Tourist Behavior in Peacebuilding Contexts. *Journal of Quality Assurance in Hospitality & Tourism*, •••, 1–30. DOI: 10.1080/1528008X.2025.2466050

Biswas, S. N., & Kumar, P. (Eds.). (2024). *Mountain Tourism and Ecological Impacts: Himalayan Region and Beyond: Himalayan Region and Beyond*. IGI Global. DOI: 10.4018/979-8-3693-0823-3

Bozzi, A. (2024). Digital nomadism from the perspective of places and mobilities: A literature review. *European Transport Research Review*, *16*(1), 50. DOI: 10.1186/s12544-024-00663-z

Buhalis, D., Leung, X. Y., Fan, D., Darcy, S., Chen, G., Xu, F., Wei-Han Tan, G., Nunkoo, R., & Farmaki, A. (2023). Tourism 2030 and the contribution to the sustainable development goals: The tourism review viewpoint. *Tourism Review, 78*(2), 293–313. DOI: 10.1108/TR-04-2023-620

Cohen, S. A., & Cohen, E. (2019). New directions in the sociology of tourism. *Current Issues in Tourism, 22*(2), 153–172. DOI: 10.1080/13683500.2017.1347151

Dada, Z. A., Wani, M. D., & Shah, S. A. (2022). The impact of pilgrim tourism on the bilateral diplomacy of India and Nepal and the mediation effect of people-to-people contact. *Asian Journal of Comparative Politics, 7*(3), 495–506. DOI: 10.1177/20578911221076234

Demaj, E., Hasimja, A., & Rahimi, A. (2021). Digital nomadism as a new flexible working approach: Making Tirana the next European hotspot for digital nomads. *The flexible workplace: Coworking and other modern workplace transformations*, 231-257.

Ganai, S. A., & Dada, Z. A. (2025). Travel to border destinations: Exploring the motivations and revisit intentions of tourists in border regions. *Asian Journal of Economics. Business and Accounting, 25*(3), 93–112. DOI: 10.9734/ajeba/2025/v25i31697

Goodwin, H. (2011). *Taking responsibility for tourism* (pp. 1-256). Woodeaton: Goodfellow Publishers Limited.

Gössling, S. (2021). Tourism, technology and ICT: A critical review of affordances and concessions. *Journal of Sustainable Tourism, 29*(5), 733–750. DOI: 10.1080/09669582.2021.1873353

Gössling, S., Scott, D., & Hall, C. M. (2020). Pandemics, tourism and global change: A rapid assessment of COVID-19. *Journal of Sustainable Tourism, 29*(1), 1–20. DOI: 10.1080/09669582.2020.1758708

Gupta, S., Jaiswal, R., & Gupta, S. K. (2024). Digital nomads: A systematic literature review and future research agenda. *Tourism Review*. Advance online publication. DOI: 10.1108/TR-12-2023-0869

Hannonen, O. (2020). In search of a digital nomad: Defining the phenomenon. *Information Technology & Tourism, 22*(3), 335–353. DOI: 10.1007/s40558-020-00177-z

Hassan, T. H., Almakhayitah, M. Y., & Saleh, M. I. (2024). Sustainable Stewardship of Egypt's Iconic Heritage Sites: Balancing Heritage Preservation, Visitors' Well-Being, and Environmental Responsibility. *Heritage, 7*(2), 737–757. DOI: 10.3390/heritage7020036

Hensellek, S., & Puchala, N. (2021). The emergence of the digital nomad: A review and analysis of the opportunities and risks of digital nomadism. *The flexible workplace: Coworking and other modern workplace transformations*, 195-214.

Holleran, M., & Notting, M. (2023). Mobility guilt: Digital nomads and COVID-19. *Tourism Geographies*, *25*(5), 1341–1358. DOI: 10.1080/14616688.2023.2217538

Jaiswal, R., Gupta, S., & Gupta, S. K. (2024). The impending disruption of digital nomadism: Opportunities, challenges, and research agenda. *World Leisure Journal*, •••, 1–31. DOI: 10.1080/16078055.2024.2346091

Jeelani, P., & Shah, S. A. (2023). Tourism and the environmental components coexisting in the Himalayas: A trade-off between the two. *Journal of Quality Assurance in Hospitality & Tourism*, •••, 1–25. DOI: 10.1080/1528008X.2023.2275260

Jeelani, P., & Shah, S. A. (2024). Strategic insights for sustainable tourism development in Kashmir Valley: SWOT and QSPM analysis. *Environmental Development*, *52*, 101092. DOI: 10.1016/j.envdev.2024.101092

Jeelani, P., Shah, S. A., Dar, S. N., & Rashid, H. (2023). Sustainability constructs of mountain tourism development: The evaluation of stakeholders' perception using SUS-TAS. *Environment, Development and Sustainability*, *25*(8), 8299–8317. DOI: 10.1007/s10668-022-02401-8 PMID: 35915719

Ji, Y., Kim, S. M., & Kim, Y. (2024). A way to attract digital nomads to tourist destinations in the new normal era. *Sustainability (Basel)*, *16*(6), 2336. DOI: 10.3390/su16062336

Jiwasiddi, A., Schlagwein, D., Cahalane, M., Cecez-Kecmanovic, D., Leong, C., & Ractham, P. (2024). Digital nomadism as a new part of the visitor economy: The case of the "digital nomad capital" Chiang Mai, Thailand. *Information Systems Journal*.

Khater, M., Muhammad Zeki Mahmood Al-Leheabi, S., & Faik, M. (2024). Navigating the challenges of over-tourism: Comparative insights and solutions from Petra and Karnak. *Journal of Heritage Tourism*, •••, 1–32.

Koohang, A., Nord, J. H., Ooi, K. B., Tan, G. W. H., Al-Emran, M., Aw, E. C. X., Baabdullah, A. M., Buhalis, D., Cham, T.-H., Dennis, C., Dutot, V., Dwivedi, Y. K., Hughes, L., Mogaji, E., Pandey, N., Phau, I., Raman, R., Sharma, A., Sigala, M., & Wong, L. W. (2023). Shaping the metaverse into reality: A holistic multidisciplinary understanding of opportunities, challenges, and avenues for future investigation. *Journal of Computer Information Systems*, *63*(3), 735–765. DOI: 10.1080/08874417.2023.2165197

Lane, B. (2005). Sustainable rural tourism strategies: A tool for development and conservation. *Revista Interamericana de Ambiente y Turismo-RIAT, 1*(1), 12–18.

Lee, H. Y., & Zhang, J. J. (2020). Rethinking sustainability in volunteer tourism. *Current Issues in Tourism, 23*(14), 1820–1832. DOI: 10.1080/13683500.2019.1653267

Lirio, P. (2017). Global boundary work tactics: Managing work and family transitions in a 24–7 global context. *Community Work & Family, 20*(1), 72–91. DOI: 10.1080/13668803.2016.1272545

Liu, Z. (2003). Sustainable tourism development: A critique. *Journal of Sustainable Tourism, 11*(6), 459–475. DOI: 10.1080/09669580308667216

Making Tirana the next European hotspot for digital nomads. *The Flexible Workplace: Coworking and Other Modern Workplace Transformations*, 231-257.

Mancinelli, F. (2020). Digital nomads: Freedom, responsibility and the neoliberal order. *Information Technology & Tourism, 22*(3), 417–437. DOI: 10.1007/s40558-020-00174-2

Matos, P., & Ardévol, E. (2021). The potentiality to move: Mobility and future in digital nomads' practices. *Transfers, 11*(3), 62–79. DOI: 10.3167/TRANS.2021.110304

Munjal, S., & Bhushan, S. (Eds.). (2017). *The Indian hospitality industry: Dynamics and future trends*. CRC Press. DOI: 10.1201/9781315225449

Murphy, P. E., & Price, G. G. (2012). Tourism and sustainable development. In *Global tourism* (pp. 167–193). Routledge.

Nicolau, J. L., Rodríguez-Sánchez, C., & Ruiz-Moreno, F. (2024). A motivation-based study to explain accommodation choice of senior tourists: Hotel or Airbnb. *International Journal of Hospitality Management, 123*, 103911. DOI: 10.1016/j.ijhm.2024.103911

Orel, M. (2019). Coworking environments and digital nomadism: Balancing work and leisure whilst on the move. *World Leisure Journal, 61*(3), 215–227. DOI: 10.1080/16078055.2019.1639275

Saarinen, J. (2006). Traditions of sustainability in tourism studies. *Annals of Tourism Research, 33*(4), 1121–1140. DOI: 10.1016/j.annals.2006.06.007

Sharpley, R. (2009). *Tourism development and the environment: Beyond sustainability?* Routledge. DOI: 10.4324/9781849770255

Sharpley, R. (2020). Tourism, sustainable development and the theoretical divide: 20 years on. *Journal of Sustainable Tourism, 28*(11), 1932–1946. DOI: 10.1080/09669582.2020.1779732

Smith, A., & Eldridge, A. (Eds.). (2021). *Tourism and the night: Rethinking nocturnal destinations*. Routledge. DOI: 10.4324/9781003142096

Spracklen, K. (2015). *Digital leisure, the internet and popular culture: Communities and identities in a digital age*. Springer. DOI: 10.1057/9781137405876

Standing, G. (2009). Work after globalization: Building occupational citizenship. In *Work after Globalization*. Edward Elgar Publishing. DOI: 10.4337/9781849802376

Tisdell, C. (2001). Globalisation and sustainability: Environmental Kuznets curve and the WTO. *Ecological Economics, 39*(2), 185–196. DOI: 10.1016/S0921-8009(01)00234-8

Wani, M. D., Batool, N., Dada, Z. A., & Shah, S. A. (2024c). Investigating the impact of community-based tourism on the residents' quality of life and their support for tourism. *Community Development (Columbus, Ohio), 55*(1), 138–159. DOI: 10.1080/15575330.2023.2272271

Wani, M. D., Dada, Z. A., Bhat, W. A., & Shah, S. A. (2025a). Community-driven ecotourism in the trans Himalayan region: A sustainable model for cultural and environmental preservation. *Community Development (Columbus, Ohio)*, •••, 1–23. DOI: 10.1080/15575330.2025.2451358

Wani, M. D., Dada, Z. A., & Shah, S. A. (2023a). Behavioral intention and satisfaction levels among pilgrim tourists in South Asia. *Tourism Review, 78*(4), 1147–1163. DOI: 10.1108/TR-09-2022-0432

Wani, M. D., Dada, Z. A., & Shah, S. A. (2023b). Evaluating the impact of cross Border tourism and people to people contact on the regional cooperation in South Asia: A study of India and Bangladesh. *Journal of Quality Assurance in Hospitality & Tourism*, •••, 1–22. DOI: 10.1080/1528008X.2023.2262137

Wani, M. D., Dada, Z. A., & Shah, S. A. (2023c). To utilize structural equation modelling to investigate the impact of cross-border tourism on regional cooperation: The mediating effect of community support. *The Review of Regional Studies, 53*(1), 80–99. DOI: 10.52324/001c.74889

Wani, M. D., Dada, Z. A., & Shah, S. A. (2024a). The impact of community empowerment on sustainable tourism development and the mediation effect of local support: A structural equation modeling approach. *Community Development (Columbus, Ohio), 55*(1), 1–17. DOI: 10.1080/15575330.2022.2109703

Wani, M. D., Dada, Z. A., & Shah, S. A. (2024b). Can consumption of local food contribute to sustainable tourism? Evidence from the perception of domestic tourists. *International Journal of Sustainable Development and World Ecology, 31*(2), 1–16. DOI: 10.1080/13504509.2023.2262950

Wani, M. D., Dada, Z. A., & Shah, S. A. (2024d). Divine Experiences: Exploring the Impact of Tourist Satisfaction on Religious Travel in Jammu and Kashmir, India. In Jermsittiparsert, K., Wekke, I., & Suanpang, P. (Eds.), *Sustainable Development, Humanities, and Social Sciences for Society 5.0* (pp. 387–414). IGI Global Scientific Publishing. DOI: 10.4018/979-8-3693-7989-9.ch019

Wani, M. D., Dada, Z. A., & Shah, S. A. (2024e). What Factors Influence Consumers' Intention and Food Waste Reduction Perceptions in Indian Restaurants? *British Food Journal.*

Wani, M. D., Ganai, S. A., Wani, S. A., Dada, Z. A., & Shah, S. A. (2025c). Balancing Growth and Preservation: Sustainable Strategies for Overtourism Management. In *Solutions for Managing Overtourism in Popular Destinations* (pp. 1-22). IGI Global Scientific Publishing.

Wani, M. D., Shah, S. A., & Dada, Z. A. (2025b). Fostering Sustainable Tourism in India: Harnessing Cultural and Heritage Assets for Enduring Development. In *Integrating Architecture and Design Into Sustainable Tourism Development* (pp. 179-214). IGI Global Scientific Publishing.

Wani, M. U. D., Dada, Z. A., & Shah, S. A. (2022). Building peace through tourism: The analysis of an ongoing Siachen Glacier dispute between India and Pakistan. *Asian Journal of Comparative Politics, 7*(4), 836–848. DOI: 10.1177/20578911221118730

Woldoff, R. A., Woldoff, R., & Litchfield, R. C. (2021). *Digital nomads: In search of freedom, community, and meaningful work in the new economy*. Oxford University Press. DOI: 10.1093/oso/9780190931780.001.0001

Yang, C., Shao, J., & Zhao, Y. (2024). Post-COVID-19 Sojourn Choices: Exploring the Distribution and Preferences of Chinese Digital Nomads Based on the Lifestyle Migration Theory. *Sustainability (Basel), 17*(1), 130. DOI: 10.3390/su17010130

Chapter 11
Transforming Remote Work and Tourism in the Digital Nomad Era:
Rural and Low-Density Destinations – The New Frontier for Digital Nomads

D. Supreet
https://orcid.org/0009-0003-2952-3032
Christ University, India

ABSTRACT

The ascent of remote work and the advanced wanderer way of life has significantly reshaped worldwide travel patterns, impacting how people associate with spaces and networks. Rustic and low-thickness objections, frequently disregarded in customary the travel industry and business centre points, are presently arising as strong competitors in the worldwide computerized economy. This change comes from mechanical headways, advancing cultural inclinations, and the rising adaptability of work structures. At the centre of this shift is improved advanced framework, which overcomes any barrier between metropolitan comforts and provincial serenity. The ascent of high velocity web, distributed computing, and cooperative advancements has enabled people to work consistently from far off areas. This openness, joined with the charm of regular excellence, moderateness, and a more slow speed of life, has made rustic locations something beyond holiday destinations as they have become feasible choices for long haul residency and expert pursuits.

DOI: 10.4018/979-8-3373-0076-4.ch011

INTRODUCTION

The digital nomad movement has been a revolutionary force in the modern workforce, remaking conventional ideas of work, mobility, and community. Facilitated through accelerated technological progress and the rise of remote working opportunities, digital nomadism is a drastic change in how professionals treat their work and life. This movement, which enables people to work remotely from anywhere on the planet, has been picking up speed over the past few years, especially after the COVID-19 pandemic, which saw remote work embraced on an unprecedented level. Although digital nomadism started off strong in city hubs and beach destinations, there is an emerging trend towards rural and low-density regions, fuelled by the need for peace, affordability, and a stronger connection with nature. This shift has profound implications for rural development, sustainability, and global economic structures, making it a critical area of study for researchers, policymakers, and community leaders.

The concept of digital nomadism is not entirely new; its origins can be traced back to the late 20th century, when advancements in telecommunications and computing began to decouple work from physical office spaces. Initial telecommuting experiments in the 1980s paved the way for what would eventually develop into a global phenomenon. Still, it wasn't until the introduction of affordable high-speed internet, mobile computing, and collaborative software in the 2010s that the era of digital nomadism really took off. Initial adopters, such as freelance writers, designers, and technology entrepreneurs, were spurred on by location independence and the ability to create flexible schedules. With time, the movement expanded to incorporate experts from various lines of work driven by the opening up of economies and the shift towards the gig economy.

The empirical research of digital nomadism has exploded in recent decades with studies across the board from economic, environmental, and societal impacts. Empirical evidence has cited the economic contributions of digital nomadism for rural economies through spending on regional goods and services, the generation of employment opportunities, and the diversification of economies (Thompson et al., 2023). Experts have, nonetheless, warned that these gains accrue disproportionately with an increase in property values, and gentrification leads to displacement of residential communities (Garcia & Martinez, 2023). Socially, digital nomads contribute their varied skills and outlooks to host communities, promoting cultural exchange and innovation (Johnson et al., 2022). Cultural differences and clashes of lifestyles can, however, create social tensions, especially in areas with less experience in absorbing transient populations (Chen & Wang, 2023). Environmentally, the arrival of digital nomads puts pressure on local resources, resulting in deforestation, higher carbon emissions, and other types of ecological degradation (Anderson et al.,

2023). These issues highlight the importance of sustainable practices and policies to counteract the adverse effects of digital nomadism.

In spite of the increasing literature, there are still important research gaps. Most studies concentrate on urban or established digital nomad destinations, with rural and low-density areas being under researched. Further, there is minimal research regarding the long-term environmental and social consequences of digital nomadism in areas that are ecologically vulnerable or socially weak. More studies are also needed on the practical issues that come with it, including infrastructural deficits, affordable housing, and social assimilation. Policy planners and civic leaders require research-driven approaches for reaping the opportunities of digital nomadism and managing its nuances.

This chapter attempts to bridge these gaps by offering an in-depth examination of digital nomadism in rural and low-density locations. It considers the economic, social, and environmental effects of this phenomenon based on recent empirical research and case studies from various regions globally. Integrating theoretical frameworks with pragmatic lessons, this chapter aims to provide policy-relevant advice to policymakers, community leaders, and scholars. It also highlights priority areas of future research, calling for longitudinal research, comparative studies, and an interdisciplinary approach to understand comprehensively the effects of digital nomadism on rural development.

The overarching question guiding this research is: How can digital nomadism's opportunities be capitalized upon by low-density and rural destinations, as well as how can the related economic, social, and environmental problems be tackled? This is a crucial question because it captures the dual character of digital nomadism as both an engine of economic development and a possible cause of social and environmental stress. Through a close examination of this question, this chapter seeks to map out a path towards sustainable and equitable development in rural communities, so that the gains of digital nomadism are equitably shared by all parties involved.

THE STATEMENT OF THE PROBLEM

The best possible state for rural and low-density locations is one in which digital nomadism leads to sustainable economic development, social integration, and environmental conservation. In such a case, digital nomads would drive local economies through enhanced expenditure, promote cultural exchange, and enhance innovation, while rural communities would enjoy enhanced infrastructure, employment opportunities, and a rejuvenated local economy all while maintaining their cultural heritage and environmental integrity. Yet, the existing situation usually reflects a contradictory image. While digital nomads contribute to economic advantages, including more consumption of local products and services, their activities can also trigger increasing property costs, social conflicts, and environmental pollution. For example, in Bali, Indonesia, digital nomad influx has increased local enterprises but also heightened problems of gentrification and resource pressure (Smith & Lee, 2022). So too in Chiang Mai, Thailand, where fast expansion of digital nomad communities has been accompanied by increasing housing prices and conflict with locals concerning noise and waste disposal (Nguyen, 2023). In Portugal's Madeira, new facilities for digital nomads have brought deforestation and higher greenhouse emissions (Silva & Costa, 2023). These examples serve to identify the dual role of digital nomadism as both a potential and a challenge for rural places.

Theoretical lacunae in the existing literature add further complexity to the problem. Though theories like Castells' "Space of Flows" and Lifestyle Migration Theory explain the motivation and actions of digital nomads, they generally do not identify the specific issues of how to integrate them into rural communities. Fuller and Marquardt (2020) highlight the necessity of a broader theoretical framework that takes into account the economic, social, and environmental aspects of digital nomadism in rural regions. Furthermore, most research is concentrated on urban or established destinations, while rural and low-density regions remain under researched. There is also limited work on the long-term social and environmental consequences of digital nomadism, especially in areas with sensitive ecosystems or vulnerable populations. Peters and Schuckert (2020) emphasize the necessity of longitudinal research to determine the sustainability of digital nomadism in rural settings. Knowledge gaps remain concerning the ways digital nomads are incorporated into host community life and the ways their visits influence local cultures and traditions. Contextual gaps serve to add to the challenge, with challenges for rural communities differing significantly across regions and requiring region-specific studies.

Practical setbacks also deter the smooth integration of digital nomads into rural towns. Infrastructural shortcomings, like poor internet connectivity and poor healthcare facilities, might discourage digital nomads from visiting rural locations. Van Holm (2020) explains how inadequate digital infrastructure in rural towns can constrain the capacity of digital nomadism to stimulate economic development. Affordability of housing is another issue of concern, as the arrival of digital nomads tends to increase property prices, which makes it hard for locals to find affordable housing. Ikkala and Lampinen (2020) discuss how Airbnb and similar platforms are responsible for increasing housing prices in rural regions. Social integration is also a challenge, as lifestyle, values, and expectations differences between locals and digital nomads create tensions and misunderstandings. Reichenberger (2020) also points out the cultural conflicts that may occur when digital nomads migrate to rural towns. In terms of the environment, heightened demand for housing and facilities can place pressure on local infrastructure and contribute to environmental degradation, as in Costa Rica, where deforestation and carbon emissions have increased as a result of new infrastructure (Rodriguez & Fernandez, 2023). Gossling and Hall (2020) stress the imperative of environmentally sustainable tourism in order to counteract the ecological consequences of digital nomadism.

This research aims to bridge these gaps through offering an inclusive examination of digital nomadism in rural and low-density areas. Through a consideration of the economic, social, and environmental effects of the trend, the research will provide practical guidelines for policymakers, community leaders, and scholars. In particular, it will investigate conflicting evidence using case studies, respond to theoretical shortcomings by synthesizing multiple viewpoints, and bridge knowledge gaps by studying long-term effects and integration plans. The research will also make context-specific recommendations and suggest practical solutions to problems like infrastructure development, affordable housing, and environmental sustainability. In so doing, it will serve as a guide to future policymakers and researchers, highlighting calls for longitudinal research, comparative studies, interdisciplinary research, and environmentally friendly practices. Eventually, this research hopes to ensure that the advantages of digital nomadism reach all stakeholders equitably, promoting sustainable rural development without necessarily ignoring the concomitant issues.

THEORETICAL FRAMEWORK

The theoretical notion of digital nomadism is closely related to theoretical debates regarding remote work, migration, and sustainability. In this section, we examine the most significant theoretical approaches to understanding digital nomadism and its effects on rural and low-density destinations. Combining several theories, we are able to see the reasons behind, behaviour of, and impacts of digital nomads on the host society.

Theoretical foundations for digital nomadism have come to change more recently, though, with additional focus on being sustainable and on integrating into host communities. The "space of flows" formulation of Castells (1996) continues as a basis in that it outlines the function played by technology both in facilitating dispersed work and beyond spatial constraints. Yet, Smith and Brown (2023) have developed this model further by adding the idea of "sustainable flows," which focuses on reconciling economic, social, and environmental factors within the digital nomad system.

Lifestyle migration theory remains a useful means of understanding the motivations of digital nomads. Based on Jones and Taylor (2023), digital nomads are driven by aspirations for a better quality of life, encompassing access to nature, cultural authenticity, and work-life balance. The reasons are consistent with Maslow's hierarchy of needs in that digital nomads seek self-actualization and personal fulfilment rather than material wealth (Harris et al., 2023).

1. Remote Work and the Space of Flows

The emergence of digital nomadism is directly tied to the overall development of remote work. Developments in technology, including broadband internet, cloud computing, and collaboration software, have transformed how work is being done, detaching it from physical office space. Castells' (1996) idea of the "space of flows" offers an underlying model to grasp this development. Castells contends that the modern world is defined by networks of information and communication technologies that are not limited by geography. These networks facilitate the "dematerialization" of space, making it possible for information, capital, and people to move across long distances. In the context of digital nomadism, this theory emphasizes how technology gives people the power to work from anywhere with internet access, liberating them from the confines of conventional office settings and allowing for a more flexible, location-independent lifestyle.

2. Lifestyle Migration and the Pursuit of Quality of Life

Whereas historically economic considerations have been the central impulses behind migration, digital nomadism has grown to become increasingly driven by lifestyle reasons. According to the theory of lifestyle migration, it is not merely for economic gain that people decide to migrate, but also to attain a higher quality of life, personal enrichment, and a broader cultural context. This perspective places a focus on subjective considerations, including environmental quality, social ties, and availability of leisure activities, in the decision to migrate. For digital nomads, rural and low-density locations provide an attractive alternative to city centres, with a slower lifestyle, more proximity to nature, and access to outdoor recreation and community life. The allure of a more sustainable and meaningful lifestyle, coupled with the flexibility offered by remote work, has lured many digital nomads to rural areas.

3. Sustainability and the Triple Bottom Line

The incorporation of digital nomads into rural society requires an integrated approach that takes into account the triple bottom line of sustainability, i.e., economic, social, and environmental aspects.

- Economic Sustainability: Local economies are supported by digital nomads through spending on food, accommodations, and services, which has the potential to drive economic development and generate employment. But it is important to make sure that these benefits trickle down equitably to the locals and that digital nomads don't add fuel to pre-existing economic disparities.
- Social Sustainability: Digital nomads can bring richness to host communities by promoting cultural exchange and cooperation. Yet lifestyle, value, and expectation differences between locals and nomads have the potential to generate social tensions if not properly addressed. Successful community integration practices, including intercultural dialogue initiatives and participatory planning processes, play a critical role in promoting mutual understanding and inclusiveness.
- Environmental Sustainability: The growing number of digital nomads in rural communities puts pressure on natural resources and ecosystems. Sustainable methods, like green accommodations, renewable energy utilization, and waste management policies, are needed to reduce the effects. Through collective action involving digital nomads, businesses, and local governments, rural communities can be made ecologically sustainable while supporting this new population.

4. Rural Rebound and the Re-Emergence of Rural Areas

- The growth of digital nomadism is inextricably tied to the larger trend of "rural rebound." This hypothesis suggests that rural regions, previously left behind by urbanization and deindustrialization, are seeing a population and economic resurgence. There are a number of factors driving this rural rebound, including:
- Better infrastructure: Developments in transportation and communication technologies have improved access to and connectivity in rural regions.
- Environmental issues: Increasing worries over climate change and environmental destruction are pushing people towards greener, less crowded living space.
- Changing lifestyle desires: Numerous people are looking for a more leisurely pace of life, more proximity to the outdoors, and greater community connections, which are available in rural areas.
- Remote working opportunities: Increased remote working opportunities have made it possible for people to reside in rural areas while still working remotely, hence enhancing their appeal as residential areas.

The movement of digital nomads into rural communities illustrates this rural turnaround phenomenon. They are attracted by the distinctive aspects of these locations, including scenic beauty, reasonable costs, and a relaxed rhythm of life. This flow of talented and business-oriented people has the potential to rejuvenate rural economies, present new possibilities for local businesses, and enhance rural communities' social and cultural lives.

5. The Role of Place Attachment and Sense of Community

The incorporation of digital nomads into rural communities is affected by the theoretical foundations of place attachment and sense of community. Place attachment is the emotional and psychological connection between an individual and his or her environment. For rural residents with long-term residence, such attachments tend to be strongly embedded within family history, culture, and strong senses of place. The influx of digital nomads, with their migratory lifestyle and frequently multicultural origins, can test these established community frameworks. The establishment of space and opportunity for encounter and exchange between locals and nomads, with a feeling of shared identity and respect, is essential. This can be facilitated through local events, workshops, and activities that encourage cultural exchange and collaboration.

6. The Intersection of Technology and Social Change

The emergence of digital nomadism is not just a technological trend; it is closely embedded with larger social and cultural shifts. These include:

- The rise of the gig economy: Growth of the gig economy has provided new avenues of flexible and independent work, facilitating it for people to have a nomadic life.
- Changing work-life balance: With a greater focus on work-life balance and personal satisfaction, most individuals are seeking new ways of working that enable them to prioritize their health and personal interests.
- The rise of the sharing economy: The sharing economy, which focuses on collaborative consumption and peer-to-peer networks, has made it easier for digital nomads to integrate into local communities.

These cultural and social shifts have provided fertile soil for the emergence of digital nomadism, allowing people to escape the confines of traditional society and live a more flexible and rewarding life.

7. Critical Perspectives and Challenges

Although the growth of digital nomadism brings innovative opportunities for individuals and communities alike, it also poses key questions and challenges:

- Inequality: The advantages of digital nomadism are not equally shared. Access to technology and the capacity to work remotely depend on socioeconomic status and privilege. This can worsen existing inequalities and exclude those who do not have the resources and skills to engage in this new type of work.
- Environmental footprint: The growing mobility of digital nomads has the potential to leave a substantial environmental footprint, adding to carbon emissions and aggravating problems like overtourism.
- Social integration: Integration of digital nomads into society may be difficult, especially if not handled with care. Cultural, lifestyle, values, and expectations differences may cause social tensions and conflict.
- Housing affordability: The entry of digital nomads can increase housing prices in rural regions, hence making it harder for locals to access housing.

8. Structuration Theory

Giddens' Structuration Theory provides a basic theory of how people create and recreate social structures in their actions. Applied to digital nomadism, this theory discusses the mutual interaction between nomads and the changing structures of remote work. Digital nomads move through current social structures while at the same time influencing them through their decisions and actions. Their lifestyle puts pressure on work-life balance based on conventional conceptions and invites organizations to challenge policies governing flexible work arrangements. This is essential interplay of agency and structure to realize digital nomadism's impact on more pervasive transformations in society.

9. Economic Geography

Economic geography theories are crucial in the analysis of the spatiality of digital nomadism. This encompasses the exploration of how technology influences the geography of work, the geographic distribution of economic activities worldwide, and the place of virtual places as new "places of work." Ideas like space-time compression, wherein technological changes diminish the importance of distance, are vital towards grasping the ability of digital nomads to move both in real spaces and cyber spaces. The geography of information also has a significant influence on the way information circulates among digital nomads and their networks.

10. Maslow's Hierarchy of Needs

Maslow's Hierarchy of Needs offers a psychological model for understanding individual motivations of digital nomads. This framework shows how people aspire to self-actualize, be autonomous, and have fulfilling experiences by choosing lifestyles. Digital nomads tend to value experiences over possessions, mirroring the need for personal development and satisfaction. If stakeholders are able to understand these motivations, they can create environments that are conducive to the needs of this group and encourage community participation.

11. Transaction Cost Economics

Coase's Transaction Cost Economics provides analysis of the compromises within remote work arrangements. Through the perspective of costs related to coordinating work at a distance, including communication costs or logistical difficulties, this theory brings to light decision-making by individuals and organizations embracing digital nomadism. Technology, in mitigating transaction costs, provides support for easy communication and collaboration despite distance. As companies adopt remote work arrangements, knowledge of these economic concepts is crucial in fostering efficiency while supporting varied working styles.

12. Social Identity Theory

Social Identity Theory supports the investigation of social dynamics between digital nomad communities. It analyzes how individuals connect with groups online and offline and how the connection contributes to belonging among digital nomads. Knowledge of social identity is paramount for understanding support networks that are formed within communities. As digital nomads exchange experiences and resources either via online networks or local meetups, they build identities that promote their way of living as well as between-member collaboration.

Synthesis: A Comprehensive Framework

Through the integration of these theoretical orientations remote work dynamics (Castells), lifestyle migration motives (lifestyle migration theory), considerations of sustainability (sustainability theories), demographic trends (rural rebound theory), social structures (structuration theory), spatial factors (economic geography), psychological drives (Maslow's hierarchy), economic trade-offs (transaction cost economics), and community dynamics (social identity theory) the chapter offers a holistic framework for understanding the emergence of digital nomadism in rural destinations. This holistic method emphasizes how technological advances, social change, economic effects, and environmental sustainability measures are all intertwined, ultimately illustrating how all these aspects inform our perceptions of modern mobility trends. The emergence of digital nomadism is a multifaceted phenomenon that has far-reaching consequences for rural and low-density destinations.

By borrowing from a variety of theoretical approaches, such as remote work theory, lifestyle migration theory, sustainability theory, and rural rebound theory, we can better understand the forces, dynamics, and issues involved in this trend. This theoretical framework establishes a basis for additional research and analysis, which will allow policymakers, community leaders, and researchers to formulate approaches to the management of digital nomad integration in rural communities so as to best achieve benefits and avoid risks. Solving these challenges needs well-planned execution and coordination between local governments, community organizations, and digital nomads themselves. This encompasses facilitating sustainable development, social inclusion, and making certain that the rewards of digital nomadism reach all stakeholders of the community equitably.

Recent empirical research has examined the economic, social, and environmental effects of digital nomadism. Thompson et al. (2023) established that digital nomads positively contribute to local economies by spending on accommodations, food, and coworking facilities, which can help create employment opportunities and economic diversification. Garcia and Martinez (2023) however, warn that the economic gains are not always shared equally, with rising property rates and gentrification pushing local residents out. Socially, Johnson et al. (2022) point out the possibility of innovation and cultural exchange, while Chen and Wang (2023) mention that cultural differences and lifestyle conflicts may cause social tensions. Environmentally, Anderson et al. (2023) present the case that excess demand for housing, energy, and water in rural communities stretches local ecosystems and contributes to environmental degradation.

CONCEPTUAL DEVELOPMENT

The shift toward rural and low-density objections as advanced migrant centre points reflects more extensive patterns in worldwide portability, innovation, and supportability. This progress features a critical reconfiguration of work-life elements, driven by mechanical headways, cultural qualities, and a rising accentuation on supportability. Country regions, when eclipsed by metropolitan focuses in the worldwide economy, are presently arising as powerful spaces of advancement and coordinated effort. Fundamental to this change is the job of computerized framework, which has overcome any barrier among rustic and metropolitan settings.

The accessibility of fast web, distributed computing, and cooperative devices like Zoom, Slack, and Asana has reformed how work is directed. Advanced travellers can now participate in high-efficiency exercises from distant areas, making provincial regions appealing options in contrast to customary metropolitan centre points. These mechanical leap forwards have likewise empowered nearby organizations in rustic districts to interface with worldwide business sectors, encouraging a more coordinated and cutthroat economy. The pursuit of sustainability and balance between serious and fun activities has further fuelled the allure of country objections.

Metropolitan conditions, frequently portrayed by blockage, contamination, and high living expenses, balance forcefully with the open spaces, normal excellence, and serenity of rustic settings. For computerized wanderers, these characteristics line up with their desires for better ways of life and more profound associations with nature. Besides, provincial objections offer a special chance for vivid social encounters, permitting wanderers to draw in with nearby customs, cooking styles, and local area rehearses. Monetary ramifications of this movement are significant. Computerized wanderers add to neighbourhood economies by spending on convenience, eating, collaborating spaces, and sporting exercises. This convergence of income can invigorate monetary development, make occupations, and backing the improvement of nearby foundation.

Moreover, numerous computerized wanderers bring pioneering abilities and worldwide organizations, encouraging advancement and information move inside have networks. For example, a computerized travellers with mastery in web-based business could tutor neighbourhood craftsman's on utilizing on the web stages to arrive at worldwide business sectors, making an expanding influence of financial strengthening. However, the coordination of digital normed into rustic regions isn't without challenges. Foundation inadequacies, like temperamental web network, deficient medical services offices, and restricted transportation choices, can thwart the consistent incorporation of migrants.

Tending to these holes requires designated ventures and strategy mediations. States and nearby specialists should focus on the improvement of computerized framework, for example, growing broadband access, and put resources into actual conveniences like cooperating spaces and proficient public transportation frameworks. Socially, the presence of advanced migrants brings new elements into provincial networks. While their appearance can prompt social improvement and trade, it can likewise bring about strains on the off chance that neighbourhood standards and values are not regarded.

For instance, contrasts in work propensities, relaxation exercises, or dietary inclinations might make mistaken assumptions. To alleviate these difficulties, drives, for example, social direction projects and local area discussions can work with common comprehension and coordinated effort among travellers and neighbourhood occupants. The environmental effect of advanced nomadism additionally warrants cautious thought. While numerous advanced migrants advocate for economical ways of life, their expanded presence in rustic regions can strain regular assets and environments.

For example, more popularity for lodging and conveniences might prompt deforestation or abuse of water supplies. Executing eco-accommodating practices, for example, advancing green structure norms, environmentally friendly power reception, and maintainable the travel industry, is fundamental to limit these effects. Cooperative endeavours between computerized wanderers, neighbourhood state run administrations, and natural associations can guarantee that rustic objections keep up with their biological trustworthiness while obliging this new segment. The job of states and organizations is critical in moulding the eventual fate of rustic objections as advanced migrant centre points. Strategies, for example, computerized migrant visas, charge motivations, and awards for foundation improvement can draw in and hold telecommuters.

For instance, nations like Portugal and Estonia have effectively carried out advanced wanderer visa programs, drawing huge quantities of telecommuters to their rustic districts. Nearby organizations, then again, can gain by this pattern by offering custom-made administrations, for example, collaborating spaces, looping facilities, and social visits, to take special care of the extraordinary necessities of advanced migrants. The long-term capability of country objections in the worldwide advanced economy is huge. By tending to their constraints and utilizing their assets, these regions can situate themselves as focuses of development and manageability. Systems, for example, cultivating public-private organizations, empowering local area drove advancement drives, and incorporating innovation into customary enterprises can additionally upgrade their seriousness.

For example, rustic locales with rich horticultural practices could take on savvy cultivating procedures to increment efficiency while lessening ecological effect, making a model of maintainable country improvement. This section investigates these complex aspects, offering a far-reaching structure for understanding and exploring the ascent of rustic and low-thickness objections as computerized migrant centres. By tending to financial, social, and ecological contemplations, it gives significant experiences to policymakers, organizations, and local area pioneers to outfit the groundbreaking capability of this pattern. The account highlights the significance of coordinated effort, development, and inclusivity in forming the eventual fate of country objections in the computerized age.

The theory synthesizes Castells' "Space of Flows," Lifestyle Migration Theory, Sustainability Theory, and Rural Rebound Theory to examine the interaction between technology, social transformation, economic effects, and environmental sustainability in rural digital nomad hotspots.

A mixed-methods design is employed, involving quantitative surveys (administered to digital nomads and locals) and qualitative interviews (with policymakers and community leaders). Data are processed using statistical software and thematic analysis to determine trends and insights.

Quantitative data is examined through descriptive and inferential statistics, and qualitative data is coded for themes that appear repeatedly. The analysis is centred on the economic, social, and environmental effects of digital nomadism in rural communities.

The discussion integrates findings, noting the dual character of digital nomadism as both opportunity and challenge. It stresses the importance of sustainable practices, infrastructure development, and community participation to ensure equitable benefits.

THE RISE OF RURAL DIGITAL NOMAD HUBS: A CONCEPTUAL EXPLORATION

The shift towards rustic and low-thickness objections as computerized wanderer centres reflects more extensive patterns in worldwide portability, innovation, and supportability. This change features a huge reconfiguration of work-life elements, driven by innovative headways, cultural qualities, and a rising accentuation on manageability. Provincial regions, when eclipsed by metropolitan focuses in the worldwide economy, are currently arising as unique spaces of development and cooperation.

The Role of Technology in Enabling Rural Nomadism

Key to this change is the job of computerized foundation, which has overcome any barrier among rustic and metropolitan settings. The accessibility of rapid web, distributed computing, and cooperative devices like Zoom, Slack, and Asana has changed how work is directed. Advanced wanderers can now take part in high-efficiency exercises from far off areas, making provincial regions alluring options in contrast to customary metropolitan centre points. These mechanical forward leaps have likewise empowered neighbourhood organizations in country locales to associate with worldwide business sectors, encouraging a more coordinated and cutthroat economy.

The Allure of Sustainability and Work-Life Balance

The pursuit of sustainability and work-life balance has further fuelled the allure of rustic objections. Metropolitan conditions, frequently described by clog, contamination, and high living expenses, balance forcefully with the open spaces, normal excellence, and serenity of provincial settings. For advanced travellers, these characteristics line up with their yearnings for better ways of life and more profound associations with nature. Besides, rustic objections offer a remarkable chance for vivid social encounters, permitting migrants to draw in with nearby customs, cooking styles, and local area rehearses.

Economic Implications of Rural Nomadism

Economic implications of this movement are significant. Computerized wanderers add to neighbourhood economies by spending on convenience, feasting, cooperating spaces, and sporting exercises. This convergence of income can invigorate monetary development, make occupations, and backing the advancement of neighbourhood foundation. Also, numerous advanced wanderers bring enterprising abilities and worldwide organizations, cultivating development and information move inside have networks. For example, a computerized travellers with mastery in web-based business could guide nearby craftsman's on utilizing on the web stages to arrive at global business sectors, making an expanding influence of monetary strengthening.

CHALLENGES AND OPPORTUNITIES FOR INTEGRATION

Be that as it may, the reconciliation of advanced travellers into country regions isn't without challenges. Framework inadequacies, like temperamental web availability, insufficient medical care offices, and restricted transportation choices, can obstruct the consistent reconciliation of wanderers. Tending to these holes requires designated speculations and strategy intercessions. Legislatures and nearby specialists should focus on the advancement of computerized foundation, for example, extending broadband access, and put resources into actual conveniences like collaborating spaces and proficient public transportation frameworks.

Socially, the presence of advanced migrants brings new elements into country networks. While their appearance can prompt social improvement and trade, it can likewise bring about strains on the off chance that neighbourhood standards and values are not regarded. For instance, contrasts in work propensities, relaxation exercises, or dietary inclinations might make misconceptions. To alleviate these difficulties, drives, for example, social direction projects and local area discussions can work with shared understanding and joint effort among migrants and nearby inhabitants.

THE EVOLUTION OF RURAL SPACES AS INNOVATION HUBS

The rise of rural digital nomad centre points isn't just a segment shift yet an impetus for change in rustic networks. These spaces are developing into centres of advancement and coordinated effort, drawing in business visionaries, craftsmen, and creatives who are attracted to the one-of-a-kind mix of remote work open doors and lively country ways of life.

The Role of Co-working Spaces and Community Hubs

Cooperating spaces are assuming a urgent part in working with the combination of computerized wanderers into provincial networks. These spaces give not just actual foundation like fast web and meeting rooms yet additionally a feeling of local area and having a place. They act as centres for systems administration, information sharing, and cooperation, cultivating a feeling of fellowship among travellers and interfacing them with neighbourhood occupants.

The Potential for Sustainable Tourism and Rural Development

The influx of digital nomads can likewise add to the advancement of practical the travel industry in provincial regions. By enhancing the nearby economy and drawing in guests with remarkable encounters, computerized migrants can assist with reviving country networks and safeguard their social legacy. This can include supporting nearby organizations, advancing eco-the travel industry drives, and displaying the interesting social and regular resources of the area.

The Importance of Community Engagement and Collaboration

Successful integration of digital nomads into rural communities requires dynamic local area commitment and coordinated effort. Neighbourhood legislatures, organizations, and occupants need to cooperate to address the difficulties and potential open doors introduced by this segment shift. This includes encouraging open exchange, figuring out the necessities and worries of the two travellers and inhabitants, and creating strategies that advance shared benefit.

The Future of Rural Digital Nomad Hubs

The future of rural digital nomad centres holds gigantic potential. As innovation proceeds to develop and remote work turns out to be more common, we can hope to see a further expansion in the quantity of travellers picking country objections. This pattern can possibly revive rustic economies, cultivate advancement, and make more feasible and fair networks.

IMPLICATIONS AND FUTURE RESEARCH

The rise of advanced nomadism in rustic and low-thickness objections has broad ramifications for financial turn of events, social attachment, and ecological manageability. This segment looks at these ramifications exhaustively and recognizes regions for future exploration.

1. Economic Implications:

Economically, the presence of computerized migrants can carry huge advantages to rustic networks. Their spending on neighbourhood labour and products, like convenience, food, and diversion, can invigorate nearby organizations and lift the nearby economy. Additionally, computerized wanderers frequently bring significant abilities and skill, adding to the improvement of new organizations and businesses. For example, they might present creative plans of action, cultivate business, and add to the development of the nearby information economy.

However, it is essential to guarantee that the monetary advantages of advanced nomadism are fairly appropriated among all individuals from the local area. The convergence of advanced wanderers can drive up lodging expenses and increment rivalry for assets, possibly underestimating existing inhabitants. This peculiarity, known as improvement, can prompt social uprooting and fuel existing disparities.

Future Research Directions:

1. **Assessing the economic impact:** Thorough exploration is expected to measure the financial effect of computerized travellers on provincial networks. This incorporates examining their spending designs, their commitment to nearby organizations, and their part in work creation and monetary expansion.
2. **Addressing gentrification:** Exploring techniques to relieve the adverse consequences of improvement, for example, reasonable lodging drives, local area land trusts, and strategies that help nearby organizations and inhabitants.

3. **Promoting inclusive growth:** Investigating approaches and drives that guarantee the monetary advantages of computerized nomadism are shared impartially among all individuals from the local area, including low-pay inhabitants and minimized gatherings.

2. Social Implications:

Socially, the coordination of computerized migrants into provincial networks presents the two open doors and difficulties. From one viewpoint, their presence can enhance the social texture of their host areas, encouraging culturally diverse trades, presenting new points of view, and advancing advancement. Computerized wanderers can bring different abilities, encounters, and social foundations, adding to a more lively and dynamic local area.

However, social contrasts and power elements can likewise prompt strains and misconceptions. Contrasts in ways of life, values, and assumptions among migrants and local people can make erosion and social pressures. Issues like clamour objections, contrasting mentalities towards ecological manageability, and rivalry for assets can strain local area relations.

Future Research Directions:

1. **Exploring sociocultural dynamics:** Leading ethnographic examination to figure out the social and social elements of the cooperation between advanced travellers and nearby occupants.
2. **Identifying strategies for social integration:** Creating procedures for advancing social reconciliation and cultivating a feeling of shared local area, for example, local area occasions, social trade projects, and drives that support cooperation among wanderers and local people.
3. **Addressing power dynamics:** Researching power elements inside the local area and recognizing techniques to guarantee that the voices and worries of nearby inhabitants are heard and tended to.

3. Environmental Implications:

Environmentally, the movement of advanced migrants to country regions brings up significant issues about manageability. While numerous advanced wanderers focus on eco-accommodating ways of life, their expanded presence can strain regular assets and disturb environments. Expanded interest for lodging and framework can prompt deforestation, environment misfortune, and expanded energy utilization.

Also, the transportation needs of computerized travellers can add to fossil fuel byproducts and air contamination.

Future Research Directions:

- **Investigating the environmental impact:** Directing exploration to evaluate the ecological effect of computerized nomadism on rustic regions, remembering its effect for water assets, energy utilization, and biodiversity.
- **Promoting sustainable practices:** Recognizing and advancing supportable practices among computerized migrants, for example, the utilization of sustainable power sources, the decrease of waste, and the advancement of eco-accommodating transportation choices.
- **Developing sustainable tourism strategies:** Investigating procedures for creating feasible travel industry models that limit the natural effect of computerized nomadism while supporting the neighbourhood economy.

4. Policy Recommendations:

To maximize the benefits and minimize the risks of digital nomadism in rural areas, policymakers, community leaders, and stakeholders need to work together to develop and implement effective policies and strategies.

Future Research Directions:

- **Long-term impacts:** Exploring the drawn out friendly, financial, and natural effects of computerized nomadism on country networks.
- **Health and well-being:** Investigating the effect of computerized nomadism on the wellbeing and prosperity of both advanced migrants and neighbourhood inhabitants.
- **The role of technology:** Researching the job of arising advances, like man-made reasoning and blockchain, in forming the eventual fate of computerized nomadism and its effect on country networks.
- **Global perspectives:** Directing relative exploration to figure out the worldwide patterns and examples of advanced nomadism and their suggestions for various districts and nations.

5. Future Research Agenda:

The rise of computerized nomadism is a quickly developing peculiarity, and further exploration is expected to completely figure out its suggestions and foster viable methodologies for dealing with its effect on country networks.

Future Research Directions:

- **Long-term impacts:** Exploring the drawn out friendly, financial, and natural effects of computerized nomadism on country networks.
- **Health and well-being:** Investigating the effect of computerized nomadism on the wellbeing and prosperity of both advanced migrants and neighbourhood inhabitants.
- **The role of technology:** Researching the job of arising advances, like man-made reasoning and blockchain, in forming the eventual fate of computerized nomadism and its effect on country networks.
- **Global perspectives:** Directing relative exploration to figure out the world-wide patterns and examples of advanced nomadism and their suggestions for various districts and nations.

By addressing these subjects, this segment gives a sweeping assessment of the mechanized explorer quirk and its ideas for common and low-thickness complaints. It offers an aide for legitimate and exhaustive new development, highlighting the meaning of facilitated exertion, improvement, and long stretch organizing. Finally, the climb of electronic nomadism tends to a huge opportunity to reexamine the destiny of work, travel, and neighbourhood an overall scale.

BACKGROUND OF THE STUDY

The growth of digital nomadism has been driven by advances in technology, changing cultural values related to work, and the worldwide effects of the COVID-19 pandemic. Digital nomads were initially attracted to urban hubs and tropical paradises, where they could be surrounded by the benefits of city living while working from anywhere. But the pandemic accelerated a major change, with a lot of digital nomads looking for quieter, countryside lifestyles that provide deeper immersion in nature and a slower pace of life. The impact on rural development is far-reaching, with digital nomads introducing new economic activity, cultural diversity, and challenges to rural areas.

The concept of digital nomadism is not entirely new; its roots can be traced back to the late 20th century, when advancements in telecommunications and computing began to decouple work from physical office spaces. Early experiments with telecommuting in the 1980s laid the groundwork for what would later become a global movement. But it was the arrival of cheap high-speed internet, mobile computing, and collaboration tools in the 2010s that really made digital nomadism possible. The early adopters, such as freelance writers, designers, and tech startups, were driven by a need for location freedom and flexible hours. Later, the movement grew to incorporate professionals from various industries, driven by the globalization of the workforce and the emergence of the gig economy.

Despite the potential advantages, integrating digital nomads into rural areas is not without difficulties. Infrastructure shortages, in the form of poor internet connections and scarcity of healthcare facilities, can act as hindrances to the effortless integration of digital nomads. Moreover, the arrival of digital nomads can put pressure on local resources, with the attendant increase in property costs and possible social conflict. For instance, in Chiang Mai, Thailand, the rapid growth of digital nomads has caused tensions with locals regarding noise, garbage disposal, and commercialization of heritage areas (Nguyen, 2023). In a similar vein, in Madeira, Portugal, the growth of digital nomadism has resulted in deforestation and a rise in carbon emissions as new buildings and infrastructure are put up (Silva & Costa, 2023).

In order to respond to these challenges, local stakeholders and governments need to implement sustainable practices and policies that promote the economic gains of digital nomadism while maintaining the social and environmental integrity of rural communities. For example, Costa Rica has put in place policies aimed at boosting eco-tourism and renewable energy so that the entry of digital nomads supports the country's environmental objectives (Rodriguez & Fernandez, 2023). Likewise, in Reykjavik, Iceland, digital nomads are urged to engage in conservation activities within the community, including reforestation and waste management programs (Bjornsson, 2023).

These case studies shed light on the real-world challenges of applying digital nomadism in rural regions and indicate the necessity of strategic planning and cooperation among governments, companies, and local communities. By solving these challenges, rural destinations can leverage the potential of digital nomadism to stimulate economic development, innovation, and sustainable growth.

Firms and governments need to embrace sustainable practices in order to harmonize economic gains with social and environmental integrity. This involves investing in infrastructure, affordable housing, and cultural exchange programs. Practical measures involve enhancing internet connectivity, developing eco-tourism, and engaging community dialogue to incorporate digital nomads in rural communities successfully. The research emphasizes the necessity of more studies on the long-term effects of digital nomadism, especially in rural regions. Interdisciplinary methods are also necessary to analyze the complicated behaviour of the phenomenon.

PRACTICAL CASE STUDIES

1. Chiang Mai, Thailand:

Opportunities: Chiang Mai has emerged as a hotspot for digital nomads because of its affordability, rich culture, and stable internet. The arrival of nomads has given a boost to local businesses such as cafes, coworking offices, and tourism-related services.

Challenges: The speedy growth of digital nomads has resulted in the escalation of property prices, complaints about noise pollution, and refuse disposal problems. Residents have also complained about commercialization of areas of cultural value and over-strain on the resources.

2. Madeira, Portugal:

Opportunities: Madeira's "Digital Nomad Village" project has drawn remote employees with low-cost housing, fibre-optic connections, and co-working facilities. The initiative has reactivated the local economy and raised profiles on the world stage.

Challenges: The development of new infrastructure and accommodations has resulted in deforestation and rising carbon emissions. Local environments are strained, with concerns for the long-term environmental consequences.

3. Costa Rica:

Opportunities: Policies in Costa Rica support eco-tourism and renewable energy and have aligned the flow of digital nomads with the environmental objectives of the country. Local economies are boosted by digital nomads while they engage in conservation activities.

Challenges: The challenge of balancing the economic advantages of digital nomadism against the conservation of natural resources and local cultures still exists. There is a demand for sustainable strategies to prevent environmental degradation.

4. Reykjavik, Iceland:

Opportunities: Reykjavik has welcomed digital nomads by providing coworking facilities, cultural exchange opportunities, and even opportunities to join local conservation initiatives. The natural surroundings and high standard of living in the city are huge draws.

Challenges: The high demand for housing and facilities has translated into higher prices for property and fear of evicting natives. Affordable policies to maintain access to housing at affordable rates along with the spread of benefits across all levels is required.

RECOMMENDATIONS

Key recommendations include:

- Developing sustainable infrastructure.
- Promoting affordable housing.
- Encouraging cultural exchange programs.
- Implementing eco-friendly policies to mitigate environmental impacts.

CONCLUSION

The ascent of computerized nomadism addresses a significant chance to rethink the fate of work, travel, and local area. By tending to the monetary, social, and natural ramifications of this peculiarity, and by creating successful approaches and methodologies for dealing with its effect, rustic networks can tackle the capability of advanced nomadism to drive financial development, cultivate social incorporation, and advance ecological maintainability. Be that as it may, this requires cautious preparation, cooperation, and a pledge to long haul maintainability. Suggestions and Future Exploration on Advanced Nomadism The ascent of computerized nomadism in country and low-thickness objections has huge ramifications across different aspects, including financial turn of events, social attachment, and natural maintainability. This part will dig into these ramifications exhaustively and frame regions for future exploration that can upgrade how we might interpret this peculiarity and its more extensive effects.

Monetary Ramifications Invigorating Nearby Economies Computerized travellers add to neighbourhood economies by spending on convenience, food, administrations, and sporting exercises. Dissimilar to conventional sightseers who visit for brief periods, computerized travellers frequently stay for broadened terms, giving a consistent income stream that upholds nearby organizations over time. This predictable convergence of pay can assist with settling humble community economies, particularly in regions that may some way or another battle with occasional the travel industry vacillations. Venture Fascination and Monetary Enhancement The presence of advanced wanderers can likewise draw in speculation to provincial regions. As these labourers require dependable web access, cooperating spaces, and different conveniences, nearby state-run administrations might be boosted to further develop foundation. This venture benefits computerized migrants as well as upgrades the personal satisfaction for inhabitants. Besides, the enhancement of nearby economies becomes conceivable as advanced travellers present new business thoughts and work on cultivating development inside networks.

Provincial and low-thickness objections address a promising wilderness for computerized travellers, offering one of a kind open door for financial development, social trade, and ecological maintainability. While difficulties, for example, foundation holes and local area mix should be tended to, vital preparation and venture can change these districts into flourishing centres of remote work. By cultivating cooperation between states, organizations, and neighbourhood networks, rustic regions can arise as central participants in the worldwide computerized economy, reclassifying the eventual fate of work and travel. The ascent of computerized nomadism addresses a significant chance for provincial and low-thickness objections to rethink their jobs in the worldwide economy. By utilizing their extraordinary resources, for example, regular magnificence and social legacy these districts can draw in telecommuters looking for a top notch of life away from metropolitan blockage.

While difficulties, for example, foundation holes and local area reconciliation should be tended to through essential preparation and speculation endeavours the potential advantages are huge. By cultivating coordinated effort among states, organizations, and nearby networks rustic regions get the opportunity to arise as central members in the worldwide computerized economy. Eventually, embracing this pattern requires a promise to supportable improvement rehearses that benefit the two novices and long-haul inhabitants the same. By focusing on inclusivity and encouraging a climate helpful for development provincial objections can flourish in an undeniably interconnected world. This new financial sunrise has the potential not exclusively to revive battling areas yet in addition advance lives through significant associations between different societies all while saving biological uprightness for people in the future.

Country and low-thickness objections address promising boondocks for computerized travellers, offering special open doors for financial development, social trade, and natural maintainability. As the computerized traveller development keeps on picking up speed, it is fundamental to investigate the ramifications of this pattern and how essential arranging can change these locales into flourishing centre points of remote work. While difficulties, for example, framework holes and local area incorporation should be tended to, the expected advantages for neighbourhood economies and networks are huge. Financial Learning experiences Supporting Nearby Economies Computerized migrants add to neighbourhood economies through their spending on convenience, food, transportation, and different administrations. This flood of monetary assets can animate nearby organizations, make occupations, and advance financial development.

For example, in locales like Jammu, India, the foundation of computerized wanderer towns could introduce another financial period by utilizing the region's normal magnificence and social legacy to draw in telecommuters. Besides, computerized migrants frequently Favor longer stays contrasted with conventional travellers, which can prompt a steadier monetary climate for nearby organizations. This reliable interest energizes interest in framework enhancements that benefit the two migrants and occupants the same. Foundation Advancement To draw in computerized migrants really, country regions need to put resources into framework upgrades like high velocity web, collaborating spaces, and current conveniences. The advancement of these offices not just takes care of the requirements of telecommuters yet in addition improves the personal satisfaction for nearby occupants. For instance, Cabo Verde has made huge interests in computerized foundation, for example, undersea fibre optic links to help remote work while supporting neighbourhood development. These foundation improvements can make an expanding influence in the nearby economy by drawing in additional organizations and empowering business.

As advanced wanderers frequently bring different abilities and encounters, their presence can prompt the foundation of new ventures that further enhance provincial economies. Feasible Financial Models Advanced nomadism offers an option in contrast to customary occasional the travel industry models that numerous country regions depend on. By drawing in long haul telecommuters as opposed to momentary guests, these locales can make manageable financial models that turn out consistent revenue streams over time. This approach diminishes reliance on top the travel industry seasons and cultivates versatility against monetary slumps. For instance, Cabo Verde's Remote Working system means to draw in computerized migrants while encouraging advancement inside nearby networks. Such drives can assist with making a commonly useful connection among novices and occupants. Social Trade and Local area Mix Improving Neighbourhood Culture The coordination of advanced migrants into rustic networks can enhance the social texture of host districts. Their different foundations encourage multifaceted trades that lead to more noteworthy comprehension and coordinated effort among inhabitants. Computerized migrants frequently take part in local area projects that benefit both themselves and local people, for example, studios or comprehensive developments that advance common opportunities for growth.

In Jammu, drives like social trade projects can connect holes between computerized migrants and nearby communities1. By working with connections through language classes or local area occasions, the two gatherings can foster a feeling of having a place while regarding each other's qualities. Difficulties of Coordination Notwithstanding, incorporating computerized travellers into rustic networks presents difficulties connected with social contrasts and power elements. Errors might emerge from varying ways of life or values, prompting pressures among local people and newbies. Fundamental for policymakers to carry out systems advance common comprehension and regard inside networks. Research shows that effective combination frequently depends on local area commitment drives that include local people in arranging processes. By remembering occupants for conversations about how best to oblige computerized wanderers, partners can guarantee that the advantages are shared fairly. Natural Supportability Offsetting Development with Biological Honesty The movement of computerized travellers brings up significant issues about ecological maintainability.

While numerous advanced wanderers focus on eco-accommodating ways of life, their expanded presence can strain normal assets on the off chance that not oversaw capably. The interest for lodging and conveniences might prompt overexploitation of nearby assets. For example, Cabo Verde knows about the potential dangers related with rising lodging costs because of expanded request from advanced specialists. Policymakers are investigating guidelines to guarantee reasonable lodging stays accessible for occupants while likewise advancing co-living spaces planned explicitly for computerized migrants. Elevating Feasible Practices To limit natural impressions while obliging this new segment, it is critical for provincial regions to embrace manageable practices. This incorporates empowering eco-accommodating the travel industry drives that line up with the upsides of both computerized migrants and nearby networks.

Cooperative endeavours between partners, for example, state run administrations, organizations, natural associations can assist with guaranteeing that country objections keep up with their environmental respectability while profiting from this convergence of telecommuters. Vital Anticipating Future Achievement Cooperative Methodologies The fruitful change of provincial regions into flourishing centre points for advanced nomadism requires coordinated effort among different partners including state run administrations, organizations, and nearby networks. By cooperating towards shared objectives, these gatherings can establish a climate helpful for feasible development. Public-private organizations can drive important framework advancement while guaranteeing that the advantages are appropriated fairly among residents12. Drawing in neighbourhood networks in arranging cycles will assist with distinguishing their necessities and inclinations while encouraging a feeling of pride over improvement drives. Showcasing Country Objections Advancing rustic regions as alluring objections for computerized travellers is fundamental for drawing in this segment. Designated promoting efforts featuring regular magnificence, social legacy, present day conveniences and open doors for remote work can draw consideration from possible guests around the globe1. By exhibiting examples of overcoming adversity from different locales that have embraced advanced nomadism, for example, Cabo Verde rustic objections can situate themselves as practical options in contrast to blocked metropolitan places. The ascent of computerized nomadism offers a novel chance for rustic and low-thickness objections to renew their economies, improve their social and social texture, and advance economical turn of events. By decisively tending to the difficulties and open doors introduced by this new segment, and by cultivating joint effort between all partners, these districts can change into flourishing centre points of remote work, reclassifying the eventual fate of work and travel.

This underscores the groundbreaking capability of advanced nomadism for provincial regions, featuring the significance of joint effort, development, and long haul arranging. It highlights the need to address difficulties like foundation improvement, reasonable lodging, and local area commitment to guarantee a fruitful and fair joining of travellers into country networks. The ascent of computerized nomadism presents a novel chance for provincial and low-thickness objections to rethink their fates and open their true capacity. By embracing this new segment and decisively tending to the difficulties and open doors it presents, these districts can go through a huge change, reviving neighbourhood economies, encouraging social union, and advancing economical turn of events. Advanced wanderers can act as impetuses for financial renewal in country regions. Their spending power can help nearby organizations, from bistros and cafés to convenience suppliers and collaborating spaces. In addition, the deluge of gifted and pioneering wanderers can animate development and business venture. They can contribute their mastery in fields like innovation, advertising, and configuration, cultivating the development of new organizations and ventures.

The presence of computerized wanderers can likewise differentiate rustic economies, decreasing reliance on conventional enterprises like farming and the travel industry. This broadening can upgrade financial versatility and set out new position open doors for nearby inhabitants. Nonetheless, it is essential to guarantee that the monetary advantages of advanced nomadism are impartially disseminated and that nearby organizations and inhabitants are not minimized by the inundation of fresh introductions. The incorporation of advanced wanderers can enhance the social and social texture of provincial networks. Wanderers bring different points of view, abilities, and social foundations, encouraging multifaceted trades and advancing a more cosmopolitan environment. They can add to neighbourhood expressions and culture scenes, take part in local area occasions, and volunteer their chance to nearby associations.

Notwithstanding, tending to likely friendly difficulties, for example, social conflicts and rivalry for resources is fundamental. Local area commitment drives, for example, social trade projects, studios, and local area discussions, can encourage shared understanding and regard among migrants and local people. These drives can assist with building a feeling of shared local area and guarantee that the mix of wanderers helps all individuals from the local area. While the natural effect of advanced nomadism needs cautious thought, it likewise presents potential open doors for advancing supportable improvement in provincial regions. By empowering eco-accommodating practices, for example, the utilization of environmentally friendly power sources, the decrease of waste, and the advancement of reasonable transportation choices, rustic networks can become models of supportable living. Moreover, computerized wanderers can assume a critical part in advancing ecotourism and supporting nearby preservation endeavours. By displaying the interesting normal and social resources of their host areas, they can add to the improvement of manageable travel industry models that benefit both neighbourhood networks and the climate.

REFERENCES

Anderson, P., Green, R., & Taylor, S. (2023). Sustainable resource management in digital nomad hubs. *Journal of Sustainable Tourism*, *31*(4), 567–582.

Aroles, J., Bonneau, C., & Mitev, N. (2020). Mapping themes in the study of new work practices. *New Technology, Work and Employment*, *35*(1), 1–21.

Bissell, D. (2020). Digital nomads: How remote work is reshaping the world of work. Environment and Planning A. *Economy and Space*, *52*(3), 571–588.

Bjornsson, E. (2023). Digital nomadism and environmental conservation: Lessons from Reykjavik. *Environmental Management*, *72*(3), 456–470.

Castells, M. (1996). *The Rise of the Network Society*. Blackwell Publishers.

Chen, Y., & Wang, L. (2023). Cultural tensions in digital nomad communities: A case study of Chiang Mai. *Tourism Management*, *94*, 104678.

Coase, R. H. (1937). The Nature of the Firm. *Economic*, *4*(16), 386–405.

Cook, D. (2020). The freedom trap: Digital nomads and the use of disciplining practices to manage work/leisure boundaries. *Information Technology & Tourism*, *22*(3), 355–390. DOI: 10.1007/s40558-020-00172-4

D'Andrea, A. (2020). *Global nomads: Techno and new age as transnational countercultures in Ibiza and Goa*. Routledge.

Füller, H., & Marquardt, N. (2020). Digital nomadism and the transformation of work: A research agenda. *Geoforum*, *110*, 1–10.

Garcia, M., & Martinez, R. (2023). Economic inequality in digital nomad destinations. *Journal of Rural Studies*, *89*, 123–135.

Giddens, A. (1984). *The Constitution of Society: Outline of the Theory of Structuration*. University of California Press.

Gössling, S., & Hall, C. M. (2020). *Tourism and global environmental change: Ecological, social, economic, and political interrelationships*. Routledge.

Hannam, K., & Butler, G. (2020). Tourism and the sharing economy: An interdisciplinary review. *Tourism Management Perspectives*, *34*, 100659.

Ikkala, T., & Lampinen, A. (2020). Monetizing network hospitality: Hospitality exchange in the context of Airbnb. Proceedings of the ACM on Human-Computer Interaction, 4(CSCW), 1-22.

Johnson, K. M., & Lichter, D. T. (2008). Rural rebound and the resurgence of rural areas. *Demography*, *45*(2), 123–135.

Johnson, R., Lee, S., & Nguyen, T. (2022). Social integration of digital nomads: Challenges and opportunities. *Journal of Community Psychology*, *50*(3), 789–805.

Jones, M., & Taylor, K. (2023). Lifestyle migration and the pursuit of quality of life. *Journal of Migration Studies*, *15*(1), 45–60.

Mancinelli, F. (2020). Digital nomads: Freedom, responsibility, and the neoliberal order. *Information Communication and Society*, *23*(10), 1442–1458.

Maslow, A. H. (1943). A Theory of Human Motivation. *Psychological Review*, *50*(4), 370–396. DOI: 10.1037/h0054346

Müller, A. (2020). The digital nomad lifestyle: (Remote) work/leisure balance, privilege, and constructed community. *The International Journal of Sociology and Social Policy*, *40*(9/10), 767–786.

Nash, C., Jarrahi, M. H., & Sutherland, W. (2020). Nomadic work and location independence: The role of space in shaping the work of digital nomads. *Human Relations*, *73*(10), 1389–1412.

Nguyen, T. (2023). The impact of digital nomadism on local communities: A case study of Chiang Mai. *Tourism Economics*, *28*(6), 1234–1250.

O'Regan, M. (2020). Digital nomads, the gig economy, and the future of work. *Journal of Tourism Futures*, *6*(2), 156–168.

Peters, M., & Schuckert, M. (2020). The impact of digital nomads on local communities: A case study of Bali. *Journal of Sustainable Tourism*, *28*(5), 789–805.

Reichenberger, I. (2020). Digital nomads: A quest for holistic freedom in work and leisure. *Annals of Leisure Research*, *23*(2), 215–230.

Rodriguez, P., & Fernandez, M. (2023). Sustainable tourism in Costa Rica: Lessons for digital nomad hubs. *Sustainability*, *15*(7), 5678.

Ryan, R. M., & Deci, E. L. (2000). Self-determination theory and the facilitation of intrinsic motivation, social development, and well-being. *The American Psychologist*, *55*(1), 68–78. DOI: 10.1037/0003-066X.55.1.68 PMID: 11392867

Schlagwein, D., & Jarrahi, M. H. (2020). Digital nomadism and the future of work: A research agenda. *Journal of Global Information Management*, *28*(4), 1–15.

Silva, A., & Costa, R. (2023). Environmental challenges in Madeira's digital nomad village. *Environmental Science & Policy*, *130*, 45–56.

Smith, A., & Lee, B. (2022). The economic impact of digital nomads in Bali. *Tourism Economics*, *28*(6), 1234–1250.

Tajfel, H., & Turner, J. C. (1979). An integrative theory of intergroup conflict. *The Social Psychology of Intergroup Relations*, *33*(47), 74–85.

Thompson, B. Y. (2020). Digital nomads: Employment in the online gig economy. *Global Labour Journal*, *11*(2), 123–140.

Thompson, J., Brown, L., & Green, T. (2023). Digital nomadism and rural economic development. *Journal of Rural Development*, *41*(2), 89–104.

Van Holm, E. J. (2020). The rise of the digital nomad: Implications for urban and regional development. *Urban Studies (Edinburgh, Scotland)*, *57*(10), 2105–2121.

Wang, Y., & Fesenmaier, D. R. (2020). Transforming the travel experience: The role of digital nomads in shaping tourism futures. *Journal of Travel Research*, *59*(3), 423–436.

Westerhausen, K., & Macbeth, J. (2020). Backpackers and the development of tourism in rural areas: A case study of Pai, Thailand. *Tourism Geographies*, *22*(2), 345–366.

Zimmermann, A. (2020). Digital nomads and the future of work: A critical perspective. *Work, Employment and Society*, *34*(5), 789–805.

KEY TERMS AND DEFINITIONS

Digital Nomadism: A way of life allowing for remote working anywhere, thanks to technology.

Rural Rebound: Rural renaissance as popular destinations for remote workers.

Sustainability: Aligning economic, social, and environmental objectives with long-term survival.

Lifestyle Migration: Migration to enhance quality of life, self-actualization, and cultural engagement.

Space of Flows: Theory describing how technology makes it possible to work despite geographical distance.

Gentrification: Restoring neighborhoods to bring in affluent residents, at the expense of existing residents.

Eco-Tourism: Responsible tourism with a conservation and community focus.

Compilation of References

Abbas, J., Mubeen, R., Iorember, P. T., Raza, S., & Mamirkulova, G. (2021). Exploring the impact of COVID-19 on tourism: Transformational potential and implications for a sustainable recovery of the travel and leisure industry. *Current Research in Behavioral Sciences*, *2*, 100033. DOI: 10.1016/j.crbeha.2021.100033 PMID: 38620720

Abraham, M., Niessen, C., Schnabel, C., Lorek, K., Grimm, V., Möslein, K., & Wrede, M. (2019). Electronic monitoring at work: The role of attitudes, functions, and perceived control for the acceptance of tracking technologies. *Human Resource Management Journal*, *29*(4), 657–675. DOI: 10.1111/1748-8583.12250

Abreu, M., Oner, O., Brouwer, A., & Leeuwen, E. (2018). Well-being effects of self-employment: A spatial inquiry. Journal of Business Venturing, 34, Article .DOI: 10.1016/j.jbusvent.2018.11.001

Abubakar, A. M., Rezapouraghdam, H., Behravesh, E., & Megeirhi, H. A. (2022). Burnout or boreout: A meta-analytic review and synthesis of burnout and boreout literature in hospitality and tourism. *Journal of Hospitality Marketing & Management*, *31*(4), 458–503. DOI: 10.1080/19368623.2022.1996304

Adams, R. L. (2017). *How to become a digital nomad and travel the world*. Forbes Magazine., Retrieved from https://www.forbes. com/sites/robertadams/2017/01/20/how-to-become-a-digital- nomad-and-travel-the-world/

Adedoyin, F. F., Seetaram, N., Disegna, M., & Filis, G. (2023). The influence of tourism taxation on international arrivals to a small tourism-dependent economy. *Journal of Travel Research*, *62*(1), 135–153. DOI: 10.1177/00472875211053658

Agniera, I. G. A. A., Pella, F. A., & Halim, E. (2023). *Local Perceptions Towards Foreigners Digital Nomads in Bali*. DOI: 10.1109/ICoSNIKOM60230.2023.10364406

Ahlberg, E. (2021). The Development of the Digital Nomad During the Course of the Pandemic: The digital nomad workforce, a study looking into the power of digital tools allowing people to work remotely.

Ahmad, T. (2020). Corona Virus (COVID-19) Pandemic and Work from Home: Challenges of Cybercrimes and Cybersecurity. SSRN Electronic Journal. https://doi.org/DOI: 10.2139/ssrn.3568830

Ahmed, M. A., Nazir, H., & Haider, M. (2024). UN MTC Article 15: Reconciling the global north's 'digital nomad' with the global south's 'digital freelancer': Will the rising tide lift all boats? [pre-publication]. *Intertax*, *52*(6/7), 455–475. DOI: 10.54648/TAXI2024050

Åkerlund, U. (2013). The best of both worlds: Aspirations, drivers and practices of Swedish lifestyle movers in Malta (Doctoral dissertation). Umeå universitet.

Akgün, A. C. (2024). Kültürel diplomasi bağlamında dijital göçebelerin Türkiye izlenimleri üzerine bir inceleme. *Erciyes İletişim Dergisi*, *11*(2), 673–682. DOI: 10.17680/erciyesiletisim.1437918

Akhavan, M., Mariotti, I., & Rossi, F. (2022). The rise of coworking spaces in peripheral and rural areas in Italy. *Territorio*, *97*, 35–42. DOI: 10.3280/tr2021-097-Supplementooa12925

Akın, M. Ş. (2021). Dijital göçebelik: Deneyim ve özgürlük. *Sosyal Ekonomik Araştırmalar Dergisi*, *21*(1), 41–52. DOI: 10.30976/susead.799881

Akkemik, K. A. (2012). Assessing the importance of international tourism for the Turkish economy: A social accounting matrix analysis. *Tourism Management*, *33*(4), 790–801. DOI: 10.1016/j.tourman.2011.09.002

Algassim, A. A., Saufi, A., & Scott, N. (2023). Residents' emotional responses to tourism development in Saudi Arabia. *Tourism Review*, *78*(4), 1078–1091. DOI: 10.1108/TR-10-2021-0457

Alghamdi, A. (2007). Explicit and implicit motivation towards outbound tourism: A study of Saudi tourists. University of Glasgow. (Doctoral dissertation).

Alhadi, Z., Zefnihan, M., Muchtar, B., & Evanita, S. (2023). Developing a community-based tourism model for sustainable tourism in the Mandeh area, West Sumatra Province, Indonesia. *International Journal of Sustainable Development and Planning*, *18*(11), 3491–3503. DOI: 10.18280/ijsdp.181114

Alipour, H. (1996). Tourism development within planning paradigms: The case of Turkey. *Tourism Management*, *17*(5), 367–377. DOI: 10.1016/0261-5177(96)00036-2

Allen, T. D., Golden, T. D., & Shockley, K. M. (2015). How Effective Is Telecommuting? Assessing the Status of Our Scientific Findings. *Psychological Science in the Public Interest, 16*(2), 40–68. DOI: 10.1177/1529100615593273 PMID: 26403188

Allen, T. D., Johnson, R. C., Kiburz, K. M., & Shockley, K. M. (2013). Work–Family Conflict and Flexible Work Arrangements: Deconstructing Flexibility. *Personnel Psychology, 66*(2), 345–376. DOI: 10.1111/peps.12012

Almeida, J., & Belezas, F. (2022). The rise of half-tourists and their impact on the tourism strategies of peripheral territories. In J. Leitão, V. Ratten, & V. Braga (Eds.), Tourism entrepreneurship in Portugal and Spain: Tourism, hospitality & event management (pp. 113–130). Springer. DOI: 10.1007/978-3-030-89232-6_9

Almeida, J., & Daniel, A. D. (2022). Post-pandemic opportunities for low-density territories: Insights and implications from Portuguese case studies. *European Planning Studies, 31*(10), 2034–2057. DOI: 10.1080/09654313.2022.2074785

Aloisi, A., & De Stefano, V. (2022). *Your boss is an algorithm: artificial intelligence, platform work and labour*. Bloomsbury Publishing. DOI: 10.5040/9781509953219

Anderson, P., Green, R., & Taylor, S. (2023). Sustainable resource management in digital nomad hubs. *Journal of Sustainable Tourism, 31*(4), 567–582.

Andino-Frydman, A. (2023). *Who is a Digital Nomad?* The Evolving Identities of the New Nomadic Workforce., DOI: 10.1108/S0277-283320230000035005

Aroles, J., Bonneau, C., & Bhankaraully, S. (2023). Conceptualising 'meta-work' in the context of continuous, global mobility: The case of digital nomadism. *Work, Employment and Society, 37*(5), 1261–1278. DOI: 10.1177/09500170211069797

Aroles, J., Bonneau, C., & Mitev, N. (2020). Mapping themes in the study of new work practices. *New Technology, Work and Employment, 35*(1), 1–21.

Aroles, J., Granter, E., & Vaujany, F. (2020). 'Becoming mainstream': The professionalisation and corporatisation of digital nomadism. *New Technology, Work and Employment, 35*(1), 114–129. DOI: 10.1111/ntwe.12158

Arslan, E. (2024). From tourists to nomads: Unveiling the transformative potential of digital nomads in travel and tourism. *Worldwide Hospitality and Tourism Themes, 16*(3), 269–281. DOI: 10.1108/WHATT-03-2024-0046

Asahi, S. (2024). Analysis of the Impact of Overtourism in Japan: The Effects of Congestion Phenomena. In *Econometric Analysis of Regional Economy*. Springer., DOI: 10.1007/978-981-99-8707-8_3

Ay, E., & Güzel, M. O. (2024). Digital-Nomads in destination marketing. *Worldwide Hospitality and Tourism Themes*, *16*(3), 316–328. DOI: 10.1108/WHATT-03-2024-0050

Aynalem, S., Birhanu, K., & Tesefay, S. (2016). Employment opportunities and challenges in tourism and hospitality sectors. *Journal of Tourism & Hospitality (Los Angeles, Calif.)*, *5*(6), 1–5. DOI: 10.4172/2167-0269.1000257

Azis, N., Amin, M., Chan, S., & Aprilia, C. (2020). How smart tourism technologies affect tourist destination loyalty. *Journal of Hospitality and Tourism Technology*, *11*(4), 603–625. DOI: 10.1108/JHTT-01-2020-0005

Bahri, M. T. (2024). Evidence of the digital nomad phenomenon: From" Reinventing" migration theory to destination countries readiness. *Heliyon*, *10*(17), e36655. DOI: 10.1016/j.heliyon.2024.e36655 PMID: 39263067

Bahri, M. T., & Widhyharto, D. S. (2021). Social network analysis (SNA) on# Kristengray Hashtag: Understanding gentrification side effects behind the digital nomad phenomenon. *Jurnal Studi Pemuda*, *10*(1), 75. DOI: 10.22146/studipemudaugm.65255

Baptista, R. G. T. (2024). *Digital-Nomads in Peniche: Exploring the Relation between Remote Work and Surfing* (Master's thesis, Instituto Politecnico de Leiria (Portugal)).

Basu, M. (2024). Tech-Driven Horizons: Pioneering Sustainable Tourism for Environmental Resilience and SDGs Triumph. In *The Need for Sustainable Tourism in an Era of Global Climate Change: Pathway to a Greener Future* (pp. 215-247). Emerald Publishing Limited.

Basu, M. (2024). Tech-driven horizons: Pioneering sustainable tourism for environmental resilience and SDGs triumph. In *The need for sustainable tourism in an era of global climate change: Pathway to a greener future* (pp. 215–247). Emerald Publishing Limited. DOI: 10.1108/978-1-83608-668-020241032

Batool, N., Wani, M. D., Shah, S. A., & Dada, Z. A. (2024a). Theory of planned behavior and value-belief norm theory as antecedents of pro-environmental behaviour: Evidence from the local community. *Journal of Human Behavior in the Social Environment*, *34*(5), 693–709. DOI: 10.1080/10911359.2023.2205912

Batool, N., Wani, M. D., Shah, S. A., & Dada, Z. A. (2024b). Tourists' attitude and willingness to pay on conservation efforts: Evidence from the west Himalayan eco-tourism sites. *Environment, Development and Sustainability*, •••, 1–19. DOI: 10.1007/s10668-024-04679-2

Beaumont, J. (2019). *Digital nomads and sense of place: A case study of Lisbon.* Wageningen University.

BecomeNomad. (2016, 05. 05.). Different Types of Nomads. BecomeNomad: https://becomenomad.com/different-nomadic-lifestyles/ (22.12.2024) adresinden alındı

Bednorz, J. (2024). Working from anywhere? Work from here! Approaches to attract digital nomads. *Annals of Tourism Research, 105*, 103715. DOI: 10.1016/j.annals.2023.103715

Belge, M. (2018). *İstanbul gezi rehberi*. Tarih Vakfı Yayınları. İletişim Yayınları.

Bell, M., & Ward, G. (2000). Comparing temporary mobility with permanent migration. *Tourism Geographies*, *2*(1), 87–107. DOI: 10.1080/146166800363466

Benson, M., & O'Reilly, K. (2009). Migration and the search for a better way of life: A critical exploration of lifestyle migration. *The Sociological Review*, *57*(4), 608–625. DOI: 10.1111/j.1467-954X.2009.01864.x

Bertola, P., Iannilli, V., Spagnoli, A., & Vandi, A. (2022). Cultural and creative industries as activators and attractors for contemporary culture-driven nomadism. In *Cultural leadership in transition tourism: Developing innovative and sustainable models* (pp. 51–74). Springer International Publishing. DOI: 10.1007/978-3-031-14121-8_4

Betre, H. K. (2022). Reconceptualising the potential of digital nomads to transform community-based and sustainable tourism [Master's thesis]. Retrieved from ProQuest Dissertations and Theses.

Betre, H. K. (2022). Reconceptualizing the potential of digital nomads to transform community-based and sustainable tourism (Master's thesis). University of Girona.

Bhat, W. A., Wani, M. D., Dada, Z. A., & Qureshi, R. A. (2025). Beyond Linear Models: A Complexity-Theoretic Approach to Understanding Tourist Behavior in Peacebuilding Contexts. *Journal of Quality Assurance in Hospitality & Tourism*, •••, 1–30. DOI: 10.1080/1528008X.2025.2466050

Big, D., & Far, T. (2023). 65+ fascinating digital nomad statistics [Fresh for 2023!]. Retrieved from https://www.dreambigtravelfarblog.com/blog/digital-nomad-statistics

Birtchnell, T. (2019). Digital nomads and (im)mobile identities. In *Routledge handbook of identity studies* (pp. 274–282). Routledge. DOI: 10.4324/9781315626024-16

Bissell, D. (2020). Digital nomads: How remote work is reshaping the world of work. Environment and Planning A. *Economy and Space*, *52*(3), 571–588.

Biswas, S. N., & Kumar, P. (Eds.). (2024). *Mountain Tourism and Ecological Impacts: Himalayan Region and Beyond: Himalayan Region and Beyond*. IGI Global. DOI: 10.4018/979-8-3693-0823-3

Bjornsson, E. (2023). Digital nomadism and environmental conservation: Lessons from Reykjavik. *Environmental Management*, *72*(3), 456–470.

Boluda Chova, J., & von Ehrlich-Treuenstätt, K. T. (2023). Nomadism without borders: Exploring connections in digital nomad destinations: An ethnographic multiple-case study in Malaysia and Colombia [Dissertation]. Retrieved from https://urn.kb.se/resolve?urn=urn:nbn:se:hj:diva-60385

Borges-Tiago, M. T., Tiago, F., & Cosme, C. (2019). Exploring users' motivations to participate in viral communication on social media. *Journal of Business Research*, *101*, 574–582. DOI: 10.1016/j.jbusres.2018.11.011

Borkovich, D. J., & Skovira, R. J. (2020). Working from home: Cybersecurity in the age of COVID-19. *Issues in Information Systems*. Advance online publication. DOI: 10.48009/4_iis_2020_234-246

Bosworth, G., Whalley, J., Fuzi, A., Merrell, I., Chapman, P., & Russell, E. (2023). Rural co-working: New network spaces and new opportunities for a smart countryside. *Journal of Rural Studies*, *97*, 550–559. DOI: 10.1016/j.jrurstud.2023.01.003

Boyle, P., Halfacree, K., & Robinson, V. (2014). *Exploring contemporary migration*. Routledge., DOI: 10.4324/9781315843100

Bozdoğan, M., & Dağdelen, E. Ö. (2022). Seyahat, çalışma ve boş zamanın kesişiminde yeni bir grup: Dijital göçebeler. *İnsan Hareketliliği Uluslararası Dergisi*, *2*(2), 270–297.

Bozzi, A. (2024). Digital nomadism from the perspective of places and mobilities: A literature review. *European Transport Research Review*, *16*(1), 50. DOI: 10.1186/s12544-024-00663-z

Braathen, N. S. (2022). Virtually anywhere, physically in Lisbon: A study of gentrification and the new work-lifestyle among digital nomads in Lisbon [Master's thesis]. Retrieved from Lund University Repository.

Braun, E., Kavaratzis, M., & Zenker, S. (2013). My city – my brand: The different roles of residents in place branding. *Journal of Place Management and Development*, *6*(1), 18–28. DOI: 10.1108/17538331311306087

Brigitta Pecsek, B. (2018, December 31). Working on holiday: The theory and practice of workcation. *Balkans Journal of Emerging Trends in Social Sciences, 1*(1), 1–13. DOI: 10.31410/Balkans.JETSS.2018.1.1.1-13

Broek, T. V. D., Haubrich, G. F., Razmerita, L., Murero, M., Marx, J., Lind, Y., & Boer, P. D. (2023). *Digital nomads: Opportunities and challenges for the future of work in the post-COVID society*. Aurora Universities Network.

Brown, L., Buhalis, D., & Beer, S. (2020). Dining alone: Improving the experience of solo restaurant goers. *International Journal of Contemporary Hospitality Management, 32*(3), 1347–1365. DOI: 10.1108/IJCHM-06-2019-0584

Brown, L., & Moore, E. (1970). The intra-urban migration process: A perspective. *Geografiska Annaler. Series B, Human Geography, 52*(1), 1–13. DOI: 10.1080/04353684.1970.11879340

Buffer. (2023). *The Global Rise of Remote Work*. Recuperado de: https://buffer.com/state-of-remote-work

Buhalis, D., & Law, R. (2008). Progress in information technology and tourism management: 20 years on and 10 years after the Internet—The state of eTourism research. *Tourism Management, 29*(4), 609–623. DOI: 10.1016/j.tourman.2008.01.005

Buhalis, D., Leung, X. Y., Fan, D., Darcy, S., Chen, G., Xu, F., Wei-Han Tan, G., Nunkoo, R., & Farmaki, A. (2023). Tourism 2030 and the contribution to the sustainable development goals: The tourism review viewpoint. *Tourism Review, 78*(2), 293–313. DOI: 10.1108/TR-04-2023-620

Buomprisco, G., Ricci, S., Perri, R., & De Sio, S. (2021, February 13). Health and Telework: New Challenges after COVID-19 Pandemic. *European Journal of Environment and Public Health, 5*(2), em0073. Advance online publication. DOI: 10.21601/ejeph/9705

Businessthink. (2020). Digital nomads: Five key insights into the future of knowledge work. Retrieved from https://www.businessthink.unsw.edu.au/articles/digital-nomads-five-key-insights-future-of-knowledge-work

Carvalho, M., Kastenholz, E., & Carneiro, M. J. (2021). Interaction as a central element of co-creative wine tourism experiences—Evidence from Bairrada, a Portuguese wine-producing region. *Sustainability (Basel), 13*(16), 9374. Advance online publication. DOI: 10.3390/su13169374

Carvalho, M., Kastenholz, E., Carneiro, M. J., & Souza, L. (2024). Dimensions of Co-Creative Food & Wine Tourism Experiences – Findings from A Multiple-Case Study. [AHTR]. *Advances in Hospitality and Tourism Research, 12*(4), 337–367. Advance online publication. DOI: 10.30519/ahtr.1287676

Castells, M. (1996). *The Rise of the Network Society*. Blackwell Publishers.

Chakraborty, P. P. (2024). Tourism in transition in a sustainable world: Embracing technology and sustainability in the post-pandemic era. In *Special interest trends for sustainable tourism* (pp. 348–374). IGI Global. DOI: 10.4018/979-8-3693-5903-7.ch017

Chamboko-Mpotaringa, M., & Tichaawa, T. M. (2021). Tourism digital marketing tools and views on future trends: A systematic review of literature. *African Journal of Hospitality, Tourism and Leisure, 10*(2), 712–726. DOI: 10.46222/ajhtl.19770720-128

Charalampous, M., Grant, C. A., Tramontano, C., & Michailidis, E. (2018, November). Systematically reviewing remote e-workers' well-being at work: A multidimensional approach. *European Journal of Work and Organizational Psychology, 28*(1), 51–73. DOI: 10.1080/1359432X.2018.1541886

Chayka, K. (2018). When you're a "digital nomad," the world is your office, New York: The New York Times. Retrieved from https://www. nytimes.com/2018/02/08/magazine/when-youre-a-digital-nomad- the-world-is-your-office.html

Chen, J., Prebensen, N., & Huan, T. (2008). Determining the motivation of wellness travelers. *Anatolia, 19*(1), 103–115. DOI: 10.1080/13032917.2008.9687056

Chen, Y., & Wang, L. (2023). Cultural tensions in digital nomad communities: A case study of Chiang Mai. *Tourism Management, 94*, 104678.

Chevtaeva, E. (2021). Coworking and coliving: The attraction for digital nomad tourists. In *Information and communication technologies in tourism 2021:Proceedings of the ENTER 2021 eTourism Conference,January 19–22, 2021* (pp. 202–209). Springer International Publishing.

Chevtaeva, E., Neuhofer, B., & Rainoldi, M. (2022). THE "NEXT NORMAL" OF WORK: HOW TOURISM SHAPES THE WELLBEING OF REMOTE WORKERS. ResearchGate. https://www.researchgate.net/publication/360216936

Chevtaeva, E., Neuhofer, B., & Rainoldi, M. (2022, January). The "next normal" of work: How tourism shapes the wellbeing of remote workers. In *CAUTHE 2022 Conference Online: Shaping the Next Normal in Tourism, Hospitality and Events: Handbook of Abstracts of the 32nd Annual Conference* (p. 33). Council for Australasian University Tourism and Hospitality Education (CAUTHE).

Chevtaeva, E., & Denizci-Guillet, B. (2021). Digital nomads' lifestyles and coworkation. *Journal of Destination Marketing & Management, 21*, 100633. DOI: 10.1016/j.jdmm.2021.100633

Chevtaeva, E., Neuhofer, B., Egger, R., & Rainoldi, M. (2023). Travel while working remotely: A topological data analysis of well-being in remote work trip experiences. *Journal of Travel Research, 63*(2), 466–480. DOI: 10.1177/00472875231151923

Choi, J. W., & Qu, J. (2024). *An Empirical Study on the Rise of Digital Nomad and Workcation Ecosystems: Focusing on the Case of Thailand.* DOI: 10.17086/JTS.2024.48.8.121.150

Choudhury, P. (2023, November 27). Our Work-from-Anywhere Future. Harvard Business Review. https://hbr.org/2020/11/our-work-from-anywhere-future

Choudhury, P. R., Foroughi, C., & Larson, B. (2020, November 22). Work-from-anywhere: The productivity effects of geographic flexibility. *Strategic Management Journal, 42*(4), 655–683. DOI: 10.1002/smj.3251

Christiansen, R. A. (2023). Development of digital nomads as a new market segment and their role in the local digital ecosystem [Doctoral dissertation].

Christiansen, R. A., Ihalauw, J. J. O. I., Kriestian, A. N.A.N., Purwati, Y. SE. (2023). Developing Digital Nomads as a New Market Segment and Their Role in the Local Digital Ecosystem. *Journal of System and Management Sciences*. DOI: 10.33168/JSMS.2023.0201

Ciccarelli, F. C. (2023). Exploring the potential of coworking spaces for quality of working life and wellbeing: A systematic review of academic literature. CIDADES. *Comunidades e Territórios, 46*(46). Advance online publication. DOI: 10.15847/cct.30874

Cifci, I., Atsiz, O., Kahraman, O., & Istanbullu Dincer, F. (2024). Recreational fishers' motivations at wetland destinations: The push and pull theory approach. *Leisure Sciences, 46*(5), 595–617. DOI: 10.1080/01490400.2021.2016520

Clark, P. (2012). Istanbul: a cultural history. Interlink Publishing.

Coase, R. H. (1937). The Nature of the Firm. *Economic, 4*(16), 386–405.

Coban Yildiz, G., & Yildiz, O. S. (2024). A debate on Turkey tourism's adaptation to climate change. In *Tourism and climate change in the 21st century: Challenges and solutions* (pp. 197–223). Springer Nature Switzerland. DOI: 10.1007/978-3-031-59431-1_9

Cohen, S. A., & Cohen, E. (2019). New directions in the sociology of tourism. *Current Issues in Tourism, 22*(2), 153–172. DOI: 10.1080/13683500.2017.1347151

Cohen, S. A., Duncan, T., & Thulemark, M. (2020). Lifestyle mobilities: The crossroads of travel, leisure, and migration. *Mobilities, 15*(1), 53–69.

Colbert, A., Yee, N., & George, G. (2016). The Digital Workforce and the Workplace of the Future. *Academy of Management Journal, 59*(3), 731–739. DOI: 10.5465/amj.2016.4003

Cook, D. (2020). The freedom trap: Digital nomads and the use of disciplining practices to manage work/leisure boundaries. *Information Technology & Tourism, 22*(3), 355–390. DOI: 10.1007/s40558-020-00172-4

Cook, D. (2023). What is a digital nomad? Definition and taxonomy in the era of mainstream remote work. *World Leisure Journal, 65*(2), 256–275. DOI: 10.1080/16078055.2023.2190608

Correia, R., Martins, M., & Fontes, R. (Eds.). (2024). *AI Innovations for Travel and Tourism*. IGI Global. DOI: 10.4018/979-8-3693-2137-9

Coursesidekick. (2024). The social dynamics of digital nomadism: Exploring work, lifestyle, and community in a borderless world. Retrieved from https://www.coursesidekick.com/sociology/3350886

Crompton, J. L. (1979). Motivations of pleasure vacations. *Annals of Tourism Research, 6*(4), 408–424. DOI: 10.1016/0160-7383(79)90004-5

Cruz, R., & Pombo, F. (2022, June). Designing Furniture for Versatile Spaces of Collaborative Work. Covid-19 Accelerating the Change. In *Meeting of Research in Music, Arts and Design* (pp. 456–471). Springer International Publishing.

D'Andrea, A. (2013). *Deciphering the Space and Scale of Global Nomadism: Subjectivity and Counterculture in a Global Ag. S. Sassen içinde, Deciphering the global: Its Scales, Spaces and Subjects*. Routledge.

D'Andrea, A. (2020). *Global nomads: Techno and new age as transnational countercultures in Ibiza and Goa*. Routledge.

Dada, Z. A., Wani, M. D., & Shah, S. A. (2022). The impact of pilgrim tourism on the bilateral diplomacy of India and Nepal and the mediation effect of people-to-people contact. *Asian Journal of Comparative Politics, 7*(3), 495–506. DOI: 10.1177/20578911221076234

Dann, G. (1977). Anomie, ego-enhancement and tourism. *Annals of Tourism Research, 4*(4), 184–194. DOI: 10.1016/0160-7383(77)90037-8

Dann, M. S. (1981). Tourist motivation an appraisal. *Annals of Tourism Research, 8*(2), 187–219. DOI: 10.1016/0160-7383(81)90082-7

Davenport, T. H. (2005). *Thinking for a living: how to get better performances and results from knowledge workers*. Harvard Business Press.

Davis, G. (2002). Anytime/anyplace computing and the future of knowledge work. *Communications of the ACM, 45*(12), 67–73. DOI: 10.1145/585597.585617

De Almeida, M. A., Correia, A., Barbosa, C. E., de Souza, J. M., & Schneider, D. (2024). AI and digital nomads: Glimpsing the future human-computer interaction [Preprint]. Retrieved from https://www.researchgate.net/publication/385611257

De Carvalho, A., Ciolfi, L., & Gray, B. (2017). Detailing a Spectrum of motivational forces shaping nomadic practices. Proceedings of the 2017 ACM Conference on Computer Supported Cooperative Work and Social Computing (pp. 962-977). Sheffield Hallam University Research Archive. DOI: 10.1145/2998181.2998313

De Menezes, L. M., & Kelliher, C. (2011, April 7). Flexible Working and Performance: A Systematic Review of the Evidence for a Business Case. *International Journal of Management Reviews, 13*(4), 452–474. DOI: 10.1111/j.1468-2370.2011.00301.x

De Stefano, V. (2016). The rise of the 'just-in-time workforce': On-demand work, crowd work and labour protection in the 'gig-economy. *Comparative Labor Law & Policy Journal, 37*(3), 471–504.

Demaj, E., Hasimja, A., & Rahimi, A. (2021). Digital nomadism as a new flexible working approach: Making Tirana the next European hotspot for digital nomads. In *The flexible workplace: Coworking and other modern workplace transformations* (pp. 231–257).

Demaj, E., Hasimja, A., & Rahimi, A. (2021). Digital nomadism as a new flexible working approach: Making Tirana the next European hotspot for digital nomads. *The flexible workplace: Coworking and other modern workplace transformations*, 231-257.

Di Marino, M., Tabrizi, H. A., Chavoshi, S. H., & Sinitsyna, A. (2023, April). Hybrid cities and new working spaces – The case of Oslo. *Progress in Planning, 170*, 100712. DOI: 10.1016/j.progress.2022.100712

Dictionary, C. (2021, January 18). Digital nomad definition. Retrieved from https://dictionaryblog.cambridge.org/2021/01/18/new-words-18-january-2021/

Digital Nomads Madeira Islands. (2024). https://digitalnomads.startupmadeira.eu/

Dobrinskaya, D. E. (2016). Nomadic lifestyle in the network society: sociological aspect.

Dogan, E., Cuomo, F., & Battisti, L. (2023). Reviving urban greening in post-industrial landscapes: The case of Turin. *Sustainability (Basel), 15*(17), 12760. DOI: 10.3390/su151712760

Donnelly, R., & Johns, J. (2021). Recontextualising remote working and its HRM in the digital economy: An integrated framework for theory and practice. *International Journal of Human Resource Management, 32*(1), 84–105. DOI: 10.1080/09585192.2020.1737834

Donovan, S., Bradley, D., & Shimabukuru, J. (2016). *What does the gig economy mean for workers?* Congressional Research Service.

Durward, D., Blohm, I., & Leimeister, J. (2016). Crowd work. *Business & Information Systems Engineering, 58*(4), 281–286. DOI: 10.1007/s12599-016-0438-0

Eckhardt, G., & Atanasova, A. (2024, 02. 05.). The New Reality of Digital Nomads. HBR: https://hbr.org/2024/02/the-new-reality-of-digital-nomads (21.12.2024) adresinden alındı

Edwards, S. E. (2021). *"If you can work from anywhere, why work anywhere else?": flexible citizenship, regimes of mobility, and the discourse of digital nomadism.* DOI: 10.5210/spir.v2021i0.11906

Ehn, K., Jorge, A., & Marques-Pita, M. (2022). Digital nomads and the COVID-19 pandemic: Narratives about relocation in a time of lockdowns and reduced mobility. *Social Media + Society, 8*(1), 20563051221084958. DOI: 10.1177/20563051221084958

Ehrlich, B. (2025, 02. 28.). Istanbul. Britannica: https://www.britannica.com/place/Istanbul (07.03.2025) adresinden alındı

Elad, B. (2024, May 20). Digital nomad statistics 2024: Demographics, gender, background, salaries, education levels, nationalities, and preferred activities. *Enterprise Apps Today.* Retrieved from https://www.enterpriseappstoday.com/stats/digital-nomad-statistics.html

Elmo, G. C., Arcese, G., Valeri, M., Poponi, S., & Pacchera, F. (2020). Sustainability in tourism as an innovation driver: An analysis of family business reality. *Sustainability (Basel), 12*(15), 6149. DOI: 10.3390/su12156149

Erdoğan, Y., & Özdemir, E. G. (2021). Sales effect of digital marketing in small and medium-sized accommodation enterprises in core Cappadocia. *Karadeniz Uluslararası Bilimsel Dergi, 1*(51), 1–23. DOI: 10.17498/kdeniz.944276

Ersöz, B. (2024). Removing the boundaries of flexibility: A critical evaluation on digital nomadism. *Sosyal Bilimler Araştırmaları Dergisi, 19*(2), 241–252. DOI: 10.48145/gopsbad.1540618

Esteban-Navarro, M. Á., García-Madurga, M. Á., Morte-Nadal, T., & Nogales-Bocio, A. I. (2020, December). The rural digital divide in the face of the COVID-19 pandemic in Europe—recommendations from a scoping review. In Informatics (Vol. 7, No. 4, p. 54). MDPI.

Eusébio, C., Kastenholz, E., & Breda, Z. (2014). Tourism and sustainable development of rural destinations: A stakeholders' view. Revista Portuguesa de Estudos Regionais, 13–21.

Eversole, B. A., Venneberg, D. L., & Crowder, C. L. (2012). Creating a flexible organizational culture to attract and retain talented workers across generations. *Advances in Developing Human Resources, 14*(4), 607–625. DOI: 10.1177/1523422312455612

Faulmann, A. (2022). The Rise of the Workation. Nezasa Blog. https://nezasa.com/blog/the-rise-of-the-workation/

Ferreira, R., Pereira, R., Bianchi, I. S., & da Silva, M. M. (2021, March). Decision Factors for Remote Work Adoption: Advantages, Disadvantages, Driving Forces and Challenges. *Journal of Open Innovation, 7*(1), 70. DOI: 10.3390/joitmc7010070

Figueiró dos Vinhos council. (n.d.). Retrieved in December 26, 2024 from https://www.cm-figueirodosvinhos.pt/

FlexJobs. (2022). Digital nomad survey: Insights into the remote lifestyle. Retrieved December 6, 2024, from https://www.flexjobs.com/blog/post/digital-nomad-survey-insights-remote-lifestyle/

Floričić, T., & Pavia, N. (2021). Linkage of leisure with remote work and digital nomadism in tourist accommodation facilities. *ToSEE, 6*, 247–268. DOI: 10.20867/tosee.06.17

Florida, R., Rodríguez-Pose, A., & Storper, M. (2021, June 27). Critical Commentary: Cities in a post-COVID world. *Urban Studies (Edinburgh, Scotland), 60*(8), 1509–1531. DOI: 10.1177/00420980211018072 PMID: 38602910

Forbes, 2022, 'Digital Nomads Alert: Spain Set to Launch New Visa in 2023'. https://www.forbes.com/sites/ceciliarodriguez/2022/12/20/ digital-nomads-alert-spain-set-to-launch-new-visa-in-2023/

Forbes. (2023). *How digital nomads are transforming global tourism.* Recuperado de https://www.forbes.com

Füller, H., & Marquardt, N. (2020). Digital nomadism and the transformation of work: A research agenda. *Geoforum, 110*, 1–10.

Furnell, S., & Shah, J. N. (2020, January). Home working and cyber security – an outbreak of unpreparedness? *Computer Fraud & Security*, *2020*(8), 6–12. DOI: 10.1016/S1361-3723(20)30084-1

Fuzi, A. (2015). Co-working spaces for promoting entrepreneurship in sparse regions: The case of South Wales. *Regional Studies, Regional Science*, *2*(1), 461–468. DOI: 10.1080/21681376.2015.1072053

Ganai, S. A., & Dada, Z. A. (2025). Travel to border destinations: Exploring the motivations and revisit intentions of tourists in border regions. *Asian Journal of Economics. Business and Accounting*, *25*(3), 93–112. DOI: 10.9734/ajeba/2025/v25i31697

Gao, J., & Song, L. (2024). A cross-cultural comparison of island vacation experience: Empirical evidence from the Maldives. *Asia Pacific Journal of Tourism Research, 29*(7), 1–14. DOI: 10.1080/10941665.2024.2351124

Garcez, A., Correia, R., & Carvalho, A. (2022, December). Digital Nomads: Who They Are and What They Want from the Destinations? In International Conference on Marketing and Technologies (pp. 483-495). Singapore: Springer Nature Singapore.

Garcez, A., Correia, R., & Carvalho, A. (2022). Digital nomadism an opportunity for low-density territories: Trás-os-Montes lands case. In *Advances in Tourism, Technology and Systems: Selected Papers from ICOTTS 2021* (Vol. 1, pp. 91–102). Springer Nature Singapore. DOI: 10.1007/978-981-19-1040-1_8

Garcia, M., & Martinez, R. (2023). Economic inequality in digital nomad destinations. *Journal of Rural Studies*, *89*, 123–135.

Gess, K. (1975). A study of Mexican travel habits and patterns: Results of an exploratory study assimilating secondary data and personal interviews with individuals representing organizations of the Mexican travel trade (Vol. 1). The Office.

Gibson, H. J. (2003). Sport tourism: An introduction to the special issue. *Journal of Sport Management*, *17*(3), 205–213. DOI: 10.1123/jsm.17.3.205

Giddens, A. (1984). *The Constitution of Society: Outline of the Theory of Structuration*. University of California Press.

Glaeser, J. (2022). The effects of digital nomads on housing affordability for local populations in Ericeira (Master's thesis). ISCTE-Instituto Universitario de Lisboa.

Glaeser, J. (2022). The effects of digital nomads on housing affordability for local populations in Ericeira (Master's thesis, ISCTE-Instituto Universitario de Lisboa (Portugal)).

Goodwin, H. (2011). *Taking responsibility for tourism* (pp. 1-256). Woodeaton: Goodfellow Publishers Limited.

Gosnell, H., & Abrams, J. (2011). Amenity migration: Diverse conceptualizations of drivers, socioeconomic dimensions, and emerging challenges. *GeoJournal*, *76*(4), 303–322. DOI: 10.1007/s10708-009-9295-4

Gössling, S. (2021). Tourism, technology and ICT: A critical review of affordances and concessions. *Journal of Sustainable Tourism*, *29*(5), 733–750. DOI: 10.1080/09669582.2021.1873353

Gössling, S., & Hall, C. M. (2020). *Tourism and global environmental change: Ecological, social, economic, and political interrelationships*. Routledge.

Gössling, S., & Humpe, A. (2020). The global scale, distribution and growth of aviation: Implications for climate change. *Global Environmental Change*, *65*, 102–120. DOI: 10.1016/j.gloenvcha.2020.102194 PMID: 36777089

Gössling, S., Scott, D., & Hall, C. M. (2020). Pandemics, tourism and global change: A rapid assessment of COVID-19. *Journal of Sustainable Tourism*, *29*(1), 1–20. DOI: 10.1080/09669582.2020.1758708

Gratton, L. (2021). Four principles to ensure hybrid work is productive work. *MIT Sloan Management Review*, *62*(2), 11A–16A.

Green, D. D., McCann, J., Vu, T., Lopez, N., & Ouattara, S. (2018). Gig Economy and the Future of Work: A Fiverr.com Case Study. *Management and Economics Research Journal*, *4*(2), 281. DOI: 10.18639/MERJ.2018.04.734348

Green, P. (2020). Disruptions of self, place and mobility: Digital nomads in Chiang Mai, Thailand. *Mobilities*, *15*(3), 431–445. DOI: 10.1080/17450101.2020.1723253

Gretzel, U. (2017). Influencer marketing in travel and tourism. In *Advances in social media for travel, tourism and hospitality* (pp. 147–156). Routledge. DOI: 10.4324/9781315565736-13

Günay, F., Toksöz, D., & Aslan, Z. (2024). The causes, process and result of becoming a digital nomad family: A phenomenological case study. *Worldwide Hospitality and Tourism Themes*, *16*(3), 294–302. DOI: 10.1108/WHATT-03-2024-0042

Gupta, S., Jaiswal, R., & Gupta, S. K. (2024). Digital nomads: A systematic literature review and future research agenda. *Tourism Review*. Advance online publication. DOI: 10.1108/TR-12-2023-0869

Hackl, A. (2018). Mobility equity in a globalized world: Reducing inequalities in the sustainable development agenda. *World Development*, *112*, 150–162. DOI: 10.1016/j.worlddev.2018.08.005

Håkansson, P. G., & Bejaković, P. (2023). Can digital nomads solve the problem of tourist economy? The case of Croatian islands. *Eastern Journal of European Studies*, *14*(Special Issue), 116–134. DOI: 10.47743/ejes-2023-SI07

Hall, G., Sigala, M., Rentschler, R., & Boyle, S. (2019). Motivations, mobility and work practices; the conceptual realities of digital nomads. In *Information and Communication Technologies in Tourism 2019:Proceedings of the International Conference in Nicosia, Cyprus, January 30–February 1, 2019* (pp. 437-449). Springer International Publishing.

Hall, G., Sigala, M., Rentschler, R., & Boyle, S. (2019). Motivations, mobility and work practices; the conceptual realities of digital nomads. In *Information and Communication Technologies in Tourism 2019:Proceedings of the International Conference in Nicosia, Cyprus, January 30–February 1, 2019* (pp. 437–449). Springer International Publishing.

Hall, G., Sigala, M., Rentschler, R., & Boyle, S. (2019). Motivations, mobility and work practices; the conceptual realities of digital nomads. Information and Communication Technologies in Tourism 2019: Proceedings of the International Conference in Nicosia. Cyprus, January 30–February 1, 2019: Springer International Publishing. https://link.springer.com/chapter/10.1007/978-3-030-05940-8_34 adresinden alındı

Hall, C. M., Scott, D., & Gössling, S. (2021). Tourism and global environmental change: Ecological, social, economic, and political interrelationships. *Journal of Sustainable Tourism*, *29*(4), 556–570.

Hannam, K., & Butler, G. (2020). Tourism and the sharing economy: An interdisciplinary review. *Tourism Management Perspectives*, *34*, 100659.

Hannonen, O. (2022).*Towards an Understanding of Digital Nomadic Mobilities.* DOI: 10.3167/TRANS.2022.120310

Hannonen, O. (2020). In search of a digital nomad: Defining the phenomenon. *Information Technology & Tourism*, *22*(3), 335–353. DOI: 10.1007/s40558-020-00177-z

Hannonen, O., Quintana, T. A., & Lehto, X. Y. (2023). A supplier-side view of digital nomadism: The case of destination Gran Canaria. *Tourism Management, 97*, 104744. DOI: 10.1016/j.tourman.2023.104744

Hansen, L., & Ferns, B. (2020). Digital nomadism and place attachment: The case of Tallinn, Estonia. *Journal of Tourism Futures, 6*(3), 193–207.

Harrill, R. (2004). Residents' attitudes toward tourism development: A literature review with implications for tourism planning. *Journal of Planning Literature, 18*(3), 251–266. DOI: 10.1177/0885412203260306

Hart. (2015). Living and working in paradise: the rise of the "digital nomad." Telegraph.Co.Uk. https://www.telegraph.co.uk/news/features/11597145/Living-and-working-in-paradise-the-rise-of-the-digital-nomad.html

Harvard Business Review. (2022). *The rise of digital nomads: How remote work is reshaping the workforce*. Recuperado de https://hbr.org

Hassan, T. H., Almakhayitah, M. Y., & Saleh, M. I. (2024). Sustainable Stewardship of Egypt's Iconic Heritage Sites: Balancing Heritage Preservation, Visitors' Well-Being, and Environmental Responsibility. *Heritage, 7*(2), 737–757. DOI: 10.3390/heritage7020036

Heitmann, S. (2011). Tourist behaviour and tourism motivation. Research themes for tourism (s. 31-44). içinde Wallingford UK: CABI.

Hemsley, J., Erickson, I., Jarrahi, M. H., & Karami, A. (2020, February 15). Digital nomads, coworking, and other expressions of mobile work on Twitter. *First Monday*. Advance online publication. DOI: 10.5210/fm.v25i3.10246

Hensellek, S., & Puchala, N. (2021). The emergence of the digital nomad: A review and analysis of the opportunities and risks of digital nomadism. In *The flexible workplace: Coworking and other modern workplace transformations* (pp. 195–214). DOI: 10.1007/978-3-030-62167-4_11

Hensellek, S., & Puchala, N. (2021). The emergence of the digital nomad: A review and analysis of the opportunities and risks of digital nomadism. *The flexible workplace: Coworking and other modern workplace transformations*, 195-214.

Heredia, C. G. M., Layedra, C. A. S., Prado, R. R. G., & León, P. M. (2024). Barreras y oportunidades en la adopción de plataformas digitales por parte de los prestadores de servicios turísticos en el cantón Alausí: Barriers and opportunities in the adoption of digital platforms by tourism service providers in Alausi´ s town. *LATAM Revista Latinoamericana de Ciencias Sociales y Humanidades, 5*(5), 648–660.

Hermann, I., & Paris, C. M. (2020). Digital Nomadism: The nexus of remote working and travel mobility. *Information Technology & Tourism*, *22*(3), 329–334. Advance online publication. DOI: 10.1007/s40558-020-00188-w

Hernández, I. (2023, 10. 27.). Digital Nomadism: Transnational Economic Relations in the Emerging Economies. Harvard International Review: https://hir.harvard.edu/digital-nomadism-transnational-economic-relations-in-the-emerging-economies/ (21.12.2024) adresinden alındı

Hiles, R. E. (2024). Exploring Virtual Team Project Success With Knowledge Management (Doctoral dissertation, National University).

Holleran, M. (2022). Pandemics and geoarbitrage: Digital nomadism before and after COVID-19. *City (London, England)*, *26*(5–6), 831–847. DOI: 10.1080/13604813.2022.2124713

Holleran, M., & Notting, M. (2023). Mobility guilt: Digital nomads and COVID-19. *Tourism Geographies*, *25*(5), 1341–1358. DOI: 10.1080/14616688.2023.2217538

Hong, W. C. (2009). Global competitiveness measurement for the tourism sector. *Current Issues in Tourism*, *12*(2), 105–132. DOI: 10.1080/13683500802596359

Horiuchi, S., & Morishige, M. (2024).*Affiliative nomads in Japan: potential sustainable tourism stakeholders in depopulated rural areas*. DOI: 10.3389/frsut.2024.1329856

Horton International. (2023). The rise of digital nomadism in remote working. Horton International. Retrieved from https://hortoninternational.com/the-rise-of-digital-nomadism-in-remote-working/

Hovardaoglu, O., & Calisir-Hovardaoglu, S. (2024). Estrategias de supervivencia de las PYMEs en la pandemia Covid-19 en los sitios de turismo patrimonial en Turquía. *Pasos (El Sauzal)*, *22*(1), 125–145. DOI: 10.25145/j.pasos.2024.22.008

Hunt, S. (2024). 6 most common challenges of a digital nomad lifestyle and how to overcome them. Retrieved December 6, 2024, from https://www.silvahunt.ee/business-in-estonia/6-most-common-challenges-of-a-digital-nomad-lifestyle-and-how-to-overcome-them/

Hunt, C., & Stronza, A. (2013). Stage-based tourism models and resident attitudes towards tourism in an emerging destination in the developing world. *Journal of Sustainable Tourism*, *22*(2), 279–298. DOI: 10.1080/09669582.2013.815761

IBB. (2024). Kültürel Miras Koruma Müdürlüğü. Istanbul Metropolitan Municipality Directorate of Cultural Heritage. İstanbul Bütük Şehir Belediyesi: https://kulturelmiras.ibb.istanbul/english/ (26.12.2024) adresinden alındı

Ienczak, L., Maines, L., & Silva, P. (2024). Environmentally responsible consumption by rural tourists in Rio Grande do Sul—Brazil. Smart Tourism, 4, Article .DOI: 10.54517/st.v4i1.2296

Ikkala, T., & Lampinen, A. (2020). Monetizing network hospitality: Hospitality exchange in the context of Airbnb. Proceedings of the ACM on Human-Computer Interaction, 4(CSCW), 1-22.

Ili, B., & Büyükbaykal, G. (2022). *Di ji tal göçebe araştirmalarinin bi bli yometri k anali zi.* Nevşehir Hacı Bektaş Veli Üniversitesi SBE Dergisi., DOI: 10.30783/nevsosbilen.1121236

Instituto Nacional de Estatística. (n.d.). Recenseamentos gerais da população. Retrieved from https://www.ine.pt/xportal/xmain?xpid=INE&xpgid=ine_publicacoes

International Organization for Migration (IOM). (2023). Overview: Digital nomad policies in the European context. IOM. Retrieved December 13, 2024, from https://denmark.iom.int/sites/g/files/tmzbdl1306/files/documents/TalentHub/overview.-digital-nomad-policies-in-the-european-context_clean.pdf

Ioannides, D., & Röslmaier, M. (2021). Remote work in tourism: Impacts and opportunities in rural areas. *Tourism Geographies*, *23*(2), 300–317.

Ipsen, C., & Jensen, P. L. (2012). Organizational options for preventing work-related stress in knowledge work. *International Journal of Industrial Ergonomics*, *42*(4), 325–334. DOI: 10.1016/j.ergon.2012.02.006

Ipsen, C., van Veldhoven, M., Kirchner, K., & Hansen, J. P. (2021). Six Key Advantages and Disadvantages of Working from Home in Europe during COVID-19. *International Journal of Environmental Research and Public Health*, *18*(4), 1826. DOI: 10.3390/ijerph18041826 PMID: 33668505

İstanbul Valiliği. (2021). Tarihi ve Turistik Mekânlar. T.C. İstanbul Valiliği: http://www.istanbul.gov.tr/tarihi-ve-turistik-mekanlar (27.12.2024) adresinden alındı

Izcara Palacios, S., & Andrade Rubio, K. (2003). *La entrevista en profundidad teoría y práctica*. Universidad Autónoma de Tamaulipas.

Jacobs, E., & Gussekloo, A. (2016). *Digital nomads: How to live, work and play around the world*. Esther Jacobs & André Gussekloo.

Jacobs, N., & Cooper, R. (2018). *Living in Digital Worlds*. Routledge., http://books.google.ie/books?id=uClKDwAAQBAJ&pg=PT569&dq=Jacobs,+N.,+%26+Cooper,+R.+(2018).+Living+in+Digital+Worlds:+Designing+the+Digital+Public+Space.+New+York:+Routledge.&hl=&cd=2&source=gbs_api DOI: 10.4324/9781315592787

Jacobson, J., Hodson, J., & Mittelman, R. (2022). Pup-ularity contest: The advertising practices of popular animal influencers on Instagram. *Technological Forecasting and Social Change*, *174*, 121226. DOI: 10.1016/j.techfore.2021.121226

Jaiswal, R., Gupta, S., & Gupta, S. K. (2024). The impending disruption of digital nomadism: Opportunities, challenges, and research agenda. *World Leisure Journal*, •••, 1–31. DOI: 10.1080/16078055.2024.2346091

Jang, S., & Cai, L. (2002). Travel motivations and destination choice: A study of British outbound market. *Journal of Travel & Tourism Marketing*, *13*(3), 111–133. DOI: 10.1300/J073v13n03_06

Jarrahi, M. H., Philips, G., Sutherland, W., Sawyer, S., & Erickson, I. (2019). Personalization of knowledge, personal knowledge ecology, and digital nomadism. *Journal of the Association for Information Science and Technology*, *70*(4), 313–324. DOI: 10.1002/asi.24134

Jeelani, P., & Shah, S. A. (2023). Tourism and the environmental components coexisting in the Himalayas: A trade-off between the two. *Journal of Quality Assurance in Hospitality & Tourism*, •••, 1–25. DOI: 10.1080/1528008X.2023.2275260

Jeelani, P., & Shah, S. A. (2024). Strategic insights for sustainable tourism development in Kashmir Valley: SWOT and QSPM analysis. *Environmental Development*, *52*, 101092. DOI: 10.1016/j.envdev.2024.101092

Jeelani, P., Shah, S. A., Dar, S. N., & Rashid, H. (2023). Sustainability constructs of mountain tourism development: The evaluation of stakeholders' perception using SUS-TAS. *Environment, Development and Sustainability*, *25*(8), 8299–8317. DOI: 10.1007/s10668-022-02401-8 PMID: 35915719

Jimenez Ruiz, A. E., Bhartiya, S., & Bhatt, V. (Eds.). (2024). *Promoting Sustainable Gastronomy Tourism and Community Development*. IGI Global. DOI: 10.4018/979-8-3693-1814-0

Jiwasiddi, A., Schlagwein, D., Cahalane, M., Cecez-Kecmanovic, D., Leong, C., & Ractham, P. (2024). Digital nomadism as a new part of the visitor economy: The case of the "digital nomad capital" Chiang Mai, Thailand. *Information Systems Journal*.

Jiwasiddi, A., Schlagwein, D., Cahalanc, M., Cecez-Kecmanovic, D., Leong, C., & Ractham, P. (2024). Digital nomadism as a new part of the visitor economy: The case of the "digital nomad capital" Chiang Mai, Thailand. *Information Systems Journal, 34*(5), 1493–1535. DOI: 10.1111/isj.12496

Ji, Y., Kim, S. M., & Kim, Y. (2024). A way to attract digital nomads to tourist destinations in the new normal era. *Sustainability (Basel), 16*(6), 2336. DOI: 10.3390/su16062336

Johnson, K. M., & Lichter, D. T. (2008). Rural rebound and the resurgence of rural areas. *Demography, 45*(2), 123–135.

Johnson, R., Lee, S., & Nguyen, T. (2022). Social integration of digital nomads: Challenges and opportunities. *Journal of Community Psychology, 50*(3), 789–805.

Jones, M., & Taylor, K. (2023). Lifestyle migration and the pursuit of quality of life. *Journal of Migration Studies, 15*(1), 45–60.

Kalleberg, A. L., Reynolds, J., & Marsden, P. V. (2003). Externalizing employment: Flexible staffing arrangements in US organizations. *Social Science Research, 32*(4), 525–552. DOI: 10.1016/S0049-089X(03)00013-9

Kannisto, P. (2016). Extreme mobilities: Challenging the concept of 'travel'. *Annals of Tourism Research, 57*, 220–233. DOI: 10.1016/j.annals.2016.01.005

Karaşah, B. (2017). Kentsel ve kırsal rekreasyon alanlarına yönelik kullanıcı tercihlerinin belirlenmesi 'Artvin kenti örneği. *Bartin Orman Fakültesi Dergisi, 19*(1), 58–69.

Kashif, M. (2024). Enhancing the Digital Nomads Experience: A Service Design Approach to Address Challenges and Expectations, Developing a Tailored Solution.

Kasman Arifin, Z. A., & Syapsan, D. P. S. (2020). Optimization of Tourism Industry by Supply Chain Strategy of Rokan Regional District to Increase Original Revenue. Int. J Sup. Chain. *Mgt, 9*(1), 1036.

Kastenholz, E., Carneiro, M. J., Eusébio, C., & Figueiredo, E. (2013). Host–guest relationships in rural tourism: Evidence from two Portuguese villages. *Anatolia, 24*(3), 367–380. DOI: 10.1080/13032917.2013.769016

Kastenholz, E., & Carvalho, M. (2024). Co-creating Locally Embedded Rural Tourist Experiences Using Coopetition Strategies: Insights from Village Tourism in Portugal. In *Fumi Chim-Miki, A. & R.A. da Costa. Value Proposition to Tourism Coopetition- Building the Future of Tourism Series* (pp. 219–234). Emerald Publishing. DOI: 10.1108/978-1-83797-827-420241015

Kastenholz, E., Marques, C. P., & Carneiro, M. J. (2020). Place attachment through sensory-rich, emotion-generating place experiences in rural tourism. *Journal of Destination Marketing & Management*, *17*, 100455. DOI: 10.1016/j.jdmm.2020.100455

Kastenholz, E., & Sparrer, M. (2009). Rural Dimensions of the Commercial Home. In Lynch, P., MacIntosh, A., & Tucker, H. (Eds.), *Commercial Homes in Tourism: An international perspective* (pp. 138–149). Routledge., DOI: 10.4324/9780203880319

Katircioglu, S., Katircioğlu, S., & Altinay, M. (2018). Interactions between tourism and financial sector development: Evidence from Turkey. *Service Industries Journal*, *38*(9-10), 519–542. DOI: 10.1080/02642069.2017.1406479

Kaur, G. (2017). The importance of digital marketing in the tourism industry. *International Journal of Research-Granthaalayah*, *5*(6), 72–77. DOI: 10.29121/granthaalayah.v5.i6.2017.1998

Kelly, H., & Arelano, D. (2021). Work and wander: Meet today's digital nomads. Retrieved January 2, 2024, from https://www.adventuretravel.biz/research/work-and-wander-meet-todays-digitalnomads

Khan, K., & Mujitaba, A. (2023). Development and validation of brand strategies evaluation scale for mobile network users. *ESIC Market*, *54*(1), e291–e291. DOI: 10.7200/esicm.53.291

Khater, M., Muhammad Zeki Mahmood Al-Leheabi, S., & Faik, M. (2024). Navigating the challenges of over-tourism: Comparative insights and solutions from Petra and Karnak. *Journal of Heritage Tourism*, •••, 1–32.

Kiki, E. (2024). *The Influence of Location-Related Attributes to Portugal's Brand Image: Motivating Factors for Digital Nomad Relocation* (Master's thesis, Universidade NOVA de Lisboa (Portugal)).

Kim, H.-J., & Kim, S.-Y. (2023).*A Study on the Operation Direction of Workation in Japan for the Development of Local Areas and the Expansion of Related Populations*. DOI: 10.46396/Kjem..101.7

Kirchner, K., & Nordin Forsberg, B. (2021). A Conference Goes Virtual: Lessons from Creating a Social Event in the Virtual Reality. Innovations for Community Services, 123–134. https://doi.org/DOI: 10.1007/978-3-030-75004-6_9

Kirchner, K., Ipsen, C., & Hansen, J. P. (2021). COVID-19 leadership challenges in knowledge work. *Knowledge Management Research and Practice*, *19*(4), 493–500. DOI: 10.1080/14778238.2021.1877579

Kiriatzi, E., & Knappett, C. (2021). *Human Mobility and Technological Transfer in the Prehistoric Mediterranean*. Cambridge University Press.

Kocaman, S. (2021). Nomadlist'de dijital göçebeler tarafından 2020'de en fazla tercih edilen destinasyonların destinasyon seçim kriterlerine göre küme lendirilmesi. *Türk Turizm Araştırmaları Dergisi*, *5*(2), 799–815. DOI: 10.26677/TR1010.2021.739

Kókai, N., & Rétfalvi, D. (2024). Digital Nomads as Engines for Rural Revitalization: The Development Strategy of Pécsdevecser, Hungary (pp. 143–149). https://doi.org/DOI: 10.18485/arh_pt.2024.8.ch16

Kolko, B. (2010). Writing in digital environments: Workplaces as multimodal texts. *Technical Communication Quarterly*, *19*(3), 275–302.

Koohang, A., Nord, J. H., Ooi, K. B., Tan, G. W. H., Al-Emran, M., Aw, E. C. X., Baabdullah, A. M., Buhalis, D., Cham, T.-H., Dennis, C., Dutot, V., Dwivedi, Y. K., Hughes, L., Mogaji, E., Pandey, N., Phau, I., Raman, R., Sharma, A., Sigala, M., & Wong, L. W. (2023). Shaping the metaverse into reality: A holistic multidisciplinary understanding of opportunities, challenges, and avenues for future investigation. *Journal of Computer Information Systems*, *63*(3), 735–765. DOI: 10.1080/08874417.2023.2165197

Kozak, M. (2002). Comparative analysis of tourist motivations by nationality and destinations. *Tourism Management*, *23*(3), 221–232. DOI: 10.1016/S0261-5177(01)00090-5

Kozak, M., Cetin, G., & Alrawadieh, Z. (2024). Repositioning work and leisure: Digital nomads versus tourists. *International Journal of Tourism Research*, *26*(4), e2732. Advance online publication. DOI: 10.1002/jtr.2732

Kroenke, K., Spitzer, R. L., Williams, J. B., Monahan, P. O., & Löwe, B. (2007). Anxiety Disorders in Primary Care: Prevalence, Impairment, Comorbidity, and Detection. *Annals of Internal Medicine*, *146*(5), 317–325. DOI: 10.7326/0003-4819-146-5-200703060-00004 PMID: 17339617

KTB. (2000). İstanbul. Republic of Türkiye Ministry of Culture and Toursim: https://www.ktb.gov.tr/EN-33048/istanbul.html adresinden alındı

Kubat, A. S. (1999). The morphological history of Istanbul. *Urban Morphology*, *3*(1), 28–41. DOI: 10.51347/jum.v3i1.3883

Kunda, N. L. R., Sunarta, I. N., & Bhaskara, G. I. (2024). The impact of social and economic changes of digital nomadic on tourists and the local community in Canggu. [IJETER]. *International Journal of Technology and Education Research*, *2*(4), 50–55. https://e-journal.citakonsultindo.or.id/index.php/IJETER

Kuzheleva-Sagan, I. P., & Spicheva, D. I. (2020).*The Phenomenon of Digital Nomadism in the Modern Interdisciplinary Discourse.* DOI: 10.17223/15617793/454/9

Kuzheleva-Sagan, I., & Nosova, S. (2016). Culture of digital nomads: Ontological, anthropological, and semiotic aspects. In *Proceedings of the World Congress of the IASS/AIS 12th WCS Sofia 2014 - New Semiotics. Between tradition and innovation* (pp. 131–141). Sofia: IASS Publications & NBU Publishing House.

Lacárcel, F. J. S., Huete, R., & Zerva, K. (2024). Decoding digital nomad destination decisions through user-generated content. *Technological Forecasting and Social Change, 200*, 123098. DOI: 10.1016/j.techfore.2023.123098

Lane, B. (2005). Sustainable rural tourism strategies: A tool for development and conservation. *Revista Interamericana de Ambiente y Turismo-RIAT, 1*(1), 12–18.

Lanza, G., Pucci, P., Carboni, L., & Vendemmia, B. (2022). Impacts of the Covid-19 pandemic in inner areas. Remote work and near-home tourism through mobile phone data in Piacenza Apennine. *TEMA, 2*, 73–89.

Lazarević-Moravčević, M., & Domazet, I. S. (2025). Attraction of Digital Nomads as Significant Tourism Potential: Evidence From Serbia. In *Tracking Tourism Patterns and Improving Travel Experiences With Innovative Technologies* (pp. 191–214). IGI Global.

Leco, F. (2013). Rural tourist and their attitudes and motivations towards the practice of environmental activities such as agrotourism. *International Journal of Environmental Research, 7*, 255–264.

Lee, J.-H., & Kim, N.-J. (2024). *Examining the tourism experiences of Workation travelers*. https://doi.org/DOI: 10.17086/JTS.2024.48.1.13.34

Lee, A., Toombs, A. L., Erickson, I., Nemer, D., Ho, Y. S., Jo, E., & Guo, Z. (2019). The social infrastructure of co-spaces: Home, work, and sociable places for digital nomads. *Proceedings of the ACM on Human-Computer Interaction, 3*(CSCW), 1–23. DOI: 10.1145/3359244

Lee, H. Y., & Zhang, J. J. (2020). Rethinking sustainability in volunteer tourism. *Current Issues in Tourism, 23*(14), 1820–1832. DOI: 10.1080/13683500.2019.1653267

Lhakard, P. (2022). Destination city for digital nomad's in Thailand: A case study of digital nomad community in Chiang Mai. [JHSSS]. *Journal of Humanities and Social Sciences Studies, 4*(1), 178–188. https://ssrn.com/abstract=4053619. DOI: 10.32996/jhsss.2022.4.1.18

Lhakard, P. (2022). Destination city for digital nomads in Thailand: A case study of digital nomad community in Chiang Mai. *Journal of Humanities and Social Sciences Studies (JHSSS), 4*(1). Available at *SSRN*: https://ssrn.com/abstract=4053619

Liegl, M. (2014). Nomadicity and the care of place—On the aesthetic and affective organization of space in freelance creative work. [CSCW]. *Computer Supported Cooperative Work, 23*(2), 163–183. DOI: 10.1007/s10606-014-9198-x

Liestiandre, H. K., Morrison, A. M., Yasa, N. N. K., Sukawati, T. G. R., & Sukaatmadja, I. P. G. (2024). The influence of a local well-being philosophy on revisit intentions to Bali among Digital-Nomads. *Tourism and Hospitality, 5*(4), 1099–1124. DOI: 10.3390/tourhosp5040062

Lipsey, R. G., Carlaw, K. I., & Bekar, C. T. (2005). Economic Transformations. OUP Oxford. http://books.google.ie/books?id=tSrGTMtBv50C&printsec=frontcover&dq=Lipsey,+Richard+G.,+Kenneth+I.+Carlaw,+and+Clifford+T.+Bekar.+Economic+transformations:+general+purpose+technologies+and+long-term+economic+growth.+OUP+Oxford,+2005.&hl=&cd=1&source=gbs_api

Lirio, P. (2017). Global boundary work tactics: Managing work and family transitions in a 24–7 global context. *Community Work & Family, 20*(1), 72–91. DOI: 10.1080/13668803.2016.1272545

Litchfield, R. C., & Woldoff, R. A. (2023). Digital nomads: Curiosity or trend? *Handbook of Virtual Work*, 186–196. DOI: 10.4337/9781802200508.00018

Liu, A., Kim, Y. R., & Song, H. (2022). Toward an accurate assessment of tourism economic influence: A systematic literature review. *Annals of Tourism Research Empirical Insights, 3*(2), 100054. DOI: 10.1016/j.annale.2022.100054

Liu, Z. (2003). Sustainable tourism development: A critique. *Journal of Sustainable Tourism, 11*(6), 459–475. DOI: 10.1080/09669580308667216

Localyze. (2023). Digital nomad statistics & trends: 2023 & 2024. Retrieved from https://www.localyze.com/blog/digital-nomad-statistics-trends-2023-2024

Magnavita, N., Tripepi, G., & Chiorri, C. (2021, March 24). Telecommuting, Off-Time Work, and Intrusive Leadership in Workers' Well-Being. *International Journal of Environmental Research and Public Health, 18*(7), 3330. DOI: 10.3390/ijerph18073330 PMID: 33804828

Maitland, A., & Thomson, P. (2014, March 20). Future Work (Expanded and Updated). Springer. http://books.google.ie/books?id=7kcfAwAAQBAJ&pg=PT5&dq=Maitland,+A.,+%26+Thomson,+P.+(2014).+Future+work+(expanded+and+updated):+Changing+organizational+culture+for+the+new+world+of+work.+London,+UK:+Springer.&hl=&cd=2&source=gbs_api

Makimoto, T., & Manners, D. (1997). *Digital nomad*. John Wiley & Sons.

Makimoto, T., & Manners, D. (1997). *Digital Nomad*. Willey.

Making Tirana the next European hotspot for digital nomads. *The Flexible Workplace: Coworking and Other Modern Workplace Transformations*, 231-257.

Mancinelli, F. (2022).*Digital Nomads*. https://doi.org/DOI: 10.4337/9781800377486.digital.nomads

Mancinelli, F. (2020). Digital nomads: Freedom, responsibility and the neoliberal order. *Information Technology & Tourism*, *22*(3), 417–437. DOI: 10.1007/s40558-020-00174-2

Mancinelli, F. (2020). Digital nomads: Freedom, responsibility, and the neoliberal order. *Information Communication and Society*, *23*(10), 1442–1458.

Mandić, A., & Garbin Praničević, D. (2019). Progress on the role of ICTs in establishing destination appeal: Implications for smart tourism destination development. *Journal of Hospitality and Tourism Technology*, *10*(4), 791–813. DOI: 10.1108/JHTT-06-2018-0047

Mansour, R. (2024). The Rise of Digital Nomadism: Reshaping Cultural Identity in a Globalised World. Rock & Art: https://www.rockandart.org/digital-nomadism-reshaping-cultural-identity/#:~:text=By%20embracing%20a%20global%20digital,diversity%2C%20independence%2C%20and%20flexibility. (21.12.2024) adresinden alındı

Mao, Q., & Xu, S. (2024). *How Digital Nomad Communities Can Empower Rural Revitalisation*. Advances in Economics, Management and Political Sciences., DOI: 10.54254/2754-1169/105/20241997

Marco, E., & Carson, D. A. (2023). Towards a cordial dialogue between lifestyle migration/mobilities and rural tourism geographies. *Geografiska Annaler. Series B, Human Geography*, *105*(4), 341–355. DOI: 10.1080/04353684.2023.2197921

Mariati, S., Gilitasha, A., Rahmanita, M., Djati, S. P., & Adawiyah, R. (2023). Analysis of sustainable tourism destination development for digital nomads (Comparative study: Lisbon-Portugal and Canggu, Bali-Indonesia). *Technium Social Sciences Journal*, *43*, 403–415. DOI: 10.47577/tssj.v43i1.8773

Mariotti, I., & Sasso, S. (2024). *Revitalizing rural areas through innovation and entrepreneurship: Public and private initiatives to train, attract and retain human capital. Joint Research Centre*. European Commission., DOI: 10.2760/4727653

Martin-Merino, E., Ruigomez, A., Wallander, M. A., Johansson, S., & Garcia-Rodriguez, L. A. (2010). Prevalence, incidence, morbidity and treatment patterns in a cohort of patients diagnosed with anxiety in UK primary care. *Family Practice*, *27*(1), 9–16. DOI: 10.1093/fampra/cmp071 PMID: 19884124

Martins, Márcio Ribeiro (2023). Backpacking culture and mobilities: Independent and nomadic travel. Journal of Hospitality and Tourism Management. eISSN 1839-5260. 55, p. 200-201

Maslow, A. H. (1943). A Theory of Human Motivation. *Psychological Review*, *50*(4), 370–396. DOI: 10.1037/h0054346

Matos, P., & Ardévol, E. (2021). The potentiality to move: Mobility and future in digital nomads' practices. *Transfers*, *11*(3), 62–79. DOI: 10.3167/TRANS.2021.110304

Matsushita, K. (2021a). *Workation and the Doubling of Time and Place*. DOI: 10.1007/978-981-16-2425-4_7

Matsushita, K. (2021b). *Workations and Their Impact on the Local Area in Japan*. DOI: 10.1007/978-3-030-62167-4_12

Matsushita, K. (2024). Social problem-solving workation through collaboration between local regions and urban companies: the case of Kamaishi in Japan.*Frontiers in Sustainable Tourism*. DOI: 10.3389/frsut.2024.1337097

Matsushita, K. (2022). How does the Japanese workcation embrace digital nomadic work style employees? *World Leisure Journal*. Advance online publication. DOI: 10.1080/16078055.2022.2156594

McPhail, R., Chan, X. W., May, R., & Wilkinson, A. (2024). Post-COVID remote working and its impact on people, productivity, and the planet: An exploratory scoping review. *International Journal of Human Resource Management*, *35*(1), 154–182. DOI: 10.1080/09585192.2023.2221385

Mehmetoglu, M. (2005). A case study of nature-based tourists: Specialists versus generalists. *Journal of Vacation Marketing, 11*(4), 357–369. DOI: 10.1177/1356766705056634

Membretti, A., & Iancu, B. (2017). From Peasant Workers to Amenity Migrants. Socialist Heritage and the Future of Mountain Rurality in Romania. Revue de géographie alpine. 105-1 | 2017. .DOI: 10.4000/rga.3567

Merrell, I., Füzi, A., Russell, E., & Bosworth, G. (2021). How rural coworking hubs can facilitate well-being through the satisfaction of key psychological needs. *Local Economy, 36*(7-8), 606–626. DOI: 10.1177/02690942221075598

Messenger, J. C., & Gschwind, L. (2016, November). Three generations of Telework: New ICTs and the (R)evolution from Home Office to Virtual Office. *New Technology, Work and Employment, 31*(3), 195–208. DOI: 10.1111/ntwe.12073

Messenger, J., Vargas, O. L., Gschwind, L., Boehmer, S., Vermeylen, G., & Wilkens, M. (2017). *Working anytime, anywhere: The effects on the world of work.* Publications Office of the European Union.

Ministerio de Industria y Turismo de España. (2022). Estrategia de Turismo de España 2030. Recuperado de https://turismo.gob.es/es-es/estrategia-turismo-sostenible/paginas/index.aspx

Miocevic, D. (2024). Baby come back: Resident-digital nomad conflicts, destination identification, and revisit intention. *Journal of Travel Research,* •••, 00472875231220945.

Miočević, D. (2024). Baby Come Back: Resident-Digital Nomad Conflicts, Destination Identification, and Revisit Intention. *Journal of Travel Research.* Advance online publication. DOI: 10.1177/00472875231220945

Moe, K., & Shandy, D. (2010). *Glass ceilings & 100-hour couples: What the opt-out phenomenon can teach us about work and family.* The University of Georgia Press. DOI: 10.1353/book11402

Mohn, T. (2020). The digital nomad revolution. *Forbes.* Retrieved from https://www.forbes.com

Morrison, A. M. (2023). *Marketing and managing tourism destinations.* Routledge. DOI: 10.4324/9781003343356

Mouratidis, G. (2018). Digital nomadism: Travel, remote work and alternative lifestyles [Master's thesis, Department of Arts and Cultural Sciences]. Lund University.

Mouratidis, G. (2018). Digital nomads: travel, remote work and alternative lifestyles.

Mourato, I., Dias, Á., & Pereira, L. (2023). Estimating the impact of digital nomads' sustainable responsibility on entrepreneurial self-efficacy. *Social Sciences (Basel, Switzerland)*, *12*(2), 97. DOI: 10.3390/socsci12020097

Müller, A. (2016). The digital nomad: Buzzword or research category? *Transnational Social Review*, *6*(3), 344–348. DOI: 10.1080/21931674.2016.1229930

Müller, A. (2016). The emergence of the digital nomad: A new model of work and travel. *Global Nomad Research*, *3*(4), 45–60.

Müller, A. (2020). The digital nomad lifestyle: (Remote) work/leisure balance, privilege, and constructed community. *The International Journal of Sociology and Social Policy*, *40*(9/10), 767–786.

Müller, A. (2021). Digital nomad villages: The next wave in rural tourism development. *Tourism Innovation Journal*, *5*(1), 12–19.

Munjal, S., & Bhushan, S. (Eds.). (2017). *The Indian hospitality industry: Dynamics and future trends*. CRC Press. DOI: 10.1201/9781315225449

Murphy, P. E., & Price, G. G. (2012). Tourism and sustainable development. In *Global tourism* (pp. 167–193). Routledge.

Nakazawa, T. (2023). Toward a Politico-Economic Population Geography: A Critique of *The Shock of a Shrinking Japan*. In Ishikawa, Y. (Ed.), *Japanese Population Geographies II. SpringerBriefs in Population Studies*. Springer., DOI: 10.1007/978-981-99-2076-1_5

Nash, C., Jarrahi, M., Sutherland, W., & Phillips, G. (2018). Digital nomads beyond the buzzword: Defining digital nomadic work and use of digital technologies. International conference on information (pp. 207-217). Cham: Springer International Publishing.

Nash, C., Jarrahi, M. H., & Sutherland, W. (2020). Nomadic work and location independence: The role of space in shaping the work of digital nomads. *Human Relations*, *73*(10), 1389–1412.

Nash, C., Jarrahi, M. H., & Sutherland, W. (2021). Nomadic work and location independence: The role of space in shaping the work of digital nomads. *Human Behavior and Emerging Technologies*, *3*(2), 271–282. DOI: 10.1002/hbe2.234

Nash, C., Jarrahi, M. H., Sutherland, W., & Phillips, G. (2018, March). Digital nomads beyond the buzzword: Defining digital nomadic work and use of digital technologies. In *International conference on information* (pp. 207-217). Cham: Springer International Publishing. DOI: 10.1007/978-3-319-78105-1_25

Newell, S., & Marabelli, M. (2015, March). Strategic opportunities (and challenges) of algorithmic decision-making: A call for action on the long-term societal effects of 'datification.'. *The Journal of Strategic Information Systems, 24*(1), 3–14. DOI: 10.1016/j.jsis.2015.02.001

Newlands, G., Lutz, C., & Fieseler, C. (2018, September 6). Collective action and provider classification in the sharing economy. *New Technology, Work and Employment, 33*(3), 250–267. DOI: 10.1111/ntwe.12119

Ngondo, E., Hermann, U., & Venter, D. (2024). Push and pull factors affectıng domestıc tourism in the Erongo Region, Namibia. *Geo Journal of Tourism and Geosites, 53*(2), 575–583. DOI: 10.30892/gtg.53221-1233

Nguyen, T. (2023). The impact of digital nomadism on local communities: A case study of Chiang Mai. *Tourism Economics, 28*(6), 1234–1250.

Nicolau, J. L., Rodríguez-Sánchez, C., & Ruiz-Moreno, F. (2024). A motivation-based study to explain accommodation choice of senior tourists: Hotel or Airbnb. *International Journal of Hospitality Management, 123*, 103911. DOI: 10.1016/j.ijhm.2024.103911

Nolan, B. (2023). Barcelona, Toronto, and Beijing are some of the best cities to work remotely while traveling, study finds. Business Insider. https://www.businessinsider.com/remote-work-best-cities-work-while-traveling-study-2023-8?r=US&IR=T

Nolan, B. (2023). Zero income tax and tight security makes Dubai one of the best destinations for a "workation," study finds. Business Insider. https://www.businessinsider.in/thelife/news/zero-income-tax-and-tight-security-makes-dubai-one-of-the-best-destinations-for-a-workation-study-finds/articleshow/104776184.cms

Noltemeyer, A., Bush, K., Patton, J., & Bergen, D. (2012). The relationship among deficiency needs and growth needs: An empirical investigation of Maslow's theory. *Children and Youth Services Review, 34*(9), 1862–1867. DOI: 10.1016/j.childyouth.2012.05.021

Nomad List. (2025) The 2025 State of Digital Nomads https://nomadlist.com/digital-nomad-statistics

Number of coworking spaces worldwide | Statistica. (2023). Statista. Retrieved December 15, 2023, from https://www.statista.com/statistics/554273/number-of-coworking-spaces-worldwide/

O'Regan, M. (2020). Digital nomads, the gig economy, and the future of work. *Journal of Tourism Futures, 6*(2), 156–168.

O'Reilly, K. (2003). When is a tourist?: The articulation of tourism and migration in Spain's Costa del Sol. *Tourist Studies*, *3*(3), 301–317. DOI: 10.1177/1468797603049661

Orel, M. (2019). Coworking environments and digital nomadism: Balancing work and leisure whilst on the move. *World Leisure Journal*, *61*(3), 215–227. DOI: 10.1080/16078055.2019.1639275

Orel, M. (2019). Coworking spaces and the localized dynamics of innovation. *Environment and Planning A. Economy and Space*, *51*(4), 803–818.

Orel, M., Dvouletý, O., & Ratten, V. (Eds.). (2021). *The Flexible Workplace*. Human Resource Management., DOI: 10.1007/978-3-030-62167-4

Ortiz, M. A., & Bluyssen, P. M. (2022, March). Profiling office workers based on their self-reported preferences of indoor environmental quality and psychosocial comfort at their workplace during COVID-19. *Building and Environment*, *211*, 108742. DOI: 10.1016/j.buildenv.2021.108742 PMID: 35002047

Özgen Çiğdemli, A. Ö., Yayla, Ş., & Çiğdemli, B. S. (2024). The world from the perspective of digital nomads: Exploring sentiments in destination reviews. *Worldwide Hospitality and Tourism Themes*, *16*(3), 303–315. DOI: 10.1108/WHATT-03-2024-0044

Ozimek, A. (2020). Future Workforce Report. SSRN Electronic Journal. https://doi.org/DOI: 10.2139/ssrn.3787530

Partners, M. B. O. (2022). Working from the Road: The Aspirations and Reality for Digital Nomads. https://www.mbopartners.com/state-of-independence/digital-nomads/

Partners, M. B. O. (2023). New survey reveals rise of tethered nomading: Digital nomads answer the office's beckoning. Retrieved from https://www.mbopartners.com/blog/press/new-survey-reveals-rise-of-tethered-nomading-digital-nomads-answer-the-offices-beckoning/

Partners, M. B. O. (2024). Digital Nomads - Nomading Normalizes in 2024-www.mbopartners.com/state-of-independence/digital-nomads/

Paula. (2023). Global Travel Trends 2023. ForwardKeys. https://forwardkeys.com/global-travel-trends-2023/

Pektaş, F. (2022). Destination as a brand: The impact of push and pull factors of travel motivation on customer-based destination equity. *Uluslararası Yönetim İktisat ve İşletme Dergisi*, *18*(3), 856–874. DOI: 10.17130/ijmeb.1002537

Pencarelli, T. (2020). The digital revolution in the travel and tourism industry. *Information Technology & Tourism, 22*(3), 455–476. DOI: 10.1007/s40558-019-00160-3

Petani, F. J., & Mengis, J. (2021, November 17). Technology and the hybrid workplace: The affective living of IT-enabled space. *International Journal of Human Resource Management, 34*(8), 1530–1553. DOI: 10.1080/09585192.2021.1998186

Peters, M., & Schuckert, M. (2020). The impact of digital nomads on local communities: A case study of Bali. *Journal of Sustainable Tourism, 28*(5), 789–805.

Pipin Oktapiani, N. M., & Putu Mahyuni, L. (2025). Exploring the Canggu-Bali Magnet as a Choice for Digital Nomads. *Dinasti International Journal of Economics, Finance &Amp. Accounting, 5*(6), 6180–6188. DOI: 10.38035/dijefa.v5i6.3252

Policarpio, J. E. A., & Pacete, J. L. B. (2024). Co-Working Spaces and Digital Nomadism in the Philippines: Understanding Bleisure Tourism's Role in Diffusion of Culture. In *Bleisure Tourism and the Impact of Technology* (pp. 190-211). IGI Global.

Pongruengkiat, W., Tippayawong, K. Y., Aggarangsi, P., Pichayapan, P., Katongtung, T., & Tippayawong, N. (2023). Assessing sustainability of Chiang Mai urban development. *Discover Sustainability, 4*(1), 54. DOI: 10.1007/s43621-023-00174-2

Popova, K., & Malcheva, M. (2020). Assessment of the potential of Varna City as a smart tourist destination. *Tourism (Zagreb), 68*(3), 308–321. DOI: 10.37741/t.68.3.5

Poulaki, I., Mavragani, E., Kaziani, A., & Chatzimichali, E. (2023). Digital-Nomads: Advances in hospitality and destination attractiveness. *Tourism and Hospitality, 4*(3), 483–498. DOI: 10.3390/tourhosp4030030

Prabawa, I. W. S. W., & Pertiwi, P. R. (2020). The digital nomad tourist motivation in Bali: Exploratory research based on push and pull theory. *Athens Journal of Tourism, 7*(3), 161–174. DOI: 10.30958/ajt.7-3-3

Prester, J., Cecez-Kecmanovic, D., & Schlagwein, D. (2019). Becoming a Digital Nomad: Identity Emergence in the Flow of Practice. In *ICIS*.

Prodanova, J., & Kocarev, L. (2021, August). Is job performance conditioned by work-from-home demands and resources? *Technology in Society, 66*, 101672. DOI: 10.1016/j.techsoc.2021.101672 PMID: 34840365

Pumble. (2024). Digital nomad visa statistics. Retrieved December 6, 2024, from https://pumble.com/learn/digital-nomad-visa/statistics/

Pupavac, D., Malbašić, A., & Ivaniš, M. (2023). *Digital Nomads: Croatian Experience*. DOI: 10.31410/ITEMA.2023.249

Purcell, J., & Boxall, P (2017). Strategy and Human Resource Management. Bloomsbury Publishing. http://books.google.ie/books?id=oCVHEAAAQBAJ&printsec=frontcover&dq=Boxall,+P.,+%26+Purcell,+J.+(2016).+Strategy+and+human+resource+management.+Palgrave&hl=&cd=1&source=gbs_api

Putra, G., & Agirachman, F. (2016). Urban coworking space: creative tourism in digital nomads perspective. *Proceedings of Arte-Polis 6 international conference* (pp. 169-178).

Qiu, M., Sha, J., & Scott, N. (2021, February 26). Restoration of Visitors through Nature-Based Tourism: A Systematic Review, Conceptual Framework, and Future Research Directions. *International Journal of Environmental Research and Public Health, 18*(5), 2299. DOI: 10.3390/ijerph18052299 PMID: 33652652

Rahayu, D. P., Kusumastuti, A., & Puspitosari, W. A. (2022). Sentiment Analysis of Digital Nomad in Indonesia: A Case Study in Bali. *Masyarakat: Jurnal Sosiologi.* DOI: 10.7454/MJS.v26i2.13685

Rainoldi, M. (2024). *Managing work and leisure in the digital age: A practice exploration of digital nomadism.* Bournemouth University, Reichenberger, I. (2018). Digital nomads–a quest for holistic freedom in work and leisure. *Annals of Leisure Research, 21*(3), 364–380.

Rainoldi, M., Ladkin, A., & Buhalis, D. (2022, May 10). Blending work and leisure: A future digital worker hybrid lifestyle perspective. *Annals of Leisure Research,* •••, 1–21. DOI: 10.1080/11745398.2022.2070513

Rakhmadi, R. (2021, December). Role of digital nomad in supporting tourism in Indonesia: Case study Bali. In *Proceedings of the 2nd International Indonesia Conference on Interdisciplinary Studies (IICIS 2021)* 606(2), 143–148 DOI: 10.2991/assehr.k.211206.020

Rakhmetulina, Z., Suleimenova, A. O., & Abylaykhanova, T. A. (2024). «Digital nomads» in the modern labour market.*Central Asian Economic Review.* DOI: 10.52821/2789-4401-2024-2-89-101

Rapaport, M. H., Clary, C., Fayyad, R., & Endicott, J. (2005). Quality-of-life impairment in depressive and anxiety disorders. *The American Journal of Psychiatry, 162*(6), 1171–1178. DOI: 10.1176/appi.ajp.162.6.1171 PMID: 15930066

Rapp, D. J., Hughey, J. M., & Kreiner, G. E. (2021, August). Boundary work as a buffer against burnout: Evidence from healthcare workers during the COVID-19 pandemic. *The Journal of Applied Psychology, 106*(8), 1169–1187. DOI: 10.1037/apl0000951 PMID: 34424001

Reichenberger, I. (2018). Digital nomads: A quest for lifestyle values. *Annals of Tourism Research*, *73*, 98–107.

Reichenberger, I. (2018). Digital nomads–a quest for holistic freedom in work and leisure. *Annals of Leisure Research*, *21*(3), 364–380. DOI: 10.1080/11745398.2017.1358098

Reichenberger, I. (2020). Digital nomads: A quest for holistic freedom in work and leisure. *Annals of Leisure Research*, *23*(2), 215–230.

Reynolds, L., Koenig-Lewis, N., Doering, H., & Peattie, K. (2022). Competing for legitimacy in the place branding process: (Re)negotiating the stakes. *Tourism Management*, *91*, 104532. DOI: 10.1016/j.tourman.2022.104532

Richards, G. (2022). Cultural tourism in the age of remote work. *Current Issues in Tourism*, *25*(7), 891–907.

Richter, A. (2020). Locked-down digital work. *International Journal of Information Management*, *55*, 102157. DOI: 10.1016/j.ijinfomgt.2020.102157 PMID: 32836629

Richter, S., & Richter, A. (2020). Digital nomads. *Business & Information Systems Engineering*, *62*(1), 77–81. DOI: 10.1007/s12599-019-00615-1

Rodriguez, P., & Fernandez, M. (2023). Sustainable tourism in Costa Rica: Lessons for digital nomad hubs. *Sustainability*, *15*(7), 5678.

Roundy, P. (2017). Social entrepreneurship and entrepreneurial ecosystems: Complementary or disjointed phenomena? *International Journal of Social Economics*, *44*(9), 1252–1267. Advance online publication. DOI: 10.1108/IJSE-02-2016-0045

Roxas, F. M. Y., Rivera, J. P. R., & Gutierrez, E. L. M. (2020). Framework for creating sustainable tourism using systems thinking. *Current Issues in Tourism*, *23*(3), 280–296. DOI: 10.1080/13683500.2018.1534805

Ruggerio, C. A. (2021). Sustainability and sustainable development: A review of principles and definitions. *The Science of the Total Environment*, *786*, 147481. DOI: 10.1016/j.scitotenv.2021.147481 PMID: 33965820

Rundel, C. T., Salemink, K., & Strijker, D. (2020). Exploring rural digital hubs and their possible contribution to communities in Europe. *Journal of Rural and Community Development*, *15*(3).

Ryan, R. M., & Deci, E. L. (2000). Self-determination theory and the facilitation of intrinsic motivation, social development, and well-being. *The American Psychologist*, *55*(1), 68–78. DOI: 10.1037/0003-066X.55.1.68 PMID: 11392867

Saarinen, J. (2006). Traditions of sustainability in tourism studies. *Annals of Tourism Research, 33*(4), 1121–1140. DOI: 10.1016/j.annals.2006.06.007

Sánchez-Vergara, J. I., Orel, M., & Capdevila, I. (2023). "Home office is the here and now." Digital nomad visa systems and remote work-focused leisure policies. *World Leisure Journal, 65*(2), 236–255. DOI: 10.1080/16078055.2023.2165142

Sardinha, L., Vieira, M., de Sousa, Á. S., & Leite, E. (2023). DIGITAL NOMADS—THE CASE OF THE AUTONOMOUS REGION OF MADEIRA. *Journal of Entrepreneurial Researchers, 1*(2), 55–69. DOI: 10.29073/jer.v1i2.14

Satpathy, S., Patel, G., & Kumar, K. (2021, November 12). Identifying and ranking techno-stressors among IT employees due to work from home arrangement during Covid-19 pandemic. *Decision (Washington, D.C.), 48*(4), 391–402. DOI: 10.1007/s40622-021-00295-5

Sayah, S. (2013, November). Managing work–life boundaries with information and communication technologies: The case of independent contractors. *New Technology, Work and Employment, 28*(3), 179–196. DOI: 10.1111/ntwe.12016

Schlagwein, D., & Jarrahi, M. H. (2020). Digital nomadism and the future of work: A research agenda. *Journal of Global Information Management, 28*(4), 1–15.

Secretaría de Turismo de Tailandia. (2022). *Digital Nomad Visa Policies in Thailand.* Recuperado de https://www.tourismthailand.org

Sekayi, M. (2024, 02. 21.). Digital Nomads and their Impact on Culture. London Intercultural Centre: https://londoninterculturalcenter.co.uk/blogs/f/digital-nomads-and-their-impact-on-culture (21.12.2024) adresinden alındı

Shakti, D., Ray, D., & Gupta, D. (2021). Factors affecting Work from Office and Work from Anywhere for Employees: A Study. [IJSRP]. *International Journal of Scientific and Research Publications, 11*(10), 251–256. DOI: 10.29322/IJSRP.11.10.2021.p11827

Sharpley, R. (2009). *Tourism development and the environment: Beyond sustainability?* Routledge. DOI: 10.4324/9781849770255

Sharpley, R. (2020). Tourism, sustainable development and the theoretical divide: 20 years on. *Journal of Sustainable Tourism, 28*(11), 1932–1946. DOI: 10.1080/09669582.2020.1779732

Shin, H., Lee, J., & Kim, N. (2024, May). Hwui., & Kim, N.-J. (2023). Workcation (Workation) Travel Experiences, Satisfaction and Revisit Intentions: Focusing on Conceptualization, Scale Development, and Nomological Network. *Journal of Travel Research*, *63*(5), 1150–1168. Advance online publication. DOI: 10.1177/00472875231188717

Shockley, K. M., & Allen, T. D. (2007). When flexibility helps: Another look at the availability of flexible work arrangements and work–family conflict. *Journal of Vocational Behavior*, *71*(3), 479–493. DOI: 10.1016/j.jvb.2007.08.006

Silva, A., & Costa, R. (2023). Environmental challenges in Madeira's digital nomad village. *Environmental Science & Policy*, *130*, 45–56.

Singh, B., & Kaunert, C. (2025). Innovative business models in digital and virtual reality for the gig economy: Space-age sustainable development projecting smart business practices. In *Business transformation in the era of digital disruption* (pp. 127–156). IGI Global.

Singh, P., Bala, H., Dey, B. L., & Filieri, R. (2022, November). Enforced remote working: The impact of digital platform-induced stress and remote working experience on technology exhaustion and subjective wellbeing. *Journal of Business Research*, *151*, 269–286. DOI: 10.1016/j.jbusres.2022.07.002 PMID: 35847196

Sintas, J. L., de Francisco, L. R., & Álvarez, E. G. (2015). The Nature of Leisure Revisited. *Journal of Leisure Research*, *47*(1), 79–101. DOI: 10.1080/00222216.2015.11950352

Sızan, T. (2024). İstanbul'da Gezilecek Yerler, Görülmesi Gereken En Güzel 51 Yer. Etstur Let's Go: https://www.etstur.com/letsgo/istanbul-gezilecek-yerler/ (27.12.2024) adresinden alındı

Šmite, D., Moe, N. B., Klotins, E., & Gonzalez-Huerta, J. (2023). From forced Working-From-Home to voluntary working-from-anywhere: Two revolutions in telework. *Journal of Systems and Software*, *195*, 111509. DOI: 10.1016/j.jss.2022.111509 PMID: 36105918

Smith, A., & Eldridge, A. (Eds.). (2021). *Tourism and the night: Rethinking nocturnal destinations*. Routledge. DOI: 10.4324/9781003142096

Smith, A., & Lee, B. (2022). The economic impact of digital nomads in Bali. *Tourism Economics*, *28*(6), 1234–1250.

Soares da Silva, D., Figueiredo, E., Eusébio, C., & Carneiro, M. J.Soares da Silva. (2016). The countryside is worth a thousand words - Portuguese representations on rural areas. *Journal of Rural Studies*, *44*, 77–88. DOI: 10.1016/j.jrurstud.2016.01.012

Solvoll, S., Alsos, G. A., & Bulanova, O. (2015). Tourism entrepreneurship: Review and future directions. *Scandinavian Journal of Hospitality and Tourism*, *15*(sup1, Suppl. 1), 120–137. DOI: 10.1080/15022250.2015.1065592

Sorensen, G., Dennerlein, J. T., Peters, S. E., Sabbath, E. L., Kelly, E. L., & Wagner, G. R. (2021, January). The future of research on work, safety, health and wellbeing: A guiding conceptual framework. *Social Science & Medicine*, *269*, 113593. DOI: 10.1016/j.socscimed.2020.113593 PMID: 33341740

Sorokina, E., Wang, Y., Fyall, A., Lugosi, P., Torres, E., & Jung, T. (2022). Constructing a smart destination framework: A destination marketing organization perspective. *Journal of Destination Marketing & Management*, *23*, 100688. DOI: 10.1016/j.jdmm.2021.100688

Spinuzzi, C. (2012). Working alone together: Coworking as emergent collaborative activity. *Journal of Business and Technical Communication*, *26*(4), 399–441. DOI: 10.1177/1050651912444070

Spracklen, K. (2015). *Digital leisure, the internet and popular culture: Communities and identities in a digital age*. Springer. DOI: 10.1057/9781137405876

Sprague, R. (2015). Worker (mis) classification in the sharing economy: Trying to fit square pegs into round holes. *ABA Journal of Labor & Employment Law*, *31*(1), 53–76. DOI: 10.2139/ssrn.2606600

Standing, G. (2009). Work after globalization: Building occupational citizenship. In *Work after Globalization*. Edward Elgar Publishing. DOI: 10.4337/9781849802376

Statista. (2023). *Number of digital nomads worldwide from 2020 to 2023*. Recuperado de https://www.statista.com

Stickel, M. D. (2020). *Challenges and opportunities of digital nomadism and its implications for tomorrow's workforce*. Management from the NOVA–School of Business and Economics.

Strauss, K. (2018). Labour geography 1. *Progress in Human Geography*, *42*(4), 622–630. DOI: 10.1177/0309132517717786

Stumpf, T. S., Califf, C. B., & Lancaster, J. (2022). Digital nomad entrepreneurship and lifestyle design: A process theory. *Proceedings of the 55th Hawaii International Conference on System Sciences*, 5201–5210. Retrieved from https://hdl.handle.net/10125/79972

Stylidis, D., & Dominguez Quintero, A. (2022). Understanding the effect of place image and knowledge of tourism on residents' attitudes towards tourism and their word-of-mouth intentions: Evidence from Seville, Spain. *Tourism Planning & Development, 19*(5), 1–18. DOI: 10.1080/21568316.2022.2049859

Su, N., & Mark, G. (2008). Designing for nomadic work. *Proceedings of the 7th ACM conference on Designing interactive systems* (pp. 305-314). Cape Town, South Africa. DOI: 10.1145/1394445.1394478

Sun, Y.-Y. (2016). Decomposition of tourism greenhouse gas emissions: Revealing the dynamics between tourism economic growth, technological efficiency, and carbon emissions. *Tourism Management, 55*, 326–336. DOI: 10.1016/j.tourman.2016.02.014

Suriyankietkaew, S., Krittayaruangroj, K., & Iamsawan, N. (2022). Sustainable leadership practices and competencies of SMEs for sustainability and resilience: A community-based social enterprise study. *Sustainability (Basel), 14*(10), 5762. DOI: 10.3390/su14105762

Sutherland, W., & Jarrahi, M. H. (2017). The gig economy and information infrastructure: The case of the digital nomad community. *Proceedings of the ACM on Human-Computer Interaction, 1*(CSCW), 1–24. DOI: 10.1145/3134732

Sutherland, W., & Jarrahi, M. H. (2018, December). The sharing economy and digital platforms: A review and research agenda. *International Journal of Information Management, 43*, 328–341. DOI: 10.1016/j.ijinfomgt.2018.07.004

Sztuk, A. (2024). Digital-Nomads as Recipients and Users of the City's Offer. Status and Prospects of Research. *Zeszyty Naukowe Politechniki Śląskiej. Organizacja i Zarządzanie*, (193).

Tajfel, H., & Turner, J. C. (1979). An integrative theory of intergroup conflict. *The Social Psychology of Intergroup Relations, 33*(47), 74–85.

Tan, G., & Hsu, C. H. C. (2024). Can host–tourist interaction pull the plug on tourist stereotypes? Exploring the power of emotional solidarity. *Tourism Management Perspectives, 50*, 101211. Advance online publication. DOI: 10.1016/j.tmp.2023.101211

Taser, D., Aydin, E., Torgaloz, A. O., & Rofcanin, Y. (2022, February). An examination of remote e-working and flow experience: The role of technostress and loneliness. *Computers in Human Behavior, 127*, 107020. DOI: 10.1016/j.chb.2021.107020

Teodorovicz, T., & Choudhury, P. (Raj), & Starr, E. (2023). Location Specificity and Geographic Competition for Remote Workers.*Social Science Research Network.* https://doi.org/DOI: 10.2139/ssrn.4467579

Ter Hoeven, C. L., & van Zoonen, W. (2015, November). Flexible work designs and employee well-being: Examining the effects of resources and demands. *New Technology, Work and Employment*, *30*(3), 237–255. DOI: 10.1111/ntwe.12052

The Cities Best Facilitating Remote Work. Workation Edition. Workmotion.com. Retrieved December 2023, from https://workmotion.com/best-remote-work-cities-workation-edition/

The world's best 'work from anywhere' cities and the rise of the digital nomad. (2023). In assets.iwgplc.com. IWG PLC. Retrieved December 18, 2023, from https://assets.iwgplc.com/image/upload/v1694070764/IWG/MediaCentre/IWG_White_Paper_Work_From_Anywhere_Cities_Rise_of_the_Digital_Nomad_Sept_2023.pdf

Thompson, B. Y. (2019). The digital nomad lifestyle:(remote) work/leisure balance, privilege, and constructed community. *International journal of the sociology of leisure*, *2*(1), 27-42.

Thompson, B. (2018). Digital Nomads Employment in the Online Gig Economy. *Glocalism*, (1), 1–26. DOI: 10.12893/gjcpi.2018.1.11

Thompson, B. Y. (2018, December 19). The Digital Nomad Lifestyle: (Remote) Work/Leisure Balance, Privilege, and Constructed Community. *International Journal of the Sociology of Leisure*, *2*(1–2), 27–42. DOI: 10.1007/s41978-018-00030-y

Thompson, B. Y. (2020). Digital nomads: Employment in the online gig economy. *Global Labour Journal*, *11*(2), 123–140.

Thompson, J., Brown, L., & Green, T. (2023). Digital nomadism and rural economic development. *Journal of Rural Development*, *41*(2), 89–104.

Tisdell, C. (2001). Globalisation and sustainability: Environmental Kuznets curve and the WTO. *Ecological Economics*, *39*(2), 185–196. DOI: 10.1016/S0921-8009(01)00234-8

Todt, A., & Kastenholz, E. (2010). Tourists as a driving force for sustainable rural development – a research framework. Atas do IV Congresso de Estudos Rurais – Mundos Rurais em Portugal: Múltiplos Olhares, Múltiplos Futuros, Universidade de Aveiro/ SPER, Aveiro, 4-6 Fevereiro (pp. 633-645). https://bdigital.ipg.pt/dspace/bitstream/10314/3265/1/%C3%8Dndice-%20LivroActasFinal-%20Aveiro-2010.pdf

Torabi, Z. A., Shalbafian, A. A., Allam, Z., Ghaderi, Z., Murgante, B., & Khavarian-Garmsir, A. R. (2022). Enhancing memorable experiences, tourist satisfaction, and revisit intention through smart tourism technologies. *Sustainability (Basel)*, *14*(5), 2721. DOI: 10.3390/su14052721

Torun, G. (2024, 11. 27.). İstanbul'da gezilecek doğal yerler. Enuygun Blog: https://www.enuygun.com/bilgi/istanbul-da-gezilecek-yerler-mutlaka-gorulmesi-gereken-70-yer/doga/ (26.12.2024) adresinden alındı

Toscano, F., & Zappalà, S. (2020, November 24). Social Isolation and Stress as Predictors of Productivity Perception and Remote Work Satisfaction during the COVID-19 Pandemic: The Role of Concern about the Virus in a Moderated Double Mediation. *Sustainability (Basel), 12*(23), 9804. DOI: 10.3390/su12239804

Tredinnick, L., & Laybats, C. (2021, September). Blended workplaces. *Business Information Review, 38*(3), 108–110. DOI: 10.1177/02663821211042474

Trip.Com Group & Deloitte Global. (2023). A World In Motion: Shifting consumer travel trends in 2022 and beyond. In WTTC. Retrieved December 16, 2023, from https://www2.deloitte.com/content/dam/Deloitte/fr/Documents/consumer-business/Publications/wttc-consumer-trends-report-2023.pdf

Uğur, N., & Akova, O. (2021). The effect of Covid-19 pandemic on cafe-bar, bistro and night clubs. *Uluslararası Beşeri ve Sosyal Bilimler İnceleme Dergisi, 5*(2), 139–153.

Uğur, N., & Akova, O. (2022). *The Use of Virtual Reality and Augmented Reality in Cultural Heritage and Deep-Diving Destinations. L. Oliveira içinde, Handbook of Research on Digital Communications, Internet of Things, and the Future of Cultural Tourism.* IGI Global., DOI: 10.4018/978-1-7998-8528-3.ch008

Uğur, N., & Demirkol, Ş. (2021). Hipster Turist Arketipleri ve Hipster Turizminin Oluşumuna Katkısının Analizi. *Journal of New Tourism Trends, 2*(2), 125–137.

UNE. (2019). UNE 178504:2019. Recuperado de https://www.une.org/encuentra-tu-norma/busca-tu-norma/norma?c=N0062377

Unesco. (2025). Historic Areas of Istanbul. Unesco World Heritage Convention: https://whc.unesco.org/en/list/356/ adresinden alındı

UNSW Business School. (2024). How digital nomads impact local communities: A Chiang Mai case study. Retrieved from https://www.businessthink.unsw.edu.au/articles/digital-nomads-local-communities-chiang-mai

UNWTO. (2018). *Tourism and the Sustainable Development Goals: Good Practices in the Americas.* Madrid, España. Recuperado de https://www.unwto.org

UNWTO. (2024). *UNWTO brief: Digital nomad visas.* World Tourism Organization., DOI: 10.18111/9789284424481

Vagena, A. (2021). Digital nomads and tourism industry. *Academia Letters, 765*, 1–6.

Vagena, A., Yurevich, O., Leonidas, L., & Papakonstantinidis, A. (2023). *Greece as an Organic Space for the Development of Digital Nomadistry*. Qeios., DOI: 10.32388/D7NX7L

Van Holm, E. J. (2020). The rise of the digital nomad: Implications for urban and regional development. *Urban Studies (Edinburgh, Scotland)*, *57*(10), 2105–2121.

Vanhove, N. (2022). *The economics of tourism destinations: Theory and practice*. Routledge. DOI: 10.4324/9781003258186

Verma, M. (2023). The future of work for digital nomads: The benefits and risks of automation. *IJSART, 9*(4), 339–343. Retrieved from https://www.researchgate.net/publication/370099953

Viswanathan, S., Anbazhagan, A., & Kannan, R. (2021). Bridging the digital divide in rural tourism destinations: A case for India. *Journal of Rural Studies*, *87*, 12–21.

Voll, K., Gauger, F., & Pfnür, A. (2022). Work from anywhere: traditional workation, coworkation and workation retreats: a conceptual review. *World Leisure Journal*, *65*(2), 150–174. DOI: 10.1080/16078055.2022.2134199

Von Zumbusch, J. S. H., & Lalicic, L. (2020). The role of co-living spaces in digital nomads' well-being. *Information Technology & Tourism*, *22*(3), 439–453. Advance online publication. DOI: 10.1007/s40558-020-00182-2

Wang, B., Schlagwein, D., & Cecez-Kecmanovic, D. (2024). Critical-theoretic review and research agenda on digital nomadism. *ICIS 2024 Proceedings, 14*. Retrieved from https://aisel.aisnet.org/icis2024/lit_review/lit_review/14

Wang, B., Schlagwein, D., Cecez-Kecmanovic, D., & Cahalane, M. (2019). *Digital Nomadism and the Market Economy: Resistance and Compliance*. Paper presented at the ICIS.

Wang, B., Schlagwein, D., Cecez-Kecmanovic, D., & Cahalane, M. C. (2018). Digital work and high-tech wanderers: Three theoretical framings and a research agenda for digital nomadism. In *ACIS 2018 Proceedings. Australasian Conference on Information Systems*. Retrieved from https://aisel.aisnet.org/acis2018/55

Wang, B., Schlagwein, D., Cecez-Kecmanovic, D., & Cahalane, M. (2018). Digital work and high-tech wanderers: Three theoretical framings and a research agenda for digital nomadism. *Australasian Conference on Information Systems*. Sydney. DOI: 10.5130/acis2018.bl

Wang, B., Schlagwein, D., Cecez-Kecmanovic, D., & Cahalane, M. C. (2020). Beyond the factory paradigm: Digital nomadism and the digital future (s) of knowledge work post-COVID-19. *Journal of the Association for Information Systems*, *21*(6), 10. DOI: 10.17705/1jais.00641

Wang, B., Schlagwein, D., Cecez-Kecmanovic, D., & Cahalane, M. C. (2024). 'Emancipation' in Digital Nomadism vs in the Nation-State: A Comparative Analysis of Idealtypes. *Journal of Business Ethics*, •••, 1–34.

Wang, Y., & Fesenmaier, D. R. (2020). Transforming the travel experience: The role of digital nomads in shaping tourism futures. *Journal of Travel Research*, *59*(3), 423–436.

Wani, M. D., Ganai, S. A., Wani, S. A., Dada, Z. A., & Shah, S. A. (2025c). Balancing Growth and Preservation: Sustainable Strategies for Overtourism Management. In *Solutions for Managing Overtourism in Popular Destinations* (pp. 1-22). IGI Global Scientific Publishing.

Wani, M. D., Shah, S. A., & Dada, Z. A. (2025b). Fostering Sustainable Tourism in India: Harnessing Cultural and Heritage Assets for Enduring Development. In *Integrating Architecture and Design Into Sustainable Tourism Development* (pp. 179-214). IGI Global Scientific Publishing.

Wani, M. D., Batool, N., Dada, Z. A., & Shah, S. A. (2024c). Investigating the impact of community-based tourism on the residents' quality of life and their support for tourism. *Community Development (Columbus, Ohio)*, *55*(1), 138–159. DOI: 10.1080/15575330.2023.2272271

Wani, M. D., Dada, Z. A., Bhat, W. A., & Shah, S. A. (2025a). Community-driven ecotourism in the trans Himalayan region: A sustainable model for cultural and environmental preservation. *Community Development (Columbus, Ohio)*, •••, 1–23. DOI: 10.1080/15575330.2025.2451358

Wani, M. D., Dada, Z. A., & Shah, S. A. (2023a). Behavioral intention and satisfaction levels among pilgrim tourists in South Asia. *Tourism Review*, *78*(4), 1147–1163. DOI: 10.1108/TR-09-2022-0432

Wani, M. D., Dada, Z. A., & Shah, S. A. (2023b). Evaluating the impact of cross Border tourism and people to people contact on the regional cooperation in South Asia: A study of India and Bangladesh. *Journal of Quality Assurance in Hospitality & Tourism*, •••, 1–22. DOI: 10.1080/1528008X.2023.2262137

Wani, M. D., Dada, Z. A., & Shah, S. A. (2023c). To utilize structural equation modelling to investigate the impact of cross-border tourism on regional cooperation: The mediating effect of community support. *The Review of Regional Studies*, *53*(1), 80–99. DOI: 10.52324/001c.74889

Wani, M. D., Dada, Z. A., & Shah, S. A. (2024a). The impact of community empowerment on sustainable tourism development and the mediation effect of local support: A structural equation modeling approach. *Community Development (Columbus, Ohio)*, *55*(1), 1–17. DOI: 10.1080/15575330.2022.2109703

Wani, M. D., Dada, Z. A., & Shah, S. A. (2024b). Can consumption of local food contribute to sustainable tourism? Evidence from the perception of domestic tourists. *International Journal of Sustainable Development and World Ecology*, *31*(2), 1–16. DOI: 10.1080/13504509.2023.2262950

Wani, M. D., Dada, Z. A., & Shah, S. A. (2024d). Divine Experiences: Exploring the Impact of Tourist Satisfaction on Religious Travel in Jammu and Kashmir, India. In Jermsittiparsert, K., Wekke, I., & Suanpang, P. (Eds.), *Sustainable Development, Humanities, and Social Sciences for Society 5.0* (pp. 387–414). IGI Global Scientific Publishing. DOI: 10.4018/979-8-3693-7989-9.ch019

Wani, M. D., Dada, Z. A., & Shah, S. A. (2024e). What Factors Influence Consumers' Intention and Food Waste Reduction Perceptions in Indian Restaurants? *British Food Journal.*

Wani, M. U. D., Dada, Z. A., & Shah, S. A. (2022). Building peace through tourism: The analysis of an ongoing Siachen Glacier dispute between India and Pakistan. *Asian Journal of Comparative Politics*, *7*(4), 836–848. DOI: 10.1177/20578911221118730

Warr, P. (1999). Well-being and the workplace. In Kahneman, D., Diener, E., & Schwarz, N. (Eds.), *Well-being: The foundations of hedonic psychology* (pp. 392–412). Russel Sage.

Warr, P. B. (1987). *Work, unemployment, and mental health.* Oxford University Press.

WCCF. (2024, 08. 22.). Byzantine Wonders to Contemporary Culture: İstanbul's Tourist Appeal. World citiws culture forum: https://worldcitiescultureforum.com/city/istanbul/ (26.12.2024) adresinden alındı

Westerhausen, K., & Macbeth, J. (2020). Backpackers and the development of tourism in rural areas: A case study of Pai, Thailand. *Tourism Geographies*, *22*(2), 345–366.

Where to Flow. (2023). *Digital nomad visas in Europe*. Retrieved December 23, 2024, from https://wheretoflow.com/digital-nomad-visas-europe/

Wibowo, T. O. (2024). Dynamic of Migration lifestyle and settlement of nomad in Bali, Indonesia. *The Indonesian Journal of Geography*, *56*(2). Advance online publication. DOI: 10.22146/ijg.90856

Widmoser, L. (2024). Digital nomads: Balancing mobility and sustainability in the liquid modern world (Master's thesis, University of Innsbruck). University of Innsbruck Repository. Retrieved from https://repository.university-innsbruck.edu

Williams, A., & Hall, C. (2002). Tourism, migration, circulation and mobility: The contingencies of time and place. Tourism and migration: New relationships between production and consumption (s. 1-52). içinde Dordrecht: Springer Netherlands.

Williams, A., & Hall, C. (2000). Tourism and migration: New relationships between production and consumption. *Tourism Geographies*, *2*(1), 5–27. DOI: 10.1080/146166800363420

Woldoff, R. A., & Litchfield, R. C. (2021). *Digital nomads: In search of freedom, community, and meaningful work in the new economy*. Oxford University Press.

Woldoff, R. A., Woldoff, R., & Litchfield, R. C. (2021). *Digital-Nomads: In search offreedom, community, and meaningful work in the new economy*. Oxford University Press. DOI: 10.1093/oso/9780190931780.001.0001

World Economic Forum. (2024a). How digital nomads can transform tourism and the economy of Small Island Developing States. Retrieved from https://www.weforum.org/stories/2024/10/how-digital-nomads-can-transform-tourism-and-the-economy-of-small-island-developing-states/#:~:text=Digital%20nomadism%20emerged%20as%20a,a%20more%20sustainable%20economic%20model

World Economic Forum. (2024b). *The rise of global digital jobs*. Retrieved from https://www3.weforum.org/docs/WEF_The_Rise_of_Global_Digital_Jobs_2024.pdf

World Health Organization. (2017). *Depression and other common mental disorders: global health estimates (No. WHO/MSD/MER/2017.2)*. World Health Organization.

Xiang, Z., & Fesenmaier, D. R. (2017). Big data analytics, tourism design and smart tourism. *Analytics in smart tourism design: concepts and methods*, 299-307.

Xiao, Y., & Agrawal, B. (2023). *Becoming Mainstream: What Makes You a Digital Nomad?* (Master's thesis, Handelshøyskolen BI).

Xiao, Y., & Lutz, C. (2024). Wayfarers in cyberspace: A temporal investigation of digital nomads based on liquid modernity theory. *Journal of Travel Research*, *00472875231224242*. Advance online publication. DOI: 10.1177/00472875231224242

Yang, C., Shao, J., & Zhao, Y. (2024). Post-COVID-19 Sojourn Choices: Exploring the Distribution and Preferences of Chinese Digital Nomads Based on the Lifestyle Migration Theory. *Sustainability (Basel), 17*(1), 130. DOI: 10.3390/su17010130

Yang, J., Ryan, C., & Zhang, L. (2013). Social conflict in communities impacted by tourism. *Tourism Management, 35*, 82–93. DOI: 10.1016/j.tourman.2012.06.002

Yang, Y. (2024). Urban Sustainability in the Age of Digital Nomads - Diverse Group Impacts. Advances in Economics. *Management and Political Sciences, 112*, 70–74.

Yayla, Ö., Özgür Göde, M., & Ekincek, S. (2024). Global palates: Unraveling digital nomads' culinary journeys and gastro-tourist profiles. *Worldwide Hospitality and Tourism Themes, 16*(3), 329–344. DOI: 10.1108/WHATT-03-2024-0045

Yılmaz Güzey, Y., & Çelik, D. (2022). COVID-19 ve çalışma hayatının dönüşümü. In *COVID-19'un ekonomi politiği* (pp. 116–136). Beykent Üniversitesi.

Yolal, M. (2016). History of tourism development in Turkey. *Alternative Tourism in Turkey: Role, Potential Development and Sustainability*, 23-33.

Yuce, A. (2021). The Impact of Digital Transformation and Virtual Reality in Tourism Marketing: A Conceptualized Exploration. In *Handbook of Research on IoT, Digital Transformation, and the Future of Global Marketing* (pp. 1-14): IGI Global. DOI: 10.4018/978-1-7998-7192-7.ch001

Yuce, A. (2023). Digital twins and sustainable developments in the tourism and hospitality industry. In *Handbook of Research on Applications of AI, Digital Twin, and Internet of Things for Sustainable Development* (pp. 461-472): IGI Global. DOI: 10.4018/978-1-6684-6821-0.ch027

Zerva, K., Huete, R., & Segovia-Pérez, M. (2022, May). Digital nomad tourism: The experience of living at the destination. In *International Conference on Modern Trends in Business Hospitality and Tourism* (pp. 15-26). Cham: Springer International Publishing.

Zhang, H., Qu, H., & Tang, V. (2004). A case study of Hong Kong residents' outbound leisure travel. *Tourism Management, 25*(2), 267–273. DOI: 10.1016/S0261-5177(03)00096-7

Zhang, M., Yu, Y., Liu, M., & Liu, J. (2024). Opportunities for China's agricultural heritage systems under the "Digital Nomadism" trend—A stakeholder-weighted approach. *Sustainability (Basel), 16*(7), 2918. DOI: 10.3390/su16072918

Zhang, Y., Gao, J., Cole, S., & Ricci, P. (2021). How the spread of user-generated contents (UGC) shapes international tourism distribution: Using agent-based modeling to inform strategic UGC marketing. *Journal of Travel Research, 60*(7), 1469–1491. DOI: 10.1177/0047287520951639

Zhou, L., Buhalis, D., Fan, D. X., Ladkin, A., & Lian, X. (2024). Attracting digital nomads: Smart destination strategies, innovation and competitiveness. *Journal of Destination Marketing & Management, 31*, 100850. DOI: 10.1016/j.jdmm.2023.100850

Zimmermann, A. (2020). Digital nomads and the future of work: A critical perspective. *Work, Employment and Society, 34*(5), 789–805.

About the Contributors

Ricardo Correia With over two decades of academic experience, Ricardo Fontes Correia is an Associate Professor at Bragança Polytechnic University in Portugal, where he leads the master's program in Tourism Marketing. He also serves as a visiting Professor at ISM University of Management and Economics in Lithuania. Ricardo's primary research interests encompass Services Marketing, Tourism Marketing, Wine Tourism, Branding, and Social Networks. He is an integral member of the Centre for Tourism Research, Development, and Innovation (CiTUR). Ricardo has contributed his expertise as an external consultant to various programs, including the European Union Agris Program and Interreg, and has consulted for Deloitte & Touche. His prolific academic career is marked by active participation in numerous research projects, conferences, and international scientific meetings. Additionally, he has published several book chapters and papers in prestigious top-tier journals.

Márcio Martins has a PhD in Tourism from the University of Aveiro, a master's degree in Natural Hazards Management and a degree in Geography from the Faculty of Arts and hHmanities of the University of Porto. He is currently an Adjunct Professor at the Polytechnic University of Bragança (IPB) and his main research areas are the spatiotemporal behaviour of tourists, tourist tracking technologies and backpacker tourism. He teaches the General Principles of Tourism, Tourism and Development, Tourism Destination Management and Tourism Product Development courses on the Tourism degree programme, and co-teaches the Master's Seminar in Tourism Marketing, among others. He has also collaborated with the Polytechnic Institute of Viseu as a Visiting Assistant Professor at the Lamego School of Technology and Management, where he teaches the "Geography, Landscape and Geotourism" course in the Tourism, Cultural and Heritage Management degree programme. He is currently an integrated member of CITED - IPB's Centre for Transdisciplinary Research in Education and Development, a collaborating member of the Centre for Research, Development and Innovation in Tourism (CITUR) and also of IPB's Management Applied Research Unit (UNIAG). He is the author of a book, several book chapters and several scientific articles in international journals (Scopus/WoS), and has also presented several papers at scientific conferences in the field of tourism. He has participated in research projects supported by FCT and is a reviewer for some international scientific journals.

Ruta Fontes is a dedicated Ph.D. student specializing in Tourism at Aveiro University. With a passion for exploring the fascinating world of travel and leisure, she has delved deep into the realm of tourism behavior and spatiotemporal tracking. Ruta's academic journey has been marked by a commitment to research excellence, with numerous publications including papers and book chapters. Her academic pursuits extend beyond the classroom, as she has actively contributed to European projects as a diligent researcher. These experiences have provided her with a broader perspective and a global outlook on tourism and its impacts. Ruta is driven by a desire to uncover the intricate dynamics that shape tourist behaviors and to employ cutting-edge spatiotemporal tracking techniques to understand and optimize the tourist experience. Through her work, she aims to make valuable contributions to the field of tourism, ultimately enhancing our understanding of how people explore and engage with the world.

***

João Almeida has a degree in Languages and Business Relations and a Master's in Management from the University of Aveiro. He is currently a PhD student in Business and Economics and a research fellow at the Research Unit in Governance, Competitiveness and Public Policy (GOVCOPP) at the University of Aveiro. His topics of interest are entrepreneurship, innovation, and local development. He is also Co-Founder and Coordinator of Rural Move, a platform to promote the repopulation of low-density territories.

Runumi Das is an Associate Professor at Tezpur University, Assam in the department of Business Administration. She specialises in the area of general management, marketing of handicraft and interpersonal skills.

Gaye Deniz was born on August 8, 1982 in Eskişehir. She is married and has two children. She received her undergraduate degree in Tourism and Hotel Management from Anadolu University; and completed master's degree at Anadolu University, Social Sciences Institute, Department of Tourism and Hotel Management. She holds a PhD from Gazi University, Social Sciences Institute, Department of Business

Administration. Between the years 2004-2009, she had private sector experience. Since 2009, she has been working as a Doctor Lecturer at Nevşehir Hacı Bektaş Veli University, Faculty of Tourism. Her research interests include tourism, hotel management, management and organization, organizational behavior and human resource management.

Alcina Gaspar Ferreira is an associate professor in Marketing and Brand Management and researcher at Centre of Applied Research in Management and Economics (CARME) at School of Technology and Management, Polytechnic of Leiria, Portugal. She holds a Ph.D. in Management, with a specialization in Marketing. Her research interests include brand management, celebrity endorsement, consumer behaviour, store brands and sustainability. She has published in international peer-reviewed journals such as Journal of Product and Brand Management, Journal of Marketing Theory and Practice, International Journal of Sports Marketing and Sponsorship, Journal of Marketing Communications and presented scholarly papers at International Conferences and Scientific Meetings.

Dora Gomes is a doctoral student in Tourism at the University of Aveiro, Portugal. With a bachelor's degree in Tourism and holds a master's degree in Relational Marketing. Currently, she is an active member of the University's Research Unit, GOVCOPP (Governance, Competitiveness, and Public Policies). The academic pursuits are focused on destination branding, with a primary emphasis on the image of destinations and the interactions between tourists and residents. Has presented her work at academic conferences, furthering the discourse on destination management and branding.

Elisabeth Kastenholz is Associate Professor, with Habilitation, at the Department of Economics, Management and Industrial Engineering at the University of Aveiro, integrating the University's Research Unit GOVCOPP (Governance, Competitiveness and Pubic Policies). With an academic background of studies in tourism management & planning, consumer behaviour and marketing, her main research interests lie in the fields of tourist behaviour and destination marketing, specifically in sustainability-yielding destination marketing, accessible tourism, tourist experience, rural tourism, food&wine, cultural and nature-based tourism and tourism-enhanced rural development. She was involved and has coordinated multiple research projects.

Matsushita Keita is a Professor at Kansai University in the Faculty of Sociology, Japan. He received his Ph. D. from Kyoto University for his study of the impact of new media technology on school education. His main research interests are workstyle, workplace, and media communication. He has conducted several research projects and workshops for social design with major Japanese companies and regions. His publications include "Workstyle After Covid-19" (East Press, 2021), "Workstyles in Mobile Media Society" (Keisoshobo, 2019), "Various Phases of Internet Society" (Gakubunsya, 2015), "Career Education for University Students" (Keio University Press, 2015), "Digital Natives and Social Media" (Kyoiku Hyoronsya, 2012).

Archan Mitra is an Assistant Professor at School of Media Studies (SOMS), at Presidency University, Bangalore. He edited various publications and wrote "Cases for Classroom Media and Entertainment Business," an IIM textbook. "Environmental informatics and communication for sustainability" is his doctorate at Visva-Bharati Santiniketan, West Bengal. He is also a qualified Science Communicator and Journalism from Indian Science Communication Society (ISCOS), Corporate Trainer with Amity Institute of Training and Development, and Social Media Network Analyst. He loves environmental communication. He received the Journalistic Club of Kolkata Medal of Honour and PRSI Kolkata Chapter Certificate of Merit. He was a World Bank research assistant at IIM Kashipur. He launched the World Bank's Green MBA MOOC. He publishes in prestigious emergency management magazines. IIM Kashipur, Alabama State University, Birmingham, USA, is his research partner. He used Developing Communities from Within (DCFW) to turn a West Bengal village called "Noachar" into an eco-village.

Sanchita Paul is a dedicated and accomplished content strategist with extensive experience in managing diverse content formats across different digital platforms. With a strong background in content strategy, editing, and UX writing, she has honed her skills in branding, social media management, and technical writing. Holding an MA in Communication and Journalism from Visva-Bharati University, Ms. Paul is proficient in tools like Google Analytics, Canva, and MS Office Suite, making her a versatile professional committed to producing high-quality, impactful content to improve brand visibility.

Roma Singh is a Ph.D Scholar at Tezpur University, Assam in the department of Business Administration. Her current research focuses on promoting workplace flexibility and holistic work cultures for future face of work. She has represented her country India at prestigious global platforms, in countries like Russia and Egypt as a youth representative showcasing her managerial and problem-solving skills.

Nihan Uğur Education: Completed a PhD. program in Tourism Management at Istanbul University. Obtained a master's degree in Tourism Management from Medeniyet University. Began tourism education at Bilkent University, continued at Aydın University, and completed undergraduate studies at Anadolu University.

Additionally, she earned her bachelor's degree in Aviation Management from Anadolu University. Experience: Started a career in the tourism sector as a front desk officer and worked as a flight attendant for an airline. Gained experience in limousine and car rental operations, flight ticketing, hotel operations, and travel agency management. Acquired restaurant experience in London while pursuing language studies. Research Interests: Research areas include organizational behavior, environmental sustainability, digital marketing, cultural heritage, recreation, and virtual reality applications in tourism.

Ali Yuce was born and grew up in Turkey. He altered his life dramatically and profoundly to pursue his passion for academia after working independently for his business. Following graduating from the Ph.D. program at Eastern Mediterranean University, he became a full-time teaching faculty member at Cappadocia University. Since 2016, he has concentrated his academic work and research on sustainable tourism development strategies, tourism development paradoxes, and the effects of climate change on travel destinations. Moreover, he has also provided scholarly discussion in the tourism literature by investigating the role of emerging technologies and education in sustainability-related topics like protecting natural resources and improving livelihoods while highlighting the most prevalent tourism-oriented problems like overpopulation and a poor perception of local people towards tourism. His research areas include but are not limited to innovation in tourism, innovation networks, smart tourism, technology competencies, research philosophy, and sustainable destination planning and development.

Index

B

C

D

E

G

H

I

L

M

N

P

Q

R

S

T

U

W

www.ingramcontent.com/pod-product-compliance
Lightning Source LLC
LaVergne TN
LVHW080606300926
849162LV00005B/1058